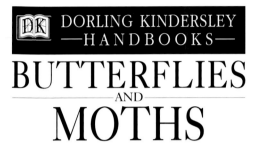

DORLING KINDERSLEY
—HANDBOOKS—

BUTTERFLIES
—AND—
MOTHS

DORLING KINDERSLEY
—HANDBOOKS—

BUTTERFLIES
—AND—
MOTHS

DAVID CARTER

Photography by
FRANK GREENAWAY

A Dorling Kindersley Book

LONDON, NEW YORK, MUNICH,
MELBOURNE, and DELHI

Editors Alison Edmonds, Heather Dewhurst
Art Editors Elaine Hewson
Consultant Editor Dr John D. Bradley
Production Caroline Webber

Caterpillar illustrations by John Still

First published in Great Britain in 1992
by Dorling Kindersley Limited
80 Strand, London WC2R ORL
Reprinted with corrections in 2000

A Penguin Company

A CIP catalogue record for this book is available
from the British Library
ISBN 0 7513 2707 7

Computer page make-up by
The Cooling Brown Partnership, Great Britain

Text film output by The Right Type, Great Britain

Reproduced by Colourscan, Singapore

Printed and bound by South China Printing Company in China

see our complete product
line at
www.dk.com

CONTENTS

AUTHOR'S INTRODUCTION

Of all the insects, butterflies and moths are the most celebrated. Butterflies are probably the most popular because they are active by day, and are renowned for their beautiful colours and graceful flight. Moths are often regarded as less engaging, but with their diversity of shapes, sizes, and colours, they are as fascinating as butterflies.

BUTTERFLIES AND MOTHS are known scientifically as Lepidoptera (meaning scaley wings), because their wings are covered with thousands of tiny, overlapping scales. These scales are often quite brilliantly coloured and account for the distinctive patterns that can be found on both butterflies and moths.

There are approximately 170,000 known species of Lepidoptera: about one tenth of these are butterflies, and the rest are moths. Butterflies and moths are amazing in their variety of size, shape, and colour. Their immense diversity, and ability to adapt to virtually any climate, has made them some of the most

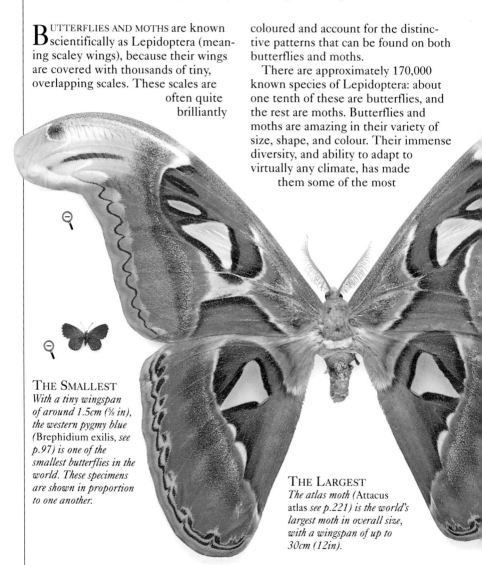

THE SMALLEST
*With a tiny wingspan of around 1.5cm (⅝ in), the western pygmy blue (*Brephidium exilis, *see p.97) is one of the smallest butterflies in the world. These specimens are shown in proportion to one another.*

THE LARGEST
*The atlas moth (*Attacus atlas *see p.221) is the world's largest moth in overall size, with a wingspan of up to 30cm (12in).*

successful creatures on earth, with
habitats ranging from arctic tundra to
alpine mountain summits, as well as
the warmer tropical rainforests and
coastal mangrove swamps.

FLOWER ASSOCIATION

As adult butterflies are only able to
feed on fluids, flower nectar is the
major source of sustenance for most
species. (Other butterfly foods range
from fermenting sap, to liquids from
dung and decaying carrion.) Plants
benefit from these associations
because, while feeding,
the insects trans-
fer pollen from
one plant to
another.
Butterflies
and moths
feed by means of
a long, hollow feed-
ing tube or proboscis. This
remains coiled up beneath
the head when not in use, but
when extended it can probe
the depths of a flower in search
of nectar. Different species
have different lengths of
tongue, a feature that is influ-
enced by the particular flowers on
which they feed.

SELECTION

The 500 or more species described
and illustrated in this book have
been selected to represent as wide
a range of different types of butterflies and moths as possible.
Emphasis has been placed on common species, or those with interest-
ing features. It would have been
impossible to include all the interest-
ing and common examples of butterflies and moths when the range is so
enormous, so I have chosen a selection
that I hope will stimulate your interest.

HABITATS

*Watching butterflies and moths in their natural
habitats is always rewarding for the interested
amateur. Learn to recognize the species in your
area, and you will build up an understanding
of their flight times, habits, and foodplants.*

HOUSE MOTH

With a wingspan of about 2cm(¾in),
the common brown house moth or false
clothes-moth *(Hofmannophila pseu-
dospretella)*, is one representative of
many thousands of small moth species
including the notorious clothes moths,
that belong to Microlepidoptera. The
smallest Microlepidoptera have a
wingspan of just a few millimetres.
  Despite their small size, many
Microlepidoptera are significant pests.
Two of the most common are the
codling moth, or apple maggot *(Cydia
pomonella)*, and the diamond back moth
(Plutella xylostella) which attacks vegetables. I have not been able cover
Microlepidoptera in this book, but a
vast number of small species exist,
often with colours and shapes that are
as beautiful as their larger cousins.

LEPIDOPTERA EVOLUTION

The earliest moth fossils are estimated to be between 100 and 140 million years old; butterflies have a fossil record that goes back 40 million years. Lepidoptera originated when flowering plants were beginning to proliferate, and have developed in close association with them. Caddis flies (Trichoptera), the most closely related group of insects to butterflies and moths, are believed to have originated about 250 million years ago, but transitional forms have yet to be identified.

FOSSILIZED MOTH
This early example of a moth has been preserved in amber (the fossilized resin of an ancient plant).

BUTTERFLY OR MOTH?

Until very recently South American *Hedylid* "moths" were believed to belong to the moth family Geometridae, but detailed study has revealed that they are more closely related to butterflies. Superficially they resemble moths, but many of their internal and external body features are like those of butterflies.

HEDYLID MOTH

THE NAMING SYSTEM

Common names vary from country to country. Thus, scientists usually use the system established in the eighteenth century by the Swedish naturalist, Carl von Linné (his name is commonly latinized as Linnaeus). The generic name, which always appears first, groups the species with others sharing similar features. The second, or specific name, differentiates the species from other members of the genus. About 170, 000 described species of butterflies and moths exist, but there are at least as many species yet to be described.

When a new species is named, it is usually described from a number of specimens. A single specimen, the type, is then selected as the one upon which the identity of the species is judged for all time.

TAGORA PALLIDA

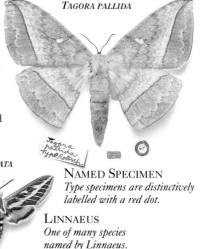

HYLES LINEATA

NAMED SPECIMEN
Type specimens are distinctively labelled with a red dot.

LINNAEUS
One of many species named by Linnaeus.

How This Book Works

THIS BOOK is arranged to include all five butterfly families, followed by twenty one of the major moth families. Each separate family has a short introduction describing its general characteristics. The entries that follow give detailed information, in words and pictures, about selected species found in that group. This annotated example shows how a typical entry is organized.

name of the family to which the butterfly or moth belongs

name of genus and species of butterfly

name of original describer

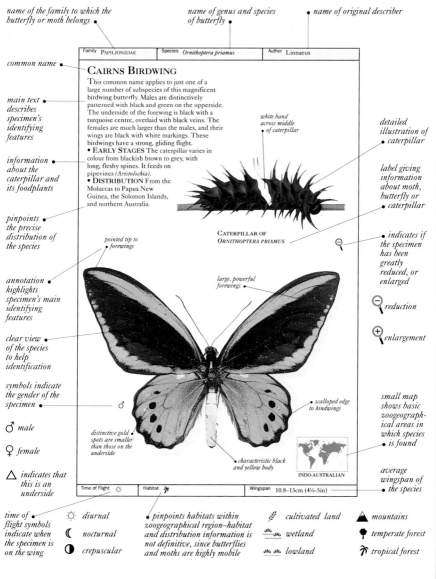

| Family PAPILIONIDAE | Species *Ornithoptera priamus* | Author Linnaeus |

common name

Cairns Birdwing

This common name applies to just one of a large number of subspecies of this magnificent birdwing butterfly. Males are distinctively patterned with black and green on the upperside. The underside of the forewing is black with a turquoise centre, overlaid with black veins. The females are much larger than the males, and their wings are black with white markings. These birdwings have a strong, gliding flight.

main text describes specimen's identifying features

• **EARLY STAGES** The caterpillar varies in colour from blackish brown to grey, with long, fleshy spines. It feeds on pipevines *(Aristolochia)*.
• **DISTRIBUTION** From the Moluccas to Papua New Guinea, the Solomon Islands, and northern Australia.

information about the caterpillar and its foodplants

white band across middle of caterpillar

detailed illustration of caterpillar

label giving information about moth, butterfly or caterpillar

pinpoints the precise distribution of the species

CATERPILLAR OF
ORNITHOPTERA PRIAMUS

indicates if the specimen has been greatly reduced, or enlarged

pointed tip to forewings

annotation highlights specimen's main identifying features

large, powerful forewings

reduction

clear view of the species to help identification

enlargement

symbols indicate the gender of the specimen

♂

scalloped edge to hindwings

small map shows basic zoogeographical areas in which species is found

♂ *male*

♀ *female*

distinctive gold spots are smaller than those on the underside

characteristic black and yellow body

INDO-AUSTRALIAN

average wingspan of the species

△ *indicates that this is an underside*

| Time of Flight ☀ | Habitat ⋔ | Wingspan 10.8–13cm (4¼–5in) |

time of flight symbols indicate when the specimen is on the wing

☀ *diurnal*

☾ *nocturnal*

◑ *crepuscular*

• *pinpoints habitats within zoogeographical region–habitat and distribution information is not definitive, since butterflies and moths are highly mobile*

🌿 *cultivated land*

〰 *wetland*

〰 *lowland*

▲ *mountains*

🌳 *temperate forest*

⋔ *tropical forest*

BUTTERFLY OR MOTH?

BUTTERFLY CHARACTERISTICS

Butterflies are a group of specialized, day-flying Lepidoptera. Generally, they can be recognized by their bright colours and clubbed antennae, but also by the way they rest, with the wings held together over the back. In butterflies, the base of the hindwing is expanded and strengthened, supporting and coupling with the forewing when in flight.

typical scale-covered wings of butterfly •

ORANGE TIP

WING SHAPE
Butterflies have a wide variety of wing shapes as shown by these two specimens.

COMMON IMPERIAL BLUE

antennae thickened at the tips •

bright colours of typical day-flying • butterfly

BUTTERFLY ANATOMY
Orange-barred giant sulphur (Phoebis philea, *see right), has all the features common to a typical butterfly.*

• *characteristic large and rounded wings*

ORANGE-BARRED GIANT

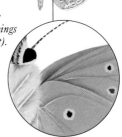

RESTING BUTTERFLY
This butterfly from the family Nymphalid is seen here resting in the typical butterfly posture, with its wings held together above its back (see left).

HINDWING COUPLING
A close look at the underside of a common blue butterfly (Polyommatus icarus) *shows the expanded hindwing base typical of butterflies (see right).*

MOTH CHARACTERISTICS

Moths are so diverse that it is difficult to give a general description. There are even many day-flying species. Moths can be distinguished by their antennae, which lack clubbed tips, and are filamentous or feathered. Most moths have a wing-coupling device consisting of bristles on the base of the hindwing that engage with a flap or "catch" on the forewing. Males have single stout bristles, whereas females have a number of slender bristles.

FIERY CAMPYLOTES

• *elongated wings typical of moths*

WING SHAPE
Moth wings vary in size, shape, and colour.

most moths have feathered antennae •

OWL MOTH

• *hook and bristle wing-coupling device hidden behind wings*

A TYPICAL MOTH
The acacia carpenter moth (Xyleutes eucalypti) *is a fairly typical moth with dull camouflage colours and a robust body.*

• *characteristically robust moth body*

ACACIA CARPENTER MOTH

RESTING MOTH
The white ermine moth (Spilosoma lubricipeda), *resting in a characteristic moth posture with its wings folded, roof-like, over the back (see left).*

WING-COUPLING
A closer look at the underside of the wings of the Jersey tiger (Euplagia quadripunctaria) *reveals the typical moth wing-coupling device (see right).*

LIFE-CYCLE

BUTTERFLIES AND MOTHS have a complex life-cycle consisting of four phases: egg, caterpillar (larva), pupa, and adult. In the egg stage, a caterpillar develops within a protective envelope. The caterpillar stage is the main feeding period. In order to grow, the caterpillar must shed its skin several times. During the pupa phase the body components are broken down and reformed into an adult butterfly or moth. This life-cycle is called a complete metamorphosis.

1 **EGG** The egg darkens and you can see the young caterpillar moving about inside, shortly before emergence time. It first cuts a circular "lid" in the tough egg shell *(A)*, and then pulls its body free of the egg with wriggling movements *(B and C)*. This is one of the most vulnerable stages. Once it has emerged *(D)*, the caterpillar usually eats its empty egg-shell *(E)*. This provides the nutrients for it to survive until it can locate its foodplant.

caterpillar enjoying its important first meal

E

a fully emerged caterpillar moves toward its egg to eat it

D

SOUTH AMERICAN OWL BUTTERFLY

the caterpillar finally breaks free of its egg

C

B

A

CHEQUERED SWALLOWTAIL

4 **ADULT** Some choose the upper surface of leaves *(O)* on which to lay their eggs, while others choose the undersides where the eggs may be better protected. Certain species lay their eggs in crevices or inside plant tissues. Females avoid plants that already have eggs laid on them. This ensures that food is there for her eggs only. The female usually glues the eggs to the surface of a leaf, or a similar support, with a viscous secretion from her body. Some butterflies lay their eggs singly, while others lay them in large batches. Butterflies and moths whose caterpillars feed on a wide range of plants often scatter eggs in flight.

O

butterflies select the right plant to lay eggs on by sight, smell, taste, and touch

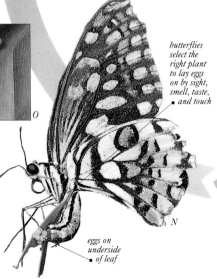

N

eggs on underside of leaf

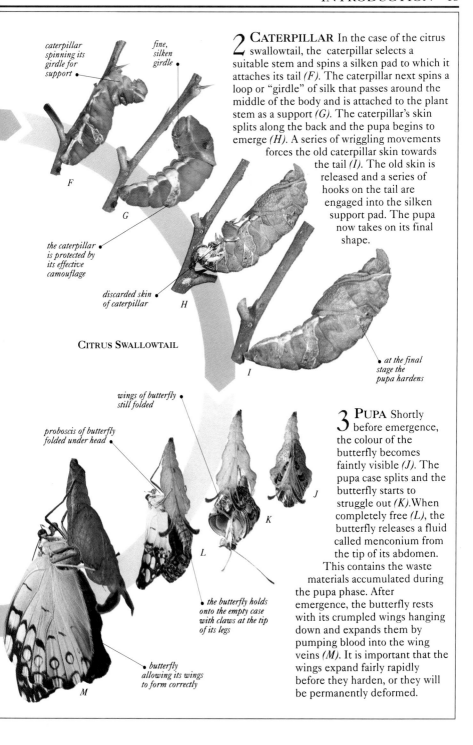

caterpillar
spinning its
girdle for
support •

fine,
silken
girdle •

2 CATERPILLAR In the case of the citrus swallowtail, the caterpillar selects a suitable stem and spins a silken pad to which it attaches its tail *(F)*. The caterpillar next spins a loop or "girdle" of silk that passes around the middle of the body and is attached to the plant stem as a support *(G)*. The caterpillar's skin splits along the back and the pupa begins to emerge *(H)*. A series of wriggling movements forces the old caterpillar skin towards the tail *(I)*. The old skin is released and a series of hooks on the tail are engaged into the silken support pad. The pupa now takes on its final shape.

F

G

the caterpillar •
is protected by
its effective
camouflage

discarded skin •
of caterpillar

H

CITRUS SWALLOWTAIL

I

• at the final
stage the
pupa hardens

wings of butterfly •
still folded

proboscis of butterfly •
folded under head

J

3 PUPA Shortly before emergence, the colour of the butterfly becomes faintly visible *(J)*. The pupa case splits and the butterfly starts to struggle out *(K)*.When completely free *(L)*, the butterfly releases a fluid called menconium from the tip of its abdomen. This contains the waste materials accumulated during the pupa phase. After emergence, the butterfly rests with its crumpled wings hanging down and expands them by pumping blood into the wing veins *(M)*. It is important that the wings expand fairly rapidly before they harden, or they will be permanently deformed.

K

L

• the butterfly holds
onto the empty case
with claws at the tip
of its legs

• butterfly
allowing its wings
to form correctly

M

EARLY STAGES

ACH STAGE of the development of a butterfly or moth is specially adapted to enable it to carry out particular functions. As many species of butterflies and moths spend most of their lives as soft bodied caterpillars, they have developed a wide range of devices to protect themselves from predators. The pupa stage is immobile and therefore even more vulnerable to attack.

CATERPILLARS

Caterpillars often blend into the background or mimic an object such as a dead leaf to conceal themselves. Looper caterpillars of the moth family Geometridae mimic twigs so that they are safe when at rest. Other caterpillars are covered with hairs or spines that make an unpleasant mouthful for a bird or small mammal. (Cuckoos are one of the few birds that will eat hairy caterpillars.) The hairs of some species are poisonous and can cause a rash if handled. Those caterpillars that are poisonous or distasteful advertise the fact with bright and distinctive wing patterns.

TWIG MIMIC
The purple thorn (Selenia tetralunaria) caterpillar has a highly developed camouflage that is hard to distinguish it from the twig on which it rests.

• *even bark blemishes are accurately reproduced*

SPINY CATERPILLAR
The bright pattern on this saddle (Sibine sp.) caterpillar warns that it has stinging spines.

POISONOUS MOUTHFUL
Most predators will avoid the pine lappet (Dendrolimus pini) caterpillar as its hairs have irritant properties.

LEAF MIMIC
This green Lycaenid caterpillar (Castalius rosimon), blends with a leaf of its foodplant.

WARNING PATTERN
This strongly patterned magpie moth (Abraxas grossulariata) caterpillar, is distasteful to birds.

FRIGHT TACTIC
The lobster moth (Stauropus fagi) caterpillar raises its head and scorpion-like tail when alarmed.

• *this caterpillar needs no camouflage, since it is such a fearsome sight*

PUPA

The pupa of a butterfly is commonly called a chrysalis, a term derived from the greek word for gold, since a number of butterfly pupae have metallic markings. Although pupae have hard, protective, outer shells, they are still vulnerable to birds, mice, and other creatures that regard them as tasty morsels. Like caterpillars, many gain protection by merging into the background, and some are even able to change their colour to match the surface on which they are resting. Others resemble dead leaves or pieces of twig, while poisonous pupae are usually quite conspicuous and brightly coloured. Moth pupae are often formed in a protective silken case called a cocoon.

LEAF MIMIC
The chrysalis of the owl butterfly (Caligo beltrao) *resembles a dead leaf.*

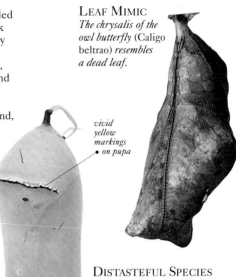

vivid yellow markings on pupa •

FRUIT MIMIC
A berry-like chrysalis of a blue morpho (Morpho *sp.*) *butterfly.*

DISTASTEFUL SPECIES
The pupae of the queen butterfly (Danaus gilippus) *are poisonous to predators.*

• the poison of this pupa comes from the plant on which it feeds

WING VEINS
The chrysalis of the cloudless giant sulphur (Phoebis sennae) *shows the developing wing veins.*

the head is at this end of the pupa •

butterfly's • developing wing veins

SILKEN SUPPORT
The giant swallowtail (Papilio cresphontes) *chrysalis is supported by a silken girdle, which was spun by the caterpillar at an earlier stage.*

BRIGHT GREEN
The chrysalis of the common bluebottle (Graphium sarpedon), *varies in colour from green to brown.*

SURVIVAL

BUTTERFLIES AND MOTHS have always been depicted as fragile creatures, and objects of great beauty; as such they have to survive in a hostile world. They have no offensive weapons such as stings, or biting jaws to defend themselves, unlike so many other insects. To protect themselves from birds and other predators they have had to adopt defensive strategies.

CAMOUFLAGE

The most universal defence tactic among adult butterflies and moths is to blend into the background, a feat achieved in various ways. When resting, butterflies hold their wings together so that only the dull underside shows. Thus, a brightly coloured butterfly seems to disappear as it lands in a hedge and closes its wings. Many moths avoid birds by flying at night, but they are then in danger from bats. However, many species are able to hear the cries of bats and therefore avoid them. Most night-flying moths have dull coloured wings that provide good camouflage when they rest on tree trunks. Other species have elaborate patterns that break up the wing and body shape so that it is difficult to recognize. Moths, in particular, are good mimics of a wide range of objects from dead twigs and leaves to wasps and spiders.

BARK MIMIC

Like many moths, this carpenter moth (Cossidae) has wings that blend with the bark on which it rests.

LEAF BUTTERFLY

So-called because of its remarkable camouflage, even the leaf veins and blemishes are accurately reproduced by the Indian leaf butterfly (Kallima inachus).

• *wing underside resembles dead leaf*

• *hindwing tip of the butterfly is just visible*

WARNING COLOURS

Most butterflies and moths defend themselves by camouflage, but those species that are poisonous advertise their defense mechanism with bright colours. Inexperienced predators, such as young birds, soon learn to leave insects with warning colours alone. Some moths have dull forewing colours that provide good camouflage when the moth is resting . If the moth is threatened, it reveals brightly coloured hindwings in a startling flash. In addition, some species have false eyespots, that create a face to startle the attacker.

forewing dull in comparison to • hindwing

FLASH COLORATION
The ilia underwing (Catocala ilia), *scares would-be attackers with the flash of bright colour.*

ILIA UNDERWING

• yellow of hindwing presents flash of colour

EYESPOTS
The twin-spotted sphinx (Smerinthus jamaicensis) *displays large eyespots on its brightly coloured hindwings to warn off predators.*

double, black- • ringed, metallic-blue hindwing eyespots

• unusual jagged shape of forewing margins

TWIN-SPOTTED SPHINX

MIMICRY

Poisonous butterflies of the same species often fly together so that their warning colours are more easily recognized. A number of poisonous species even share a similar warning pattern. In this way, birds have only to learn that one species is poisonous to avoid all the rest. Some non-poisonous species mimic poisonous species so that they too are left alone. In the past, these mimicry associations have confused entomologists who have only recognized one species where several in fact existed.

vivid red of inner margins is a deterrent to would-be • predators

SMALL POSTMAN BUTTERFLY

MIMICRY ASSOCIATIONS
These two species of distasteful butterfly are difficult to tell apart. By sharing the same pattern, they help to protect each other.

• these butterflies are very difficult to tell apart, and would fool most hungry birds

POSTMAN BUTTERFLY

CONSERVATION

IN MANY PARTS of the world, butterfly and moth numbers have decreased alarmingly in recent times and many species have become extinct. It is essential that we take steps to find out what is going wrong before it is too late to save these fascinating creatures for future generations. In the Victorian era, when collectors had their hey-day, their activities had little effect on butterfly and moth populations. This is hardly surprising since each insect lays many, and often hundreds, of eggs in the expectation that only one or two will survive to maturity. However, today when the numbers of some species are dangerously low, even collecting a few specimens of a rare species may be enough to tip the balance against survival. Some conservation organisations are recommending that certain species should be protected from collection. There is little that can be done to save our butterflies and moths if their habitats are destroyed, so it is important that we manage our environment, and avoid further damaging the already fragile, balance of nature.

APOLLO BUTTERFLY

LARGE COPPER

EXTINCTION
These two butterflies are at risk from changes in their habitats; the large copper due to drainage of wetlands for farming, and the apollo because of tourism in mountainous areas.

BUTTERFLIES, MOTHS, AND MAN

Butterflies and moths can be both allies and enemies of man. When we grow vast areas of the same type of plants, for example fields of wheat and rice or plantations of conifers, we create the ideal conditions for certain species to build up huge populations and become pests. In some cases, an insect may be accidentally introduced to another country and become a pest because its natural predators and competition are absent. Butterflies are valuable pollinators when they move from plant to plant gathering nectar. Some caterpillars feed on weeds and are agents of control. Other species have been cultivated for centuries for their silk.

PEACOCK

GYPSY MOTH

FRIEND OR FOE?
The peacock (Inachis io), pollinates plants, thus indirectly helping man. The gypsy moth, (Lymantria dispar), is a common pest in fruit orchards.

MARSH
FRITILLARY

The countryside is now an environment controlled by man. Many butterfly and moth habitats have been destroyed by clearing and draining of land to cultivate crops. The marsh fritillary (above) is at risk from land-drainage.

INSECTICIDES
The use of sprays and herbicides has become a great threat to the habitats of butterflies and moths. Not only insects, but other animals too are killed, which interferes with the balance of nature.

TROPICAL
FORESTS
Destruction of the world's tropical forests imperils the many varied species that live within them.

AFRICAN GIANT
SWALLOWTAIL

Tropical rainforests, with their huge variety of plants and wonderful fauna, are the richest habitats for butterflies, providing homes for some of the most spectacular species. Their continued destruction for growing crops and the logging industry threatens these species. Much has yet to be learned about the complex communities of insects that live in tropical forests. Butterflies and moths are now an integral part of this research, because they are relatively easy to recognize, and are already well-documented. Threatened species of birdwing are being farmed in an effort to ensure their survival.

OBSERVATION

THE STUDY of butterflies and moths in their natural environment is always rewarding. The first close-up view of a live butterfly through a magnifying glass is an amazing experience that can never be matched by looking at preserved specimens.

As butterflies and day-flying moths are such active creatures, it is best to observe them when they are feeding or drinking. The flower garden is one of the easiest places to start butterfly watching. Patience is essential. Stand close to a group of nectar-bearing flowers and wait for a butterfly to visit. When it is well settled, it is possible to approach without disturbing it. Remember that butterflies are very sensitive to even the slightest movement, and take care not to cast your shadow over them.

With experience, you soon learn to recognize a good butterfly site. Hedgerows, forest margins, and any sheltered, sunny spot will usually

WHERE TO LOOK
Butterflies often gather to drink from puddles on muddy ground, and this is an ideal opportunity to study these beautiful creatures.

• *these leaves conceal several species from the Papilionidae family, but at this early stage they are hard to identify*

• *by looking like bird droppings these caterpillars are not attracting the attention of birds, or other predators*

these caterpillars are all tropical
• *species*

FINDING SPECIMENS
When looking for caterpillars remember the effectiveness of their camouflage. These swallowtail caterpillars disguise themselves by resembling bird droppings.

prove to be fruitful. Damp areas by streams and puddles can be popular drinking places for butterflies, particularly in the tropics.

Many butterflies and moths are attracted to fermenting fruit or to sap oozing from wounds in tree trunks. Moth hunters have taken advantage of this to attract moths for study. They smear a "treacle" of sugars, molasses, rum, and beer onto tree trunks or fenceposts at dusk and then visit at hourly intervals throughout the night.

By torchlight they can watch moths gorging themselves on the sweet alcoholic mixture.

Moths are dazzled and disorientated by lights, not, as many people think, attracted to them, so they often tend to fly

NIGHT LIGHT
Any ordinary lamp will attract moths at night, but mercury vapour lamps are by far the most efficient.

this paraffin lamp is easily portable

flat-bottom gives lamp stability, and prevents it becoming a fire-risk

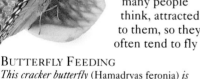

BUTTERFLY FEEDING
This cracker butterfly (Hamadryas feronia) *is feeding on the juices from a piece of fruit. Both butterflies and moths enjoy feeding on fruits.*

towards them. Using this principle, many different forms of light traps have been devised, and these are used to enable scientists both to collect moths, and to monitor numbers and species, in biological surveys. However, a simple lantern or light bulb in front of a white sheet will attract many different species.

EQUIPMENT FOR THE FIELD

One of the best ways to keep a record of butterflies and moths you have seen, is to take photographs of them. You can equip most modern single lens reflex cameras with a macro lens for butterfly close-ups, and achieve excellent results with practice and patience. A simple snap-shot camera is useful for recording butterfly habitats. Write down times of appearance, distribution, mating behaviour, and food-plants, to build up a picture of the species' habits. Many students have made important discoveries in this way.

tape recorder

notebook and field guides

short-focus telescope

camera

REARING

ONE OF THE BEST ways to learn more about butterflies and moths is to rear them from eggs. There are a number of large and spectacular exotic species, including silkmoths and moonmoths, that are relatively easily reared in captivity, as well as the more common and native species.

Keep eggs in small transparent plastic boxes until they hatch. If left in too large a container, they may dry up and die. As soon as the tiny caterpillars hatch, transfer them into a container that holds some of their foodplant. While small, you can keep most caterpillars in plastic boxes lined with absorbent paper. Provide

them with a regular supply of fresh foliage. At this stage, there is no need to punch holes in the lid for ventilation, as this causes the food to dry up too rapidly. Condensation can endanger small caterpillars, but the paper lining should prevent this from happening. As caterpillars grow, it will be necessary to transfer them to larger containers or

twigs of oak are used to rear the oak (Antheraea harti) *silkmoth*

silkmoth caterpillar

foodplant must be changed regularly to ensure fresh food for the caterpillar

twigs reach down to ground, so that caterpillars can climb back on plant if they fall off

KEEPING CATERPILLARS
When rearing caterpillars on cut food, it is essential to plug the neck of the water jar. Otherwise the caterpillars will crawl in and drown.

cages. Some caterpillars require a growing plant. Place a potted plant in the cage or make a cage by tying a sleeve of netting over the branch of a shrub.

PUPA STAGE

Many butterfly species will simply attach their pupae to the foodplant, but some moths form their pupae below ground or under bark. To provide a pupation site, place a thick layer of slightly damp peat on the floor of the cage. Some pupae overwinter with the adults emerging in the following year. In the spring you

should transfer them to a spacious emergence cage, and spray them from time to time with a fine mist of water. The balance of moisture is critical at all stages of development, as too much will encourage mould. Cages should be cleaned regularly. It is essential to provide twigs for the newly emerged butterflies and moths to cling to while they are expanding their wings. Not all adults will feed, but those that do will take nectar from cut flowers provided, or substitute nectar that can be made quite easily from a diluted honey or sugar solution.

RANGE OF CAGES
Commercially made cages are available for rearing caterpillars; alternatively, improvise with a card shoe box covered with mesh on one side.

a zip-fastener allows easy access to the cage

CAGE DESIGN
Where possible, cages should always provide the caterpillar with light and ventilation. They must also be easy to clean.

fresh or cut plants make suitable food for the caterpillars

mesh cage provides adequate ventilation

HANDLING CATERPILLARS

Try to avoid handling caterpillars, but if it is necessary, move smaller ones with a fine paintbrush. Many caterpillar species have stinging hairs- these should be handled with caution. When caterpillars are about to moult, they usually look dull and shrunken. They must not be moved at this stage as any disturbance is likely to prevent moulting.

BUTTERFLY GARDEN

ONE WAY IN WHICH you can contribute towards conservation is to make your garden as attractive as possible to butterflies and moths. In doing this, you will encourage a range of other wildlife so that your garden will be an even more enjoyable place.

The first step is to grow flowers that provide a rich source of nectar. Night scented flowers, such as honeysuckle, are usually attractive to moths. Make sure that you grow plants that flower at different times of year to provide a continuous food supply throughout the seasons.

It is also desirable to grow caterpillar foodplants, as these will encourage female butterflies to lay their eggs in your garden. With a little research you can find out which butterfly and moth species inhabit your area so that you can provide them with a range of suitable plants. If space permits, you could develop an area of wild garden for native plants to flourish.

If you plan to attract butterflies and moths to your garden, you should avoid using insecticides if possible. Those that kill aphids are said to be harmless to caterpillars, but all garden chemicals should be used with care.

PIPEVINE SWALLOWTAIL

BUDDLEIA
Also called the butterfly bush, the flowers of this shrub attract many butterfly and moth species, including the pipevine swallowtail.

honey-
scented
buddleia
bush flowers
in summer •

ICEPLANT
Small tortoiseshells (Aglais urticae) *enjoying the iceplant's nectar (see left).*

HONEYSUCKLE
This attracts long tongued moths, like this hawk-moth (Macroglossum stellatarum).

APPLE
Moth caterpillars like the foliage of this tree; the fallen fruit attracts butterflies like the Camberwell beauty (Nymphalis antiopa).

HUMMINGBIRD HAWK-MOTH

MARJORAM
A herb that is attractive to butterflies such as the meadow brown (Maniola jurtina).

CAMBERWELL BEAUTY

HEBE
This is a useful plant for attracting such butterflies as the peacock (Inachis io).

MEADOW BROWN

PEACOCK

WILD FLOWERS
A small area devoted to wild flowers and grasses will also attract butterflies and moths.

this plant attracts a wide variety of insects

PALAEARCTIC REGION

THE PALAEARCTIC REGION is the largest of the zoogeographic regions, extending across the northern hemisphere from Europe to China and Japan, and extending southwards to north Africa, including the Sahara. The climate of this region is mainly temperate but ranges from arctic to subtropical. As temperature and climate are distinctly seasonal, butterflies and moths usually have a constant number of generations each year and their

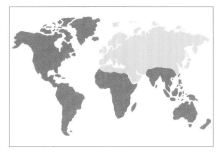

ZOOGEOGRAPHICAL PALAEARCTIC REGION

flight periods can be predicted with some accuracy. Butterflies and moths of the Palaearctic region are better known than those in any other part of the world because the study of these insects first started in Europe. The fauna in parts of this region, for instance central Asia, is still very poorly known.

AGRICULTURE
Many areas of the Palaearctic region have been subjected to intense agricultural activity for some centuries, and this has had a profound effect on the fauna.

Maniola jurtina
(Nymphalidae)

Cerura vinula
(Notodontidae)

Orgyia antiqua
(Lymantriidae)

Sphinx ligustri
(Sphingidae)

Arctia caja
(Arctiidae)

Parnassius apollo
(Papilionidae)

Argynnis lathonia
(Nymphalidae)

Ochlodes venatus
(Hesperiidae)

Inachis io
(Nymphalidae)

Polyommatus icarus
(Lycaenidae)

Pieris brassicae
(Pieridae)

Boarmia roboraria
(Geometridae)

Zygaena filipendulae
(Zygaenidae)

Papilio machaon
(Papilionidae)

Bombyx mori
(Bombycidae)

Saturnia pyri
(Saturniidae)

Noctua pronuba
(Noctuidae)

Lycaena dispar
(Lycaenidae)

Anthocharis
cardamines
(Pieridae)

Lasiocampa
quercus
(Lasiocampidae)

AFROTROPICAL REGION

THE AFROTROPICAL REGION includes the whole of Africa south of the Sahara. Madagascar is normally placed in a zoogeographic region of its own because so many of its species occur nowhere else in the world. However, for the purposes of this book, it is included with the Afrotropical region. This region boasts more than 2,500 described species of butterflies, and many more species of moths, although little is known about the smaller

ZOOGEOGRAPHICAL AFROTROPICAL REGION

moths. The richest parts of the region are the lowland tropical rainforests, with those in west Africa having the most species. The other major habitat for Lepidoptera is grassland and savanna, which has a smaller but characteristic butterfly and moth fauna of its own.

SAVANNA
Grassland with trees and scrub is just one of the many habitats of the African continent.

Lampides boeticus
(Lycaenidae)

Papilio demodocus
(Papilionidae)

Colotis danae
(Pieridae)

Anaphe panda
(Notodontidae)

Dactylocerus swanzii
(Brahmaeidae)

Poecilmitis thysbe
(Lycaenidae)

Dasychira pyrosoma
(Lymantridae)

Bunaea alcinoe
(Saturniidae)

Eurytela dryope
(Nymphalidae)

*Grammodora
nigrolineata*
(Lasiocampidae)

Coeliades forestan
(Hesperiidae)

Anaphe panda
(Notodontidae)

Omphax plantaria
(Geometridae)

Catopsilia florella
(Pieridae)

Chrysiridia rhiphearia
(Uraniidae)

Danaus chrysippus
(Nymphalidae)

Acherontia atropos
(Sphingidae)

INDO-AUSTRALIAN REGION

THE INDO-AUSTRALIAN region encompasses two zoogeographical areas known as the Oriental and Australian regions. It stretches from Pakistan and India to Australia and New Zealand. There are profound differences in the faunas of the two regions, but many butterfly species extend from the Oriental to the Australian region, and I have found it practical to consider them together. This is one of the richest parts of the world for butterflies and moths.

ZOOGEOGRAPHICAL INDO-AUSTRALIAN REGION

Virtually the whole of this region lies within the tropics, excepting parts of Australia and New Zealand. However, many habitats are represented, from tropical forest to plains, swamps, and mountains.

PADDY FIELDS
This is a typical man-made landscape in the Oriental region.

Danis danis
(Lycaenidae)

Papilio paris
(Papilionidae)

Cethosia biblis
(Nymphalidae)

Danima banksiae
(Notodontidae)

Crypsiphona ocultaria
(Geometridae)

Ogyris genoveva
(Lycaenidae)

Gangara thyrsis
(Hesperiidae)

Teia anartoides
(Lymantridae)

Tisiphone abeone
(Nymphalidae)

Actias selene
(Saturniidae)

Utetheisa species
(Arctiidae)

Appias nero
(Pieridae)

Digglesia australasiae
(Lasiocampidae)

Achaea janata
(Noctuidae)

Coequosa triangularis
(Sphingidae)

Delias mysis
(Pieridae)

NEARCTIC REGION

THE NEARCTIC REGION is largely temperate in climate but extends from arctic Canada and Alaska to subtropical Florida and southern California. It bears many resemblances in climate and fauna to the Palaearctic region, and a number of species are common to both regions. Insects occurring in both the Nearctic and Palaearctic regions, (of which there are many), are said to have a Holarctic distribution. About 700 species of butterfly occur in the

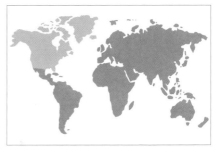

ZOOGEOGRAPHICAL NEARCTIC REGION

Nearctic region, but the moth fauna is very much more extensive than this. Probably the best known of all the butterflies occurring in this region, is the monarch, famed for its annual migration from Canada to Mexico.

FOREST
Many species in this region inhabit temperate forests, or areas bordering agricultural land .

Schizura ipomoeae
(Notodontidae)

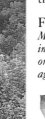

Prochoerodes transversata
(Geometridae)

Danaus plexippus
(Nymphalidae)

Cercyonis pegala
(Nymphalidae)

Apantesis virgo
(Arctiidae)

Hemiargus isola
(Lycaenidae)

Prionoxystus robiniae
(Cossidae)

Zerene eurydice
(Pieridae)

Epargyreus clarus
(Hesperiidae)

Peridroma saucia
(Noctuidae)

Atlides halesus
(Lycaenidae)

Megathymus yuccae
(Hesperiidae)

Eurytides marcellus
(Papilionidae)

Malacosoma americanum
(Lasiocampidae)

Agrius cingulata
(Sphingidae)

Lymantria dispar
(Lymantriidae)

Hyalophora cecropia
(Saturniidae)

Sibine stimulea
(Limacodidae)

Junonia coenia
(Nymphalidae)

Neophasia menapia
(Pieridae)

NEOTROPICAL REGION

THE NEOTROPICAL REGION extends from Mexico, to Tierra del Fuego in South America. It covers a wide range of habitats and climates, but the tropical rainforests of South America have the greatest diversity of species.

The Lycaenid butterflies, represented on p.35 by *Thecla coronata*, include some of the most beautiful and jewel-like species, yet they are so little studied that there is no reliable guide for their identification. The moths include

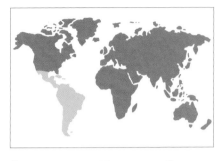

ZOOGEOGRAPHICAL NEOTROPICAL REGION

some distinctive species such as the giant agrippa *(Thysania agrippina)*, and the giant grey sphinx *(Pseudosphinx tetrio)*, but many of the smaller moth species have yet to be identified.

RAINFOREST
This area contains the richest butterfly and moth populations in the world.

Premolis semirufa (Arctiidae)

Eupackardia calleta (Saturniidae)

Battus philenor (Papilionidae)

Heliconius charitonius (Nymphalidae)

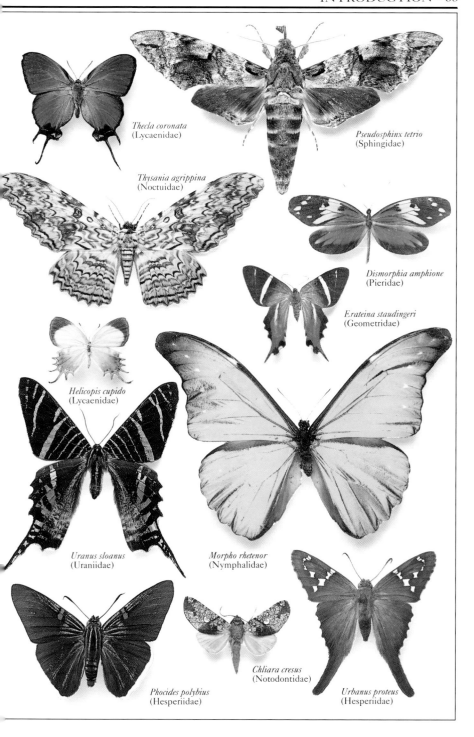

Thecla coronata
(Lycaenidae)

Pseudosphinx tetrio
(Sphingidae)

Thysania agrippina
(Noctuidae)

Dismorphia amphione
(Pieridae)

Erateina staudingeri
(Geometridae)

Helicopis cupido
(Lycaenidae)

Uranus sloanus
(Uraniidae)

Morpho rhetenor
(Nymphalidae)

Chliara cresus
(Notodontidae)

Phocides polybius
(Hesperiidae)

Urbanus proteus
(Hesperiidae)

BUTTERFLIES

HESPERIIDAE

T HE FAMILY Hesperiidae, more familiarly referred to as skippers, is a large, primitive group of some 3,000 species occurring throughout the world. Although generally considered to be butterflies, they frequently lack butterfly-style clubs to the antennae. They can be recognized by their large heads, stout bodies, and rather short, triangular-shaped forewings. They are mostly small- to medium-sized insects with drab colours, although a few of the larger species are quite brightly coloured, and attractively patterned.

———— • ————

Skippers earned their common name from the characteristic way they dart from flower to flower.

Family HESPERIIDAE	Species *Urbanus proteus*	Author Linnaeus

LONG-TAILED SKIPPER

This is one of the most recognizable skippers, and can be distinguished from other North American long-tails by the iridescent green on the upperside of the wings and body. It is an erratic flier.
• **EARLY STAGES** The caterpillar is olive-green with brown lines and yellow and black spotting. The head is brown with two yellow spots. It often feeds on varieties of cultivated bean *(Phaseolus)*.
• **DISTRIBUTION** Widespread in South America, from Argentina, extending northwards into the USA as far as Texas and Connecticut.

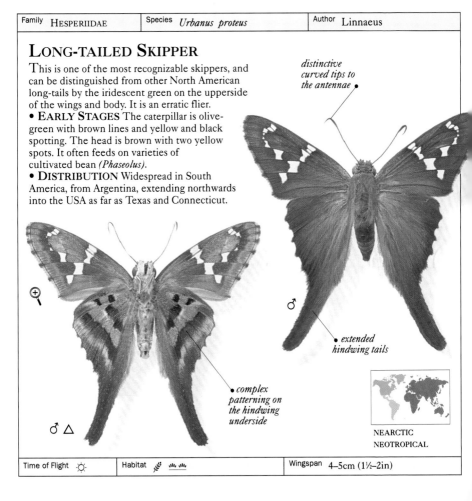

distinctive curved tips to the antennae

♂

extended hindwing tails

complex patterning on the hindwing underside

♂ △

NEARCTIC
NEOTROPICAL

Time of Flight ☀	Habitat	Wingspan 4–5cm (1½–2in)

Family HESPERIIDAE	Species *Zophopetes dysmephila*	Author Trimen

PALM SKIPPER

The robust, chocolate-brown palm skipper is one of several similar species found in Africa. The underside of the hindwing is brown with scattered black dots and a purplish tinge. The adult palm skippers are active at dusk.
• **EARLY STAGES** The caterpillar is apparently undescribed, but feeds on date palm *(Phoenix dactylifera)* and other palms.
• **DISTRIBUTION** Widespread at low altitudes in savanna country, riversides, and forests, from South Africa to Eritrea and Senegal, south of the Sahara.

white clubs on the antennae •

triangular-shaped forewings •

white margins on the forewings •

♂

three white patches on the forewings •

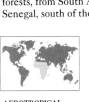

AFROTROPICAL

Time of Flight ◑	Habitat ⸰⸰ ⸰⸰	Wingspan 4–4.5cm (1½–1¾in)

Family HESPERIIDAE	Species *Epargyreus clarus*	Author Cramer

SILVER-SPOTTED SKIPPER

This large skipper is dark brown with orange markings on the forewings, and a small cluster of white eyespots at the forewing tip.
• **EARLY STAGES** The caterpillar is light green with darker markings and has a reddish brown head. There is one generation a year in the temperate north, and two or three in warmer, southern regions.
• **DISTRIBUTION** Found in North America.

curved tip to antennae •

♂

• both sexes have small, blunt, curved tails

silvery white patch on the hindwing • underside

♂ △

NEARCTIC
NEOTROPICAL

Time of Flight ☼	Habitat ♚	Wingspan 4.5–6cm (1¾–2½in)

Family HESPERIIDAE	Species *Euschemon rafflesia*	Author Macleay

REGENT SKIPPER

This large, black and yellow skipper is represented
by two subspecies in Australia. Regent skippers
visit the flowers of many plants, often feeding on
Lantanas. They are active in bright sunlight and
have a distinctive swift and jerky flight. They rest
on leaves with their wings outspread. An unusual
feature of the male is its wing-coupling mechanism,
which is similar to that of many moths.
• **EARLY STAGES** The stout caterpillar is
greenish or bluish grey in colour, but yellow
with two reddish black stripes behind
the head. It feeds at
night on *Wilkiea*.
• **DISTRIBUTION**
Queensland to NSW
in Australia.

INDO-AUSTRALIAN

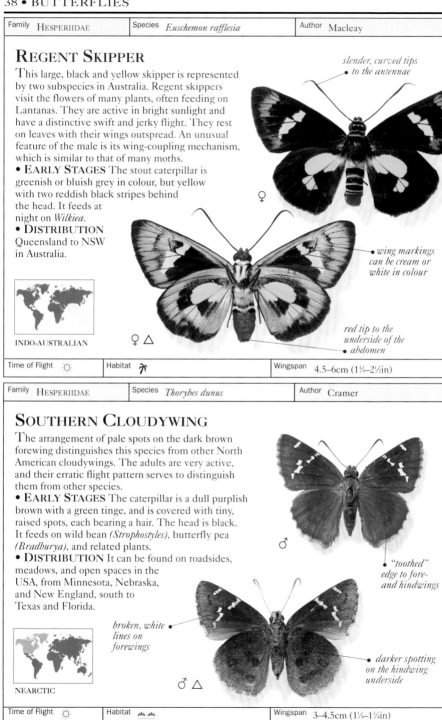

*slender, curved tips
to the antennae*

♀

*wing markings
can be cream or
white in colour*

*red tip to the
underside of the
abdomen*

♀ △

Time of Flight ☼	Habitat 🌴	Wingspan 4.5–6cm (1¾–2½in)

Family HESPERIIDAE	Species *Thorybes dunus*	Author Cramer

SOUTHERN CLOUDYWING

The arrangement of pale spots on the dark brown
forewing distinguishes this species from other North
American cloudywings. The adults are very active,
and their erratic flight pattern serves to distinguish
them from other species.
• **EARLY STAGES** The caterpillar is a dull purplish
brown with a green tinge, and is covered with tiny,
raised spots, each bearing a hair. The head is black.
It feeds on wild bean *(Strophostyles)*, butterfly pea
(Bradburya), and related plants.
• **DISTRIBUTION** It can be found on roadsides,
meadows, and open spaces in the
USA, from Minnesota, Nebraska,
and New England, south to
Texas and Florida.

*broken, white
lines on
forewings*

NEARCTIC

♂

*"toothed"
edge to fore-
and hindwings*

*darker spotting
on the hindwing
underside*

♂ △

Time of Flight ☼	Habitat 〜〜	Wingspan 3–4.5cm (1¼–1¾in)

Family HESPERIIDAE	Species *Heteropterus morpheus*	Author Pallas

LARGE CHEQUERED SKIPPER

The underside of the hindwing has a chequered pattern.
• **EARLY STAGES** The caterpillar has a greyish white body
and feeds on various grasses. There is one generation a year.
• **DISTRIBUTION** Widely distributed in scattered colonies
from southern Scandinavia
to the Mediterranean.

PALAEARCTIC

♀ △

♀

*large, ringed
spots on the
hindwing
underside*

Time of Flight ☼	Habitat	Wingspan 3–4cm (1¼–1½in)

Family HESPERIIDAE	Species *Metisella metis*	Author Linnaeus

GOLD-SPOTTED SYLPH

This group of small brown skippers has reddish
orange spots on the uppersides of the fore- and
hindwings. The species are difficult to distinguish
from one another, and the sexes look similar.
• **EARLY STAGES** The caterpillar is dark green
above, with white lines along the
back, and pale green below. It
feeds on various grasses.
• **DISTRIBUTION** Found by
muddy streams in South Africa,
from Cape Province and
Natal to Transvaal.

AFROTROPICAL

♂

*unusually large,
rounded hindwings*

Time of Flight ☼	Habitat 🌳	Wingspan 2.5–3cm (1–1¼in)

Family HESPERIIDAE	Species *Oreisplanus munionga*	Author Olliff

ALPINE SKIPPER

The dark brown uppersides of the wings of this butterfly
are patterned with angular, orange spots. The undersides
are mainly yellow with dark brown markings.
• **EARLY STAGES** The caterpillar
is striped with greenish grey. It
feeds on sedge *(Carex)*.
• **DISTRIBUTION**
Occurs in the
mountains of
south-east
Australia, from
NSW to Victoria
and Tasmania.

INDO-AUSTRALIAN

♂ △

♂

*yellow underside
gives camouflage when
the skipper feeds from
yellow plants*

Time of Flight ☼	Habitat ▲	Wingspan 2.5–3cm (1–1¼in)

Family HESPERIIDAE	Species *Gangara thyrsis*	Author Fabricius

GIANT REDEYE

One of the largest skippers, this species can be distinguished by its blood-red eyes. Females are slightly larger than males, and lack the characteristic male hair patches on the wing bases.
• **EARLY STAGES** The caterpillar is blood-red, covered with a filamentous, white, waxy coating which is easily rubbed off if touched. It feeds chiefly on banana leaves *(Musa)*. The pupae, which are formed among the leaves, produce a rattling noise if disturbed.
• **DISTRIBUTION** Widely distributed from Sri Lanka and India to the Philippines and Sulawesi.

caterpillar in a rolled leaf

large, translucent, pale patches on the forewings

♂

distinctive angular-shaped hindwings

elongate, dark brown abdomen

CATERPILLAR OF GANGARA THYRSIS

INDO-AUSTRALIAN

Time of Flight ☼ ◑	Habitat 🐦	Wingspan 7–7.5cm (2¾–3in)

Family HESPERIIDAE	Species *Hesperilla picta*	Author Leach

PAINTED SKIPPER

The wings of this skipper are dark brown, with yellow patches nearer the body. The forewings are yellow spotted, the hindwings have a central, orange patch.
• **EARLY STAGES** The caterpillar is yellow or green, with yellow markings, and has a dark stripe along its back edged by white lines. It feeds on sword-grasses.
• **DISTRIBUTION** Coastal areas in Australia from Queensland to Victoria, and the Blue Mountains in NSW.

♂

chequered fringe on the hindwings

white patterning on the hindwing underside

INDO-AUSTRALIAN

♀ △

Time of Flight ☼	Habitat 〰️	Wingspan 3–4cm (1¼–1½in)

Family HESPERIIDAE	Species *Carterocephalus palaemon*	Author Pallas

CHEQUERED SKIPPER

The wings of this aptly named skipper are dark
chocolate-brown with a chequered pattern. The sexes
look similar, but females are slightly larger. Chequered
skippers make only short flights. The American common
name for the butterfly is arctic skipper.
• **EARLY STAGES** The caterpillar is pale yellowish
brown with pink stripes when fully grown. It feeds
on grasses, such as false-brome
(Brachypodium).
• **DISTRIBUTION** North-
east to central Europe, and
Canada, and northern America.

paler underside
markings still
show the chequered
pattern

♀

⊕

♂ △

HOLARCTIC

Time of Flight ☼	Habitat ♣	Wingspan 2–3cm (¾–1¼in)

Family HESPERIIDAE	Species *Netrocoryne repanda*	Author Felder

EASTERN FLAT

The broad wings of this skipper have a distinctly angular
appearance. The forewings are brown with three or four
prominent, translucent spots edged with brown. The
sexes look similar, but females are larger with more
extensive translucent spots. Butterflies are on the
wing from late autumn to late winter.
• **EARLY STAGES** The stout caterpillar is bluish
grey, except for a yellow first segment, and is striped
with black and grey. The head is black. It feeds mostly
on spun leaves of *Callicoma serratifolia.*
• **DISTRIBUTION** Widely distributed in Australia, in
north-east and central Queensland, to Victoria.

distinctively
curved tips to
the antennae

♂

characteristic,
small white spot
on the hindwings

♀

INDO-AUSTRALIAN

Time of Flight ☼	Habitat 🌴 ♣	Wingspan 4–5cm (1½–2in)

Family HESPERIIDAE	Species *Phocides polybius*	Author Fabricius

GUAVA SKIPPER

A striking skipper, this species has
sharply angled fore- and hindwings
which are black with metallic, greenish
blue streaks. Each forewing has two
vermilion spots which distinguish this
skipper from similar species. The
upperside of the body is black with
metallic-blue, the underside is black.
• **EARLY STAGES** The young
caterpillar is red with yellow rings,
becoming white with a brown and yellow
head as it develops. It feeds on guava
(Psidium guajava) and related species.
• **DISTRIBUTION** South and Central
America extending to Argentina.

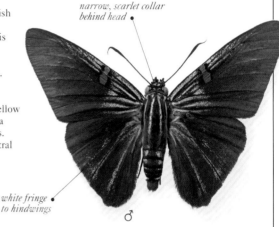

*narrow, scarlet collar
behind head*

*white fringe
to hindwings*

♂

NEOTROPICAL

Time of Flight ☼	Habitat 🦋	Wingspan 5–6cm (2–2½in)

Family HESPERIIDAE	Species *Coeliades forestan*	Author Stoll

STRIPED POLICEMAN

This robust species has greyish brown,
triangular forewings, which are centrally
suffused with white on the undersides. The
rounded hindwings with their broad, short tails
are characteristic of this mainly African genus
of skippers. Striped policemen have a rapid
flight, and their habit of patrolling over their
territory from dawn to dusk gives rise to their
common name. They are attracted to the
flowers of various low-growing plants.
• **EARLY STAGES**
The caterpillar is pale
yellow with purplish red
bands. Its head is red or
yellow, with black spots.
It feeds on geranium.
• **DISTRIBUTION** Found
in Africa south of the Sahara,
including Madagascar and
the Seychelles.

♂

*• chrome-yellow
scaling of the
tail fringes*

*large, white stripes on the •
hindwing undersides*

♂ △

AFROTROPICAL

Time of Flight ☼	Habitat 🦋	Wingspan 4.5–5cm (1¾–2in)

Family HESPERIIDAE	Species *Pyrrhochalcia iphis*	Author Drury

GIANT AFRICAN SKIPPER

This is the largest skipper in Africa and probably in the
world. The males are black and purplish blue, while the
beautiful females are strongly rayed with metallic-bluish
green. The undersides are more striking, males having
dark blue forewings and brilliant metallic-blue hindwings.
Females are a metallic-yellowish with black veins. These
huge, slow-flying skippers are probably mimics of
Agaristid moths. They often fly at night.
• **EARLY STAGES** The caterpillar is black with a
chequered, creamy white pattern. It feeds on the foliage
of cashew trees *(Anacardium occidentale)*.
• **DISTRIBUTION** Gambia to Nigeria, Zaire and Angola.

*• striking black
and white
caterpillar*

**CATERPILLAR OF
PYRRHOCHALCIA IPHIS**

*distinctive
• orange-scaled head*

*• cream tips
to wings*

*paler shading •
to fore- and
hindwings*

*rounded lobes on
the hindwings •*

♀

AFROTROPICAL

Time of Flight ◐	Habitat 🎋	Wingspan 7–8cm (2¾–3¼in)

Family HESPERIIDAE	Species *Erynnis tages*	Author Linnaeus

DINGY SKIPPER

The dingy skipper is dull-coloured, but it
is nevertheless a distinctive species with
delicate white patterning on a greyish
brown background.
• **EARLY STAGES** The caterpillar
is green with a dark line along its
back, and has a black head. It feeds
at night on bird's foot-trefoil
(Lotus corniculatus) and other
plants of the pea family.
• **DISTRIBUTION** Occurs on
open heaths and
downlands throughout
Europe, extending into
temperate Asia.

*large rounded
hindwings •*

♀

*small, white •
markings on the
underside*

♀ △

PALAEARCTIC

Time of Flight ☼	Habitat 🌿🌿	Wingspan 2.5–3cm (1–1¼in)

Family HESPERIIDAE	Species *Calpodes ethlius*	Author Stoll

BRAZILIAN SKIPPER

This skipper has dark brown wings, spotted with silvery white. The forewings are narrow and pointed in contrast with the broad, lobed hindwings. It can fly over large distances.
• **EARLY STAGES** The caterpillar is greyish green with a white line down the back and brown spots along the sides. The head is orange and black. It feeds on canna leaves *(Canna flaccida)*, and sometimes damages cultivated forms of this plant. It is known as the canna leaf roller. The pale green pupa is camouflaged in a leaf roll.
• **DISTRIBUTION** Widely distributed in South America, and the West Indies. Occurs in southern parts of the USA .

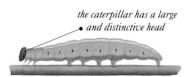

the caterpillar has a large and distinctive head

CATERPILLAR OF CALPODES ETHLIUS

large, robust head and body

three white spots on the hindwing

♂

NEOTROPICAL

Time of Flight ☼	Habitat 〰 〰	Wingspan 4.5–5.5cm (1¾–2¼in)

Family HESPERIIDAE	Species *Megathymus yuccae*	Authors Boisduval & Le Conte

YUCCA GIANT SKIPPER

Large-bodied and hairy, this skipper has blackish brown wings, which are distinctively patterned with yellow and white. Males are generally much smaller than females. They can be seen from midwinter to early summer. These skippers do not feed as adults, although related species have been observed drinking on moist ground.
• **EARLY STAGES** The caterpillar is large and grub-like with a small head. It feeds on yucca.
• **DISTRIBUTION** This is the most widespread of the North American giant skippers. It lives in various habitats, including forest margins where the foodplants grow. Its range extends from Utah and Kansas in the USA, south to Florida and Mexico.

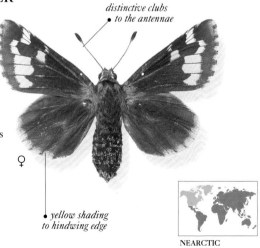

distinctive clubs to the antennae

♀

yellow shading to hindwing edge

NEARCTIC

Time of Flight ☼	Habitat 〰 〰 〰	Wingspan 4.5–8cm (1¾–3¼in)

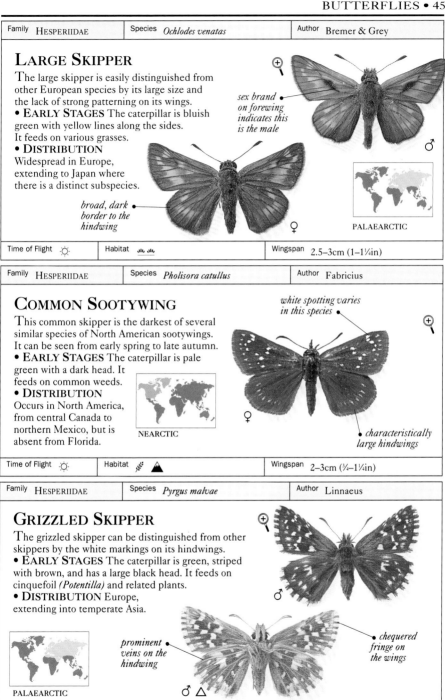

Family	HESPERIIDAE	Species	*Ochlodes venatas*	Author	Bremer & Grey

LARGE SKIPPER

The large skipper is easily distinguished from
other European species by its large size and
the lack of strong patterning on its wings.
• **EARLY STAGES** The caterpillar is bluish
green with yellow lines along the sides.
It feeds on various grasses.
• **DISTRIBUTION**
Widespread in Europe,
extending to Japan where
there is a distinct subspecies.

*sex brand
on forewing
indicates this
is the male*

♂

*broad, dark
border to the
hindwing*

♀

PALAEARCTIC

Time of Flight ☼	Habitat 〰 〰	Wingspan	2.5–3cm (1–1¼in)

Family	HESPERIIDAE	Species	*Pholisora catullus*	Author	Fabricius

COMMON SOOTYWING

This common skipper is the darkest of several
similar species of North American sootywings.
It can be seen from early spring to late autumn.
• **EARLY STAGES** The caterpillar is pale
green with a dark head. It
feeds on common weeds.
• **DISTRIBUTION**
Occurs in North America,
from central Canada to
northern Mexico, but is
absent from Florida.

*white spotting varies
in this species*

♀

NEARCTIC

*characteristically
large hindwings*

Time of Flight ☼	Habitat 〰 ▲	Wingspan	2–3cm (¾–1¼in)

Family	HESPERIIDAE	Species	*Pyrgus malvae*	Author	Linnaeus

GRIZZLED SKIPPER

The grizzled skipper can be distinguished from other
skippers by the white markings on its hindwings.
• **EARLY STAGES** The caterpillar is green, striped
with brown, and has a large black head. It feeds on
cinquefoil *(Potentilla)* and related plants.
• **DISTRIBUTION** Europe,
extending into temperate Asia.

♂

*prominent
veins on the
hindwing*

*chequered
fringe on
the wings*

PALAEARCTIC

♂ △

Time of Flight ☼	Habitat 〰〰 〰〰	Wingspan	2–2.5cm (¾–1in)

PAPILIONIDAE

T HIS LARGE family of butterflies contains some of the biggest and most beautiful species in the world. It is also the most widely studied and well-known of all the butterfly groups.

•

Most species occur in the tropics, but some are also found in temperate climates. Because many Papilionidae species have tailed hindwings, their popular name is swallowtail. However, not all Papilionids have tailed wings, for example the birdwings of tropical Australasia. Swallowtail butterflies can be recognized by their large, striking wings and by the fact that they have three fully developed pairs of legs. They are usually strong fliers.

Family PAPILIONIDAE	Species *Papilio aegeus*	Author Donovan

ORCHARD SWALLOWTAIL

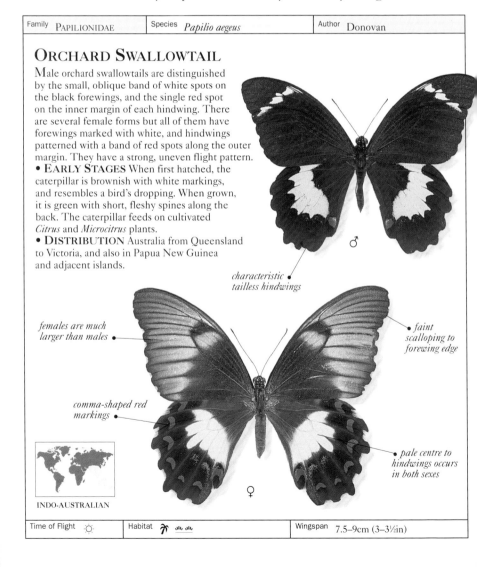

Male orchard swallowtails are distinguished by the small, oblique band of white spots on the black forewings, and the single red spot on the inner margin of each hindwing. There are several female forms but all of them have forewings marked with white, and hindwings patterned with a band of red spots along the outer margin. They have a strong, uneven flight pattern.
• **EARLY STAGES** When first hatched, the caterpillar is brownish with white markings, and resembles a bird's dropping. When grown, it is green with short, fleshy spines along the back. The caterpillar feeds on cultivated *Citrus* and *Microcitrus* plants.
• **DISTRIBUTION** Australia from Queensland to Victoria, and also in Papua New Guinea and adjacent islands.

characteristic • tailless hindwings

females are much larger than males •

comma-shaped red markings •

INDO-AUSTRALIAN

• faint scalloping to forewing edge

• pale centre to hindwings occurs in both sexes

Time of Flight ☼	Habitat 🌴	Wingspan 7.5–9cm (3–3½in)

| Family PAPILIONIDAE | Species *Papilio paris* | Author Linnaeus |

PARIS PEACOCK

The striking patches of
metallic colour found on the
hindwings place this butterfly in
a group called the gloss papilios.
Female Paris peacocks are usually
yellower than the males.
• **EARLY STAGES** The caterpillar
is green with white or yellow
markings, and yellow scent horns.
It feeds on a wide range of plants,
including *Citrus*.
• **DISTRIBUTION** Mainly at low
altitudes in India, Thailand, Sumatra,
and Java, although absent from the
Malay Peninsula. It occurs at higher
altitudes in south-west China.

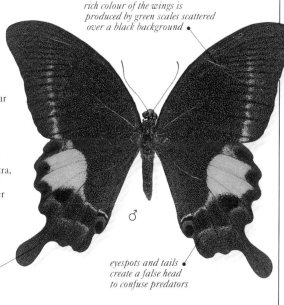

*rich colour of the wings is
produced by green scales scattered
over a black background*

♂

*distinctive
curved shape
of hindwings*

*eyespots and tails
create a false head
to confuse predators*

INDO-AUSTRALIAN

| Time of Flight ☼ | Habitat 🌴 | Wingspan 8–13.5cm (3¼–5¼in) |

| Family PAPILIONIDAE | Species *Papilio polytes* | Author Linnaeus |

COMMON MORMON

The very variable female has
three different colour forms. One
form resembles the male, the
others mimic different species of
swallowtail. Males have a swifter
flight than females.
• **EARLY STAGES** The caterpillar
is green with brown markings, very
similar to that of the chequered
swallowtail (*P. demoleus*, see p.48). It
feeds on cultivated *Citrus*, especially
orange (*C. sinensis*), and lime (*C.
aurantifolia*), as well as on related native
plants such as *Murraya* and *Triplasia*.
• **DISTRIBUTION**
Widespread
throughout India
and Sri Lanka to
China, Japan,
Malaysia, the
Philippines, and
the Moluccas.

*pale hindwing markings
continue on the forewings*

♂

*band of cream
spots on the
hindwings*

INDO-AUSTRALIAN

| Time of Flight ☼ | Habitat | Wingspan 9–10cm (3½–4in) |

Family PAPILIONIDAE	Species *Papilio demoleus*	Author Linnaeus

CHEQUERED SWALLOWTAIL

This distinctively patterned, black and yellow
butterfly has an elongated, red eyespot on
the inner corner of its
hindwing. It has no tails
on its hindwing. It is also
called the lime swallowtail.
• **EARLY STAGES** At
first, the caterpillar is dark
brown with white markings
and it resembles a bird's
dropping. Later, it becomes
green with dark brown
markings, that give it good
camouflage. It feeds on *Citrus*
and plants of the pea family.
• **DISTRIBUTION** From
Iran, India, and Malaysia, to
Papua New Guinea and
northern Australia.

*lacy, black and
yellow patterning on
the inner forewings*

♂

*chequered fringes
on the wings*

INDO-AUSTRALIAN

Time of Flight ☀	Habitat	Wingspan 8–10cm (3¼–4in)

Family PAPILIONIDAE	Species *Papilio anchisiades*	Author Esper

RUBY-SPOTTED SWALLOWTAIL

This largely black species
can have pink, ruby, or
purplish patches on the
hindwings. The butterflies
mimic swallowtails of
the genus *Parides*.
• **EARLY STAGES** The
caterpillar is green and brown with
white markings and bulges on its
back. It feeds on cultivated *Citrus*.
• **DISTRIBUTION** Central America
and tropical South America.

*tailless
hindwings*

♂

*bright patches
on the hindwings*

NEOTROPICAL

Time of Flight ☀	Habitat	Wingspan 6–9.5cm (2½–3¾in)

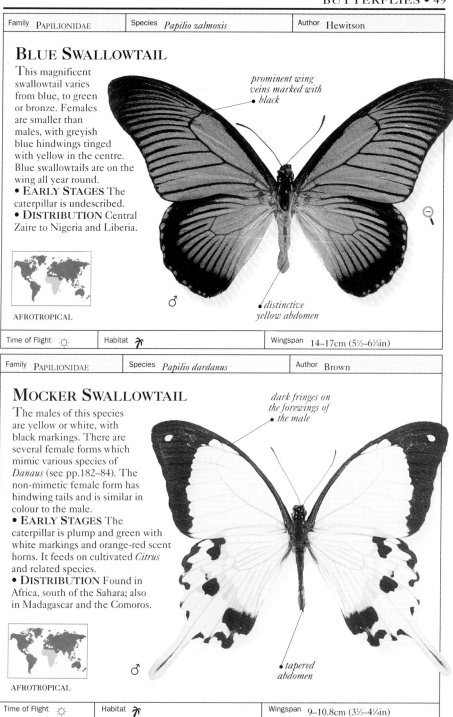

| Family PAPILIONIDAE | Species *Papilio zalmoxis* | Author Hewitson |

BLUE SWALLOWTAIL

This magnificent swallowtail varies from blue, to green or bronze. Females are smaller than males, with greyish blue hindwings tinged with yellow in the centre. Blue swallowtails are on the wing all year round.
• **EARLY STAGES** The caterpillar is undescribed.
• **DISTRIBUTION** Central Zaire to Nigeria and Liberia.

prominent wing veins marked with black

distinctive yellow abdomen

♂

AFROTROPICAL

| Time of Flight ☼ | Habitat 🌴 | Wingspan 14–17cm (5½–6¾in) |

| Family PAPILIONIDAE | Species *Papilio dardanus* | Author Brown |

MOCKER SWALLOWTAIL

The males of this species are yellow or white, with black markings. There are several female forms which mimic various species of *Danaus* (see pp.182–84). The non-mimetic female form has hindwing tails and is similar in colour to the male.
• **EARLY STAGES** The caterpillar is plump and green with white markings and orange-red scent horns. It feeds on cultivated *Citrus* and related species.
• **DISTRIBUTION** Found in Africa, south of the Sahara; also in Madagascar and the Comoros.

dark fringes on the forewings of the male

tapered abdomen

♂

AFROTROPICAL

| Time of Flight ☼ | Habitat 🌴 | Wingspan 9–10.8cm (3½–4¼in) |

| Family PAPILIONIDAE | Species *Papilio cresphontes* | Author Cramer |

GIANT SWALLOWTAIL

A distinctive black and
yellow-coloured
swallowtail, this is
one of the largest
species to be found
in North America.
• **EARLY STAGES** The
caterpillar is brown with dirty
white markings. It feeds on
various wild plants.
• **DISTRIBUTION** Occurs from
Central America to Mexico and
southern parts of the USA.

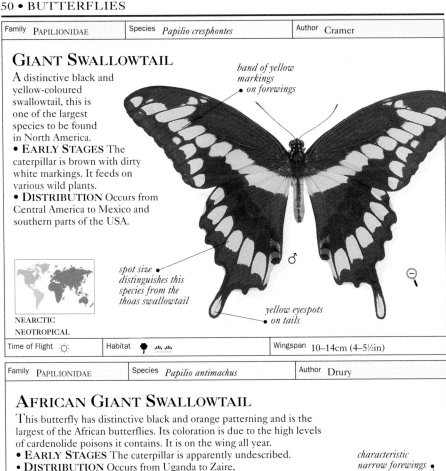

band of yellow
markings
• on forewings

spot size •
distinguishes this
species from the
thoas swallowtail

yellow eyespots
• on tails

NEARCTIC
NEOTROPICAL

| Time of Flight ☀ | Habitat 🌳 ⸲⸲ ⸲⸲ | Wingspan 10–14cm (4–5½in) |

| Family PAPILIONIDAE | Species *Papilio antimachus* | Author Drury |

AFRICAN GIANT SWALLOWTAIL

This butterfly has distinctive black and orange patterning and is the
largest of the African butterflies. Its coloration is due to the high levels
of cardenolide poisons it contains. It is on the wing all year.
• **EARLY STAGES** The caterpillar is apparently undescribed.
• **DISTRIBUTION** Occurs from Uganda to Zaire,
Angola, and Sierra Leone.

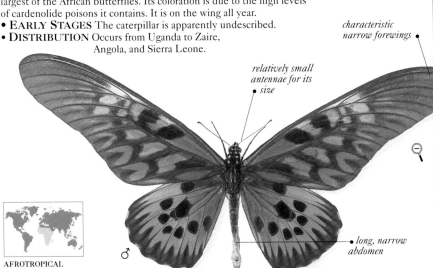

characteristic
narrow forewings •

relatively small
antennae for its
• size

long, narrow
abdomen

AFROTROPICAL

| Time of Flight ☀ | Habitat 🌿 ⸲⸲ ⸲⸲ | Wingspan 15–25cm (6–10in) |

| Family PAPILIONIDAE | Species *Papilio demodocus* | Author Esper |

CITRUS SWALLOWTAIL

This black and yellow butterfly is tailless. It is the African counterpart of *Papilio demoleus* (see p.48), but it is generally larger with a band of black on the hindwing. It is also called the Christmas butterfly.

• **EARLY STAGES** The caterpillar feeds on cultivated *Citrus* and legumes.

• **DISTRIBUTION** Occurs in tropical Africa, and is a pest in South Africa. Also found in Madagascar.

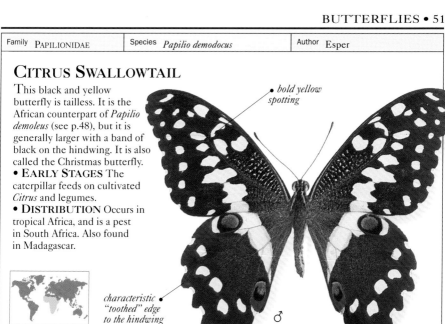

• *bold yellow spotting*

characteristic "toothed" edge to the hindwing

♂

AFROTROPICAL

| Time of Flight ☼ | Habitat | Wingspan 9–12cm (3½–4¾in) |

| Family PAPILIONIDAE | Species *Papilio machaon* | Author Linnaeus |

SWALLOWTAIL

This butterfly has a singular bold patterning of black on yellow. The hindwings have fairly short tails and are variably marked with orange patches. In the USA this species is also known as the old world swallowtail.

• **EARLY STAGES** The caterpillar has bright green and black bands, spotted with red. It feeds on milk parsley *(Peucedanum palustre)* and other related plants.

• **DISTRIBUTION** Found in fen and meadowland in Europe, across temperate Asia to Japan. Also occurs in subarctic and Arctic regions of Canada and the USA.

thin, pale leading edge to forewings

♀

broad, black band is dusted with blue

red eyespot in the corner of each hindwing

HOLARCTIC

| Time of Flight ☼ | Habitat | Wingspan 7–10cm (2¾–4in) |

Family PAPILIONIDAE	Species *Papilio glaucus*	Author Linnaeus

TIGER SWALLOWTAIL

Males and some females of this species are yellow with tiger stripes. A female form occurs in which the ground colour is dark brown or black. This form is found most frequently in the southern parts of the species' range, where it is believed to be a mimic of the poisonous pipevine swallowtail (*Battus philenor*, see p.55). Further north the butterfly becomes smaller and paler. Tiger swallowtails have a strong, sailing flight.
• **EARLY STAGES** The plump caterpillar is green with bright yellow and black eyespots. The caterpillars when they are young, resemble bird droppings. They feed on willows *(Salix)* and cottonwoods *(Populus)*. There are one to three broods a year depending on location.
• **DISTRIBUTION** This is the most widely distributed North American swallowtail, extending south from Alaska, the USA, and Canada, to the Gulf of Mexico.

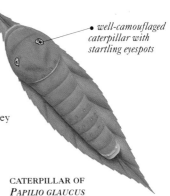

• *well-camouflaged caterpillar with startling eyespots*

CATERPILLAR OF
PAPILIO GLAUCUS

*striking tiger striping
• on forewings*

*forewing •
eyespots
fade at
base of
margin*

• *unusual
V-shaped
marking
on inner
margin of
hindwings*

♂

• *black stripe
along length of
body matches wings*

• *hooked
hindwing
tails*

• *yellow spotting
along wing margins*

NEARCTIC

Time of Flight ☼	Habitat 🌳 🌿 🌿	Wingspan 9–16.5cm (3½ –6½ in)

Family PAPILIONIDAE	Species *Eurytides marcellus*	Author Cramer

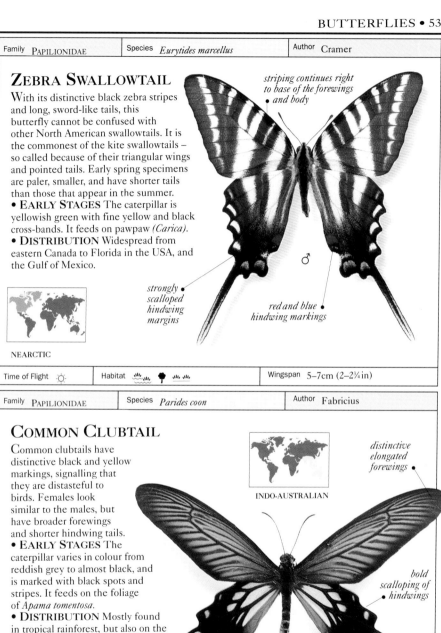

ZEBRA SWALLOWTAIL

With its distinctive black zebra stripes and long, sword-like tails, this butterfly cannot be confused with other North American swallowtails. It is the commonest of the kite swallowtails – so called because of their triangular wings and pointed tails. Early spring specimens are paler, smaller, and have shorter tails than those that appear in the summer.
• **EARLY STAGES** The caterpillar is yellowish green with fine yellow and black cross-bands. It feeds on pawpaw *(Carica)*.
• **DISTRIBUTION** Widespread from eastern Canada to Florida in the USA, and the Gulf of Mexico.

striping continues right to base of the forewings • and body

strongly • scalloped hindwing margins

red and blue • hindwing markings

♂

NEARCTIC

Time of Flight ☼	Habitat 〰️🌿 🌳 🌿🌿	Wingspan 5–7cm (2–2¾in)

Family PAPILIONIDAE	Species *Parides coon*	Author Fabricius

COMMON CLUBTAIL

Common clubtails have distinctive black and yellow markings, signalling that they are distasteful to birds. Females look similar to the males, but have broader forewings and shorter hindwing tails.
• **EARLY STAGES** The caterpillar varies in colour from reddish grey to almost black, and is marked with black spots and stripes. It feeds on the foliage of *Apama tomentosa*.
• **DISTRIBUTION** Mostly found in tropical rainforest, but also on the plains, throughout northern India and Burma to Malaysia, Sumatra, and Java, but absent in Borneo.

INDO-AUSTRALIAN

distinctive elongated forewings •

bold scalloping of • hindwings

clubbed hindwing tails •

♂

• markings vary from yellow to orange

Time of Flight ☼	Habitat 🌴	Wingspan 9–13cm (3½–5in)

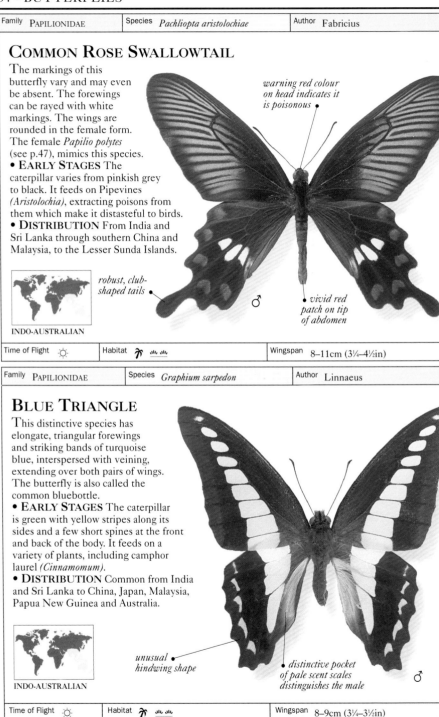

| Family PAPILIONIDAE | Species *Pachliopta aristolochiae* | Author Fabricius |

COMMON ROSE SWALLOWTAIL

The markings of this butterfly vary and may even be absent. The forewings can be rayed with white markings. The wings are rounded in the female form. The female *Papilio polytes* (see p.47), mimics this species.
• **EARLY STAGES** The caterpillar varies from pinkish grey to black. It feeds on Pipevines *(Aristolochia)*, extracting poisons from them which make it distasteful to birds.
• **DISTRIBUTION** From India and Sri Lanka through southern China and Malaysia, to the Lesser Sunda Islands.

warning red colour on head indicates it is poisonous

robust, club-shaped tails

vivid red patch on tip of abdomen

♂

INDO-AUSTRALIAN

| Time of Flight ☼ | Habitat 🌴 ⸜⸜ ⸜⸜ | Wingspan 8–11cm (3¼–4½in) |

| Family PAPILIONIDAE | Species *Graphium sarpedon* | Author Linnaeus |

BLUE TRIANGLE

This distinctive species has elongate, triangular forewings and striking bands of turquoise blue, interspersed with veining, extending over both pairs of wings. The butterfly is also called the common bluebottle.
• **EARLY STAGES** The caterpillar is green with yellow stripes along its sides and a few short spines at the front and back of the body. It feeds on a variety of plants, including camphor laurel *(Cinnamomum)*.
• **DISTRIBUTION** Common from India and Sri Lanka to China, Japan, Malaysia, Papua New Guinea and Australia.

unusual hindwing shape

distinctive pocket of pale scent scales distinguishes the male

♂

INDO-AUSTRALIAN

| Time of Flight ☼ | Habitat 🌴 ⸜⸜ ⸜⸜ | Wingspan 8–9cm (3¼–3½in) |

| Family PAPILIONIDAE | Species *Battus philenor* | Author Linnaeus |

PIPEVINE SWALLOWTAIL

The male butterfly has a metallic-blue sheen on the hindwings. This swallowtail is mimicked by several other butterfly species. It is also called the blue swallowtail.
• **EARLY STAGES** The caterpillar is reddish brown, with rows of black or red, fleshy tentacles on its back. It feeds on the foliage of pipevines *(Aristolochia)*, and other plants.
• **DISTRIBUTION** From southern Canada to Mexico and Costa Rica.

forewings much duller than hindwings

pale, arrow-shaped markings on hindwings

♂

NEARCTIC
NEOTROPICAL

| Time of Flight ☼ | Habitat 🌳 🌱 🌱 | Wingspan 7.5–11cm (3–4½in) |

| Family PAPILIONIDAE | Species *Battus polydamas* | Author Linnaeus |

POLYDAMAS SWALLOWTAIL

This golden-yellow fringed butterfly has no tails. It is dark and the hindwings usually have a green lustre. The underside is patterned with red. These swallowtails are distasteful to birds.
• **EARLY STAGES** The caterpillar is black, and feeds on pipevines *(Aristolochia)*.
• **DISTRIBUTION** From northern Argentina to the West Indies, Central America, and southern parts of the USA.

distinctive yellow band on both wings

strongly scalloped hindwings

♀

NEARCTIC
NEOTROPICAL

| Time of Flight ☼ | Habitat 🌴 🌱 🌱 | Wingspan 7–9cm (2¾–3½in) |

Family PAPILIONIDAE	Species *Iphiclides podalirius*	Author Scopoli

SCARCE SWALLOWTAIL

This pale yellow species has slender, transverse stripes and long tails. In some forms, the background colour is almost white and the black stripes are much heavier.
• **EARLY STAGES** The caterpillar is slug-like. Its body is green with yellow lines, often spotted with red. It feeds on blackthorn *(Prunus spinosa)*.
• **DISTRIBUTION** Despite its common name, this species is widespread in Europe. Its range extends to North Africa and across temperate Asia to China.

black, V-shaped markings angled towards forewing edge

♀

PALAEARCTIC

blue markings stop before front edge of hindwing

long hindwing tails

orange and blue eyespots on hindwing

Time of Flight ☼	Habitat 🌳 ⚘ ⚘	Wingspan 7–8cm (2¾–3¼in)

Family PAPILIONIDAE	Species *Zerynthia rumina*	Author Linnaeus

SPANISH FESTOON

A very distinctive black and yellow butterfly with an intricate, lace-like and delicate pattern, the Spanish festoon belongs to a very easily recognized group of tailless swallowtails. It can be distinguished from other closely related festoons by the vivid, and conspicuous red markings on the forewing. Spanish festoons can be seen on the wing from late winter to late spring. Females are usually larger than the males, and are a darker shade of yellow.
• **EARLY STAGES** The caterpillar is pale brown with rows of blunt, red spines along its body. It feeds on birthwort *(Aristolochia)*.
• **DISTRIBUTION** This butterfly species can be found among the rough, stony hillsides of south-eastern France, Spain, and Portugal. It is particularly common around coastal regions within its habitat.

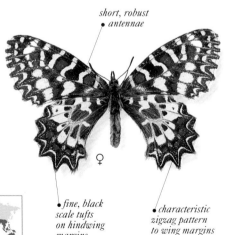

short, robust antennae

♀

PALAEARCTIC

fine, black scale tufts on hindwing margins

characteristic zigzag pattern to wing margins

Time of Flight ☼	Habitat ⚘ ⚘	Wingspan 4.5–5cm (1¾–2in)

Family PAPILIONIDAE	Species *Lamproptera meges*	Author Zincken

GREEN DRAGONTAIL

This butterfly is easily recognized by its translucent forewings and drooping tail. The only other species in this genus *(Lamproptera curius)* can be distinguished by the presence of a transverse white band on the wings. Green dragontails resemble dragonflies in flight, and have a very rapid wingbeat. Even when resting, they vibrate their wings and, unlike the majority of butterflies, they hover over flowers while feeding.

• **EARLY STAGES** Although the caterpillar does not appear to be known, the related *Lamproptera curius* has a dark apple-green caterpillar that feeds on *Illigera cordata* foliage.

• **DISTRIBUTION** Usually found in sunlit forest clearings from India to southern China, Malaysia, the Philippines, and Sulawesi.

antennae are almost as • long as forewings

white margins to • hindwings

scattered white • or pale yellow scales on hindwing

long, feather- • like tails

♂

INDO-AUSTRALIAN

Time of Flight ☼	Habitat 🜪	Wingspan 4–5cm (1½–2in)

Family PAPILIONIDAE	Species *Parnassius apollo*	Author Linnaeus

APOLLO

Although the pattern of this butterfly is distinctive, it is also very variable. It can be distinguished from similar species by the absence of red markings on the forewing. Males are smaller than females.

• **EARLY STAGES** The caterpillar is a velvety black colour with a line of orange-red spots along its sides. It is known to feed on stonecrop *(Sedum)* and houseleek *(Sempervivum)*.

• **DISTRIBUTION** In mountain districts in Europe, extending into central Asia.

subtle grey dusting on • wing edges

distinctive, grey antennae with • dark rings

hindwing • markings vary in colour from red to orange-yellow

grey hairs on • tip of body

♂

PALAEARCTIC

Time of Flight ☼	Habitat ▲	Wingspan 5–10cm (2–4in)

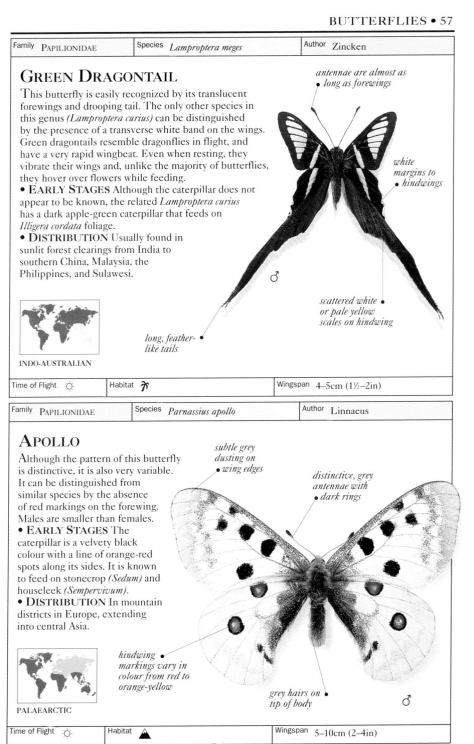

Family PAPILIONIDAE	Species *Cressida cressida*	Author Fabricius

BIG GREASY BUTTERFLY

The male butterfly has transparent forewings with two large, black spots on each. Freshly emerged females are dark grey with a distinctive pattern, but most of the wing scales are soon shed and the wings take on a paler, greasy appearance.
• **EARLY STAGES** The caterpillar is dark brown, often mottled with creamy white, but is variable in colour and pattern. It feeds on pipevines *(Aristolochia)*.
• **DISTRIBUTION** There are two subspecies of this butterfly found in Australia. A third subspecies occurs in Papua New Guinea.

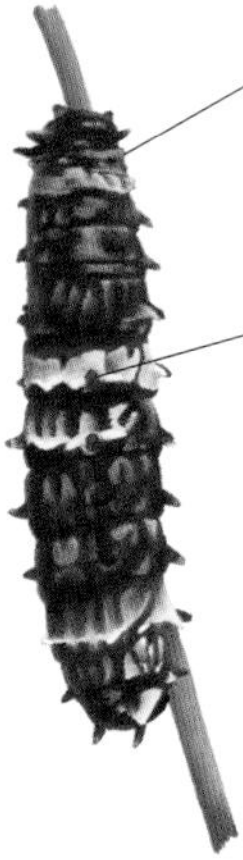

distinctive brown and cream caterpillar

red spots on cream bands

CATERPILLAR OF CRESSIDA CRESSIDA

the male has narrower forewings than the female

red spots on hindwings

♂

dull appearance due to loss of scales

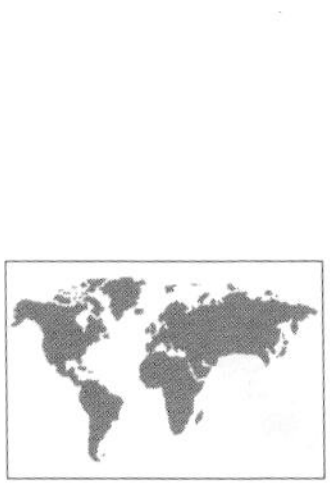

black and red body indicates that this is a poisonous species

♀

INDO-AUSTRALIAN

Time of Flight ☀	Habitat 🌿	Wingspan 7–7.5cm (2¾–3in)

Family PAPILIONIDAE	Species *Ornithoptera alexandrae*	Author Rothschild

QUEEN ALEXANDRA'S BIRDWING

This is the largest known butterfly in the world. The males are considerably smaller than the females and are distinguishable from related species by their striking wing pattern and colour. The underside of the male hindwing is golden-yellow with black veining, and is shaded with green.

• **EARLY STAGES** The caterpillar is reddish black with bright red, fleshy, pointed tentacles and a cream-coloured saddle marking in the middle of its body. It feeds on *Aristolochia schlecteri*.

• **DISTRIBUTION** Confined to south-east Papua New Guinea, east of the Owen Stanley Ranges. This species is rare and is now protected.

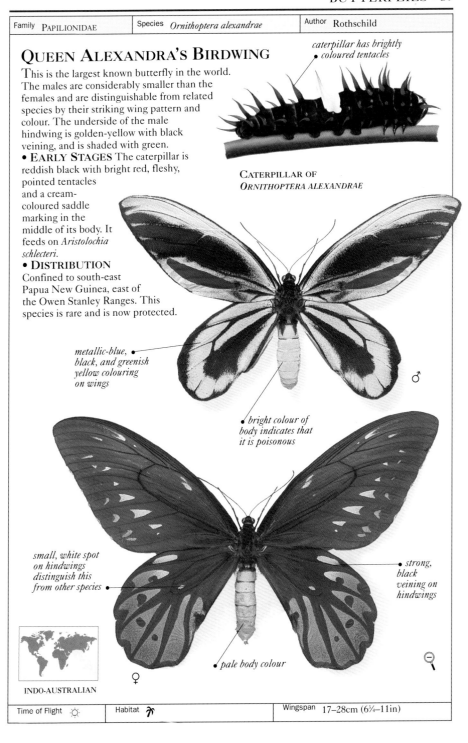

caterpillar has brightly coloured tentacles

CATERPILLAR OF
ORNITHOPTERA ALEXANDRAE

metallic-blue, black, and greenish yellow colouring on wings

♂

bright colour of body indicates that it is poisonous

small, white spot on hindwings distinguish this from other species

strong, black veining on hindwings

pale body colour

♀

INDO-AUSTRALIAN

Time of Flight ☼	Habitat 🌴	Wingspan 17–28cm (6¾–11in)

Family PAPILIONIDAE	Species *Ornithoptera priamus*	Author Linnaeus

CAIRNS BIRDWING

This common name applies to just one of a large number of subspecies of this magnificent birdwing butterfly. Males are distinctively patterned with black and green on the upperside. The underside of the forewing is black with a turquoise centre, overlaid with black veins. The females are much larger than the males, and their wings are black with white markings. These birdwings have a strong, gliding flight.

• **EARLY STAGES** The caterpillar varies in colour from blackish brown to grey, with long, fleshy spines. It feeds on pipevines *(Aristolochia)*.

• **DISTRIBUTION** From the Moluccas to Papua New Guinea, the Solomon Islands, and northern Australia.

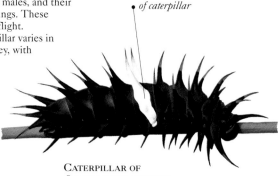

white band across middle of caterpillar

CATERPILLAR OF
ORNITHOPTERA PRIAMUS

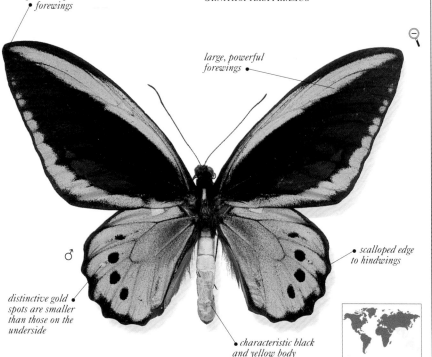

pointed tip to forewings

large, powerful forewings

scalloped edge to hindwings

♂

distinctive gold spots are smaller than those on the underside

characteristic black and yellow body

INDO-AUSTRALIAN

Time of Flight ☼	Habitat 🌴	Wingspan 10.8–13cm (4¼–5in)

Family PAPILIONIDAE	Species *Troides brookiana*	Author Wallace

RAJAH BROOKE'S BIRDWING

Although there are several named subspecies, all
males are similar in appearance, with a distinctive
green pattern on a black background. Females vary
in colour from olive-green with white or green
markings, to black with coppery green markings.
The hindwings of the females are often flushed
with metallic-blue at the base. These birdwings
have a powerful, soaring flight. Males can often
be found drinking from wet mud; both sexes
are attracted to flowers.

• **EARLY STAGES** The caterpillar is dark
brown to grey with a lighter saddle marking
in the middle of the body. It has long,
tentacle-like projections which are a pale
yellowish brown. The shorter "tentacles"
are the same colour as the body. The head
is large, black, and shiny. The caterpillar
eats pipevines *(Aristolochia)*.

• **DISTRIBUTION** Occurs from
Malaysia to Sumatra and Borneo.

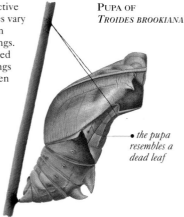

PUPA OF
TROIDES BROOKIANA

• *the pupa
resembles a
dead leaf*

*typical elongated
forewing shape of
• birdwing butterflies*

*striking contrast
of green on solid
black base •*

• red collar

*• characteristic
wing pattern is
also present in
some females*

♂

• jet-black body

INDO-AUSTRALIAN

Time of Flight ☼	Habitat 🜨	Wingspan 12–17.8cm (4¾–7in)

PIERIDAE

T HIS IS A LARGE family of more than 1,000 species of butterfly. Most of the species are predominantly white, yellow, or orange in colour and are often referred to collectively as whites, yellows, or sulphurs. Pigments that are derived from the body's waste products explain the distinct colouring, which is a feature peculiar to this family of butterflies. It is believed that the name "butterfly" originates from a member of the Pieridae – the bright yellow brimstone *(Gonepteryx rhamni)* that was known to the early British naturalists as the butter-coloured fly.

———— • ————

This family includes the cabbage white butterflies *(Pieris brassicae* and *Pieris rapae)*, which are commonly seen in gardens, and are notorious pests.

Family PIERIDAE	Species *Appias nero*	Author Fabricius

ORANGE ALBATROSS

This most striking butterfly is probably the only species in the world that is entirely orange in colour. Females look similar to males but have a black border around the wings and a black band on the hindwing. Males are often seen drinking from the moist sand of river banks. Females are much more retiring and tend to keep high in the tree canopy. They are known to feed from the flowers of a variety of trees.
• **EARLY STAGES** Little seems to be known about the early stages of this species except that the caterpillar feeds on plants of the family Capparidaceae.
• **DISTRIBUTION** Widely distributed from northern India to Burma, Malaysia, the Philippines, and Sulawesi.

INDO-AUSTRALIAN

long, slender antennae •

characteristic sharply pointed forewings •

black veining on forewing •

♂

yellow shading on inner hindwing margin •

• *dark-coloured body*

Time of Flight ☼	Habitat 🌶	Wingspan 7–7.5cm (2¾–3in)

Family PIERIDAE	Species *Mylothris chloris*	Author Fabricius

COMMON DOTTED BORDER

This species of butterfly has two distinct geographical forms (the race shown here is from western Africa). The upperside of the female's forewing is similar to the underside but the hindwing upperside is a pale salmon-pink. Males of the east and the South African races differ. They have the base of the forewings flushed with pink and the black markings on the hindwings reduced to black dots.

• **EARLY STAGES** The caterpillar is black with transverse, reddish bands. It feeds on the foliage of various mistletoes (Loranthaceae).

• **DISTRIBUTION** Very common in woodland, savanna, parks, and gardens throughout Africa, south of the Sahara.

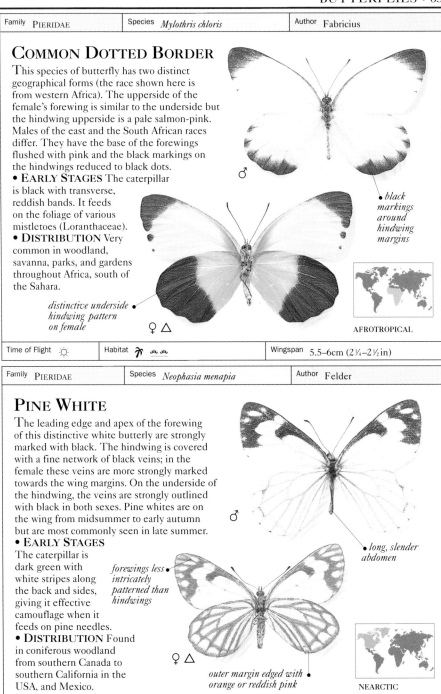

black markings around hindwing margins

distinctive underside hindwing pattern on female

♀ △

♂

AFROTROPICAL

Time of Flight ☼	Habitat 🦅 ⚘ ⚘	Wingspan 5.5–6cm (2¼–2½ in)

Family PIERIDAE	Species *Neophasia menapia*	Author Felder

PINE WHITE

The leading edge and apex of the forewing of this distinctive white butterly are strongly marked with black. The hindwing is covered with a fine network of black veins; in the female these veins are more strongly marked towards the wing margins. On the underside of the hindwing, the veins are strongly outlined with black in both sexes. Pine whites are on the wing from midsummer to early autumn but are most commonly seen in late summer.

• **EARLY STAGES** The caterpillar is dark green with white stripes along the back and sides, giving it effective camouflage when it feeds on pine needles.

• **DISTRIBUTION** Found in coniferous woodland from southern Canada to southern California in the USA, and Mexico.

long, slender abdomen

♂

forewings less intricately patterned than hindwings

♀ △

outer margin edged with orange or reddish pink

NEARCTIC

Time of Flight ☼	Habitat ▲ 🌲	Wingspan 4–5cm (1½–2in)

Family PIERIDAE	Species *Anaphaeis java*	Author Sparrmann

CAPER WHITE

In the male form the distinctive black bands on the forewings and hindwings of this butterfly are patterned with a row of white streaks and spots. There are two female forms: one similar to the male but more strongly marked; the other with black bands, and almost devoid of white markings.

• **EARLY STAGES** The caterpillar is olive-green to brown. It feeds on capers *(Capparis)* and related plants.

• **DISTRIBUTION** About ten different subspecies are recognized ranging from Java to Papua New Guinea, Fiji, Samoa, and Australia.

♂

• *extent of black on hindwings is very variable in this species*

•*wedge-shaped markings*

INDO-AUSTRALIAN

♀ △

Time of Flight ☼	Habitat 🌿 ⚊ ⚊	Wingspan 4.5–5.5cm (1¾–2¼in)

Family PIERIDAE	Species *Anaphaeis aurota*	Author Fabricius

BROWN-VEINED WHITE

This pure white butterfly is strongly marked on the upperside margins of the forewings with black or blackish brown bands, patterned with large, white, elongate spots. Females of the species tend to be more heavily marked than males.

• **EARLY STAGES** The caterpillar is yellowish green with black stripes along its side. It feeds on various species of *Capparis*, *Boscia*, and *Maerua*.

• **DISTRIBUTION** This species ranges from Africa to the Middle East, and India.

• *characteristic dark markings on the forewing*

♂

yellow streaks on the hindwing •

AFROTROPICAL
INDO-AUSTRALIAN

♀ △

Time of Flight ☼	Habitat ⚊ ⚊	Wingspan 5–5.5cm (2–2¼in)

Family PIERIDAE	Species *Delias mysis*	Author Fabricius

UNION JACK

The Union Jack has distinctive black tips on
the forewings, marked with four white spots. The
hindwing is marked with black along the margins.
• **EARLY STAGES** The caterpillar is yellowish
green with long, white hairs. Its head is black.The
caterpillar feeds on mistletoe *(Viscum)*.
• **DISTRIBUTION** Found in rainforests of northern
Australia, Papua New Guinea, and adjacent islands.

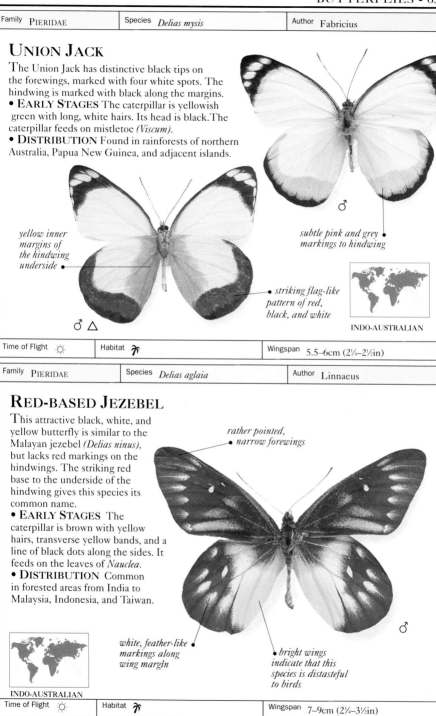

*yellow inner
margins of
the hindwing
underside* •

*subtle pink and grey •
markings to hindwing*

♂ △

• *striking flag-like
pattern of red,
black, and white*

INDO-AUSTRALIAN

Time of Flight ☼	Habitat 🐦	Wingspan 5.5–6cm (2¼–2½in)

Family PIERIDAE	Species *Delias aglaia*	Author Linnaeus

RED-BASED JEZEBEL

This attractive black, white, and
yellow butterfly is similar to the
Malayan jezebel *(Delias ninus),*
but lacks red markings on the
hindwings. The striking red
base to the underside of the
hindwing gives this species its
common name.
• **EARLY STAGES** The
caterpillar is brown with yellow
hairs, transverse yellow bands, and a
line of black dots along the sides. It
feeds on the leaves of *Nauclea.*
• **DISTRIBUTION** Common
in forested areas from India to
Malaysia, Indonesia, and Taiwan.

*rather pointed,
• narrow forewings*

♂

INDO-AUSTRALIAN

*white, feather-like •
markings along
wing margin*

• *bright wings
indicate that this
species is distasteful
to birds*

Time of Flight ☼	Habitat 🐦	Wingspan 7–9cm (2¾–3½in)

Family PIERIDAE	Species *Aporia crataegi*	Author Linnaeus

BLACK-VEINED WHITE

Aptly named, this butterfly is unlikely to be confused with any other species. Females tend to be larger and more transparent than males. The underside of both sexes is lightly suffused with black scaling.

• **EARLY STAGES** The caterpillar is grey and hairy with a black back, covered with broad, reddish brown lines. It feeds on hawthorn *(Crataegus monogyna)* and blackthorn *(Prunus spinosa)*.

• **DISTRIBUTION** Occurs throughout mainland Europe. Range extends to North Africa, and across temperate Asia to Japan.

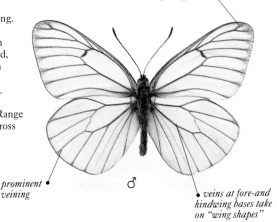

grey scaling at tips of wing veins •

prominent veining •

♂

• veins at fore-and hindwing bases take on "wing shapes"

PALAEARCTIC

Time of Flight ☼	Habitat	Wingspan 6–7.5cm (2½–3in)

Family PIERIDAE	Species *Pereute leucodrosime*	Author Kollar

RED-BANDED PEREUTE

This unusual black Pierid butterfly belongs to a small genus of about ten species, all confined to South America. It can be distinguished by its relatively large size, the red band on the forewing, and the bluish grey patch on the hindwing, although all of these markings are variable in extent. The underside of the hindwing lacks the bluish patch but has a small red spot at the base. The sexes look similar.

• **EARLY STAGES** The caterpillar and foodplants of this species appear to be unknown, but related species feed on plants of the family Loranthaceae.

• **DISTRIBUTION** Widespread in South America, from Brazil to Colombia.

characteristic white antennae •

striking red band startles predators when the butterfly opens its wings to fly •

♂

bluish grey coloration continues on body hair •

NEOTROPICAL

Time of Flight ☼	Habitat	Wingspan 6–7cm (2½–2¾in)

Family PIERIDAE	Species *Pieris brassicae*	Author Linnaeus

LARGE WHITE

Females can be recognized by the presence of two black spots and a black streak on the forewing. The undersides of the hindwings of both sexes are bright yellow with slight black scaling.
• **EARLY STAGES** The caterpillar is pale green, heavily spotted with black, with yellow lines along the back and sides. It feeds on cabbage *(Brassica oleracea)*, completely stripping the leaves. This is a notorious agricultural pest, commonly known as the cabbage white.
• **DISTRIBUTION** Common in Europe, the Mediterranean, and North Africa.

black
• wing-tips

greyish black leading
edge to forewing •

creamy white •
hindwings

♂

PALAEARCTIC

Time of Flight ☼	Habitat	Wingspan 5.5–7cm (2¼–2¾in)

Family PIERIDAE	Species *Pieris rapae*	Author Linnaeus

SMALL WHITE

This is an uninspiring but well-known and widely distributed species, distinguished by its small size and simple black wing markings. Females have a yellow hue, and two black spots on the forewing. Small whites are on the wing from spring to autumn.
• **EARLY STAGES** The caterpillar is yellowish green. It feeds on cultivated and wild cabbage *(Brassica oleracea)* and other related plants.
• **DISTRIBUTION** Widespread throughout Europe, and across temperate Asia to Japan. It also occurs in Australia and North America.

grey shading
• on wings

♂

yellow forewing tip •
and leading edge

underside of
hindwing finely
dusted with
black scales •

bright yellow
hindwing
• underside

WORLDWIDE

♂ △

Time of Flight ☼	Habitat	Wingspan 4.5–5.5cm (1¾–2¼in)

Family PIERIDAE	Species *Leptosia nina*	Author Fabricius

PSYCHE BUTTERFLY

This small, white butterfly has black markings on the wing-tips. The underside of the hindwing is faintly marked with green. The sexes are similar. They seldom fly more than 1m (3ft) above the ground.
• **EARLY STAGES** The caterpillar is pale green and feeds on *Capparis heyneana* and *Crataeva religiosa*.
• **DISTRIBUTION** Found in bamboo thickets from India to Malaysia, into southern China, as far as Indonesia.

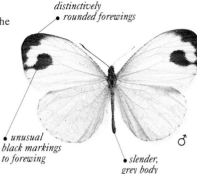

distinctively rounded forewings

unusual black markings to forewing

slender, grey body

♂

INDO-AUSTRALIAN

Time of Flight ☼	Habitat 🌿 🌴	Wingspan 4–5cm (1½–2in)

Family PIERIDAE	Species *Zerene eurydice*	Author Boisduval

CALIFORNIA DOG-FACE

A distinctive butterfly, the California dog-face gets its unusual common name from the yellow "face" on the black forewings of the male, which are sometimes shot with a beautiful reddish purple lustre. The butterfly is also known as the flying pansy. The hindwings are a rich golden-yellow, sometimes with black margins. Females are a much paler yellow. These butterflies are on the wing from spring to autumn.
• **EARLY STAGES** The caterpillar is dull green with an orange-edged, white stripe along its sides. It feeds on clover *(Trifolium)*.
• **DISTRIBUTION** Widespread in the USA in California, and sometimes as far afield as western Arizona.

black spot in centre of forewing

♂

hindwings much brighter on males

reddish brown, scalloped margin to forewing

plain wings on female

♀

NEARCTIC

Time of Flight ☼	Habitat ▲ 🌳	Wingspan 4–6cm (1½–2½ in)

| Family PIERIDAE | Species *Catopsilia florella* | Author Fabricius |

AFRICAN MIGRANT

The African migrant is a fairly common butterfly. The males are white with a greenish yellow tint and have a small, black spot in the middle of the forewing. Pale female forms can also occur, some of which are almost white.
• **EARLY STAGES** The caterpillar is greenish yellow with small, black spots. It feeds on sennas *(Cassia)*.
• **DISTRIBUTION** Occurs throughout Africa, and the Canary Islands. Also extends eastwards across India to China and Malaysia.

AFROTROPICAL
INDO-AUSTRALIAN

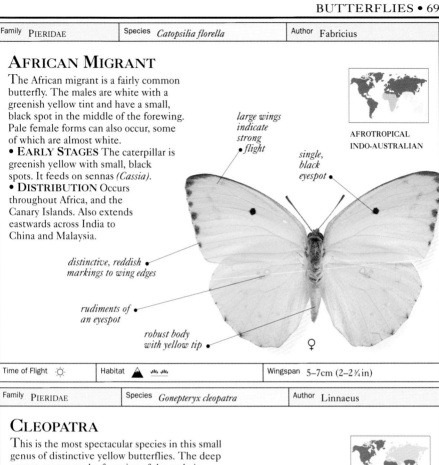

large wings indicate strong *flight*

single, black eyespot •

distinctive, reddish • markings to wing edges

rudiments of • an eyespot

robust body with yellow tip •

♀

| Time of Flight ☼ | Habitat ▲ ⫶⫶ | Wingspan 5–7cm (2–2¾in) |

| Family PIERIDAE | Species *Gonepteryx cleopatra* | Author Linnaeus |

CLEOPATRA

This is the most spectacular species in this small genus of distinctive yellow butterflies. The deep orange centre on the forewing of the male is characteristic, as are the slight hindwing tails. Females are larger and much paler, with only a trace of colour. Cleopatras can be distinguished from other species by the presence of a faint orange streak on the underside of the forewing. They are on the wing from late winter to autumn, particularly in Mediterranean coastal areas.
• **EARLY STAGES** The caterpillar is bluish green, with a white stripe along the sides. It feeds on buckthorn *(Rhamnus)*.
• **DISTRIBUTION** Occurs in lightly wooded areas in Spain, southern France, and Italy, to Greece, North Africa, and the Canary Islands where there is a distinct race known as the Canary Island brimstone.

PALAEARCTIC

small, reddish brown markings • on wing margins

♂

| Time of Flight ☼ | Habitat ♣ | Wingspan 5–7cm (2–2¾in) |

Family PIERIDAE	Species *Phoebis philea*	Author Johansson

ORANGE-BARRED GIANT SULPHUR

Males of this species have a broad, orange bar on the forewing, giving rise to the common name. Females are yellow or white with brown or black markings on both the fore- and hindwing borders. The underside is variably coloured with salmon-pink and purplish hues. The butterfly is also commonly known as the yellow apricot.

NEOTROPICAL

• **EARLY STAGES** The caterpillar is yellowish green with transverse wrinkles and a brownish black band along the sides. It feeds on sennas *(Cassia)*.

• **DISTRIBUTION** Widespread from southern Brazil to Central America and southern Florida, in the USA, where it often occurs in parks and gardens. It also strays as far north as New York.

traces of dark markings on forewing tips of male •

V-shaped marking to forewing •

♂

• *dark shading to hindwing margin*

• *central spot in forewing of female*

• *slight scalloping to hindwings*

smoky-red hindwing borders •

♀

Time of Flight ☼	Habitat 🌴	Wingspan 7–8cm (2¾–3¼in)

Family PIERIDAE	Species *Eurema brigitta*	Author Cramer

BROAD-BORDERED GRASS YELLOW

A very distinctive little butterfly varying in colour
from yellow to deep orange. The black margins of the
forewing and narrower margins of the hindwing are
characteristic of males of this species. Females are
usually paler with more diffuse, dark markings.
• **EARLY STAGES** The
caterpillar is green with a
stripe on its back and a
yellow stripe on its sides.
It feeds on sennas *(Cassia)*.
• **DISTRIBUTION** From
Africa to India, China, Papua
New Guinea, and Australia.

AFROTROPICAL
INDO-AUSTRALIAN

*broad, black
forewing
• markings*

♂

Time of Flight ☼	Habitat 〰 〰	Wingspan 4–5cm (1½–2in)

Family PIERIDAE	Species *Anteos clorinde*	Author Godart

YELLOW-SPOTTED GONATRYX

This large and distinctive species belongs to a small
genus of mainly South American butterflies known as
the mammoth sulphurs. They are rather similar in
appearance to the Palaearctic genus, *Gonepteryx*, but are
not closely related. This butterfly can be recognized by
the large, bright golden-yellow patch on the forewing of
the male, and by the small, yellow-ringed black spots
in the centre of each wing. Females lack the yellow
forewing marking, or merely
show slight traces of it.
Another common name
for the butterfly is the
white-angled sulphur.
• **EARLY STAGES**
Although the caterpillar
appears to be undescribed,
it is known to feed on
senna *(Senna spectabilis)*,
and *Pithecellobium*.
• **DISTRIBUTION** Found
from Brazil northwards to
Central America, the West
Indies, and the USA in
southern Texas, Arizona,
and Colorado.

*curved
wing-tips •*

*bright golden
patch on forewing
of male •*

*thin, faint
hindwing
margin •*

♂

small, pointed tails •

NEOTROPICAL

Time of Flight ☼	Habitat 🌳 🌷	Wingspan 7–9cm (2¾–3½in)

| Family PIERIDAE | Species *Colias eurytheme* | Author Boisduval |

ORANGE SULPHUR

Females are larger than males and are more extensively marked with black on the forewing margins. Spring examples are sometimes yellow, flushed with orange in the centre of the wings.
• **EARLY STAGES** The caterpillar is dark green with a black-edged, white stripe along the sides and a pink stripe lower down. It feeds on alfalfa *(Medicago sativa)*, white clover *(Trifolium repens)*, and related plants.
• **DISTRIBUTION** Common in many parts of the USA, becoming scarcer in Canada and towards southern Florida.

orange spot distinguishes this from the common sulphur •

characteristic black spot in centre of forewings •

♂

♀

NEARCTIC

| Time of Flight ☼ | Habitat 🌾 🌿 🌿 | Wingspan 4–6cm (1½–2½in) |

| Family PIERIDAE | Species *Pontia daplidice* | Author Linnaeus |

BATH WHITE

The distinctive black markings on the forewings of the bath white, particularly the large, squarish, central spot, separate this species from related European species. The pale, olive-green underside markings effectively camouflage it when at rest. Females are larger than males and have more extensive dark markings, particularly on the hindwings. Bath whites are on the wing from late winter to early autumn.
• **EARLY STAGES** The caterpillar is bluish grey with raised, black dots and yellow stripes along the back and sides. It feeds on mignonette *(Reseda lutea)*, mustard *(Sinapis)*, and related plants.
• **DISTRIBUTION** From central and southern Europe across temperate Asia to Japan.

distinguishing central, black spot on forewing • upperside

♀

females have an extra dark spot on the forewing underside •

distinctive white spots on hindwing margin

♀ △

• olive-green markings provide effective camouflage

PALAEARCTIC

| Time of Flight ☼ | Habitat 🌾 🌿 🌿 | Wingspan 4–5cm (1½–2in) |

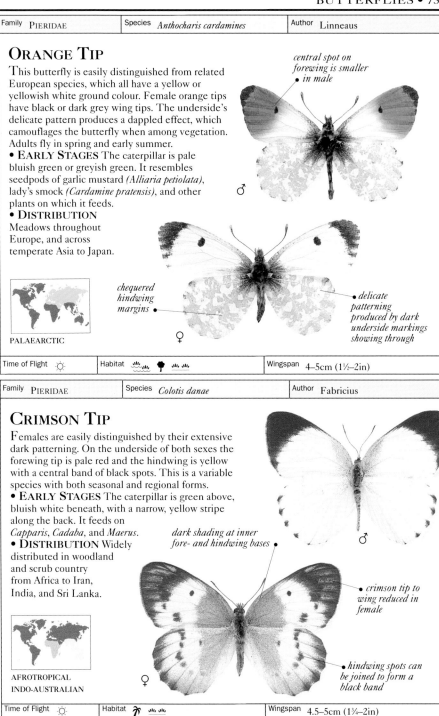

| Family PIERIDAE | Species *Anthocharis cardamines* | Author Linneaus |

ORANGE TIP

This butterfly is easily distinguished from related European species, which all have a yellow or yellowish white ground colour. Female orange tips have black or dark grey wing tips. The underside's delicate pattern produces a dappled effect, which camouflages the butterfly when among vegetation. Adults fly in spring and early summer.
• **EARLY STAGES** The caterpillar is pale bluish green or greyish green. It resembles seedpods of garlic mustard *(Alliaria petiolata)*, lady's smock *(Cardamine pratensis)*, and other plants on which it feeds.
• **DISTRIBUTION** Meadows throughout Europe, and across temperate Asia to Japan.

central spot on forewing is smaller in male

♂

PALAEARCTIC

chequered hindwing margins

delicate patterning produced by dark underside markings showing through

♀

| Time of Flight ☼ | Habitat | Wingspan 4–5cm (1½–2in) |

| Family PIERIDAE | Species *Colotis danae* | Author Fabricius |

CRIMSON TIP

Females are easily distinguished by their extensive dark patterning. On the underside of both sexes the forewing tip is pale red and the hindwing is yellow with a central band of black spots. This is a variable species with both seasonal and regional forms.
• **EARLY STAGES** The caterpillar is green above, bluish white beneath, with a narrow, yellow stripe along the back. It feeds on *Capparis*, *Cadaba*, and *Maerus*.
• **DISTRIBUTION** Widely distributed in woodland and scrub country from Africa to Iran, India, and Sri Lanka.

♂

dark shading at inner fore- and hindwing bases

crimson tip to wing reduced in female

AFROTROPICAL
INDO-AUSTRALIAN

♀

hindwing spots can be joined to form a black band

| Time of Flight ☼ | Habitat | Wingspan 4.5–5cm (1¾–2in) |

Family PIERIDAE	Species *Dismorphia amphione*	Author Cramer

TIGER PIERID

This unusual Pierid butterfly belongs to a large genus of about 40 species of South American butterfly that are remarkable mimics of various distasteful butterflies. The striking black, orange, and yellow patterning of both sexes, which has earned them their common name, is very variable and there are many named forms and subspecies. They are mostly seen flying along forest edges from sea level to about 1,000m (3,300ft).

• **EARLY STAGES**
The caterpillar is a dark, translucent green. It feeds on *Inga sapindoides*, *Inga densiflora*, and related species.

• **DISTRIBUTION**
Widespread and common in South and Central America, and also in the West Indies, and Mexico.

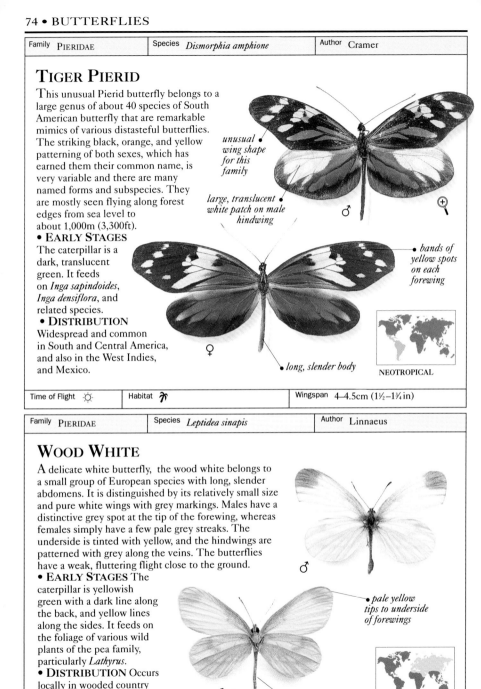

unusual wing shape for this family

large, translucent white patch on male hindwing ♂

♀

long, slender body

bands of yellow spots on each forewing

NEOTROPICAL

Time of Flight ☼	Habitat 🎋	Wingspan 4–4.5cm (1½–1¾in)

Family PIERIDAE	Species *Leptidea sinapis*	Author Linnaeus

WOOD WHITE

A delicate white butterfly, the wood white belongs to a small group of European species with long, slender abdomens. It is distinguished by its relatively small size and pure white wings with grey markings. Males have a distinctive grey spot at the tip of the forewing, whereas females simply have a few pale grey streaks. The underside is tinted with yellow, and the hindwings are patterned with grey along the veins. The butterflies have a weak, fluttering flight close to the ground.

• **EARLY STAGES** The caterpillar is yellowish green with a dark line along the back, and yellow lines along the sides. It feeds on the foliage of various wild plants of the pea family, particularly *Lathyrus*.

• **DISTRIBUTION** Occurs locally in wooded country in many areas of Europe, including the British Isles.

♂

♂ △

pale yellow tips to underside of forewings

slender body is typical of this group

PALAEARCTIC

Time of Flight ☼	Habitat ♣	Wingspan 4–5cm (1½–2in)

Family PIERIDAE	Species *Hebomoia glaucippe*	Author Linnaeus

GREAT ORANGE TIP

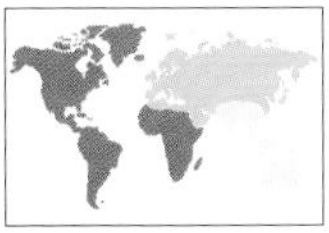

This handsome species is the largest Pierid
butterfly in Asia. Females are much darker than
males and have an extensive pattern of dark spots
on the hindwings. The undersides of both sexes are
similar, but strikingly different from the uppersides.
The entire hindwing and the outer half of the
forewing are delicately patterned with shades of
brown and buff, creating the appearance of a dead
leaf when the butterfly rests on the ground with
its wings closed. Great orange tips have a fast
and powerful flight. Males are often seen
congregating on moist
ground by streams,
but females seldom
leave the shelter of
the forest.

INDO-AUSTRALIAN
PALAEARCTIC

• **EARLY STAGES**
The caterpillar is green
with a pale stripe along
each side. It feeds on
Crataeva religiosa and
Capparis moonii.

• **DISTRIBUTION** Occurs
from India to Malaysia,
China, and Japan.

*brown
leading
edge to
forewing*

orange wing-tip

*large wings
indicate strong
flight*

♂

*pointed
wing-tips*

*red shading
less distinct
than on males*

*diamond
patterns on
hindwings
of females*

*black, V-shaped
markings on
hind margins*

♀

Time of Flight ☼	Habitat 🌴	Wingspan 7–10cm (2¾–4in)

LYCAENIDAE

THIS is a large family of more than 5,000 small, brightly coloured butterflies that occur throughout the world, but mostly in tropical and subtropical regions. The sexes often differ in coloration, and the undersides usually differ from the upper surfaces. There are several distinct groups of Lycaenidae. One large group, the hairstreaks, have tails and bright eyespot markings on their hindwings, which create a false "head" at the rear, thus diverting attackers from this area.

———— • ————

The caterpillars are often described as "slug-like". Many draw their head back into the body when threatened or resting, and some of them secrete a sweetish substance, which is very attractive to various species of ant.

Family LYCAENIDAE	Species *Liphyra brassolis*	Author Westwood

MOTH BUTTERFLY

This very large orange and black butterfly has an almost moth-like appearance and behaviour, hence its common name. The males are much more extensively marked with black than the females.

• **EARLY STAGES** The caterpillar is smooth, elliptical in shape, and very flattened. It lives in the nests of tree ants, and feeds on the larvae. When the butterfly emerges from the pupa, the wings and body are covered with highly adhesive scales, which will stick to any ants that may attack it.

• **DISTRIBUTION** From India, across South-east Asia to northern Australia.

extensive black markings on wings of male

♂

• small lobes on male hindwings

• forewings of females more rounded than those of males

♀

robust, moth-like body denotes a strong-flying species

INDO-AUSTRALIAN

Time of Flight ◑ ☼	Habitat 🏃	Wingspan 6–9cm (2½–3½in)

Family LYCAENIDAE	Species *Liptena simplicia*	Author Möschler

MÖSCHLER'S LIPTENA

This species belongs to a genus of more than 50 species living in the tropics of Africa. It has satin-white wings with broad, black borders to the front of the forewings. The underside is similarly marked, but there is an additional black band on the hindwings. The sexes look similar.

• **EARLY STAGES** The hairy caterpillar feeds on various lichens and fungi.
• **DISTRIBUTION** Widespread in Africa, south of the Sahara.

AFROTROPICAL

wing pattern continues on to head

♂

characteristic black fringes to hindwings

Time of Flight ☼	Habitat 🌴	Wingspan 2.5–3cm (1–1¼in)

Family LYCAENIDAE	Species *Spalgis epeus*	Author Westwood

APEFLY

Male apeflies have pointed, triangular forewings with one white marking, while those of the females are broader and more rounded. The hindwings of females are a paler brown.

• **EARLY STAGES** The caterpillar is undescribed, but it is known to feed on scale insects and mealy bugs.
• **DISTRIBUTION** From India and Sri Lanka, through Malaysia to Sulawesi.

INDO-AUSTRALIAN

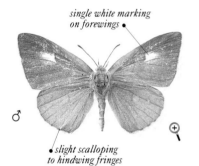

single white marking on forewings

♂

slight scalloping to hindwing fringes

Time of Flight ☼	Habitat 🌴	Wingspan 2–3cm (¾–1¼in)

Family LYCAENIDAE	Species *Lachnocnema bibulus*	Author Fabricius

WOOLLY LEGS

The upperside of the male butterfly is entirely blackish brown while the female has large patches of white or bluish white. The underside of both sexes is patterned with brown, with metallic scales on the hindwings. The legs are very hairy, hence the common name.

• **EARLY STAGES** The hairy, buff-coloured caterpillar feeds on aphids and scale insects.
• **DISTRIBUTION** Tropical Africa, south of the Sahara.

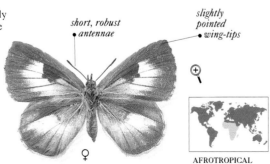

short, robust antennae

slightly pointed wing-tips

♀

AFROTROPICAL

Time of Flight ☼	Habitat 🌴	Wingspan 2–3cm (¾–1¼in)

Family LYCAENIDAE	Species *Megalopalpus zymna*	Author Westwood

SMALL HARVESTER

Easily recognizable by its strong, black forewing markings, this butterfly also has unusually shaped hindwings. The underside of this species lacks the strong, dark forewing markings that are evident on the upperside, but these show through as greyish shading. The sexes of this species are similar.
♂

• **EARLY STAGES** The caterpillar is predacious and feeds on the nymphs and adults of various plant bugs.
• **DISTRIBUTION** Western tropical Africa, south of the Sahara.

AFROTROPICAL

• *tear-shaped hindwings*

• *brown hindwing margins*

Time of Flight ☼	Habitat 🐾	Wingspan 3–4cm (1¼–1½in)

Family LYCAENIDAE	Species *Miletus boisduvali*	Author Moore

BOISDUVAL'S MILETUS

This rather drab-coloured butterfly resembles the apefly (*Spalgis epeus*, see p.77) in that the sexes are distinguished by differing wing shape and the extent of white markings. The Boisduval's miletus does have longer antennae and a more slender body.

• **EARLY STAGES** The caterpillar is undescribed, but is known to feed on aphids.
• **DISTRIBUTION** Widely distributed, mainly in lowland rainforests, from Java to Borneo, and Papua New Guinea.

pointed forewings of male

INDO-AUSTRALIAN

♂

Time of Flight ☼	Habitat 🐾	Wingspan 3–4cm (1¼–1½in)

Family LYCAENIDAE	Species *Feniseca tarquinius*	Author Fabricius

HARVESTER

This distinctive butterfly varies in colour from orange-brown to pale orange-yellow with blackish brown forewing borders, with other markings. The sexes look similar.

• **EARLY STAGES** The greenish brown caterpillar is known to feed on woolly aphids. It covers itself with loosely spun webbing, to which the empty shells of its prey are attached.
• **DISTRIBUTION** Occurs in alder swamps and wet woodland in North America from Canada, to Florida and Texas.

distinctive black markings on forewings

NEARCTIC

♂

Time of Flight ☼	Habitat 〰️🌳	Wingspan 2.5–3cm (1–1¼in)

| Family LYCAENIDAE | Species *Loxura atymnus* | Author Stoll |

YAMFLY

A very distinctive butterfly, the yamfly is orange-red with strong black margins to the forewings. The hindwings taper strongly to a fairly robust tail. The sexes are similar, but females are slightly darker on the hindwings. The underside is orange-yellow with faint, dark markings. These butterflies fly high above the ground.

• **EARLY STAGES** The caterpillar is green with ridges along the back. It feeds on the young shoots of yam *(Dioscorea)* and *Smilax*. The caterpillars are often attended by red ants.

• **DISTRIBUTION** Occurs in lowland forest and wasteland from India and Sri Lanka, to Malaysia and the Philippines.

INDO-AUSTRALIAN

♂

• *hindwing tails*

• *dark brown border to hindwings*

♀

• *distinctive lobe at base of hindwings*

| Time of Flight ☼ | Habitat 🌿 🌴 | Wingspan 3–4cm (1¼–1½in) |

| Family LYCAENIDAE | Species *Cheritra freja* | Author Fabricius |

COMMON IMPERIAL

Both sexes of this distinctive hairstreak are dark blackish brown above with white tails. The wings of males are often shot with purple, while females have more white on the hindwings. The underside is white with the forewings shaded an orange-brown colour: the hindwings are lined and spotted with black.

• **EARLY STAGES** The caterpillar varies from pink to green. It has brown markings, and six protrusions on its back.

• **DISTRIBUTION** Common in forested areas at various altitudes from India and Sri Lanka, to Malaysia and Borneo.

♀

• *double hindwing tails, one much smaller than the other*

• *two eyespots either side of hindwing tails*

♀ △

INDO-AUSTRALIAN

| Time of Flight ☼ | Habitat 🌴 | Wingspan 4–4.5cm (1½–1¾in) |

| Family LYCAENIDAE | Species *Jalmenus evagoras* | Author Donovan |

COMMON IMPERIAL BLUE

All nine species of this genus come from Australia. This is a particularly beautiful species, with metallic-blue scaling on the upperside, and a distinctive underside pattern of black and orange-brown lines on a buff background. In one subspecies, the blue upperside patches are replaced by greenish white.
• **EARLY STAGES** The caterpillar is apparently undescribed, but is known to feed on acacia and the waxy secretions of scale insects. It is gregarious, and is attended by colonies of black ants. The pupae are formed in webs spun by the fully grown caterpillars.
• **DISTRIBUTION** Occurs throughout eastern and south-eastern Australia.

♀

slender, wavy tails

two orange eyespots on each hindwing

♂ △

INDO-AUSTRALIAN

| Time of Flight ☀ | Habitat 🍄 | Wingspan 3–4cm (1¼–1½in) |

| Family LYCAENIDAE | Species *Virachola isocrates* | Author Fabricius |

COMMON GUAVA BLUE

Males of this species are dark purplish blue, while females are a pale brown with a small, orange spot in the centre of each forewing, and a black and orange eyespot at the base of the hindwing tails. The underside is pale buff with darker brown scalloped bands and white vertical lines.
• **EARLY STAGES** The caterpillar is apparently undescribed, but is known to feed inside the fruit of pomegranate *(Punica granatum)* and guava *(Psidium)*. The pupae are later formed inside the shell-like remains of the eaten fruit.
• **DISTRIBUTION** Widespread and common from India to Sri Lanka and Burma. It frequents the plains, and also occurs up to an altitude of 2,000m (6,560ft) in the Himalayas.

♀

angular forewings

paler inner margin to forewings

short, slender tails

♀ △

INDO-AUSTRALIAN

| Time of Flight ☀ | Habitat 🌿 ⚘ ⚘ | Wingspan 3–5cm (1¼–2in) |

Family LYCAENIDAE	Species *Deudorix antalus*	Author Hopffer

BROWN PLAYBOY

The upperside of this butterfly is a delicate,
bluish brown, with an iridescent, purplish sheen
which can be seen in certain lights. Some
specimens are almost white. The underside is
pale brown with dark brown and white lines.
• **EARLY STAGES** The
caterpillar of this species is
apparently undescribed, but
is known to feed on the fruits
of *Crotalaria* and acacia.
• **DISTRIBUTION** Common in
African scrubland and savanna.

AFROTROPICAL

♀

• *lobe bears large,
round, black spot*

Time of Flight ☼	Habitat	Wingspan 2.5–3cm (1–1¼ in)

Family LYCAENIDAE	Species *Strymonidia w-album*	Author Knoch

WHITE-LETTER HAIRSTREAK

Both the common and scientific names refer to the
white "W" on the underside of the hindwing.
The uppersides of both sexes are blackish brown.
• **EARLY STAGES** The caterpillar is coloured
yellowish green with dark green lines and diagonal
markings, which are sometimes tinged with
a pinkish colour. It
feeds on elm *(Ulmus)*.
• **DISTRIBUTION**
This butterfly is
distributed throughout
Europe, and across
temperate Asia to Japan.

*uniform colour
of forewings* •

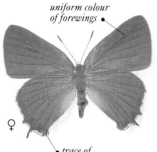

♀

• *trace of
orange eyespot*

PALAEARCTIC

Time of Flight ☼	Habitat	Wingspan 3–4cm (1¼–1½ in)

Family LYCAENIDAE	Species *Spindasis natalensis*	Author Westwood

NATAL BARRED BLUE

The upperside of this pretty species is suffused
with blue, and barred with blackish brown. By
contrast, the underside is creamy white with
spectacular bars of metallic-silver, edged with
reddish brown or black. Females are larger than
males, and have slightly duller colouring.
• **EARLY STAGES** The
caterpillar is apparently
undescribed, but it feeds
on *Mundulea* and *Vigna*.
• **DISTRIBUTION**
Scrubland from South Africa
to Mozambique and Zimbabwe.

*broken orange triangle
at forewing tip* •

*unusual
double
• tails*

AFROTROPICAL

♂

Time of Flight ☼	Habitat	Wingspan 2.5–4cm (1–1½ in)

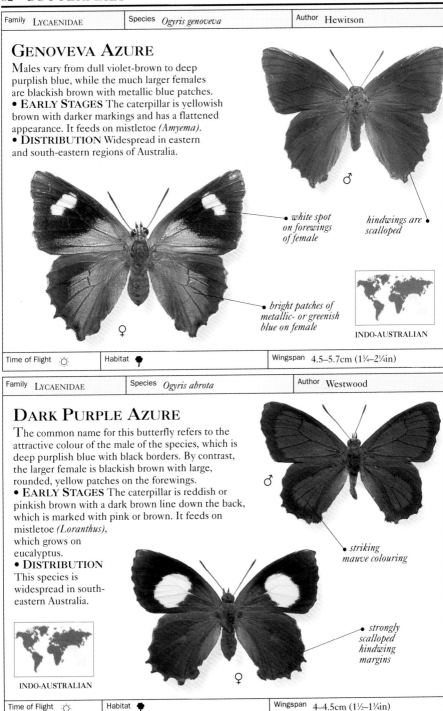

Family LYCAENIDAE	Species *Ogyris genoveva*	Author Hewitson

GENOVEVA AZURE

Males vary from dull violet-brown to deep
purplish blue, while the much larger females
are blackish brown with metallic blue patches.
• **EARLY STAGES** The caterpillar is yellowish
brown with darker markings and has a flattened
appearance. It feeds on mistletoe *(Amyema)*.
• **DISTRIBUTION** Widespread in eastern
and south-eastern regions of Australia.

♂

• *white spot
on forewings
of female*

*hindwings are •
scalloped*

• *bright patches of
metallic- or greenish
blue on female*

♀

INDO-AUSTRALIAN

Time of Flight ☼	Habitat 🌱	Wingspan 4.5–5.7cm (1¾–2¼in)

Family LYCAENIDAE	Species *Ogyris abrota*	Author Westwood

DARK PURPLE AZURE

The common name for this butterfly refers to the
attractive colour of the male of the species, which is
deep purplish blue with black borders. By contrast,
the larger female is blackish brown with large,
rounded, yellow patches on the forewings.
• **EARLY STAGES** The caterpillar is reddish or
pinkish brown with a dark brown line down the back,
which is marked with pink or brown. It feeds on
mistletoe *(Loranthus)*,
which grows on
eucalyptus.
• **DISTRIBUTION**
This species is
widespread in south-
eastern Australia.

♂

• *striking
mauve colouring*

• *strongly
scalloped
hindwing
margins*

INDO-AUSTRALIAN

♀

Time of Flight ☼	Habitat 🌱	Wingspan 4–4.5cm (1½–1¾in)

Family LYCAENIDAE	Species *Hypochrysops ignita*	Author Leach

FIERY JEWEL

The upper surfaces of all wings have broad borders. The centres of the forewings are azure and those of the hindwings are violet. The fiery red and blue underside gives rise to its name.

• **EARLY STAGES** The caterpillar feeds on acacia, camellia, and various other plants.

• **DISTRIBUTION** Widespread throughout Australia and Papua New Guinea.

silvery white underside of body

black and white fringes

♀

♀ △

INDO-AUSTRALIAN

Time of Flight ☼	Habitat 🌿	Wingspan 2.5–3cm (1–1¼in)

Family LYCAENIDAE	Species *Scoptes alphaeus*	Author Cramer

ORANGE-BANDED PROTEA

The upperside is marked with red bands on all the wings. On the underside the red colour is restricted to a triangle on the forewings. Both the fore- and hindwings are slightly scalloped.

• **EARLY STAGES** The caterpillar is a pale grey colour with bluish spots. It can be found feeding inside the flower heads of sugarbushes *(Protea)*.

• **DISTRIBUTION** Widespread throughout hilly and mountainous country in South Africa.

AFROTROPICAL

♂

chequered wing fringes

characteristic small tails

Time of Flight ☼	Habitat ⛰ 〰 〰	Wingspan 3–4cm (1¼–1½in)

Family LYCAENIDAE	Species *Tajuria cippus*	Author Fabricius

PEACOCK ROYAL

The colour of the male gives this species its name. Females are paler and have more rounded wings. The underside is grey with black lines, with an orange and black eyespot on the hindwings.

• **EARLY STAGES** The caterpillar is brown with pinkish markings. It feeds on mistletoes *(Dendrophthoe, Loranthus)*.

• **DISTRIBUTION** This species of butterfly is found in India, Sri Lanka, across to southern China, Malaysia, as far as the island of Borneo.

INDO-AUSTRALIAN

long, narrow hindwings of male

♂

slender tails on both sexes

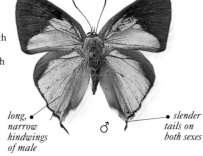

Time of Flight ☼	Habitat 🌿	Wingspan 3–4.5cm (1¼–1¾in)

Family LYCAENIDAE	Species *Chrysozephyrus syla*	Author Kollar

SILVER HAIRSTREAK

Males are metallic golden-green with narrow, brown borders. Females have purplish blue forewings with broad, black margins. The hindwings are dark brown with greenish blue rays towards the margins. The common name derives from the silvery underside of both sexes, which has brown markings and orange and black eyespots at the tail bases.

- **EARLY STAGES** The caterpillar is apparently undescribed, but is known to feed on oak *(Quercus).*
- **DISTRIBUTION** Between 1,800 and 3,500m (5,900–11,480ft) in the Himalayas.

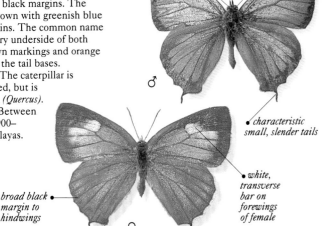

PALAEARCTIC
INDO-AUSTRALIAN

characteristic small, slender tails

white, transverse bar on forewings of female

broad black margin to hindwings

Time of Flight ☼	Habitat ▲ ♠	Wingspan 4–4.5cm (1½–1¾in)

Family LYCAENIDAE	Species *Bindahara phocides*	Author Fabricius

PLANE BUTTERFLY

Males of this species are blackish brown with white tails. Females are a paler or reddish brown with a large, black spot at the base of the tails. The underside of this butterfly is pale brown with darker bands and spots.

- **EARLY STAGES** The hairy caterpillar is dark brown and marked with yellowish white. It feeds inside fruits of creepers or lianes *(Salacia).*
- **DISTRIBUTION** From India and Sri Lanka, through Malaysia to Papua New Guinea and northern Australia.

INDO-AUSTRALIAN

narrow patch of metallic-blue on margin of hindwings

delicate, silvery white hindwing tails

characteristic lobes at base of hindwing

Time of Flight ☼	Habitat 🌴	Wingspan 4–4.5cm (1½–1¾in)

| Family LYCAENIDAE | Species *Poecilmitis thysbe* | Author Linnaeus |

COMMON OPAL

The opalescent blue that gives this butterfly its common name is more extensive in the male than the female. Females are mainly orange with black markings.
• **EARLY STAGES** The caterpillar is green with dark lines along the back. It feeds on *Zygophyllum* and numerous other plants of arid grassland.
• **DISTRIBUTION** Occurs in dry, sandy areas; common in dunes in South Africa.

AFROTROPICAL

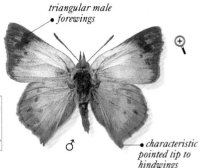

triangular male forewings

♂

characteristic pointed tip to hindwings

| Time of Flight ☀ | Habitat ⠇⠇ ⠇⠇ | Wingspan 2.5–3cm (1–1¼in) |

| Family LYCAENIDAE | Species *Hemiolaus coeculus* | Author Hopffer |

AZURE HAIRSTREAK

Males have bright violet-blue wings with blackish brown borders. Females are less vivid and have broader, paler wing margins. In contrast, the underside of both sexes is greyish white, with lines of brownish red. The hindwings have two tails, each with a turquoise and black eyespot at its base.
• **EARLY STAGES** Undescribed, but it feeds on mistletoe (Loranthaceae).
• **DISTRIBUTION** Occurs in scrubland, savanna, and forests in tropical and southern Africa.

AFROTROPICAL

♂

two tails on hindwings

eyespots and tails form false "head"

| Time of Flight ☀ | Habitat 🌴 ⠇⠇ ⠇⠇ | Wingspan 3–4cm (1¼–1½in) |

| Family LYCAENIDAE | Species *Rapala iarbus* | Author Fabricius |

COMMON RED FLASH

The male has coppery red wings. Females are pale brown. The underside is pale buff with white lines and a black and orange eyespot at the base of the hindwing tails.
• **EARLY STAGES** The caterpillar is red or brownish yellow in colour, with black markings and two stripes on the back.
• **DISTRIBUTION** Widespread in forests from India and Sri Lanka, to Malaysia, and the Lesser Sunda Islands.

INDO-AUSTRALIAN

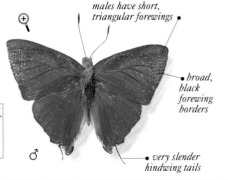

males have short, triangular forewings

broad, black forewing borders

♂

very slender hindwing tails

| Time of Flight ☀ | Habitat 🌴 | Wingspan 3–4cm (1¼–1½in) |

Family LYCAENIDAE	Species *Mimacraea marshalli*	Author Trimen

MARSHALL'S FALSE MONARCH

This species is a mimic of *Danaus chrysippus* (see p.182). The uppersides of both the fore- and hindwings are orange with black margins. The underside is similar to some *Acraea* species. The sexes are similar.
• **EARLY STAGES** The hairy caterpillar feeds at night on lichens growing on tree trunks.
• **DISTRIBUTION** Forests of eastern and central Africa, from Mozambique to Kenya and Zaire.

bright warning colours indicate the butterfly is • distasteful to birds

AFROTROPICAL

♂

Time of Flight ☼	Habitat 🐾	Wingspan 4.5–5.5cm (1¾–2¼in)

Family LYCAENIDAE	Species *Quercusia quercus*	Author Linnaeus

PURPLE HAIRSTREAK

The upperside of the male is deep purple with black borders. Females are blackish brown with vivid patches of purple. The underside of both sexes is pale greyish brown with white lines.
• **EARLY STAGES** The caterpillar is reddish brown with dark brown markings. It feeds on the flower buds and foliage of oak *(Quercus)*.
• **DISTRIBUTION** Occurs from Europe to North Africa and temperate Asia.

• splash of bright purple on female forewings

PALAEARCTIC

small tail present • on hindwings

♀

Time of Flight ☼	Habitat ❦	Wingspan 2.5–3cm (1–1¼in)

Family LYCAENIDAE	Species *Palaeochrysophanus hippothoe*	Author Linnaeus

PURPLE-EDGED COPPER

The deep coppery red males have black borders and are shot with iridescent purple on the hindwings. The females are less vivid and lack the purple sheen. The hindwings of the female are coloured brown with an orange spotted border. The underside of both sexes is grey with an orange band on the hindwings and an orange centre to the forewings.
• **EARLY STAGES** The caterpillar is green, and feeds on docks *(Rumex)* and knotgrass *(Polygonum)*.
• **DISTRIBUTION** Occurs in boggy areas across much of Europe and temperate Asia, to Siberia.

black spots and dark • veining on forewings

PALAEARCTIC

♂

traces of • orange band

Time of Flight ☼	Habitat	Wingspan 3–4cm (1¼–1½in)

Family LYCAENIDAE	Species *Amblypodia anita*	Author Hewitson

LEAF BLUE

Males are a dull purplish blue with a black border. Females are either blackish brown over the entire upperside or have large patches of brilliant metallic-blue on the forewings and smaller patches on the hindwings. The underside is patterned with brown and resembles a dead leaf when the butterfly is at rest.
• **EARLY STAGES** The caterpillar is undescribed, but is known to feed on young shoots of a climbing shrub *(Olax scandens)*.
• **DISTRIBUTION** Occurs from India and Sri Lanka, to Malaysia and Java.

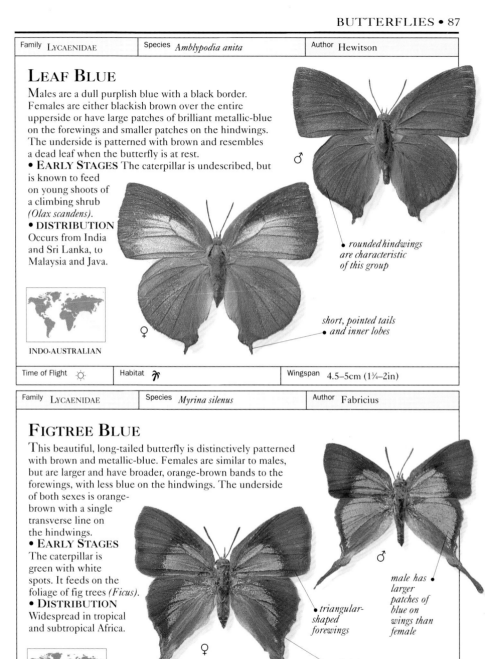

♂

rounded hindwings are characteristic of this group

short, pointed tails and inner lobes

♀

INDO-AUSTRALIAN

Time of Flight ☼	Habitat 🌱	Wingspan 4.5–5cm (1¾–2in)

Family LYCAENIDAE	Species *Myrina silenus*	Author Fabricius

FIGTREE BLUE

This beautiful, long-tailed butterfly is distinctively patterned with brown and metallic-blue. Females are similar to males, but are larger and have broader, orange-brown bands to the forewings, with less blue on the hindwings. The underside of both sexes is orange-brown with a single transverse line on the hindwings.
• **EARLY STAGES** The caterpillar is green with white spots. It feeds on the foliage of fig trees *(Ficus)*.
• **DISTRIBUTION** Widespread in tropical and subtropical Africa.

♂

male has larger patches of blue on wings than female

triangular-shaped forewings

♀

slightly scalloped hindwings

distinctive, long tails

AFROTROPICAL

Time of Flight ☼	Habitat 🌱	Wingspan 3–4cm (1¼–1½in)

| Family LYCAENIDAE | Species *Thecla coronata* | Author Hewitson |

HEWITSON'S BLUE HAIRSTREAK

Females differ from the males by the broader, black borders to the wings and a large, brick-red patch at the base of the hindwing tails. The underside is dark green with a black line extending over fore- and hindwings. This species is one of many South American Lycaenid butterflies incorrectly placed in the genus *Thecla*, that still need to be more accurately classified.

• **EARLY STAGES** Nothing is known of the caterpillar or its foodplants.

• **DISTRIBUTION** Occurs from tropical South America to Mexico.

♂

strongly indented inner edge of hindwings

narrow, black borders are characteristic of males of this species

♀

dark patch at base of hindwing tails

NEOTROPICAL

| Time of Flight ☼ | Habitat 🐾 | Wingspan 4.5–6cm (1¾–2½in) |

| Family LYCAENIDAE | Species *Thecla betulae* | Author Linnaeus |

BROWN HAIRSTREAK

Males lack the strong, orange markings on the forewing, although traces of orange may still remain.

• **EARLY STAGES** The caterpillar is green with yellowish lines.

• **DISTRIBUTION** Europe to temperate Asia.

PALAEARCTIC

♀ △

♀

orange markings on tails are variable in extent

| Time of Flight ☼ | Habitat ♠ | Wingspan 3–4cm (1¼–1½in) |

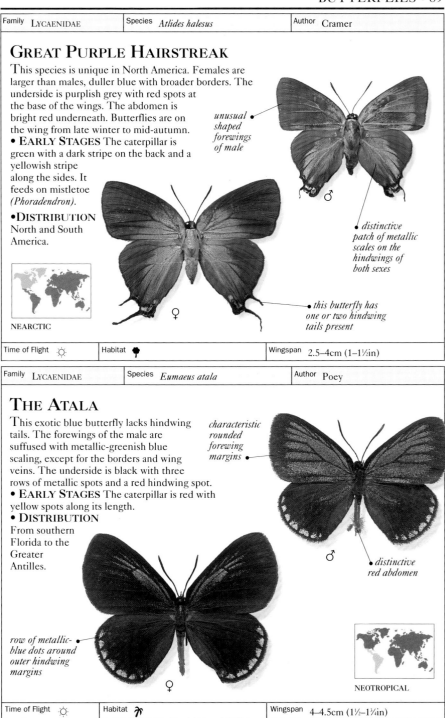

Family LYCAENIDAE	Species *Atlides halesus*	Author Cramer

GREAT PURPLE HAIRSTREAK

This species is unique in North America. Females are larger than males, duller blue with broader borders. The underside is purplish grey with red spots at the base of the wings. The abdomen is bright red underneath. Butterflies are on the wing from late winter to mid-autumn.

• **EARLY STAGES** The caterpillar is green with a dark stripe on the back and a yellowish stripe along the sides. It feeds on mistletoe *(Phoradendron)*.

• **DISTRIBUTION** North and South America.

NEARCTIC

unusual shaped forewings of male

distinctive patch of metallic scales on the hindwings of both sexes

this butterfly has one or two hindwing tails present

♂

♀

Time of Flight ☀	Habitat 🌶	Wingspan 2.5–4cm (1–1½in)

Family LYCAENIDAE	Species *Eumaeus atala*	Author Poey

THE ATALA

This exotic blue butterfly lacks hindwing tails. The forewings of the male are suffused with metallic-greenish blue scaling, except for the borders and wing veins. The underside is black with three rows of metallic spots and a red hindwing spot.

• **EARLY STAGES** The caterpillar is red with yellow spots along its length.

• **DISTRIBUTION** From southern Florida to the Greater Antilles.

characteristic rounded forewing margins

distinctive red abdomen

row of metallic-blue dots around outer hindwing margins

♂

♀

NEOTROPICAL

Time of Flight ☀	Habitat 🌴	Wingspan 4–4.5cm (1½–1¾in)

Family LYCAENIDAE	Species *Strymon melinus*	Author Hübner

GREY HAIRSTREAK

Males are slate-grey with a distinctive orange spot marked with black on the hindwing. Females are similar, but browner in colour.
• **EARLY STAGES** The caterpillar is green with diagonal, white or mauve markings on the sides. It feeds on many plants, including maize *(Zea mays)* and cotton *(Gossypium)*.
• **DISTRIBUTION** Occurs from southern Canada to Central America and north-western South America.

NEARCTIC
NEOTROPICAL

♀

• *black and orange markings at bases of hindwing tails*

Time of Flight ☼	Habitat 🌿 🌳 🌾 🌾	Wingspan 2.5–3cm (1–1¼ in)

Family LYCAENIDAE	Species *Callophrys rubi*	Author Linnaeus

GREEN HAIRSTREAK

The upperside of this common hairstreak is a dull brown. Males can be distinguished by the small, oval patch of scent scales on the forewing. Both sexes have a beautiful, green underside.
• **EARLY STAGES** The caterpillar is green with a dark line down the back and oblique yellow and green markings on either side. It feeds on gorse *(Ulex)*, broom *(Cytisus scoparius)*, and other herbs and shrubs.
• **DISTRIBUTION** Widespread in Europe, ranging to North Africa and temperate Asia.

PALAEARCTIC

♂

• *scalloped edge to hindwing is less distinct than in female*

Time of Flight ☼	Habitat 🌳 🌾 🌾	Wingspan 2.5–3cm (1–1¼ in)

Family LYCAENIDAE	Species *Lycaena phlaeas*	Author Linnaeus

SMALL COPPER

This little butterfly is one of the commonest species in the northern hemisphere. The forewings are bright orange-red with black spots and dark grey borders. The hindwings are predominantly dark grey.
• **EARLY STAGES** The caterpillar is green and variably marked with purplish pink. It feeds on dock *(Rumex)*.
• **DISTRIBUTION** Europe to Africa and across temperate Asia to Japan. Also in North America.

• *black forewing markings, variable in extent*

♀ △

HOLARCTIC

broken, • *orange-red line*

Time of Flight ☼	Habitat 🌾 🌾	Wingspan 2.5–3cm (1–1¼ in)

Family LYCAENIDAE	Species *Lycaena dispar*	Author Haworth

LARGE COPPER

Males of this magnificent species are a brilliant
orange-red with narrow, black borders and a single
black spot in the centre of the forewing. Females are
duller in colour and have broader, black borders and
a row of black spots on the forewing. The hindwing
underside of both sexes is a beautiful, pale bluish
grey with black spots and an orange band.

• **EARLY STAGES** The caterpillar of this species
is bright green and covered with small, white, raised
spots. It feeds on water dock *(Rumex hydrolapathum)*
and related species.

• **DISTRIBUTION**
Large coppers occur
from Europe, into
temperate Asia.

PALAEARCTIC

♂

• *black spots
along hindwing
margin*

• *characteristic
arrangement
of pale-ringed,
black spots*

• *female hindwings
much duller than
those of male*

♀

Time of Flight ☀	Habitat 〰	Wingspan 3–4cm (1¼–1½in)

Family LYCAENIDAE	Species *Arhopala amantes*	Author Hewitson

LARGE OAK BLUE

The males of this striking species are
coloured a deep metallic-blue with
narrow, black borders, while the
females are an intense metallic-blue
with much broader, black borders. In
contrast, the undersides of both sexes
are greyish brown with brown lines
and irregular spots, producing a
confusing camouflage pattern when
the butterfly is at rest. These butterflies
often gather together in large numbers
on nutmeg *(Myristica)* trees and
cinnamon *(Cinnamomum)* trees.

• **EARLY STAGES** The caterpillar
appears to be undescribed, but both the
caterpillar and the pupa are attended
by green tree ants.

• **DISTRIBUTION**
From northern India to
Sri Lanka, Malaysia, and
Timor. Common in the
Himalayas at altitudes of
up to 1,500m (4,920ft).

INDO-AUSTRALIAN

♂

• *broad, black
inner margin
to hindwing*

*small tail on •
hindwing*

Time of Flight ☀	Habitat ▲ 🌿	Wingspan 4.5–5.5cm (1¾–2¼in)

| Family LYCAENIDAE | Species *Parrhasius m-album* | Author Boisduval & Le conte |

WHITE "M" HAIRSTREAK

Males of this species are a brilliant, iridescent blue with black borders on the upperside. Females are similar but larger and less brightly coloured. On the underside of both sexes is a thin, white line that runs across both fore- and hindwings and forms an "M" shape near the tails. The hindwings have a black and orange eyespot on the underside. These fast-flying butterflies are on the wing from late winter to mid-autumn.
• **EARLY STAGES** The caterpillar of this species is light yellow with a darker stripe along its back and diagonal bars along its sides. It feeds on oak *(Quercus)*. There are normally one or two broods a year.
• **DISTRIBUTION** Occurs from Iowa and Connecticut in the USA, south to Mexico and the mountainous regions of Guatemala.

♀

black and orange eyespot on • hindwings

NEARCTIC
NEOTROPICAL

| Time of Flight ☼ | Habitat ▲ 🌢 | Wingspan 2.5–3cm (1–1¼in) |

| Family LYCAENIDAE | Species *Jamides alecto* | Author Felder |

METALLIC CAERULEAN

This butterfly is one of several similar species from South-east Asia with distinctive, metallic, pale blue wings, finely lined with white. This species can be recognized by the characteristic spots on the margin of the hindwings. Females are generally darker than males and have much broader, dark bands on the forewings. The underside is brown with white, wavy lines and a black and orange eyespot near the hindwing tails.
• **EARLY STAGES** The caterpillar is known to feed on the flowers and young fruit of cardamon *(Elettaria cardamomum)*, and is sometimes a minor pest. It is apparently undescribed, but the caterpillar of the closely related common caerulean *(Jamides celeno)* is a dull reddish green, covered with small, white, raised spots. It is attended by ants.
• **DISTRIBUTION** Widespread in wooded, hilly localities from India and Sri Lanka, to Burma, and Malaysia.

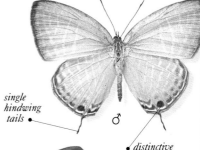

single hindwing tails •

♂

• distinctive black spot at base of hindwing tails

♀

INDO-AUSTRALIAN

| Time of Flight ☼ | Habitat 🌾 🎋 | Wingspan 3–4.5cm (1¼–1¾in) |

Family LYCAENIDAE	Species *Albulina orbitulus*	Author De Prunner

ALPINE ARGUS

Males are a deep blue with narrow black
borders. Females are dark brown. The
underside is pale brown with black spots on the
forewings and white patches on the hindwings.
• **EARLY STAGES** The
green caterpillar feeds on
milk vetches *(Astragalus
alpinus* and *A. frigidus).*
• **DISTRIBUTION**
Occurs in alpine meadows
of Norway and Sweden.
Also in mountainous areas
of temperate Asia.

*narrow, black
borders to
wings of male* •

♂

*white
wing
• fringes*

PALAEARCTIC

♀

Time of Flight ☼	Habitat ▲	Wingspan 2.5–3cm (1–1¼in)

Family LYCAENIDAE	Species *Everes comyntas*	Author Godart

EASTERN TAILED BLUE

Males are purplish blue with narrow black borders,
while females are slate grey, sometimes shot with
blue. The underside is greyish white with a curved
row of dark grey spots and hindwing eyespots.
• **EARLY STAGES** The
caterpillar is usually dark green
with brown stripes and pale
green stripes on the sides. It
feeds on clover *(Trifolium).*
• **DISTRIBUTION** Eastern
regions from southern Canada
to Central America.

♂

NEARCTIC
NEOTROPICAL

• *grey and
white wing
fringes*

• *two orange and
black spots on
each hindwing*

Time of Flight ☼	Habitat 🌿 ⸰⸰ ⸰⸰	Wingspan 2–2.5cm (¾–1in)

Family LYCAENIDAE	Species *Glaucopsyche alexis*	Author Poda

GREEN-UNDERSIDE BLUE

Unlike the male, the female is dark brown,
sometimes with a bluish suffusion near the
wing bases. The distinctive feature is the
greenish blue base of the wings' undersides.
• **EARLY STAGES** The caterpillar is green
or brown in colour, with a dark line along the
back and black stripes along
the sides. It is known to feed
on *Astralagus* and *Cytisus.*
• **DISTRIBUTION** This
butterfly occurs in southern
and central Europe, and
temperate Asia.

♂

• *narrow, brown
wing borders of male*

PALAEARCTIC

Time of Flight ☼	Habitat 🌳 ⸰⸰ ⸰⸰	Wingspan 2.5–4cm (1–1½in)

Family LYCAENIDAE	Species *Iolana iolas*	Author Ochsenheimer

IOLAS BLUE

The beautiful, purplish blue males of this species have an iridescent sheen. Females are larger, darker and have broad, greyish brown borders and black dots around the margin of the hindwing. The underside is pale buff with white-ringed, black spots. The bases of the wings are sometimes suffused with blue.

• **EARLY STAGES** The caterpillar is purplish pink and feeds inside the pods of bladder senna *(Colutea zarborescens)*.

• **DISTRIBUTION** Rocky areas or open woodland, up to an altitude of 2,000m (6,560ft) in southern and eastern Europe, Turkey, Iran, and North Africa.

narrow, dark wing borders of males •

♂

PALAEARCTIC

marginal spots show through faintly on the underside •

♀

Time of Flight ☼	Habitat ▲ ⸜⸝ ⸜⸝	Wingspan 3–4cm (1¼–1½in)

Family LYCAENIDAE	Species *Agrodiaetus dolus*	Author Hübner

FURRY BLUE

The silvery blue males of this species have large patches of brown scent scales on the forewings which create the distinctive furry appearance alluded to in the common name. The wing veins and narrow margins are blackish brown. The upperside of the female is entirely dark brown. The underside of the male is pale buff with black spots and there is sometimes a white streak on the hindwing.

• **EARLY STAGES** The caterpillar is apparently undescribed, but is known to feed on sainfoin *(Onobrychis)* and alfalfa *(Medicago sativa)*.

• **DISTRIBUTION** Grassland and hillsides in northern Spain, southern France, and central Italy.

in some males the • ground colour is almost white

♂

PALAEARCTIC

♂ △

characteristic spotting of • hindwing

Time of Flight ☼	Habitat ▲ ⸜⸝ ⸜⸝	Wingspan 2.5–4cm (1–1½in)

Family LYCAENIDAE	Species *Danis danis*	Author Cramer

LARGE GREEN-BANDED BLUE

This spectacular tropical blue belongs to a
genus confined largely to Australasia. Males
have narrower, black margins, while females are
generally larger and darker and often have a flash
of metallic-turquoise on the forewing.
The hindwing border bears a series of
large, black spots on the underside.

*narrow, black
wing margins
on males*

• **EARLY STAGES** The caterpillar
feeds on red ash *(Alphitonia excelsa)*. It is
apparently undescribed but caterpillars of
Danis hymetus, which feed on the same host plant,
are flattened and pale green.

• **DISTRIBUTION** Occurs from north-
eastern Australia to Papua New
Guinea and the Moluccas.

*white centre
to forewing more
developed in
some species*

*distinctive white
abdomen reflects
hindwing pattern*

INDO-AUSTRALIAN

Time of Flight ☼	Habitat 🐦	Wingspan 4–4.5cm (1½–1¾in)

Family LYCAENIDAE	Species *Lampides boeticus*	Author Linnaeus

LONG-TAILED BLUE

Males of this species are violet-blue with narrow,
blackish brown borders. Females have dark forewing
margins, while the hindwings are dark brown, variably
suffused with blue towards the base. The underside of
both sexes is pale brown with a series of wavy, white lines
and two black and orange eyespots on the hindwing tails.

• **EARLY STAGES** The caterpillar is pale to yellowish
green, with a dark stripe along the back. It feeds on beans
(Vicia), pea *(Pisum)*, and other legumes. It is often an
agricultural pest.

• **DISTRIBUTION** From
Europe to Africa, Asia,
Australia, and the
Pacific Islands.

*the tails are
short, despite the
common name*

PALAEARCTIC
AFROTROPICAL
INDO-AUSTRALIAN

*two large, black
spots at base of
hindwings of
both sexes*

*extent of dark
colouring in the
female is
variable*

Time of Flight ☼	Habitat 🌾	Wingspan 2.5–4cm (1–1½in)

| Family LYCAENIDAE | Species *Candalides xanthospilos* | Author Hübner |

YELLOW-SPOT BLUE

The males of this species are black with a slight purplish blue suffusion in the centre of each wing. Females are similar except they lack the purplish blue suffusion. The undersides of the wings of both sexes are bluish white with pure white centres and small, black dots along the outer margins.
• **EARLY STAGES** The caterpillar is green to bluish green with oblique, dark green markings and a yellow line along its sides. It feeds at night on the foliage of *Pimelea*.
• **DISTRIBUTION** Found in wooded country in Australia.

orange-yellow patch on forewings gives this species its common name

♂

• large, faint white marking on forewing

• characteristic central hindwing spots

♂ △

INDO-AUSTRALIAN

| Time of Flight ☼ | Habitat 🌳 | Wingspan 2.5–3cm (1–1¼in) |

| Family LYCAENIDAE | Species *Celastrina argiolus* | Author Linnaeus |

HOLLY BLUE

Males of this distinctively coloured species are pale lilac-blue with narrow, black borders, while females have broad, blackish brown borders. The underside of both sexes is bluish white with a line of elongated, black spots on the forewings and a pattern of small, black dots on the hindwings.
• **EARLY STAGES** The caterpillar is green with a yellowish green or white line along the sides, and white and purplish pink markings on the back.
• **DISTRIBUTION** Widespread throughout Europe, extending right across to North Africa and across much of temperate Asia as far as Japan.

♂

black and • white wing fringes

series of diffuse, marginal spots on female • hindwings

♀

PALAEARCTIC

| Time of Flight ☼ | Habitat 🌳 | Wingspan 2–3cm (¾–1¼in) |

Family LYCAENIDAE	Species *Castalius rosimon*	Author Fabricius

COMMON PIERROT

This attractive little butterfly is strongly patterned with large black spots on a white background. Females are larger than males and have broader wing borders.
• **EARLY STAGES** The caterpillar is green with two yellow lines along the back and small, yellow spots along the sides. It is known to feed on jujube or Chinese date *(Ziziphus jujuba)*.
• **DISTRIBUTION** India and Sri Lanka, to Malaysia and the Lesser Sundas.

INDO-AUSTRALIAN

♂

small hindwing tails

base of wings shot with metallic-blue scales

Time of Flight ☼	Habitat 🦋 ⚘ ⚘	Wingspan 2.5–3cm (1–1¼in)

Family LYCAENIDAE	Species *Philotes sonorensis*	Author Felder

SONORAN BLUE

This striking metallic-blue and orange butterfly is unlike any other North American blue. The females are more strongly marked with orange than males. The underside is brown-grey with black spots and orange forewing markings.
• **EARLY STAGES** The caterpillar is pale green and red. It feeds on stonecrops *(Sedum)*.
• **DISTRIBUTION** California to northern areas of Mexico.

NEARCTIC

♂

distinctive, chequered wing fringes

Time of Flight ☼	Habitat ▲ ⚘ ⚘	Wingspan 1.5–2cm (⅝–¾in)

Family LYCAENIDAE	Species *Brephidium exilis*	Author Boisduval

WESTERN PYGMY BLUE

This is a very tiny butterfly. Females are larger than males but are not as blue. The underside of both sexes is pale brown with grey markings. There are black, metallic blue-centred spots on the hindwing margins.
• **EARLY STAGES** The pale green caterpillar feeds on pickleweed *(Salicornia ambigua)* and saltbush *(Atriplex)*.
• **DISTRIBUTION** Occurs from the western USA, through to South America.

black and white fringes to forewings

♀

♀ △

NEARCTIC
NEOTROPICAL

Time of Flight ☼	Habitat ⚘ ⚘ ⚘	Wingspan 1–2cm (⅜–¾in)

Family LYCAENIDAE	Species *Syntarucus pirithous*	Author Linnaeus

LANG'S SHORT-TAILED BLUE

Males are violet-blue, while females are brown
with a blue sheen to the centre of the forewings
and base of the hindwings. The underside of both
sexes is pale greyish brown with white, wavy lines.
• **EARLY STAGES** The green caterpillar feeds
on the buds of plumbago (*P. europaea*), alfalfa
(*Medicago sativa*), and
other plants of the pea
family (Leguminosae).
• **DISTRIBUTION** This
species occurs in southern
Europe and Africa,
extending into Asia.

PALAEARCTIC

♂

• *black spots
at base of tails*

• *this species has
minute tails*

Time of Flight ☼	Habitat ⚬ ⅏ ⅏	Wingspan 2.5–3cm (1–1¼in)

Family LYCAENIDAE	Species *Freyeria trochylus*	Author Freyer

GRASS JEWEL

This is one of the smallest species in the world.
The sexes are similar although the males have paler
brown wings. There are two to four orange lunules
with black centres on each of the hindwings. The
underside is coloured a silvery grey with brown
and black spots.
• **EARLY STAGES** The
caterpillar is undescribed. It feeds
on heliotrope (*Heliotropium*).
• **DISTRIBUTION** Confined to
Greece in Europe, but widespread
in Africa and parts of Asia.

AFROTROPICAL

♀

• *distinctive, metallic-black
spots outlined with orange*

Time of Flight ☼	Habitat ⅏ ⅏	Wingspan 1–1.5cm (⅜–⅝in)

Family LYCAENIDAE	Species *Aricia agestis*	Author Denis & Schiffermüller

BROWN ARGUS

Both sexes are brown with marginal, orange-red
lunules. Females are larger than males and have
bigger spots. The underside is greyish brown
with black and orange spots.
• **EARLY STAGES** The caterpillar is coloured
green with purple stripes and oblique, dark
green lines. It feeds on rock
rose (*Helianthemum*) and
cranesbill (*Geranium*).
• **DISTRIBUTION** Occurs
in heathland throughout
Europe, extending across
temperate Asia.

PALAEARCTIC

♂

• *pale wing fringes*

Time of Flight ☼	Habitat ⅏ ⅏	Wingspan 2–3cm (¾–1¼in)

| Family LYCAENIDAE | Species *Leptotes cassius* | Author Cramer |

CASSIUS BLUE

Males of this little American butterfly are pale lilac-blue, while females are mainly white. The underside is white with brown markings and two black and orange hindwing eyespots.
• **EARLY STAGES** The caterpillar is green tinged with reddish brown. It feeds on flowers of Lima bean *(Phaseolus limensis)* and other plants of the pea family.
• **DISTRIBUTION** Occurs in warm, southern parts of North America, to Central and South America.

NEARCTIC
NEOTROPICAL

blue suffusion at
• base of wings

♂

• *underside pattern shows through translucent wings*

| Time of Flight ☼ | Habitat | Wingspan 1.5–2cm (⅝–¾in) |

| Family LYCAENIDAE | Species *Polyommatus icarus* | Author Rottemburg |

COMMON BLUE

This is one of the commonest European butterflies. Males are bright violet-blue, while females are brown with marginal, orange spots. The underside is pale greyish brown with black spots and marginal, orange spots.
• **EARLY STAGES** The green caterpillar feeds on various trefoils *(Lotus)* and related plants.
• **DISTRIBUTION** Grassy areas of Europe, North Africa, and temperate Asia.

PALAEARCTIC

♂

• *body covered with hair-like white scales*

| Time of Flight ☼ | Habitat | Wingspan 2.5–4cm (1–1½in) |

| Family LYCAENIDAE | Species *Plebejus argus* | Author Linnaeus |

SILVER-STUDDED BLUE

Males are a deep purplish blue with white wing margins while females are brown with marginal, orange spots. The underside is greyish brown with black spots and marginal, orange markings.
• **EARLY STAGES** The caterpillar is green with a dark brown stripe down the back, and a white stripe along each side. It feeds on gorse *(Ulex)* and various heathland plants.
• **DISTRIBUTION** Heaths and grassland throughout Europe, extending across temperate Asia to Japan.

PALAEARCTIC

♂

*wide, blackish •
markings on
inner hindwing*

*deep, white •
margin to
hindwing*

| Time of Flight ☼ | Habitat | Wingspan 2–3cm (¾–1¼in) |

Family LYCAENIDAE	Species *Lysandra bellargus*	Author Rottemburg

ADONIS BLUE

Males are a brilliant, clear blue, while females are
dark brown, dusted with blue scales, with orange,
black, and blue marginal spots on the hindwings.
The underside of both sexes is coloured pale
brown with black spots and orange markings.
• **EARLY STAGES** The
green and yellow caterpillar
feeds on horseshoe vetch
(Hippocrepis comosa).
• **DISTRIBUTION**
Widespread in Europe,
to Turkey and Iran.

PALAEARCTIC

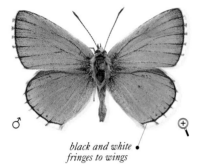

♂

*black and white •
fringes to wings*

Time of Flight ☼	Habitat ⸬ ⸬	Wingspan 3–4cm (1¼–1½in)

Family LYCAENIDAE	Species *Zizina otis*	Author Fabricius

COMMON GRASS BLUE

*silvery leading edges
• to forewings*

Males are dark lilac-blue, while females are dull brown
with a slight suffusion of blue towards the wing bases.
The underside of both sexes is a pale grey colour
with brown markings.
• **EARLY STAGES** The caterpillar is green with dark
green markings and a white line
along each side. It is covered with
minute, white hairs. It feeds
on alfalfa *(Medicago sativa)*
and other legumes.
• **DISTRIBUTION** Ranges
from Africa, throughout India
to Japan and Australia.

AFROTROPICAL
INDO-AUSTRALIAN

♂

*dark brown •
hindwing margins*

Time of Flight ☼	Habitat 🌿 ⸬ ⸬	Wingspan 3–4cm (1¼–1½in)

Family LYCAENIDAE	Species *Zizeeria knysna*	Author Trimen

AFRICAN GRASS BLUE

*triangular-shaped
forewing •*

Males of this widespread butterfly are violet-blue while
the females are dull brown. The underside of both sexes
is greyish brown with black spots. It is also known as the
dark grass blue, and the sooty blue.
• **EARLY STAGES** The caterpillar
is green and covered with short
hairs. It feeds on devil's thorn
(Tribulus terrestris) and other plants.
• **DISTRIBUTION** Range extends
from Mediterranean Europe to
Africa, India, and Australia. Some
consider the Australian subspecies
to be a distinct species.

PALAEARCTIC
AFROTROPICAL
INDO-AUSTRALIAN

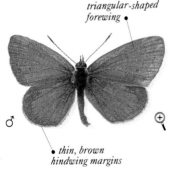

♂

*• thin, brown
hindwing margins*

Time of Flight ☼	Habitat ⸬⸬ ⸬ ⸬	Wingspan 2–2.5cm (¾–1in)

Family LYCAENIDAE	Species *Hemiargus isola*	Author Reakirt

REAKIRT'S BLUE

Males are lilac-blue with greyish brown margins. Females are similarly marked, but are dusky brown with a bluish suffusion of the wing bases. The underside of both sexes is pale brown with white markings and white-ringed, black spots on the forewings.
• **EARLY STAGES** This caterpillar is undescribed but is known to feed on mesquite *(Prosopis)* and related plants.
• **DISTRIBUTION** From southern USA to Costa Rica.

♂

NEOTROPICAL
NEARCTIC

characteristic arrangement of black spots on each hindwing

Time of Flight ☼	Habitat	Wingspan 2–3cm (¾–1¼in)

Family LYCAENIDAE	Species *Agriades franklinii*	Author Curtis

HIGH MOUNTAIN BLUE

Males are bluish grey; females are reddish brown. The underside of both sexes is greyish brown with white markings and black spots on the forewings.
• **EARLY STAGES** The caterpillar is undescribed, but feeds on various alpine plants, including *Androsace*, *Dodecatheon*, and *Diapensia*.
• **DISTRIBUTION** Found from Labrador and Alaska to the high mountains of Arizona and New Mexico, in the USA.

variable extent of blue colouring on wings of males

♂

black spots in centre of forewings

♀

NEARCTIC

Time of Flight ☼	Habitat 🔺 🌱	Wingspan 2–2.5cm (¾–1in)

Family LYCAENIDAE	Species *Maculinea arion*	Author Linnaeus

LARGE BLUE

Both sexes of this species are bright blue with black markings on the forewings. Females are larger than the males and have broader margins. The underside is greyish brown with black spots.
• **EARLY STAGES** The yellowish white caterpillar feeds at first on thyme *(Thymus)*, then on ant eggs and grubs.
• **DISTRIBUTION** Europe, but extinct in the British Isles, extends to Siberia and China.

pear-shaped forewing spots

PALAEARCTIC

♀

Time of Flight ☼	Habitat	Wingspan 3–4cm (1¼–1½in)

Family LYCAENIDAE	Species *Mesene phareus*	Author Cramer

CRAMER'S MESENE

Males are deep red with black borders. Females are paler and larger. The forewing undersides are suffused with reddish black. The hindwing undersides are similar to those of the uppersides.

• **EARLY STAGES** The caterpillar is apparently undescribed but is known to feed on the highly poisonous foliage of *Pallinia pinnata*.

• **DISTRIBUTION** This butterfly is fairly common in tropical regions of Central and South America.

bright colour of wings indicates that this butterfly • is poisonous to predators

sharply pointed forewings •

NEOTROPICAL

♂

Time of Flight ☼	Habitat 🦋	Wingspan 2–2.5cm (¾–1in)

Family LYCAENIDAE	Species *Theope eudocia*	Author Westwood

ORANGE THEOPE BUTTERFLY

Both sexes of this striking butterfly have black borders to the forewings. The underside is pale lemon-yellow and the abdomen is bright orange. They have a darting flight and settle on the undersides of leaves. Males are larger than females.

• **EARLY STAGES** The hairy, green caterpillar feeds on the foliage of cocoa *(Theobroma cacao)*.

• **DISTRIBUTION** Tropical Central and South America, including Trinidad.

patch of purple at wing-tips of male butterfly •

NEOTROPICAL

♂

Time of Flight ☼	Habitat 🦋	Wingspan 2.5–4cm (1–1½in)

Family LYCAENIDAE	Species *Hamearis lucina*	Author Linnaeus

DUKE OF BURGUNDY FRITILLARY

This species is not in fact a fritillary; it belongs to the same family as the blues. The sexes are similar except that the forewings of the female are more rounded than those of the male.

• **EARLY STAGES** The caterpillar is pale brown with a darker stripe on its back. It feeds on cowslip and primrose *(Primula)*.

• **DISTRIBUTION** Widespread in Europe.

PALAEARCTIC

♀

• distinctive marginal band of black-dotted, orange spots

Time of Flight ☼	Habitat 🌳	Wingspan 3–4cm (1¼–1½in)

Family LYCAENIDAE	Species *Syrmatia dorilas*	Author Cramer

WHITE-SPOTTED TADPOLE BUTTERFLY

This is one of a genus of about five species confined to tropical Central and South America.
They are slow-flying but their rapid wingbeat is like that of wasps. Females have broader forewings with orange spots.
• **EARLY STAGES** Undescribed.
• **DISTRIBUTION** Brazil and Venezuela.

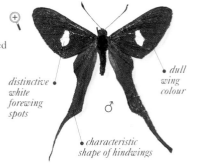

distinctive • white forewing spots

• dull wing colour

♂

• characteristic shape of hindwings

NEOTROPICAL

Time of Flight ☼	Habitat 🌴	Wingspan 1.5–2cm (⅝–¾in)

Family LYCAENIDAE	Species *Menander menander*	Author Stoll

BLUE THAROPS

One of about ten species in this South and Central American genus of brightly coloured, iridescent metalmark butterflies. Males are greenish blue with black streaks, while females are darker metallic-blue. The underside of both sexes is yellowish white with reddish brown spots forming broken lines across the fore- and hindwings. Blue tharops are fast-flying and feed at flowers of agrimony *(Eupatorium)*.
• **EARLY STAGES** Nothing appears to be known of the appearance of the caterpillar or its foodplants.
• **DISTRIBUTION** Occurs from Panama to the tropical regions of northern South America, and also in Trinidad.

blackish brown forewing • tips of male

males are a lighter colour than females •

black wing • margins

♂

vivid blue on • leading edge

blue • coloration ceases at wing-tips

• wings have fringed appearance

• broken black lines running across wings of female

♀

NEOTROPICAL

Time of Flight ☼	Habitat 🌴	Wingspan 3–4cm (1¼–1½in)

Family LYCAENIDAE	Species *Apodemia nais*	Author Edwards

NAIS METALMARK

The upperside of this species is mainly brownish orange with a distinctive pattern of brown spots and bars that form zigzag lines and bands across both wings. Females are larger and paler than males and have slightly rounded forewings. The underside of both sexes is greyish white, strongly suffused with orange over most of the forewings, and with an orange band along the hindwing margins. The wings are patterned with black spots. Adults are on the wing in summer; they visit flowers and settle on damp ground.
• **EARLY STAGES** The caterpillar is pale green with small tufts of bristles over the upper surface. It feeds on buckbrush *(Ceanothus fendleri)*.
• **DISTRIBUTION** Found in the USA from Colorado, extending south to New Mexico, and Mexico.

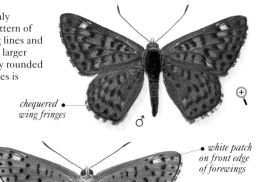

chequered wing fringes

♂

• white patch on front edge of forewings

♂ △

NEARCTIC

Time of Flight ☼	Habitat ⬚ ⬚	Wingspan 3–4cm (1¼–1½in)

Family LYCAENIDAE	Species *Helicopis cupido*	Author Linnaeus

GOLD-DROP HELICOPIS

The forewings of the males are yellowish white, edged with brown, while the bases are orange-yellow. The hindwings are dark brown with an orange-yellow base. The females are lighter, and are marked with brown around the hindwing margins. The undersides are similar to the uppersides except for several metallic spots on the inner hindwing, and margins.
• **EARLY STAGES** The caterpillar appears to be undescribed, but is known to feed on wild tania *(Montrichardia)*.
• **DISTRIBUTION** Found in tropical South America, from Venezuela to Trinidad and Brazil.

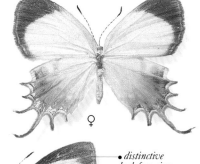

♀

• distinctive dark forewing borders

striking pattern of "metalmarks" on hindwing underside is present in both sexes

♂ △

NEOTROPICAL

Time of Flight ☼	Habitat ⬚ ⬚	Wingspan 3–4cm (1¼–1½in)

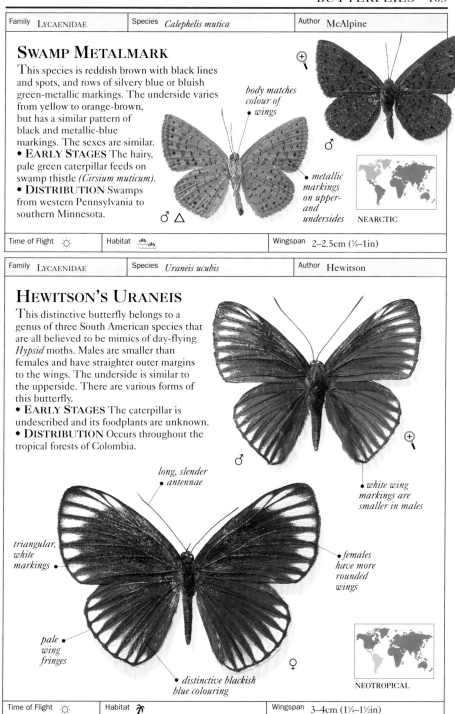

| Family | LYCAENIDAE | Species | *Calephelis mutica* | Author | McAlpine |

SWAMP METALMARK

This species is reddish brown with black lines and spots, and rows of silvery blue or bluish green-metallic markings. The underside varies from yellow to orange-brown, but has a similar pattern of black and metallic-blue markings. The sexes are similar.
• **EARLY STAGES** The hairy, pale green caterpillar feeds on swamp thistle *(Cirsium muticum)*.
• **DISTRIBUTION** Swamps from western Pennsylvania to southern Minnesota.

body matches colour of • wings

♂

• metallic markings on upper- and undersides

NEARCTIC

♂ △

| Time of Flight | ☼ | Habitat | 〰〰 | Wingspan | 2–2.5cm (¾–1in) |

| Family | LYCAENIDAE | Species | *Uraneis ucubis* | Author | Hewitson |

HEWITSON'S URANEIS

This distinctive butterfly belongs to a genus of three South American species that are all believed to be mimics of day-flying *Hypsid* moths. Males are smaller than females and have straighter outer margins to the wings. The underside is similar to the upperside. There are various forms of this butterfly.
• **EARLY STAGES** The caterpillar is undescribed and its foodplants are unknown.
• **DISTRIBUTION** Occurs throughout the tropical forests of Colombia.

long, slender • antennae

♂

• white wing markings are smaller in males

triangular, white markings •

• females have more rounded wings

pale • wing fringes

♀

• distinctive blackish blue colouring

NEOTROPICAL

| Time of Flight | ☼ | Habitat | 🌴 | Wingspan | 3–4cm (1¼–1½in) |

NYMPHALIDAE

A HUGE FAMILY comprised of over 5,000 species, the Nymphalidae contains some of the world's most beautiful and spectacular butterflies, incorporating emperors, monarchs, fritillaries, admirals, and many others.

The most important characteristic that separates this large group from other species of butterfly is the front pair of legs, which are usually undeveloped so they no longer have a walking function. In males they are often covered with dense tufts of scales, giving rise to the term "brush-footed butterflies" that is commonly applied to this family. The Nymphalidae is divided into numerous subfamilies, most of which, at one time, were regarded as distinct in their own right.

Family NYMPHALIDAE	Species *Cethosia biblis*	Author Drury

RED LACEWING

There are two female forms of this butterfly: one resembles the male, the other has a dull green ground colour. The undersides of both sexes are orange-red with lacy patterns of white lines outlined with black. Several species in the genus are similar. These butterflies are on the wing throughout the year.
• **EARLY STAGES** The caterpillar is reputed to have poisonous, branched spines. It lives gregariously on passion flowers *(Passiflora)*.
• **DISTRIBUTION** Widespread from northern India to China, Malaysia, Indonesia, and the Philippines.

males of this species are rich, reddish brown •

♂

• V-shaped, white markings along margin

♀

INDO–AUSTRALIAN

Time of Flight ☼	Habitat 🎋	Wingspan 8–9cm (3¼–3½in)

Family NYMPHALIDAE	Species *Anartia jatrophae*	Author Johansson

WHITE PEACOCK

The sexes of this butterfly are quite similar, although females tend to be larger and have slightly less angular wings. The wings are shaded and overlaid with a brown pattern.
• **EARLY STAGES** The spiny caterpillar is black, spotted with silver. It feeds on water hyssop *(Bacopa monnieri)*.
• **DISTRIBUTION** South and Central America, the West Indies, into southern Texas and Florida, USA.

shining white ground colour on wings

NEOTROPICAL

♂

Time of Flight ☼	Habitat	Wingspan 5–5.5cm (2–2¼ in)

Family NYMPHALIDAE	Species *Pantoporia hordonia*	Author Stoll

BURMESE LASCAR

This is one of a group of very distinctive species. The underside is pale straw-yellow with brown lines and narrow marginal bands.
• **EARLY STAGES** The caterpillar is greenish grey with bands along the sides. There are four pairs of points on the back. It feeds on acacia.
• **DISTRIBUTION** Found throughout India and Sri Lanka, and right through to Malaysia.

black and orange bars across wings

INDO–AUSTRALIAN

♀

Slight scalloping to hindwings

Time of Flight ☼	Habitat 🌳	Wingspan 4.5–5.7cm (1¾–2¼ in)

Family NYMPHALIDAE	Species *Cyrestis thyodamas*	Author Boisduval

COMMON MAP

The intricate and distinctive pattern of map-like markings on the white wings of this butterfly gives rise to its common name. The butterfly has a jerky flight.
• **EARLY STAGES** The caterpillar is very unusual because it is smooth, but has two long, fleshy projections on the back. It feeds on fig *(Ficus)*.
• **DISTRIBUTION** North India and Pakistan to Japan.

indented forewing tips

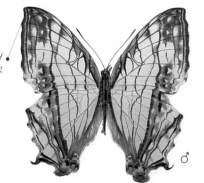

INDO–AUSTRALIAN
PALAEARCTIC

♂

Time of Flight ☼	Habitat 🌳	Wingspan 6–7cm (2½–2¾ in)

Family NYMPHALIDAE	Species *Araschnia levana*	Author Linnaeus

EUROPEAN MAP BUTTERFLY

This butterfly is remarkable for having quite distinct
spring and summer seasonal forms. Spring forms are orange
with dark brown markings, while summer forms are dark
chocolate-brown with white bands. There is a
characteristic, map-like pattern of yellowish white lines on
the dark underside that gives rise to the common name.
• **EARLY STAGES** The black, spiny caterpillar
feeds on stinging nettle *(Urtica dioica)*.

SPRING BROOD ♂

• **DISTRIBUTION**
Widespread in
Europe. Range
extends across
temperate Asia.

*distinctively
scalloped
forewing* •

SUMMER BROOD

*characteristic
black and white
wing fringes* •

♂

PALAEARCTIC

Time of Flight ☼	Habitat ❦	Wingspan 3–4cm (1¼–1½in)

Family NYMPHALIDAE	Species *Polyura delphis*	Author Doubleday

JEWELLED NAWAB

The characteristic hindwing
tails of this butterfly are similar
to those of the closely related
Charaxes butterflies. The
upperside is pale, greenish
yellow to white, with a black,
triangular tip to the forewing.
The underside is pale blue
with brown, green, and darker
blue markings. This species
varies in pattern.
• **EARLY STAGES** The
caterpillar is undescribed; other
caterpillars of this group have
distinctive horned heads. The
foodplant is unknown.
• **DISTRIBUTION** Extends from
north India and Pakistan to Burma.

*triangular, dark •
tip to forewing*

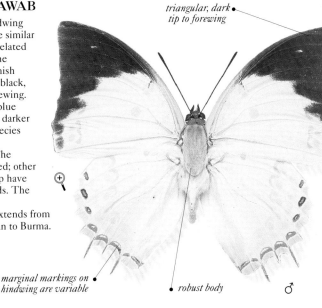

*marginal markings on •
hindwing are variable*

• robust body

♂

INDO-AUSTRALIAN

Time of Flight ☼	Habitat 🜂	Wingspan 9.5–10cm (3¾–4in)

| Family NYMPHALIDAE | Species *Polyura pyrrhus* | Author Linnaeus |

TAILED EMPEROR

The extent of black on the upperside of this butterfly is very variable and some specimens are predominantly creamy yellow with narrow, black margins. There is always a marginal band of blue on the hindwing that runs into the distinctive paired tails. The underside is brown with a creamy white centre, banded with black. The outer margin of the hindwing is orange with a black border on either side, and inside this is a series of striking, maroon-red spots. The sexes are similar. These butterflies have a powerful flight. They rest high up in tree tops, descending to feed on rotting fruit. Some subspecies, including *Semproneus fabricius* from Australia, are now regarded as distinct species.

• **EARLY STAGES** The caterpillar is green and finely speckled with white spots. There is a yellow line along the sides and two or more striking yellow transverse bands on the back. It feeds on acacia.

• **DISTRIBUTION** Occurs from the Moluccas to Papua New Guinea and Australia.

the caterpillar is well camouflaged on its foodplant •

CATERPILLAR OF
POLYURA PYRRHUS

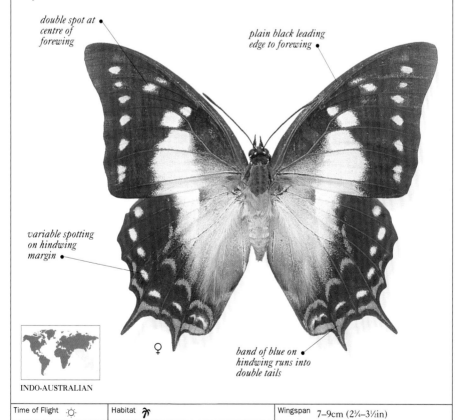

double spot at •
centre of
forewing

plain black leading
edge to forewing •

variable spotting
on hindwing
margin •

♀

band of blue on •
hindwing runs into
double tails

INDO-AUSTRALIAN

| Time of Flight ☼ | Habitat 🌴 | Wingspan 7–9cm (2¾–3½in) |

| Family NYMPHALIDAE | Species *Aglais urticae* | Author Linnaeus |

SMALL TORTOISESHELL

One of the most common European butterflies, this species is relatively small and bright. A distinctive marginal row of blue spots extends across the fore- and hindwing. The sexes are very similar. Butterflies are on the wing from spring to autumn. Those that emerge in late summer hibernate.

• **EARLY STAGES** The spiny caterpillar is black with broken, yellow bands. It feeds on stinging nettle *(Urtica dioica).*

• **DISTRIBUTION** Widespread across Europe, extending through temperate Asia to Japan.

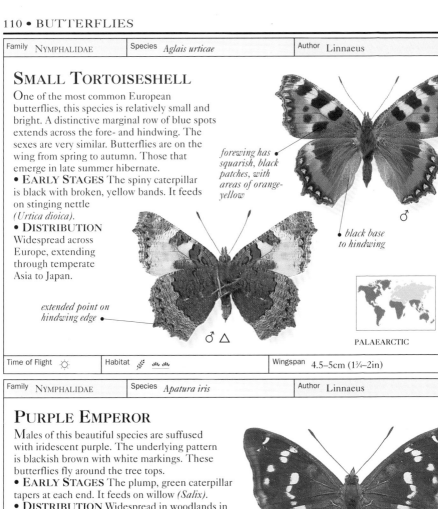

forewing has squarish, black patches, with areas of orange-yellow

black base to hindwing

♂

extended point on hindwing edge

♂ △

PALAEARCTIC

| Time of Flight ☼ | Habitat 🌾 | Wingspan 4.5–5cm (1¾–2in) |

| Family NYMPHALIDAE | Species *Apatura iris* | Author Linnaeus |

PURPLE EMPEROR

Males of this beautiful species are suffused with iridescent purple. The underlying pattern is blackish brown with white markings. These butterflies fly around the tree tops.

• **EARLY STAGES** The plump, green caterpillar tapers at each end. It feeds on willow *(Salix).*

• **DISTRIBUTION** Widespread in woodlands in Europe, and across temperate Asia to Japan.

♂

large orange, black, and purple eyespot on each hindwing

♂ △

the undersides of both sexes are shaded brown, and marked with white

PALAEARCTIC

| Time of Flight ☼ | Habitat 🌳 | Wingspan 6–7.5cm (2½–3in) |

Family NYMPHALIDAE	Species *Asterocampa celtis*	Authors Boisduval & Leconte

HACKBERRY BUTTERFLY

This brown butterfly is intricately and variably patterned with dark brown spots and bands. The tip of the forewing is characteristically spotted with white. Females are larger and paler than males, and their hindwings are more rounded. Butterflies are on the wing from spring to autumn, depending on the locality.

• **EARLY STAGES** The caterpillar is bright green with yellow stripes. The head has small branched horns. It feeds on hackberry *(Celtis)*.

• **DISTRIBUTION** Widespread in North America, from northern Ontario to Florida and Texas.

slight scalloping to wings •

♂

• distinctive angular hindwings

black and white eyespots on hindwing underside •

NEARCTIC

♂ △

Time of Flight ☼	Habitat ♣		Wingspan 4–5.5cm (1½–2¼in)

Family NYMPHALIDAE	Species *Argynnis lathonia*	Author Linnaeus

QUEEN OF SPAIN FRITILLARY

One of the most distinctive European fritillaries, this species has pointed forewings and angular hindwings. The uppersides of both sexes are orange-red, with black. The undersides are marked with silver. Butterflies are on the wing from spring to autumn.

• **EARLY STAGES** The brown-spined caterpillar is black, spotted with white, with a double white line down the back. It feeds on violets *(Viola)*.

• **DISTRIBUTION** Widespread in southern Europe and North Africa, migrating northwards. Range extends across temperate Asia to western China.

double black line around wing margin •

♂

♂ △

• large, silvery patches on hindwing underside

PALAEARCTIC

Time of Flight ☼	Habitat ⸰⸰		Wingspan 4–4.5cm (1½–1¾in)

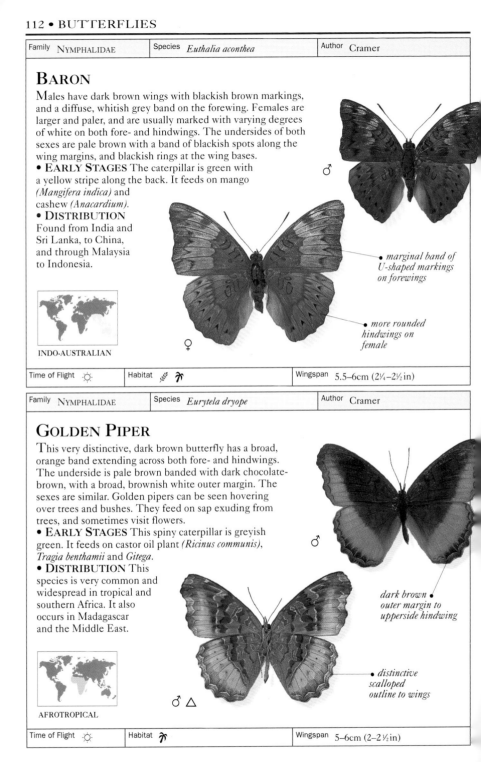

Family NYMPHALIDAE	Species *Euthalia aconthea*	Author Cramer

BARON

Males have dark brown wings with blackish brown markings, and a diffuse, whitish grey band on the forewing. Females are larger and paler, and are usually marked with varying degrees of white on both fore- and hindwings. The undersides of both sexes are pale brown with a band of blackish spots along the wing margins, and blackish rings at the wing bases.

• EARLY STAGES The caterpillar is green with a yellow stripe along the back. It feeds on mango *(Mangifera indica)* and cashew *(Anacardium)*.

• DISTRIBUTION Found from India and Sri Lanka, to China, and through Malaysia to Indonesia.

♂

• *marginal band of U-shaped markings on forewings*

• *more rounded hindwings on female*

♀

INDO-AUSTRALIAN

Time of Flight ☼	Habitat 🌾 🌴	Wingspan 5.5–6cm (2¼–2½ in)

Family NYMPHALIDAE	Species *Eurytela dryope*	Author Cramer

GOLDEN PIPER

This very distinctive, dark brown butterfly has a broad, orange band extending across both fore- and hindwings. The underside is pale brown banded with dark chocolate-brown, with a broad, brownish white outer margin. The sexes are similar. Golden pipers can be seen hovering over trees and bushes. They feed on sap exuding from trees, and sometimes visit flowers.

• EARLY STAGES This spiny caterpillar is greyish green. It feeds on castor oil plant *(Ricinus communis)*, *Tragia benthamii* and *Gitega*.

• DISTRIBUTION This species is very common and widespread in tropical and southern Africa. It also occurs in Madagascar and the Middle East.

♂

dark brown • outer margin to upperside hindwing

• *distinctive scalloped outline to wings*

♂ △

AFROTROPICAL

Time of Flight ☼	Habitat 🌴	Wingspan 5–6cm (2–2½ in)

Family NYMPHALIDAE	Species *Phyciodes tharos*	Author Drury

PEARL CRESCENT

This is a common North American butterfly. The upperside is orange with blackish brown borders and black markings at the wing bases. The forewing underside is pale orange with two black patches on the hind margin. It also has crescent-shaped markings on the hindwing. Another name for the butterfly is the pearly crescentspot.
• **EARLY STAGES** The caterpillar is apparently undescribed, and its food-plants are unknown.
• **DISTRIBUTION** Widespread from Newfoundland to Mexico.

series of spots on hindwing •

NEARCTIC

♂

white crescent on hindwing • margin

♂ △

Time of Flight ☼	Habitat ♒♒ ♒♒	Wingspan 2.5–4cm (1–1½ in)

Family NYMPHALIDAE	Species *Charaxes jasius*	Author Linnaeus

TWO-TAILED PASHA

Of this group of butterflies, the two-tailed pasha is the only member to occur in Europe. The upperside is dark brown with orange borders. There are blue spots at the base of the paired tails. The underside is banded with reddish brown, pale yellow, and white, and there are broken bands of purplish grey. Females are larger than males. Another common name for the butterfly is the foxy charaxes.
• **EARLY STAGES** The caterpillar is green, speckled with white. It feeds on strawberry tree *(Arbutus unedo)*.
• **DISTRIBUTION** This species occurs from the Mediterranean coast of Europe to tropical and southern Africa.

smoky yellow hindwing margins •

dark blackish brown • upperside

hindwing outlined with black •

♀

pale inner margins to hindwings

AFROTROPICAL

Time of Flight ☼	Habitat 🌴 🌳 ♒♒	Wingspan 7.5–8cm (3–3¼ in)

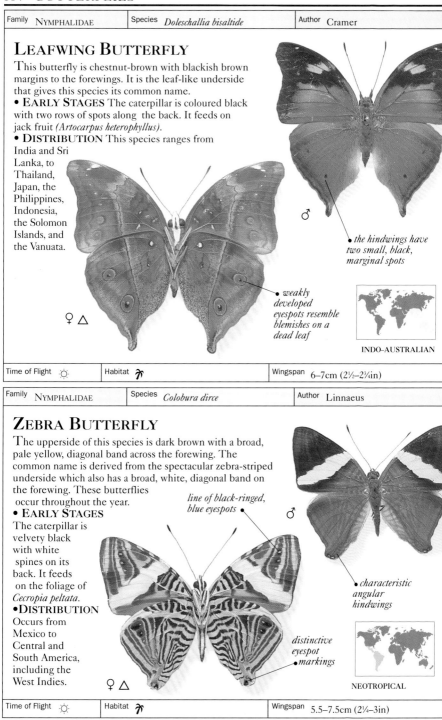

Family NYMPHALIDAE	Species *Doleschallia bisaltide*	Author Cramer

LEAFWING BUTTERFLY

This butterfly is chestnut-brown with blackish brown margins to the forewings. It is the leaf-like underside that gives this species its common name.

• **EARLY STAGES** The caterpillar is coloured black with two rows of spots along the back. It feeds on jack fruit *(Artocarpus heterophyllus)*.

• **DISTRIBUTION** This species ranges from India and Sri Lanka, to Thailand, Japan, the Philippines, Indonesia, the Solomon Islands, and the Vanuata.

♂

• *the hindwings have two small, black, marginal spots*

♀ △

• *weakly developed eyespots resemble blemishes on a dead leaf*

INDO–AUSTRALIAN

Time of Flight ☼	Habitat 🌴	Wingspan 6–7cm (2½–2¾in)

Family NYMPHALIDAE	Species *Colobura dirce*	Author Linnaeus

ZEBRA BUTTERFLY

The upperside of this species is dark brown with a broad, pale yellow, diagonal band across the forewing. The common name is derived from the spectacular zebra-striped underside which also has a broad, white, diagonal band on the forewing. These butterflies occur throughout the year.

• **EARLY STAGES** The caterpillar is velvety black with white spines on its back. It feeds on the foliage of *Cecropia peltata*.

•**DISTRIBUTION** Occurs from Mexico to Central and South America, including the West Indies.

line of black-ringed, blue eyespots •

♂

• *characteristic angular hindwings*

♀ △

distinctive eyespot •markings

NEOTROPICAL

Time of Flight ☼	Habitat 🌴	Wingspan 5.5–7.5cm (2¼–3in)

Family NYMPHALIDAE	Species *Rhinopalpa polynice*	Author Cramer

THE WIZARD

The upperside of this rather strangely shaped butterfly is a rich orange-brown with blackish brown margins and hindwing spots. The underside is intricately patterned with brown and reddish brown bands and lines, interspersed with fine lines of silvery blue. There is a line of black and white eyespots.
• **EARLY STAGES** The caterpillar is apparently undescribed, but is known to feed on *Poikilospermum suaveolens*.
• **DISTRIBUTION** Well-wooded areas of India and Malaysia to Indonesia.

unusual concave margin to forewing

characteristic short hindwing tails

INDO-AUSTRALIAN

♂

Time of Flight ☀	Habitat 🌴	Wingspan 7–8cm (2¾–3¼in)

Family NYMPHALIDAE	Species *Parathyma nefte*	Author Cramer

COLOUR SERGEANT

This butterfly is coloured a very distinctive orange and brown. The underside of the male is orange-brown with white markings, similar to the upperside, and has a striking band of black spots on the hindwing, which also has a band of larger, pinkish orange markings. Female butterflies are often attracted to the flowers of *Lantanas*.
• **EARLY STAGES** The spiny caterpillar is mainly brown, with a large, dark red patch in the middle of the back. It feeds on *Glochidion* and *Mussaenda*.
• **DISTRIBUTION** Common on the plains and in dense rainforest in India, Pakistan, Burma, and Malaysia.

♂

orange marginal line present in both sexes

females are similar to the males but they are paler and suffused with yellow

♀

INDO-AUSTRALIAN

Time of Flight ☀	Habitat 🌴 ⸎ ⸎	Wingspan 5.5–7cm (2¼–2¾in)

| Family NYMPHALIDAE | Species *Charaxes bernardus* | Author Fabricius |

TAWNY RAJAH

This beautiful Asian *Charaxes* butterfly is orange with a broad, white, central band and a blackish brown border to the forewing. The underside is greyish brown with an irregular pattern of darker lines. Females are similarly patterned to males, but are larger and have more developed hindwing tails. Butterflies fly rapidly around the tree tops.

• **EARLY STAGES** The caterpillar is dark green with red spots on the body, and four red horns on the head. It feeds on various tropical trees and shrubs, including red sandalwood (*Adenanthera pavonia)* and albizzias.

• **DISTRIBUTION** Occurs in the jungles of India, Pakistan, Sri Lanka, Burma, and Malaysia.

reddish brown leading edge to forewings

triangular-shaped forewings

hindwings have marginal band of white-centred, blackish-brown spots

two white spots on forewing tip

♂

slightly clubbed antennae

male has small triangular tails

white forewing bands continue on hindwings

♀

white patches on hindwing base

INDO-AUSTRALIAN

| Time of Flight ☼ | Habitat 🌴 | Wingspan 9–12cm (3½–4¾in) |

Family NYMPHALIDAE	Species *Brenthis ino*	Author Rottemburg

LESSER MARBLED FRITILLARY

This little butterfly has typical fritillary markings of black spots on an orange ground. The undersides of the hindwings are yellow. Several geographical forms are known, but the species can usually be recognized by its small size and the solid black margins to the wings. The sexes are similar. These butterflies have a weak flight.

• **EARLY STAGES** The caterpillar is black with a double white stripe and orange-brown spines along its back. It feeds on great burnet *(Sanguisorba officinalis)*, meadowsweet *(Filipendula ulmaria)*, and raspberry *(Rubus idaea)*.

• **DISTRIBUTION** The lesser marbled fritillary is widespread across marshy areas of Europe, but not the British Isles. The range extends from temperate Asia to Japan.

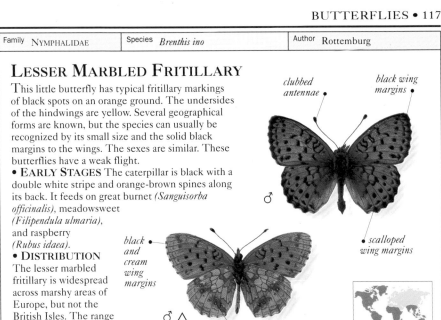

clubbed antennae

black wing margins

♂

scalloped wing margins

black and cream wing margins

♂ △

characteristic brown-ringed spots on hindwings

PALAEARCTIC

Time of Flight ☼	Habitat	Wingspan 3–4cm (1¼–1½in)

Family NYMPHALIDAE	Species *Charaxes bohemani*	Author Felder

LARGE BLUE CHARAXES

The blue on the upperside of this beautiful *Charaxes* butterfly is slightly iridescent, and is broadly bordered with black. Females are larger than males and have characteristic white, diagonal forewing bands and longer hindwing tails. The underside of both sexes is dull purplish grey.

• **EARLY STAGES** The green caterpillar feeds on mahogany bean *(Afzelia quanzensis)* and related plants.

• **DISTRIBUTION** Occurs in open woodland and areas of scrub, throughout tropical Africa from Kenya to Malawi, Zambia, and Angola.

AFROTROPICAL

distinctive, white forewing spots

♂

two small, pointed tails

pale brown inner margin

Time of Flight ☼	Habitat 🌴	Wingspan 7.5–10.8cm (3–4¼in)

Family NYMPHALIDAE	Species *Hypolimnas bolina*	Author Linnaeus

GREAT EGG-FLY

The males of this geographically variable butterfly are
generally velvety black with purple-edged, white patches
in the middle of each wing. The larger females are blackish
brown with a much more complex pattern of white markings;
they have an orange-red patch on the forewing. In some
forms of this species, females lack the orange markings,
and the white markings are greatly reduced. The
undersides of both sexes are rather similar – they are
brown, with bands of white spots and patches. The
forewing is suffused towards the base with reddish
brown. These butterflies are attracted to *Lantanas*.

• **EARLY STAGES** The caterpillar is dark brown or black
with orange-yellow, branched spines and a yellow line along
the side. It feeds on various tropical plants.

• **DISTRIBUTION** A very widespread species occurring
from India to Taiwan, Malaysia, Indonesia, and Australia.
There are many described subspecies.

*spiny, black
caterpillar*

**CATERPILLAR OF
*HYPOLIMNAS BOLINA***

♂

*wavy, black and
white fringes are
characteristic of
both sexes*

*concave
margin to
forewing*

*the forewing is
suffused with
reddish brown
towards the base*

♀

INDO-AUSTRALIAN

Time of Flight ☼	Habitat 🌴 ⚜ ⚜	Wingspan 7–11cm (2¾–4½in)

Family NYMPHALIDAE	Species *Hypolimnas salmacis*	Author Drury

BLUE DIADEM

Males of this appropriately named butterfly are rich blue with black wing margins and bases, and white dots. Females are often suffused with yellow. The underside is chocolate-brown with white bands and elongate, purple spots.
- **EARLY STAGES** The blue diadem caterpillar is dark brown with red spines. It feeds on *Urera hypselodendron* and *Fleurya*.
- **DISTRIBUTION** Lowland forests from tropical west to east Africa.

white spots at tip of forewing distinguish this butterfly from similar species

wavy, black and white wing fringes

AFROTROPICAL

♂

Time of Flight ☼	Habitat 🌴	Wingspan 9–9.5cm (3½–3¾in)

Family NYMPHALIDAE	Species *Prepona meander*	Author Cramer

BANDED KING SHOEMAKER

This beautiful butterfly belongs to a group of similar species. The pattern of metallic, greenish blue on black is very striking and quite variable, and many forms have been named. The underside by contrast is greyish brown, with a dark brown central band. The sexes are similar. When in flight these butterflies make a crackling sound.
- **EARLY STAGES** The caterpillar's head has two spiny horns. It feeds on plants of the family Annonaceae.
- **DISTRIBUTION** Widespread in Central and South America, including the West Indies.

blue band broken at top, leaving two floating spots of colour

slight scalloping to hindwing edge

NEOTROPICAL

robust body

♀

Time of Flight ☼	Habitat 🌴	Wingspan 8–10.8cm (3¼–4¼in)

Family NYMPHALIDAE	Species *Junonia coenia*	Author Hübner

BUCKEYE

The striking eyespots of this butterfly make it easy to recognize, although the markings can be quite variable. The sexes are similar.
• **EARLY STAGES** The caterpillar is green to blackish grey, marked with orange and yellow. It feeds on plantains *(Plantago)*.
• **DISTRIBUTION**
Can be found throughout North America from Ontario to Florida, and down to Mexico, in fields and along shorelines.

NEARCTIC

characteristic, orange bands on forewings

♂

large hindwing eyespots

Time of Flight ☼	Habitat ⸖ ⸖	Wingspan 5–6cm (2–2½in)

Family NYMPHALIDAE	Species *Junonia villida*	Author Fabricius

MEADOW ARGUS

This species has a pair of black and violet eyespots on each wing, with three distinctive cream markings at the wing-tip. The underside is coloured a greyish brown with darker markings, but there are no eyespots on the hindwings. Females are similar to males but have more rounded wings.
• **EARLY STAGES**
The caterpillar feeds on plantains *(Plantago)*.
• **DISTRIBUTION**
Papua New Guinea to Australia, and the islands of the South-east Pacific.

INDO-AUSTRALIAN

orange bars on forewings

♂

brown and white pattern on outer margin of hindwings

Time of Flight ☼	Habitat ⸖ ⸖	Wingspan 4–5.5cm (1½–2¼in)

Family NYMPHALIDAE	Species *Charidryas nycteis*	Author Doubleday

SILVERY CRESCENTSPOT

The hindwing row of small, black spots on this black and orange butterfly is very distinctive. The undersides of the forewings are similar to the uppersides, but the hindwing undersides are coloured yellowish white with orange and black markings and silvery spots.
• **EARLY STAGES**
The caterpillar is black and it is also spiny.
• **DISTRIBUTION**
Meadows from Canada, south to Arizona, Texas, and Georgia, in the USA.

NEARCTIC

chequered wing margins

♂

row of white-centred, black spots on hindwings

black and orange patterning extends over fore- and hindwings

Time of Flight ☼	Habitat ⸖🌳 ⸖ ⸖	Wingspan 3–5cm (1¼–2in)

Family NYMPHALIDAE	Species *Salamis parhassus*	Author Drury

MOTHER-OF-PEARL BUTTERFLY

In nature this beautiful butterfly is a
translucent pale green, suffused with
iridescent purple. Both the fore- and
hindwings have dark eyespots, but
those near the hindwing tails are
brightly coloured and prominent. The
underside is similar to the upperside but
lacks dark wing margins and has smaller,
red eyespots. The sexes are alike.
• **EARLY STAGES** The spiny caterpillar
is dark brown with a band of orange-red
markings along its back.
• **DISTRIBUTION** Common in dense
woodland, particularly along forest rivers, in
tropical Africa, extending into South Africa.

*strongly hooked
wing-tips*

AFROTROPICAL

*short, dagger-like
hindwing tails*

*brightly coloured
eyespots divert predators*

♂

Time of Flight ☼	Habitat 🌴	Wingspan 7.5–10cm (3–4in)

Family NYMPHALIDAE	Species *Junonia orithya*	Author Linnaeus

BLUE PANSY

Males have predominantly black forewings
with white, transverse bands and orange-ringed
eyespots. It is the beautiful hindwings that give
rise to its other common name, the blue argus.
Females are larger than males. Their colours tend
to be duller and their hindwings have only a slight
suffusion of blue. The underside of both sexes is
greyish brown, marked with white.
• **EARLY STAGES** The short-spined caterpillar
is black with orange and yellow markings. It feeds
on a wide and varied
range of plants.
• **DISTRIBUTION**
Extends from Africa
to India, Malaysia,
and Australia.

♂

*• black and white
hindwing margins
present in both sexes*

*female •
has larger
hindwing
eyespots*

♀

*female
has more
rounded
• wings*

AFROTROPICAL
INDO-AUSTRALIAN

Time of Flight ☼	Habitat 🌾 🌾	Wingspan 4–6cm (1½–2½in)

Family NYMPHALIDAE	Species *Poladryas minuta*	Author Edwards

DOTTED CHECKERSPOT

With its pretty, chequered pattern of black and orange, this is a typical fritillary. The underside is mainly pale orange with a series of large, white, marginal markings on both wings, and distinctive black spots. Females are considerably larger than males.
• **EARLY STAGES** The caterpillar is orange with orange and black spines. It feeds on beardtongue *(Penstemon)*. There are several broods a year.
• **DISTRIBUTION** Found in limestone and chalk districts where the foodplant flourishes; in the USA, in New Mexico and Texas, and in Mexico.

♂

clubbed antennae

tooth-like pattern on forewing edge

chequered wing fringes

characteristic triple band of black spots on underside of hindwing

♀ △

NEARCTIC

Time of Flight ☼	Habitat 🌳 ⸖ ⸖	Wingspan 3–4cm (1¼–1½in)

Family NYMPHALIDAE	Species *Nymphalis antiopa*	Author Linnaeus

CAMBERWELL BEAUTY

This unmistakeable species has a dark maroon upperside with blue, marginal spots and broad, pale yellow borders to the wings. The underside is dark grey, lined with black, and the margins are yellowish white, speckled with black. The sexes are similar. The butterfly is known in the USA as the mourning cloak.
• **EARLY STAGES** The spiny caterpillar is velvety black, finely spotted with white, with a row of reddish brown patches along the back. It feeds on various deciduous trees.
• **DISTRIBUTION** Found in Europe and temperate Asia. Also occurs from North America to northern South America.

unusual outline to forewings

♂

speckled effect to yellow borders

distinctive row of black-ringed, blue spots

HOLARCTIC

Time of Flight ☼	Habitat 🌳 ⸖ ⸖	Wingspan 6–8cm (2½–3¼in)

Family NYMPHALIDAE	Species *Nymphalis polychloros*	Author Linnaeus

LARGE TORTOISESHELL

This butterfly can be distinguished from the small tortoiseshell (*Aglais urticae*, see p.110) by its larger size, its hairy appearance, and the lack of white markings on the leading edge of its forewing. The underside is patterned with various shades of brown, and has a distinctive marginal band of slate-grey.

• **EARLY STAGES** The caterpillar is black, speckled finely with white, and has orange-brown spines. Orange lines extend along the back and sides. It feeds on the foliage of various broadleaves.

• **DISTRIBUTION** Widespread in Europe, extending to North Africa and the Himalayas.

characteristic spotting on forewing

scalloped hindwing

blue crescent-shaped markings on hindwing edge

♂

PALAEARCTIC

Time of Flight ☀	Habitat 🌳 🌿 🌿	Wingspan 5–6cm (2–2½in)

Family NYMPHALIDAE	Species *Marpesia petreus*	Author Cramer

RUDDY DAGGER WING

The distinctive shape of both fore- and hindwings make this butterfly easy to recognize. The upperside is orange with brown cross-lines and brown tails. The underside is pale pinkish brown with brown markings. The sexes are similar. Adults are attracted to flowers and over-ripe fruit, particularly figs.

• **EARLY STAGES** The caterpillar is reddish brown and yellow, spotted and lined with black. The head has distinctive spiny horns. It feeds on the leaves of fig *(Ficus)*, cashew *(Anacardium)*, and mulberry *(Mora)*.

• **DISTRIBUTION** South and Central America, extending into the USA, in Florida and Texas.

strongly hooked forewing

striking hindwing extension

false head on hindwing distracts predators

pale inner margin to hindwing

♂

NEOTROPICAL

Time of Flight ☀	Habitat 🌴	Wingspan 7–7.5cm (2¾–3in)

Family NYMPHALIDAE	Species *Basilarchia archippus*	Author Cramer

THE VICEROY

Also known as the mimic because of its remarkable resemblance to the monarch butterfly (*Danaus plexippus*, see p.184), the viceroy can be distinguished by the black line that crosses the wing veins. These butterflies are on the wing from spring to autumn. They are attracted to honeydew secreted by aphids.
• **EARLY STAGES** The humped caterpillar is mottled olive-green and brown, and has a pair of bristly tufts behind the head. It feeds on the foliage of willow *(Salix)*, and related deciduous trees.
• **DISTRIBUTION** Range extends from Canada, right through the USA, down to Mexico.

NEARCTIC
NEOTROPICAL

♂

♂

black cross-line on hindwing

Time of Flight ☼	Habitat 〰〰 〰〰	Wingspan 7–7.5cm (2¾–3in)

Family NYMPHALIDAE	Species *Precis octavia*	Author Cramer

THE GAUDY COMMODORE

This beautiful butterfly occurs in two distinct seasonal forms. The dry season form (shown right) is dark brown, variably suffused with blue. The wet season form is orange-red with dark brown spotting and borders. There is geographic variation in this species.
• **EARLY STAGES** The spiny caterpillar is dark brown with a reddish brown head. It feeds on *Coleus*, and Labiatae.
• **DISTRIBUTION** Wooded localities in tropical and southern Africa.

AFROTROPICAL

marginal band of red-ringed, black spots

distinctive scalloped outline to hindwing

♂

Time of Flight ☼	Habitat 🌴	Wingspan 5–6cm (2–2½in)

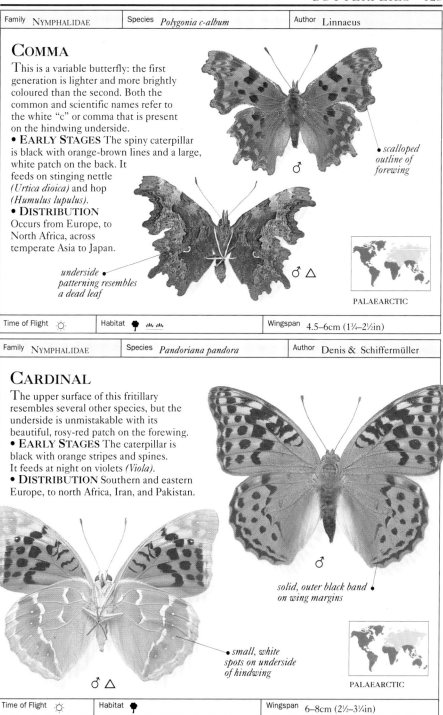

| Family NYMPHALIDAE | Species *Polygonia c-album* | Author Linnaeus |

COMMA

This is a variable butterfly: the first generation is lighter and more brightly coloured than the second. Both the common and scientific names refer to the white "c" or comma that is present on the hindwing underside.
• **EARLY STAGES** The spiny caterpillar is black with orange-brown lines and a large, white patch on the back. It feeds on stinging nettle *(Urtica dioica)* and hop *(Humulus lupulus).*
• **DISTRIBUTION** Occurs from Europe, to North Africa, across temperate Asia to Japan.

♂

• *scalloped outline of forewing*

underside • *patterning resembles a dead leaf*

♂ △

PALAEARCTIC

| Time of Flight ☼ | Habitat ♣ ᶦᶫᵎ ᶦᶫᵎ | Wingspan 4.5–6cm (1¾–2½in) |

| Family NYMPHALIDAE | Species *Pandoriana pandora* | Author Denis & Schiffermüller |

CARDINAL

The upper surface of this fritillary resembles several other species, but the underside is unmistakable with its beautiful, rosy-red patch on the forewing.
• **EARLY STAGES** The caterpillar is black with orange stripes and spines. It feeds at night on violets *(Viola).*
• **DISTRIBUTION** Southern and eastern Europe, to north Africa, Iran, and Pakistan.

♂

solid, outer black band • *on wing margins*

♂ △

• *small, white spots on underside of hindwing*

PALAEARCTIC

| Time of Flight ☼ | Habitat ♣ | Wingspan 6–8cm (2½–3¼in) |

| Family NYMPHALIDAE | Species *Palla ussheri* | Author Butler |

PALLA BUTTERFLY

Males are very distinctive with white-barred, black forewings. The hindwings are dark brown with broad, central bands of deep orange. Females are larger and have brown wings with pale orange central bands. Palla butterflies are fast and powerful fliers.
• **EARLY STAGES** The caterpillar is patterned with green and brown. It resembles a dying leaf, and feeds on *Porana densifolia*, *Bonamia poranoides*, and *Toddalia*.
• **DISTRIBUTION** Occurs in tropical forest in western, eastern, and central Africa.

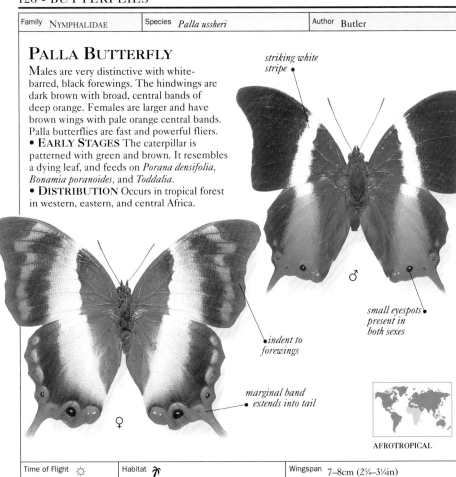

striking white stripe

♂

small eyespots present in both sexes

indent to forewings

marginal band extends into tail

♀

AFROTROPICAL

| Time of Flight ☼ | Habitat 🌳 | Wingspan 7–8cm (2¾–3¼in) |

| Family NYMPHALIDAE | Species *Inachis io* | Author Linnaeus |

PEACOCK

The patterning on this exquisite butterfly is unique. In contrast to the striking upperside, the underside is dark brown with purplish black lines, which provides good camouflage. The females are slightly larger than the males.
• **EARLY STAGES** The caterpillar is black and spiny. It feeds on nettle (*Urtica dioica*) and hop (*Humulus lupulus*).
• **DISTRIBUTION** Widespread in gardens in Europe, temperate areas of Asia, and Japan.

eyespots divert birds from attacking vulnerable body

♂

PALAEARCTIC

| Time of Flight ☼ | Habitat 🌾 🌾 | Wingspan 5.5–6cm (2¼–2½in) |

Family NYMPHALIDAE	Species *Kallima inachus*	Author Boisduval

INDIAN LEAF BUTTERFLY

The uppersides of both the male and the female butterfly are brightly and attractively coloured with orange and purplish blue. However, the brown patterning of the underside, coupled with the unusual wing shape, makes this one of the most remarkable leaf mimics of all. This facility for camouflage has given the Indian leaf butterfly its very apt common name.
• **EARLY STAGES** The caterpillar is velvety black with red spines and long yellow hairs. It feeds on *Girardinia* and *Strobilanthes*, as well as other plants.
• **DISTRIBUTION** This species is widespread from India and Pakistan, to southern China and Taiwan.

bright, colourful uppersides of males • and females

distinctive, pointed • forewings

extended • hindwing tails

♂

false "midrib" extends right •along tails

unusual angular forewing shape

♂ △

hindwing tails resemble the stem of a leaf

INDO-AUSTRALIAN

Time of Flight ☀	Habitat 🌴	Wingspan 9–12cm (3½–4¾in)

Family NYMPHALIDAE	Species *Vindula erota*	Author Fabricius

CRUISER BUTTERFLY

Males are orange-brown with a paler, central band. The underside is similar but with reddish brown lines. Females are greyish brown with orange on the hindwing and a central, white band. The underside has red lines and pale patches.
• **EARLY STAGES** The caterpillar is pale yellow with brown markings and feeds on *Adenia* and passion flower *(Passiflora)*.
• **DISTRIBUTION** Occurs in forest, from India and Pakistan, to Malaysia and Indonesia.

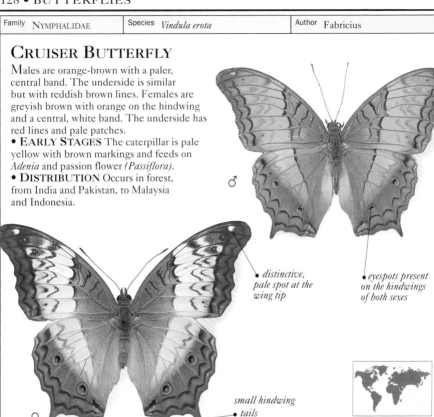

♂

distinctive, pale spot at the wing tip

eyespots present on the hindwings of both sexes

small hindwing tails

♀

INDO–AUSTRALIAN

Time of Flight ☼	Habitat 🦋 ⸲⸲ ⸲⸲	Wingspan 7–9.5cm (2¾–3¾in)

Family NYMPHALIDAE	Species *Neptis sappho*	Author PALLAS

COMMON GLIDER

This distinctive European species belongs to a genus of butterflies occurring throughout Africa and South-east Asia. Its wing pattern of black and white bands distinguishes it from other European butterflies. The underside of the common glider is a rusty, reddish brown.
• **EARLY STAGES** The caterpillar is smooth with four pairs of spiny projections on the back. It feeds on spring pea *(Lathyrus)*.
• **DISTRIBUTION** Found in woodland and on scrub-covered hillsides in central and eastern Europe.

central forewing streak

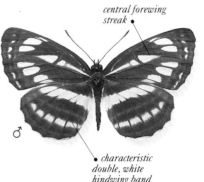

♂

characteristic double, white hindwing band

PALAEARCTIC

Time of Flight ☼	Habitat 🌳	Wingspan 4.5–5cm (1¾–2in)

Family NYMPHALIDAE	Species *Sasakia charonda*	Author Hewitson

JAPANESE EMPEROR

This beautiful species is the national butterfly of Japan. Male Japanese emperors have distinctive, dark brown wings with a bronze-green sheen, richly suffused with iridescent purple. The females are brown, but without the purple iridescence. In both sexes the underside of the forewing is blackish brown with white spots and pale greyish green tips. The underside of the hindwing is pale, greyish green with paler spots and a pink spot on the base of the hindwing. This is quite a variable butterfly with several named subspecies. Japanese emperors are powerful fliers and can be seen on the wing in the summer months.

- **EARLY STAGES** The caterpillar is coloured green and has several pairs of pointed, fleshy protuberances along its back. The green head has a pair of long horns. The caterpillar feeds on *Celtis*.
- **DISTRIBUTION** Occurs in China and Japan.

CATERPILLAR OF
SASAKIA CHARONDA

• *caterpillar blends with leaf on which it feeds*

white spotting along • margins of both wings

slightly indented forewing •

long slender • antennae

♂

shallow scalloping to wing margin

robust body, typical of a strong flier

pink • hindwing patch

PALAEARCTIC

Time of Flight ☼	Habitat 🌳	Wingspan 9.5–12cm (3¾–4¾in)

Family NYMPHALIDAE	Species *Kallimoides rumia*	Author Westwood

AFRICAN LEAF BUTTERFLY

The males of the species are dark brown with purple and red markings on the forewings. The females are larger than the males and are marked with pale blue on the forewings and cream on the hindwings. The underside of this species has the typical leaf-like, brown pattern of this particular group. It is this distinctive underside that gives the African leaf butterfly its common name.

• **EARLY STAGES** The caterpillar is reddish grey with black lines. Its foodplant is apparently unknown.

• **DISTRIBUTION** This species is found in tropical eastern and western Africa

strongly angled leading edge to • forewings

red, crescent-shaped flash • across forewings

forewings are less • pointed than those of most Kallima species

hindwings much plainer than forewings •

small, white spots • at forewing tips

♂

purple streak • in hindwing tips

yellow-ringed, black eyespots • on hindwings

central line down hindwings resembles leaf vein

♂ △

AFROTROPICAL

Time of Flight ☼	Habitat 🏃		Wingspan 7–8cm (2¾–3¼in)

Family NYMPHALIDAE	Species *Eurodryas aurinia*	Author Rottemburg

MARSH FRITILLARY

The upperside of both sexes is orange, cream, and brown. The underside is paler with fewer black markings. Females are larger than males.
• **EARLY STAGES** The spiny caterpillar is black with white spots. It normally feeds on the leaves of devil's bit scabious *(Succisa pratensis)*.
• **DISTRIBUTION** Widespread in Europe, and extending to temperate Asia.

intricate patterning varies within the species

PALAEARCTIC

♀

black spotting on hindwings

Time of Flight ☼	Habitat	Wingspan 3–4.5cm (1¼–1¾in)

Family NYMPHALIDAE	Species *Speyeria cybele*	Author Fabricius

GREAT SPANGLED FRITILLARY

Females of this large American fritillary can be identified by the strong, black suffusion of the basal half of both the fore- and hindwings. In males this suffusion is much less distinct. The underside of this fritillary can be distinguished by its pale orange colour, with black markings on the forewings and silvery patches on the hindwings.
• **EARLY STAGES** The caterpillar is black with orange-based spines. It feeds on the leaves of violet *(Viola rotundifolia)*.
• **DISTRIBUTION** Occurs from southern Canada to New Mexico, and Georgia, in the USA.

NEARCTIC

characteristic fritillary wingspots

scalloped fore- and hindwings

♀

orange ground colour can sometimes be a pale straw colour

Time of Flight ☼	Habitat ❦	Wingspan 5.5–7.5cm (2¼–3in)

Family NYMPHALIDAE	Species *Hamadryas arethusa*	Author Cramer

QUEEN CRACKER

This species belongs to a group called the cracker butterflies, so-named because they produce a clicking noise when flying. It has distinctive, metallic-blue spotting on both the fore- and hindwings. Females are larger than males, and have a diagonal white band on the forewing and metallic-blue markings on the hindwing.
• **EARLY STAGES** Little is known about the early stages of this particular butterfly, but caterpillars of related species are spiny and have curved, knobbed horns on the head.
• **DISTRIBUTION** Extends from Mexico to Bolivia.

very long antennae

strongly rounded hindwing

metallic-blue spots extend on to body

♂

NEOTROPICAL

Time of Flight ☼	Habitat 🌴	Wingspan 6–7cm (2½–2¾in)

Family NYMPHALIDAE	Species *Euphaedra neophron*	Author Hopffer

GOLD-BANDED FORESTER

The common name of this butterfly, which belongs to a group of some 125 species of African forest butterfly, derives from the broad, diagonal forewing band on a blackish brown background. The base of the forewing, and the greater part of the hindwing, is usually purplish blue, although in some forms they are green. The underside is pale orange-brown with lighter bands.
• **EARLY STAGES** The caterpillar is green with two large, pinkish red patches on the back, and longer, feathered spines along the sides. It feeds on *Deinbollia*.
• **DISTRIBUTION** Found in tropical, eastern Africa.

orange tip to forewing

♂

scalloped hindwings

pale inner margins to hindwing

AFROTROPICAL

Time of Flight ☼	Habitat 🌴	Wingspan 6–7.5cm (2½–3in)

Family NYMPHALIDAE	Species *Agrias claudia*	Author Schulze

SCHULZE'S AGRIAS

One of the more striking members of a large group of very brightly coloured South American butterflies, Schulze's agrias has striking vermilion patches of colour on its forewings. Intricate patterning on the hind-wing underside is a trait of many similar species of this genus. The females have orange markings on the forewings, and lack a coloured hindwing patch.

• **EARLY STAGES** Little is known of the early stages of this butterfly.

• **DISTRIBUTION** Widespread in tropical South America.

vivid, semi-circular crimson
• patch on forewing

♂

scalloped •
hindwing edge

• pale scent brushes
on male hindwing

NEOTROPICAL

Time of Flight ☼	Habitat 🌿	Wingspan 7–9cm (2¾–3½ in)

Family NYMPHALIDAE	Species *Diaethria clymena*	Author Cramer

88 BUTTERFLY

This butterfly is one of several species with similar wing markings (see *Callicore maimuna* p.135). The common name refers to the distinctive, black and white "88" pattern displayed on the underside of the hindwing. The underside of the forewing is strikingly patterned with red, black, and white. In contrast, the upperside is more sombre in colour, although the black wings can sometimes be marked with bands of metallic-blue. The sexes are similar.

• **EARLY STAGES** The caterpillar of this species is green with yellow markings, and has two short spines at the tail. The head has two long, spined horns. It feeds on *Trema micrantha*.

• **DISTRIBUTION** Widespread in South America, and common in Brazil.

♂

• white wing
fringes

red colour extends
on to leading edge
• of hindwing

♂ △

distinctive •
"88" markings

NEOTROPICAL

Time of Flight ☼	Habitat 🌿	Wingspan 4–4.5cm (1½–1¾ in)

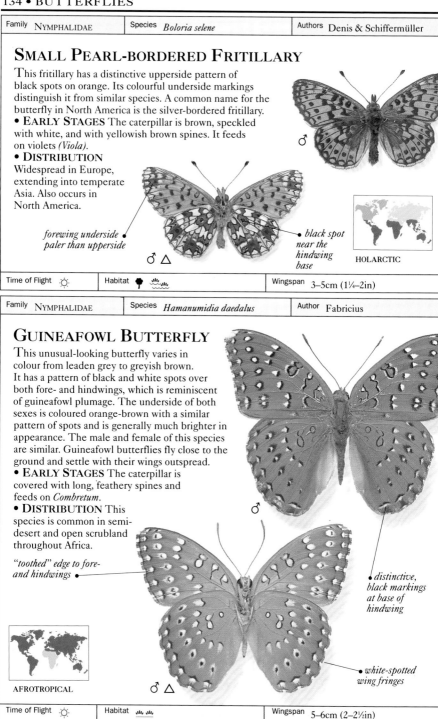

Family NYMPHALIDAE	Species *Boloria selene*	Authors Denis & Schiffermüller

SMALL PEARL-BORDERED FRITILLARY

This fritillary has a distinctive upperside pattern of
black spots on orange. Its colourful underside markings
distinguish it from similar species. A common name for the
butterfly in North America is the silver-bordered fritillary.
• **EARLY STAGES** The caterpillar is brown, speckled
with white, and with yellowish brown spines. It feeds
on violets *(Viola)*.
• **DISTRIBUTION**
Widespread in Europe,
extending into temperate
Asia. Also occurs in
North America.

♂

*forewing underside
paler than upperside*

♂ △

*black spot
near the
hindwing
base*

HOLARCTIC

Time of Flight ☼	Habitat 🌱 〰	Wingspan 3–5cm (1¼–2in)

Family NYMPHALIDAE	Species *Hamanumidia daedalus*	Author Fabricius

GUINEAFOWL BUTTERFLY

This unusual-looking butterfly varies in
colour from leaden grey to greyish brown.
It has a pattern of black and white spots over
both fore- and hindwings, which is reminiscent
of guineafowl plumage. The underside of both
sexes is coloured orange-brown with a similar
pattern of spots and is generally much brighter in
appearance. The male and female of this species
are similar. Guineafowl butterflies fly close to the
ground and settle with their wings outspread.
• **EARLY STAGES** The caterpillar is
covered with long, feathery spines and
feeds on *Combretum*.
• **DISTRIBUTION** This
species is common in semi-
desert and open scrubland
throughout Africa.

♂

*"toothed" edge to fore-
and hindwings*

*distinctive,
black markings
at base of
hindwing*

AFROTROPICAL

♂ △

*white-spotted
wing fringes*

Time of Flight ☼	Habitat 〰 〰	Wingspan 5–6cm (2–2½in)

| Family NYMPHALIDAE | Species *Callicore maimuna* | Author Hewitson |

EIGHTY-EIGHT BUTTERFLY

This butterfly is one of forty species from Central and South America, which are distinguished by the striking "88" pattern on the underside of the hindwing. The upperside surface is black with diagonal, orange markings at the wing-tips and a large, basal patch of red on the forewing. The hindwing often has an iridescent purplish sheen in males.

• **EARLY STAGES** Little is known of the early stages of this butterfly, but other *Callicore* butterflies have long, slender caterpillars.

• **DISTRIBUTION** Throughout tropical South America, from Brazil to Colombia, and up to the West Indies.

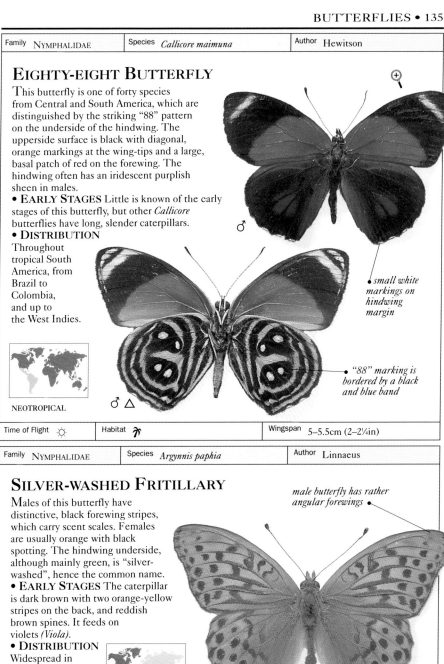

NEOTROPICAL

♂ △

• *small white markings on hindwing margin*

• *"88" marking is bordered by a black and blue band*

| Time of Flight ☼ | Habitat 🌿 | Wingspan 5–5.5cm (2–2¼in) |

| Family NYMPHALIDAE | Species *Argynnis paphia* | Author Linnaeus |

SILVER-WASHED FRITILLARY

male butterfly has rather angular forewings •

Males of this butterfly have distinctive, black forewing stripes, which carry scent scales. Females are usually orange with black spotting. The hindwing underside, although mainly green, is "silver-washed", hence the common name.

• **EARLY STAGES** The caterpillar is dark brown with two orange-yellow stripes on the back, and reddish brown spines. It feeds on violets *(Viola)*.

• **DISTRIBUTION** Widespread in Europe, extending to north Africa, and across temperate Asia to Japan.

PALAEARCTIC

♂

| Time of Flight ☼ | Habitat ♣ | Wingspan 5.5–7cm (2¼–2¾in) |

Family NYMPHALIDAE	Species *Catacroptera cloanthe*	Author Cramer

PIRATE BUTTERFLY

This reddish brown butterfly has distinctive rows of black-ringed, blue spots on both the fore- and hindwings. The leading edge of the forewing is speckled with black, and all wings have dark bases and outer margins. Males have a distinct, iridescent, purple sheen but this is absent from the larger females. The underside is variable in colour. Adults drink from damp mud, and are attracted to flowers.

• **EARLY STAGES** The caterpillar is greyish yellow with black spines. The head is brown with two bulbous horns. It feeds on *Gomphocarpus* and *Justicia*.

• **DISTRIBUTION** Common in grasslands and swampy areas in Africa.

leading edge of the forewing speckled with black

♂

scale tufts on wing fringes

small hindwing tail

AFROTROPICAL

Time of Flight ☼	Habitat 〰 〰	Wingspan 5.5–7cm (2¼–2¾in)

Family NYMPHALIDAE	Species *Siproeta epaphus*	Author Latreille

BROWN SIPROETA

This striking, blackish brown butterfly with its bright orange-brown wing-tips and white bands is easily recognizable. Females are similar to males but larger. The underside pattern is paler and duller than the upperside, and the white hindwing band is margined with orange-brown. Adults tend to fly close to the ground, where they feed from forest flowers.

• **EARLY STAGES** The caterpillar is very distinctive, and has a maroon-coloured body with long, branched, bright yellow spines. Its head is shiny black. It feeds on *Ruellia*.

• **DISTRIBUTION** Occurs in tropical rainforest in Central and South America, where it flies at high altitudes.

dark wing veins and forewing fringes

♂

small but distinct hindwing tail

NEOTROPICAL

Time of Flight ☼	Habitat 🌿	Wingspan 7–7.5cm (2¾–3in)

Family NYMPHALIDAE	Species *Melitaea didyma*	Author Esper

SPOTTED FRITILLARY

Males are bright orange-red and have strong, black margins. Females are generally larger and paler than males. The forewing underside is pale orange with black spots, while the hindwing underside is predominantly cream with orange and black.
• **EARLY STAGES** The spiny caterpillar is white with black lines and red-orange spots on the back. It feeds on plantains *(Plantago)*.
• **DISTRIBUTION** Found in Europe, North Africa, and temperate Asia.

♂

strongly clubbed antennae
female's forewings are paler than the hindwings
♀

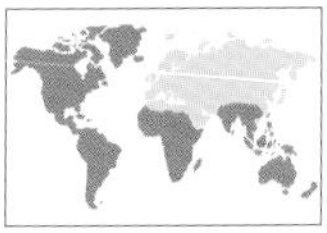

PALAEARCTIC

Time of Flight ☼	Habitat	Wingspan 3–4.5cm (1¼–1¾in)

Family NYMPHALIDAE	Species *Ladoga camilla*	Author Linnaeus

WHITE ADMIRAL

The upperside of this attractive butterfly is entirely black and white, while the underside is patterned with reddish brown and white. The inner margin of the hindwing is flushed with pale blue. Females are larger and slightly paler in colour than males. Butterflies are on the wing in early and mid-summer, and are attracted to flowers of bramble *(Rubus)*.
• **EARLY STAGES** The caterpillar is green above and brown beneath, with two rows of brown spines on the back, and a brown, spiny head. It feeds on honeysuckle *(Lonicera)*.
• **DISTRIBUTION** Widespread in Europe, extending across temperate Asia to Japan.

♀

distinctive row of black spots on hindwing margin
inner margin of hindwing flushed with pale blue
♀ △

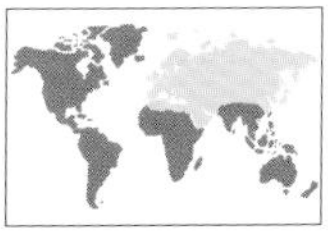

PALAEARCTIC

Time of Flight ☼	Habitat	Wingspan 5–6cm (2–2½in)

Family NYMPHALIDAE	Species *Vanessa atalanta*	Author Linnaeus

RED ADMIRAL

The distinctive, red-barred, black forewings with white spots make this an easy butterfly to recognize. The underside of the forewing is similar to, though paler than, the upperside, while the hindwing underside is patterned with brown and black. The sexes are similar. Red admirals are strong-flying butterflies and often migrate.

• **EARLY STAGES** The spiny caterpillar is variable in colour, ranging from greyish black to greyish green or pale yellowish brown. It feeds on stinging nettle (*Urtica*).

• **DISTRIBUTION** Extends from Europe to North Africa and northern India, and from Canada through the USA to Central America.

♂

♂ △

• *small, black spots in red hindwing band*

• *intricate patterning of hindwing underside*

HOLARCTIC

Time of Flight ☼	Habitat 〽 〽	Wingspan 5.5–6cm (2¼–2½in)

Family NYMPHALIDAE	Species *Vanessa indica*	Author Herbst

INDIAN RED ADMIRAL

This butterfly is similar to the red admiral (*Vanessa atalanta*, see above) but has a broad, red forewing band, and black spots on the hindwing band.

• **EARLY STAGES** The spiny caterpillar is either black, speckled with yellow, or yellow, speckled with black. It feeds on plants of the nettle family (*Urtica*).

• **DISTRIBUTION** From India and Pakistan, through to Japan, and the Philippines.

distinctive, black forewing spots •

♂

large, black spots on wing margin •

• *small, blue spots on hindwing*

INDO-AUSTRALIAN
PALAEARCTIC

Time of Flight ☼	Habitat 〽 〽	Wingspan 5.5–7.5cm (2¼–3in)

Family NYMPHALIDAE	Species *Vanessa canace*	Author Johanssen

BLUE ADMIRAL

This bluish black butterfly has pale, marginal bands. These bands vary in width, and the large forewing spot is either white or blue, according to the subspecies.
• **EARLY STAGES** The caterpillar is coloured orange-yellow with black spots. It feeds on the foliage of *Smilax*.
• **DISTRIBUTION** Ranges from India and Sri Lanka, to Malaysia, the Philippines, and Japan.

ragged edge to wings, typical of this species

♂

pale blue marginal band

INDO-AUSTRALIAN

Time of Flight ☼	Habitat 🏃	Wingspan 6–7.5cm (2½–3in)

Family NYMPHALIDAE	Species *Catonephele numili*	Author Cramer

GRECIAN SHOEMAKER

Males of this striking species are velvety black with brilliant orange spots and purplish markings on the hindwings. By contrast, females have yellowish white markings on the forewings and the hindwings are largely brownish orange with black spots and bands. The underside is brown with a patch on the forewing: orange for the male, and yellow for the female. It is believed that females may mimic one of the distasteful *Heliconia* butterflies.
• **EARLY STAGES** The caterpillar is green with white spots and short spines that are orange and black, or green and black. Its head is reddish orange with spined horns. It feeds on *Alchornea* and *Citharexylum*.
• **DISTRIBUTION** Occurs in Central and South America, including the West Indies.

rounded hindwings on male

♂

indented forewing margin on female

♀

NEOTROPICAL

Time of Flight ☼	Habitat 🏃	Wingspan 7–7.5cm (2¾–3in)

Family NYMPHALIDAE	Species *Pseudacraea boisduvali*	Author Doubleday

BOISDUVAL'S FALSE ACRAEA

The bright orange, red, and black colours of this butterfly
are typical of a distasteful species, and closely mimic the
pattern of the poisonous *Acraea* butterflies. The front part
of the forewing is grey with striking, black wing veins. The
hindwing is rich orange-red with black markings.
The underside is paler than the upperside. Females
are larger and paler, and have more rounded
hindwings than males.

• **EARLY STAGES** The caterpillar is very
unusual in appearance. It has a spiny head and
large, fleshy, spiny projections along its dark
brown body. It is quite difficult to distinguish
the head from the tail. It feeds on *Chrysophyllum*
and *Mimusops*.

• **DISTRIBUTION**
Found in
tropical rainforest,
particularly in
clearings and
near streams,
in tropical Africa,
south to Natal.

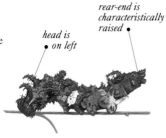

rear-end is characteristically raised

head is on left

CATERPILLAR OF
PSEUDACRAEA BOISDUVALI

patch of red at rear corner of forewing

♂

orange spots on black border

black and red pattern extends on to body

darker tip to forewing

scalloped hindwing margins

♀

AFROTROPICAL

Time of Flight ☼	Habitat 🌿	Wingspan 7–8cm (2¾–3¼in)

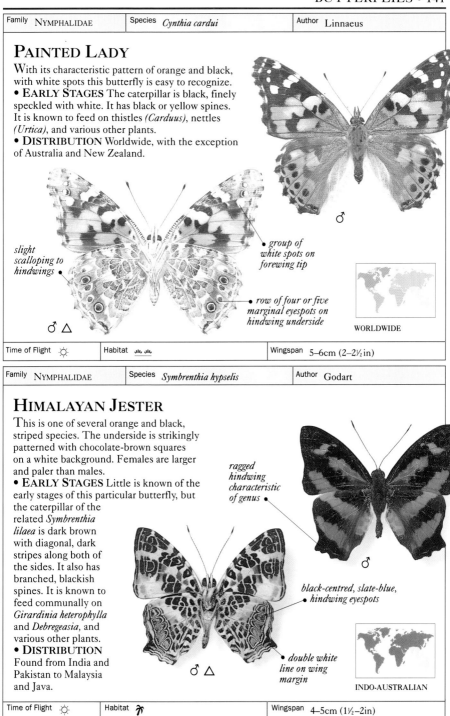

| Family NYMPHALIDAE | Species *Cynthia cardui* | Author Linnaeus |

PAINTED LADY

With its characteristic pattern of orange and black, with white spots this butterfly is easy to recognize.
• **EARLY STAGES** The caterpillar is black, finely speckled with white. It has black or yellow spines. It is known to feed on thistles *(Carduus)*, nettles *(Urtica)*, and various other plants.
• **DISTRIBUTION** Worldwide, with the exception of Australia and New Zealand.

slight scalloping to hindwings

group of white spots on forewing tip

row of four or five marginal eyespots on hindwing underside

♂ △

WORLDWIDE

| Time of Flight ☼ | Habitat ☵, ☵ | Wingspan 5–6cm (2–2½in) |

| Family NYMPHALIDAE | Species *Symbrenthia hypselis* | Author Godart |

HIMALAYAN JESTER

This is one of several orange and black, striped species. The underside is strikingly patterned with chocolate-brown squares on a white background. Females are larger and paler than males.
• **EARLY STAGES** Little is known of the early stages of this particular butterfly, but the caterpillar of the related *Symbrenthia lilaea* is dark brown with diagonal, dark stripes along both of the sides. It also has branched, blackish spines. It is known to feed communally on *Girardinia heterophylla* and *Debregeasia*, and various other plants.
• **DISTRIBUTION** Found from India and Pakistan to Malaysia and Java.

ragged hindwing characteristic of genus

♂

black-centred, slate-blue, hindwing eyespots

double white line on wing margin

♂ △

INDO-AUSTRALIAN

| Time of Flight ☼ | Habitat ☂ | Wingspan 4–5cm (1½–2in) |

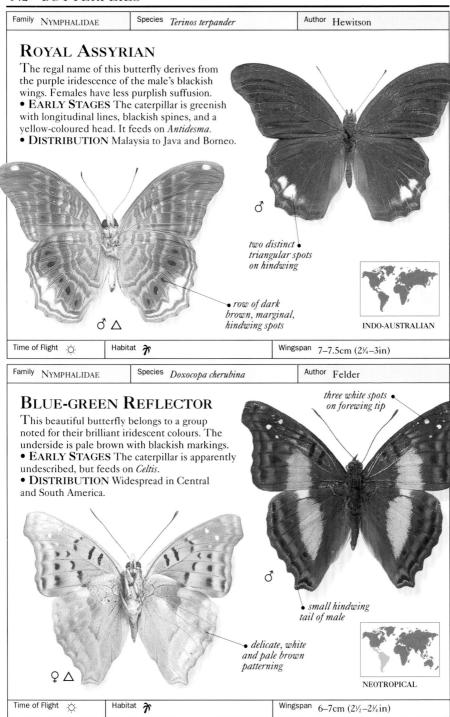

Family NYMPHALIDAE	Species *Terinos terpander*	Author Hewitson

ROYAL ASSYRIAN

The regal name of this butterfly derives from the purple iridescence of the male's blackish wings. Females have less purplish suffusion.
- **EARLY STAGES** The caterpillar is greenish with longitudinal lines, blackish spines, and a yellow-coloured head. It feeds on *Antidesma*.
- **DISTRIBUTION** Malaysia to Java and Borneo.

♂

two distinct triangular spots on hindwing

♂ △

row of dark brown, marginal, hindwing spots

INDO-AUSTRALIAN

Time of Flight ☼	Habitat 🌴	Wingspan 7–7.5cm (2¾–3in)

Family NYMPHALIDAE	Species *Doxocopa cherubina*	Author Felder

BLUE-GREEN REFLECTOR

three white spots on forewing tip

This beautiful butterfly belongs to a group noted for their brilliant iridescent colours. The underside is pale brown with blackish markings.
- **EARLY STAGES** The caterpillar is apparently undescribed, but feeds on *Celtis*.
- **DISTRIBUTION** Widespread in Central and South America.

♂

small hindwing tail of male

♀ △

delicate, white and pale brown patterning

NEOTROPICAL

Time of Flight ☼	Habitat 🌴	Wingspan 6–7cm (2½–2¾in)

Family NYMPHALIDAE	Species *Euxanthe wakefieldii*	Author Ward

FOREST QUEEN

This species belongs to a group of African butterflies noted for their distinctively rounded wings. The white markings on the black wings of the male have a bluish green iridescence. The underside is similar, but the black colouring is largely replaced by brown. The butterflies tend to fly in dappled shade, where their black and white pattern blends into the background. Females are larger and paler, and lack the bluish tint of the males.

• **EARLY STAGES** The caterpillar is green with two black-ringed, white spots on the back, each spot having two green markings within. The head is green and pale brown with four large, curved horns. It feeds on *Deinbollia*.

• **DISTRIBUTION** Tropical East Africa to Mozambique and Natal in South Africa.

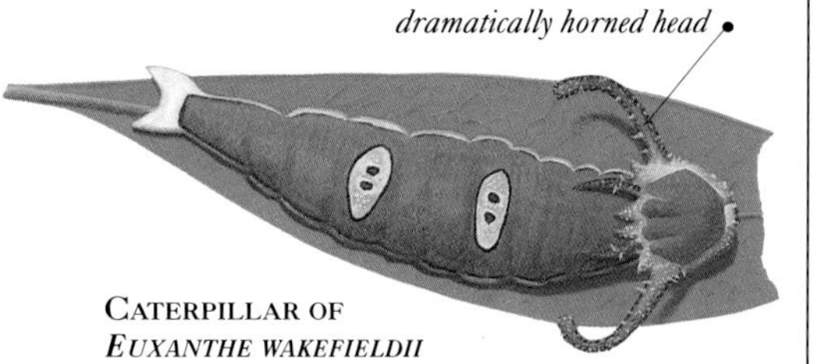

dramatically horned head

CATERPILLAR OF
EUXANTHE WAKEFIELDII

marginal row of rounded, white spots on hindwing

body tipped with brownish yellow in both sexes

♂

forewing tip of female is fuller than in male

slight scalloping to hindwings

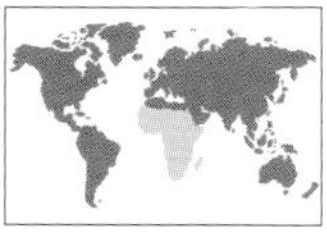

♀ △

AFROTROPICAL

Time of Flight ☼	Habitat 🌾	Wingspan 8–10cm (3¼–4in)

Family NYMPHALIDAE	Species *Limenitis zayla*	Author Doubleday & Hewitson

BI-COLOUR COMMODORE

This dark brown butterfly has a striking, orange-yellow band on the forewing which continues on the hindwing as a white band, tapering towards the rear. A scalloped red line extends along the margins of both wings. The forewing bases are suffused with orange-brown. The sexes are alike.
• **EARLY STAGES** Nothing seems to be known about the early stages of this butterfly.
• **DISTRIBUTION** Common in forests up to altitudes of 2,500m (8,200ft) in India, Pakistan, and Burma.

two pale, marginal lines on both wings

sharply pointed, triangular forewings

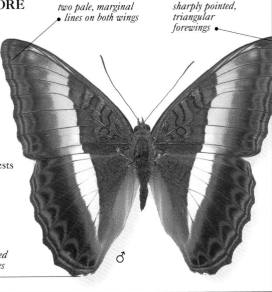

♂

INDO-AUSTRALIAN

white-flecked wing fringes at base

Time of Flight ☼	Habitat 🌴 ⛰	Wingspan 8–9.5cm (3¼–3¾in)

Family NYMPHALIDAE	Species *Metamorpha stelenes*	Author Linnaeus

MALACHITE

The upperside of this butterfly is a very pale green with distinctive, black markings. The underside is also pale with orange-brown lines. Malachites are on the wing all year in the tropics. They feed on fermenting fruit.
• **EARLY STAGES** The caterpillar is black with red spines. It feeds on *Blechnum* and *Ruellia*.
• **DISTRIBUTION** Widespread in South and Central America, migrating northwards to the USA, as far as Texas and southern Florida.

short, slender antennae

♂

♂ △

strongly scalloped hindwing margin with slight tail

NEOTROPICAL

Time of Flight ☼	Habitat 🌴	Wingspan 6–8cm (2½–3¼in)

Family NYMPHALIDAE	Species *Parthenos sylvia*	Author Cramer

CLIPPER

The clipper is an extremely
variable butterfly with the
background colour ranging
from blue, to green or
orange. However, the
translucent, white forewing
patches and dark markings are
characteristic. The underside
pattern is much paler. The
sexes are similar. Clipper
butterflies are attracted to
Lantanas blossom.
• **EARLY STAGES** The caterpillar
is green to yellowish brown with
dark purple spines. It feeds on
Adenia palmata and
Tinospora cordifolia.
• **DISTRIBUTION**
From India and Sri
Lanka through
Malaysia to Papua
New Guinea.

*pattern of translucent,
white patches*

*distinctive
black and orange
striped body*

♂

INDO-AUSTRALIAN

Time of Flight ☼	Habitat 🌴	Wingspan 10–10.8cm (4–4¼in)

Family NYMPHALIDAE	Species *Libythea celtis*	Author Laicharting

NETTLE-TREE BUTTERFLY

This is the only European representative of a
group known as snout butterflies. The dark
brown pattern and distinctive wing shape
make it easy to recognize. The underside of the
forewing is similar to the upperside but the
hindwing is entirely greyish brown. These
butterflies are on the wing from early
summer to early autumn, and again in early
and mid-spring, after hibernation.
• **EARLY STAGES** The caterpillar is brown
or green. It feeds in small groups on
nettle-tree *(Celtis australis).*
• **DISTRIBUTION** Central and
southern Europe to North
Africa, Japan, and Taiwan, with
several described subspecies.

*distinctive "snout",
characteristic of this
group of butterflies*

♂

♂ △

*strongly
"toothed"
forewing*

PALAEARCTIC

Time of Flight ☼	Habitat 🌳 ⚘ ⚘	Wingspan 5.5–7cm (2¼–2¾in)

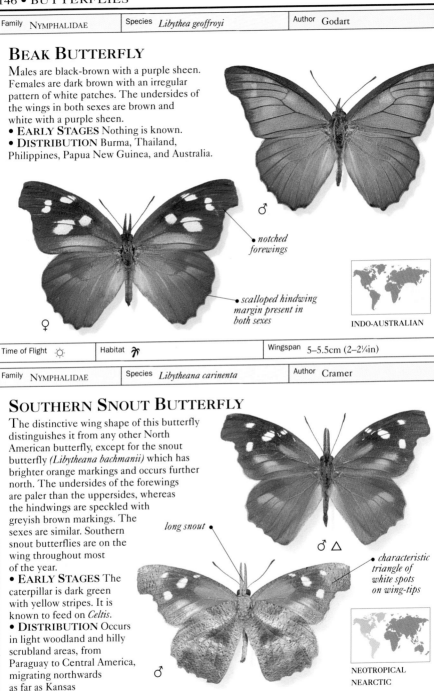

| Family NYMPHALIDAE | Species *Libythea geoffroyi* | Author Godart |

BEAK BUTTERFLY

Males are black-brown with a purple sheen.
Females are dark brown with an irregular
pattern of white patches. The undersides of
the wings in both sexes are brown and
white with a purple sheen.
- **EARLY STAGES** Nothing is known.
- **DISTRIBUTION** Burma, Thailand,
Philippines, Papua New Guinea, and Australia.

♂

notched
forewings

scalloped hindwing
margin present in
both sexes

♀

INDO-AUSTRALIAN

| Time of Flight ☼ | Habitat 🌳 | Wingspan 5–5.5cm (2–2¼in) |

| Family NYMPHALIDAE | Species *Libytheana carinenta* | Author Cramer |

SOUTHERN SNOUT BUTTERFLY

The distinctive wing shape of this butterfly
distinguishes it from any other North
American butterfly, except for the snout
butterfly *(Libytheana bachmanii)* which has
brighter orange markings and occurs further
north. The undersides of the forewings
are paler than the uppersides, whereas
the hindwings are speckled with
greyish brown markings. The
sexes are similar. Southern
snout butterflies are on the
wing throughout most
of the year.
- **EARLY STAGES** The
caterpillar is dark green
with yellow stripes. It is
known to feed on *Celtis*.
- **DISTRIBUTION** Occurs
in light woodland and hilly
scrubland areas, from
Paraguay to Central America,
migrating northwards
as far as Kansas

long snout

♂ △

characteristic
triangle of
white spots
on wing-tips

♂

NEOTROPICAL
NEARCTIC

| Time of Flight ☼ | Habitat 🌳 🌿 🌿 | Wingspan 4–5cm (1½–2in) |

Family NYMPHALIDAE	Species *Morpho aega*	Author Hübner

BRAZILIAN MORPHO

Male Brazilian morpho butterflies are distinguished by their brilliant
metallic-blue wings, which, in the past, were used to make butterfly
jewellery. Females are very different to males, displaying a
characteristic pattern of pale orange with blackish brown margins.
They also have quite different forewing shapes, and altogether
stronger patterning on the fore- and hindwings.
• **EARLY STAGES** The caterpillar is yellow, becoming white
towards the tail. It is hairy, and has two red and
black stripes on the back. This species is known to
feed on bamboo *(Chusquea)*.
• **DISTRIBUTION**
Common in Brazil.

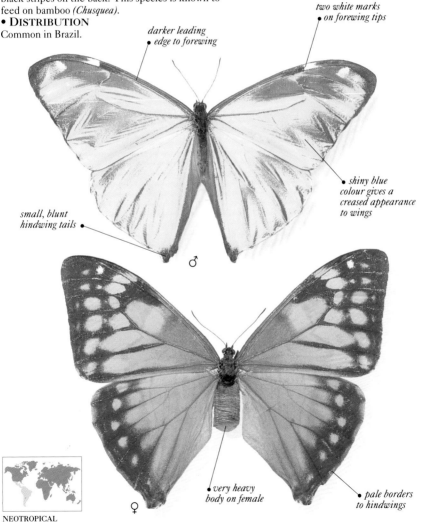

*darker leading
• edge to forewing*

*two white marks
• on forewing tips*

*shiny blue
colour gives a
creased appearance
to wings*

*small, blunt
hindwing tails •*

♂

*very heavy
body on female*

*pale borders
to hindwings*

♀

NEOTROPICAL

Time of Flight ☼	Habitat 🎋	Wingspan 8–9cm (3¼–3½in)

Family NYMPHALIDAE	Species *Morpho menelaus*	Author Linnaeus

BLUE MORPHO

Both males and females of this beautiful species are deep metallic-blue, but females have broad, black margins with white spots. The undersides of both sexes are brown with a row of brown-ringed, orange eyespots, outlined with pale, metallic-bronze. Females also have a broken band of metallic-yellow bronze. Blue morphos fly rapidly through dense forest and feed on the juices of fallen fruit. Males are particularly active, chasing each other in bright sunlight. They will even chase a blue cloth waved in the air; this device has been used by collectors to lure these fast-moving butterflies that are otherwise difficult to catch.

• **EARLY STAGES** The hairy caterpillar is reddish brown with brilliant, leaf-shaped patches of lime-green on the back. It feeds at night on *Erythroxylum pulchrum* and various other plants.

• **DISTRIBUTION** Widespread in the South American rainforest from Venezuela to Brazil.

outer edges of forewings are black with two white marks

dark leading edge to forewings

wings of female have a more scalloped appearance than on male

characteristic elongated hindwings

♂

"toothed" white markings on wing margins

♀

NEOTROPICAL

Time of Flight ☼	Habitat 🌳	Wingspan 13–14cm (5–5½in)

Family NYMPHALIDAE	Species *Morpho peleides*	Author Kollar

COMMON MORPHO

The male of this beautiful species of butterfly has more blue on the upperside than its female counterpart. The undersides of the wings have a distinctive, striking pattern of black- and yellow-ringed eyespots on a brown background. Common morphos are attracted to fermenting fruit.

• **EARLY STAGES** The caterpillar has fine brown, red, and black lines, and has two yellow patches on the back with red lines running through them. The body is covered with reddish brown and white hairs, which form tufts on the back. It feeds on the foliage of *Machaerium seemannii, Lonchocarpus,* and other plants of the pea family. If threatened, it is able to release a strong-smelling scent from a gland situated between the forelegs, which is intended to deter predators.

• **DISTRIBUTION** Common and widespread in Central and South America as well as the islands of the West Indies.

thick, dark fore- and hindwing margin

solid, black inner margin to forewings

♂

black- and yellow- ringed eyespots

small, white fringe to wings

minute white markings on black wing margins

♂ △

NEOTROPICAL

Time of Flight ☼	Habitat 🌴	Wingspan 9.5–12cm (3¾–4¾in)

Family NYMPHALIDAE	Species *Morpho rhetenor*	Author Cramer

CRAMER'S BLUE MORPHO

Males are a spectacular metallic-blue colour. By contrast, the more robust females are orange-brown and black with a pale orange-yellow triangle on the forewing undersides. The undersides of both sexes are silvery greyish brown with dark spots near the wing bases.

• **EARLY STAGES** The pale, yellowish brown caterpillar has purplish brown markings and two pale, diamond-shaped patches on the back. It feeds on *Macrolobium bifolium*.

• **DISTRIBUTION** Found in the jungles of Colombia, Venezuela, Ecuador, French Guiana, Surinam, and Guyana.

NEOTROPICAL

darker blue tinge to forewing tips •

white mark on otherwise black
• leading edge of forewings

• forewings of
male extend
into dark
curved points

• white spots
on forewing
absent in some
subspecies

curved tip to
forewings •

♂

• pale
yellow
spot on
forewing
tips

double row •
of orange
markings on
hindwings

♀

Time of Flight ☼	Habitat 🌴	Wingspan 13–15cm (5–6in)

Family NYMPHALIDAE	Species *Morpho laertes*	Author Druce

MOTHER-OF-PEARL MORPHO

This distinctive pale morpho has silvery white wings with a mother-of-pearl sheen. The upperside is marked with blackish brown on the forewing tips; the underside is more extensively marked with black, and there is a striking band of elongate golden eyespots on the hindwing. The sexes are similar. These morphos are attracted to fermenting fruit, particularly jackfruit *(Artocarpus)*.
• **EARLY STAGES** The caterpillar is greyish brown to dark fawn, tinted with yellow, and has reddish brown spots on the back. The body is covered with hairs. It feeds on the foliage of *Inga*.
• **DISTRIBUTION** Confined to the forests of Brazil.

characteristic short, slender antennae

row of black, marginal spots on hindwings

NEOTROPICAL

♂

Time of Flight ☼	Habitat 🐦	Wingspan 10–10.8cm (4–4¼in)

Family NYMPHALIDAE	Species *Faunis canens*	Author Hübner

COMMON FAUN

This is an inconspicuous species. The uppersides of both sexes are a uniform brown, while the undersides are dark brown with blackish brown lines and white dots along the wing margins.
• **EARLY STAGES** The caterpillar is pale green and hairy. It feeds on wild banana *(Musa)*.
• **DISTRIBUTION** Found in the jungles of India, Burma, and Malaysia.

♂

orange-brown colouring extends to body

white dots along wing margins of underside

♂ △

INDO-AUSTRALIAN

Time of Flight ☼	Habitat 🐦	Wingspan 6–7.5cm (2½–3in)

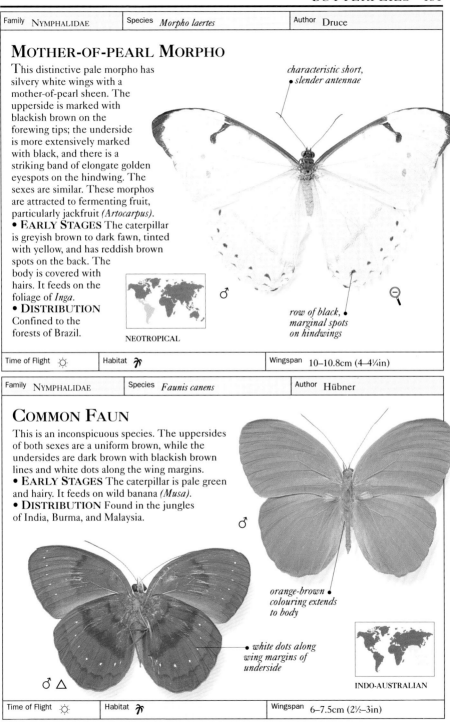

Family NYMPHALIDAE	Species *Amathuxidia amythaon*	Author Doubleday

KOH-I-NOOR BUTTERFLY

Males of this handsome and distinctive butterfly are
blackish brown with a broad, diagonal band of pale blue
on the forewings. Females, on the other hand, have a band
of dark yellow. The underside ranges in colour from brown
to pinkish blue with black lines, and there are two eyespots
on each hindwing. These butterflies are reluctant to fly
unless disturbed, but seem to be most active towards dusk –
even then, however, they do not fly very far. They tend to
be attracted to fermenting fruit. Males are reputed to give
off a sweet odour that persists, even after they are dead.
• **EARLY STAGES** Nothing seems to be known about the
early stages of this butterfly.
• **DISTRIBUTION** This species occurs from India and
Pakistan to Malaysia, Indonesia, and the Philippines. There
are several described subspecies.

INDO-AUSTRALIAN

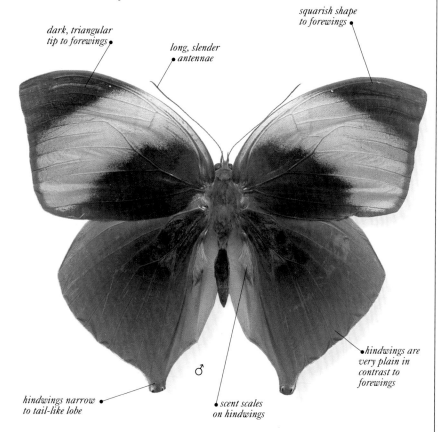

*dark, triangular
tip to forewings* •

*long, slender
• antennae*

*squarish shape
to forewings* •

*hindwings are
very plain in
contrast to
forewings*

♂

hindwings narrow •
to tail-like lobe

*• scent scales
on hindwings*

Time of Flight ◐	Habitat 🏃		Wingspan 11–12cm (4½–4¾in)

Family NYMPHALIDAE	Species *Stichophthalma camadeva*	Author Westwood

NORTHERN JUNGLE QUEEN

This species is very distinctive with its bluish white forewings spotted with black along the margin, and blackish brown hindwings with pale blue and white, marginal bands. The undersides are pale yellowish brown patterned with black and brown lines, white bands, and a row of black-ringed, orange eyespots. The sexes are alike. These butterflies do not visit flowers, but are attracted to rotting fruit, fermenting sap, and cattle dung. They are powerful fliers, usually keeping close to the ground. Males are more active than females. There are generally two broods a year, with butterflies on the wing during the summer months.

• **EARLY STAGES** The caterpillar is apparently undescribed but it is most likely that it feeds on palms (Palmae) or bamboos *(Chusquea)*.

• **DISTRIBUTION** Occurs in dense jungle from northern India and Pakistan to northern Burma.

diamond-shaped black markings on forewings

single brown spot on forewings

blackish brown colour of hindwings continues on to body

♂

characteristic white hindwing margins

striking eyespots on underside divert attackers from delicate body

♂ △

INDO-AUSTRALIAN

Time of Flight ☼	Habitat 🌴	Wingspan 12–13cm (4¾–5in)

Family NYMPHALIDAE	Species *Thauria aliris*	Author Westwood

TUFTED JUNGLE QUEEN

This large butterfly has square forewings, which are mainly black with a diagonal, white band. Males have a large patch of hair-like, specialized scales on their black and orange hindwings, but these are absent in the larger, but otherwise similar, females. The underside is strikingly patterned with orange, brown, and white. Tufted jungle queens fly just before sunset. They are attracted to fermenting fruit. They belong to the subfamily Amathusiinae, part of a small group confined to South-east Asia.

• **EARLY STAGES**
Little is known of the early stages of this butterfly, but it has been suggested that the foodplant may be bamboo *(Chusquea)*.

• **DISTRIBUTION**
Widespread from Burma to Thailand, Malaysia, and Borneo. There are several similar species in India.

INDO-AUSTRALIAN

white spot has a faded appearance •

scale patches on hindwings •

feather-like brown patterning on forewing •

♂

• *orange marking at hindwing base*

• *large eyespots on hindwings to divert predators*

♂ △

Time of Flight ◑	Habitat 🦅	Wingspan 11–13cm (4½–5in)

| Family NYMPHALIDAE | Species *Zeuxidia amethystus* | Author Butler |

SATURN BUTTERFLY

Males of this attractive species have sharply pointed forewings and a violet-blue patch on the hindwings. Females are larger than males. They are brown with yellowish brown markings and a diagonal, cream band on the forewing. The species is well camouflaged, as the undersides of both sexes are brown and patterned to resemble leaves.
• **EARLY STAGES** Little is known of the early stages, but caterpillars of other *Zeuxidia* species are known to be hairy with horns on both head and tail.
• **DISTRIBUTION** Found in forests in Thailand, Malaysia, and Sumatra.

pointed forewing tips

scale patches on hindwings only present in males

♂

INDO-AUSTRALIAN

| Time of Flight ☼ | Habitat 🦋 | Wingspan 7–10cm (2¾–4in) |

| Family NYMPHALIDAE | Species *Dynastor napoleon* | Author Westwood |

BRAZILIAN DYNASTOR

This orange and brown butterfly is a rare species. The wings are dark brown and the undersides of the forewings are paler than the uppersides. The undersides of the hindwings have dark brown wing veins that give a leaf-like impression. Females are larger than males and their forewings are more rounded.
• **EARLY STAGES** Little is known of the early stages, but related species are green or brown with ring-like markings on the back. They feed on plants of the pineapple family Bromeliaceae.
• **DISTRIBUTION** Found in high-altitude rainforests in Brazil.

band of white patches on forewings

small, orange markings on wing-tips

broad, orange band on hindwings

♂

NEOTROPICAL

| Time of Flight ◑ | Habitat 🦋 | Wingspan 12–16cm (4¾–6¼in) |

| Family NYMPHALIDAE | Species *Caligo idomeneus* | Author Linnaeus |

OWL BUTTERFLY

This striking species belongs to a genus of large butterflies characterized by enormous owl-like eyespots on the undersides of the hindwings. In both sexes, the uppersides of the forewings are dark brown with a bluish suffusion and a white line running through. The hindwings are black with a dull blue base. The undersides of the wings have an intricate brown and white, feather-like pattern. Owl butterflies fly early in the morning and towards dusk.

• **EARLY STAGES** The large caterpillar is pale greyish brown, shaded with dark brown towards the head and the forked tail. It feeds on the foliage of Banana *(Musa)*, and can often be a pest in plantations.

• **DISTRIBUTION** Widespread throughout South America, from Argentina up to Surinam.

white, longitudinal line on forewing upperside

♂

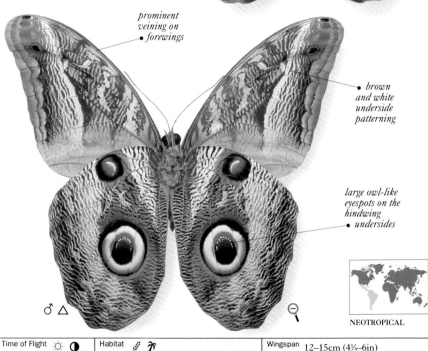

prominent veining on forewings

brown and white underside patterning

large owl-like eyespots on the hindwing undersides

♂ △

NEOTROPICAL

| Time of Flight ☀ ◑ | Habitat 🌿 🌴 | Wingspan 12–15cm (4¾–6in) |

Family NYMPHALIDAE	Species *Caligo teucer*	Author Linnaeus

COCOA MORT BLEU

The male of the cocoa mort bleu butterfly is blackish brown with a yellowish band and pale base to the forewing, while the base of the hindwing is shot with iridescent violet-blue. The female is larger than the male and has a darker forewing base. The undersides of both sexes are more ornate than the uppersides. They are intricately patterned with brown and have large, owl-like eyespots on the hindwings. These butterflies avoid bright sunlight and are on the wing in the afternoon and at dusk. They are attracted to fermenting fruit.

• **EARLY STAGES** The large caterpillar is pale brown with approximately five slender, dark bristles along the back and a pale, central oval, ringed with black. The tail is forked, and the head has a number of curved spines. It feeds on the foliage of various species of banana *(Musa)*.

• **DISTRIBUTION** Occurs from Costa Rica to Guiana, Surinam, Guyana, and Ecuador.

veins are quite prominent on forewings

yellow-coloured band on forewings of male

♂

narrow, yellow wing margins on upperside

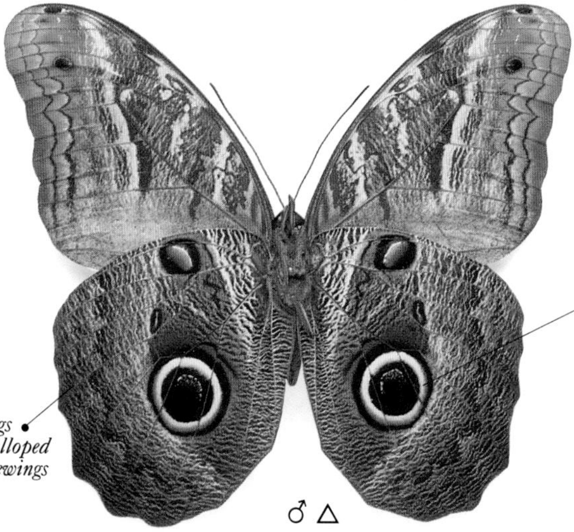

characteristic owl-like eyespots on hindwings

hindwings more scalloped than forewings

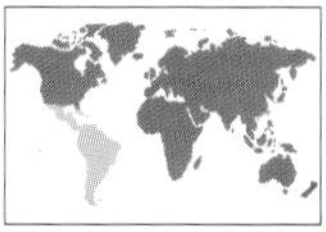

♂ △

NEOTROPICAL

Time of Flight ☀ ◑	Habitat 🏃	Wingspan 9.5–11cm (3¼–4½in)

Family NYMPHALIDAE	Species *Eryphanis polyxena*	Author Meerburg

PURPLE MORT BLEU

This beautiful butterfly has
iridescent, deep purple
wings with black borders.
Females are larger and lack
the brilliant purple colour of
the male, although they often
have a purplish blue sheen.
The undersides of both sexes,
by contrast, are various shades
of brown, with large eyespots
on the hindwings. These
butterflies have a rapid,
dipping flight and frequent
forest clearings in the late
afternoon and at dusk.
• **EARLY STAGES** The
caterpillar is pale brown with a
series of five black bristles along
the back. The long, forked tail is
covered with hair, and the head
has six short, curved spines. It
feeds on bamboo *(Chusquea)*.
• **DISTRIBUTION** Widely
distributed in Central and South
America, including the West Indies.

*curved
forewing tips*

♂

*patch of
yellowish scent
scales on inner
hindwing
margins
of male*

*brown, leaf-
like pattern
on undersides
of wings*

♂ △

NEOTROPICAL

Time of Flight ☼ ◑	Habitat 🌴	Wingspan 8.25–10cm (3¼–4in)

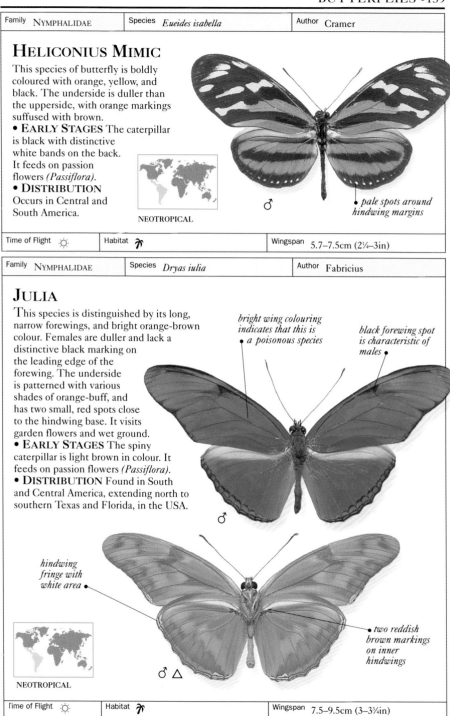

Family NYMPHALIDAE	Species *Eueides isabella*	Author Cramer

HELICONIUS MIMIC

This species of butterfly is boldly coloured with orange, yellow, and black. The underside is duller than the upperside, with orange markings suffused with brown.
• **EARLY STAGES** The caterpillar is black with distinctive white bands on the back. It feeds on passion flowers *(Passiflora)*.
• **DISTRIBUTION** Occurs in Central and South America.

NEOTROPICAL

♂

pale spots around hindwing margins

Time of Flight ☼	Habitat 🌴	Wingspan 5.7–7.5cm (2¼–3in)

Family NYMPHALIDAE	Species *Dryas iulia*	Author Fabricius

JULIA

This species is distinguished by its long, narrow forewings, and bright orange-brown colour. Females are duller and lack a distinctive black marking on the leading edge of the forewing. The underside is patterned with various shades of orange-buff, and has two small, red spots close to the hindwing base. It visits garden flowers and wet ground.
• **EARLY STAGES** The spiny caterpillar is light brown in colour. It feeds on passion flowers *(Passiflora)*.
• **DISTRIBUTION** Found in South and Central America, extending north to southern Texas and Florida, in the USA.

bright wing colouring indicates that this is a poisonous species

black forewing spot is characteristic of males

♂

hindwing fringe with white area

NEOTROPICAL

♂ △

two reddish brown markings on inner hindwings

Time of Flight ☼	Habitat 🌴	Wingspan 7.5–9.5cm (3–3¼in)

Family NYMPHALIDAE	Species *Agraulis vanillae*	Author Linnaeus

GULF FRITILLARY

The long-winged butterfly is bright orange-red with black spots and wing veins. It is the striking, silver-spotted underside that distinguishes this species and gives rise to its other common name, the silver-spotted flambeau.

• **EARLY STAGES** The spiny, black caterpillar has two brownish red stripes along each side. It feeds on passion flower *(Passiflora)*. Butterflies are strongly attracted to such flowers as a source of nectar.

• **DISTRIBUTION** This species is widespread and common from South America to the southern USA, migrating further north as far as the Rockies and the Great Lakes.

dark spotting on inner forewings •

striking, dark wing veins •

black-ringed • orange spots

♀

sharply • indented forewings

comma-shaped • marking

thin, silver fringe to hindwings •

♂ △

NEOTROPICAL
NEARCTIC

Time of Flight ☼	Habitat 🌴 🌱 🌱	Wingspan 6–7.5cm (2½–3in)

Family NYMPHALIDAE	Species *Heliconius charithonia*	Author Linnaeus

ZEBRA

The striking black and yellowish bands on the upperside of this butterfly give rise to the common name. The underside is similar, but there are red spots at the wing bases.

• **EARLY STAGES** The caterpillar is white with black spines and black spots. It feeds on passion flowers *(Passiflora)*.

• **DISTRIBUTION** Central and South America to southern parts of the USA.

NEOTROPICAL
NEARCTIC

elongated shape • of forewing

♂

• long, slender abdomen, typical of Heliconius species

Time of Flight ☼	Habitat 🌴	Wingspan 7.5–8cm (3–3¼in)

Family NYMPHALIDAE	Species *Eueides heliconius*	Author Godart

SMALL FLAMBEAU

This orange and black butterfly is a miniature replica of southern forms of the Julia (*Dryas iulia*, see p.159), and is part of a mimetic group.
• **EARLY STAGES** The caterpillar is black with long spines, and has a broad, white or yellow band along the sides. It feeds on passion flowers *(Passiflora)*.
• **DISTRIBUTION** Southern Mexico to tropical South America, and includes Trinidad.

long forewings

black wing margins

NEOTROPICAL

♂

warning colours also on body

Time of Flight ☼	Habitat 🏃	Wingspan 4.5–5cm (1¾–2in)

Family NYMPHALIDAE	Species *Dione juno*	Author Cramer

SCARCE SILVER-SPOTTED FLAMBEAU

Often occurring in the same places as the very similar Gulf fritillary, this butterfly may be distinguished by its longer forewings and extensive dark brown markings on the underside. The scarce silver-spotted flambeau is attracted to red and blue flowers.
• **EARLY STAGES** The caterpillar is mottled with light brown and covered with short hairs. The head is dark brown with short horns. The caterpillar feeds gregariously on passion flowers *(Passiflora)*.
• **DISTRIBUTION** It is widely distributed in Central and tropical South America.

dark markings distinguish this from other species

solid black leading edge to forewings

scalloped fore- and hindwings

♂

solid black hindwing fringe

elongate forewing

"notched" appearance to hindwings

♂ △

wing pattern continues on body

NEOTROPICAL

Time of Flight ☼	Habitat 🏃	Wingspan 6–7.5cm (2½–3in)

Family NYMPHALIDAE	Species *Heliconius doris*	Author Linnaeus

DORIS BUTTERFLY

This beautiful butterfly has three major colour
forms. In all three the forewings are
similar in their patterning of black
and pale yellow, but the hindwing
markings may be orange, blue,
or green. The underside of the
forewing is similar to the upperside;
the hindwing is black with white rays.
The sexes are alike.

• **EARLY STAGES** The greenish
yellow caterpillar has black bands and
black spines. It feeds gregariously on old
leaves of passion flowers *(Passiflora)*.

• **DISTRIBUTION** Forest margins and
clearings from Central to South America.

*forewing colours remain
the same in all forms •*

♀

*• distinctive,
fan-shaped
marking*

*• two white markings
on forewing*

*marginal •
row of
small, white
spots on
hindwing*

*• slight scalloping
to hindwings*

♀

NEOTROPICAL

Time of Flight ☼	Habitat 🌿	Wingspan 8–9cm (3¼–3½in)

Family NYMPHALIDAE	Species *Heliconius melpomene*	Author Linnaeus

THE POSTMAN

Many species of this genus have forms
that match so closely that they are very
difficult to distinguish. The underside
of the form illustrated is similar to the
upperside, but is paler and has red
spots at the base of the hindwing. These
butterflies fly with the small postman
(Heliconius erato, see p.163), but tend
to avoid direct sunlight.

• **EARLY STAGES** The
caterpillar feeds on
passion flower *(Passiflora)*.

• **DISTRIBUTION**
From Central America to
southern Brazil.

*long antennae are
characteristic of this
group of species •*

♂

*this colour variety is •
just one of the many
forms in this species*

NEOTROPICAL

Time of Flight ☼	Habitat 🌿	Wingspan 6–8cm (2½–3¼in)

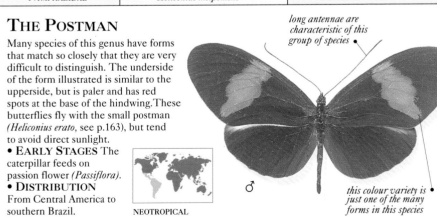

Family NYMPHALIDAE	Species *Heliconius ricini*	Author Linnaeus

SMALL HELICONIUS

This butterfly has black forewings marked with cream, and orange hindwings with broad black borders. The underside is similar but duller, lacking the orange hindwing markings.
• **EARLY STAGES** Little is known of the early stages, although it is known to feed on passion flower *(Passiflora)*.
• **DISTRIBUTION** Central and South America to the Amazon Basin.

NEOTROPICAL

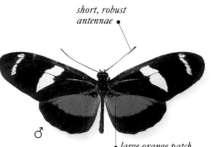

short, robust antennae •

♂

• large orange patch on the hindwing

Time of Flight ☼	Habitat 🌴	Wingspan 5.5–7cm (2¼–2¾in)

Family NYMPHALIDAE	Species *Heliconius erato*	Author Linnaeus

SMALL POSTMAN

This is an amazingly variable butterfly. Almost all variations are matched by parallel forms in the postman *(Heliconius melpomene*, see p.162), and the two species occur in the same habitats. Similar forms occur in both sexes. Butterflies fly close to the ground along forest margins and open ground. They roost communally at night.
• **EARLY STAGES** The caterpillar of the species is white with black spots and spines, and a buff-coloured head. It feeds on various passion flowers *(Passiflora)*.
• **DISTRIBUTION** A common species from Central America to southern Brazil.

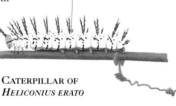

the distinctive spiny caterpillar of the • small postman

**CATERPILLAR OF
*HELICONIUS ERATO***

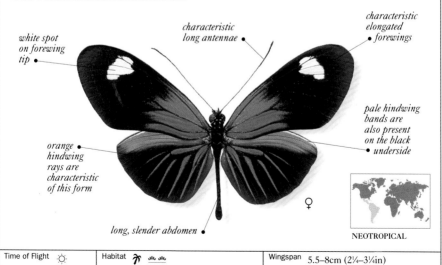

white spot on forewing tip •

characteristic long antennae •

characteristic elongated • forewings

pale hindwing bands are also present on the black • underside

orange • hindwing rays are characteristic of this form

♀

long, slender abdomen •

NEOTROPICAL

Time of Flight ☼	Habitat 🌴 ⸰ ⸰	Wingspan 5.5–8cm (2¼–3¼in)

Family NYMPHALIDAE	Species *Philaethria dido*	Author Linnaeus

SCARCE BAMBOO PAGE

Belonging to a complex of almost identical species, this butterfly is characterized by its beautiful, bluish green colour, and blackish brown markings. The underside is paler and has reddish brown and greyish brown markings. The sexes are similar. These butterflies feed on the nectar of *Lantana* and other flowers, preferring white, blue, and yellow varieties. They generally fly high in the tree canopy, but at times descend to drink and take in salts from damp ground.

• **EARLY STAGES** The caterpillar is pale green with blackish red markings and black-tipped, red spines. It feeds on passion flowers *(Passiflora)*.

• **DISTRIBUTION** This complex of species occurs from Mexico to Argentina.

NEOTROPICAL

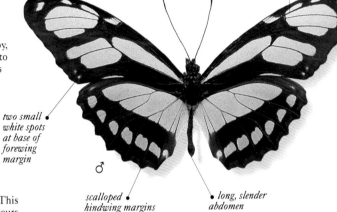

species has exceptionally long forewings for its group

smaller blue spots on forewing leading edge

two small white spots at base of forewing margin

♂

scalloped hindwing margins

long, slender abdomen

Time of Flight ☼	Habitat 🦋		Wingspan 8–9.5cm (3¼–3¾ in)

Family NYMPHALIDAE	Species *Acraea andromacha*	Author Fabricius

GLASSWING

Appropriately named, this butterfly has transparent forewings, and white hindwings with black borders. The underside is similar, but the hindwing has larger white spots in the black marginal band. The sexes are similar, but females are larger.

• **EARLY STAGES** The caterpillar of this species is a glossy, yellowish brown, with long, black, branched spines arising from raised, bluish black spots. It feeds on passion flowers *(Passiflora)*.

• **DISTRIBUTION** Found from Indonesia to Papua New Guinea, Fiji, and Australia. The glasswing has a number of described subspecies.

INDO-AUSTRALIAN

spotting from underside shows through on pale forewing

♀

band of marginal white spots less developed than on underside

Time of Flight ☼	Habitat 🦋		Wingspan 5–6cm (2–2½ in)

| Family NYMPHALIDAE | Species *Acraea acerata* | Author Hewitson |

SWEET POTATO ACRAEA

This common little African butterfly varies from pale yellow to orange-brown. The underside is paler and has distinctive, elongate, orange spots in the dark marginal band.
• **EARLY STAGES** The caterpillar is pale green with yellow and black spines. It feeds on sweet potatoes *(Ipomoea)* and can be a pest.
• **DISTRIBUTION** Tropical Africa from Ghana to eastern Africa.

short, robust antennae typical of this butterfly group

AFROTROPICAL

warning colours indicate butterfly is distasteful

♂

| Time of Flight ☼ | Habitat | Wingspan 3–4cm (1¼–1½in) |

| Family NYMPHALIDAE | Species *Acraea vesta* | Author Fabricius |

YELLOW COSTER

This orange and dark brown butterfly is quite variable, and some specimens are almost entirely black. The underside is similar to the upperside, but is paler and lacks the dark marginal bands. Females are generally larger and more heavily marked.
• **EARLY STAGES** The spiny, black caterpillars have red heads. They live gregariously, which maximizes their unpleasant warning smell. They feed on *Boehmenia*, *Debregeasia*, and *Buddleia*. Butterflies are most often found near the caterpillar's foodplant.
• **DISTRIBUTION** Open scrub country from northern India to Pakistan, Burma, and southern China.

dark brown leading edge to forewing

distinctive red spots

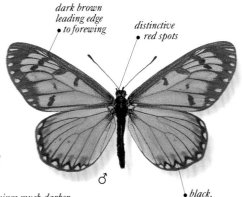

♂

black, U-shaped markings surrounding pale, marginal spots

forewings much darker than hindwings

reddish brown tinge to hindwing margin

♀

INDO-AUSTRALIAN

| Time of Flight ☼ | Habitat | Wingspan 4.5–8cm (1¾–3¼in) |

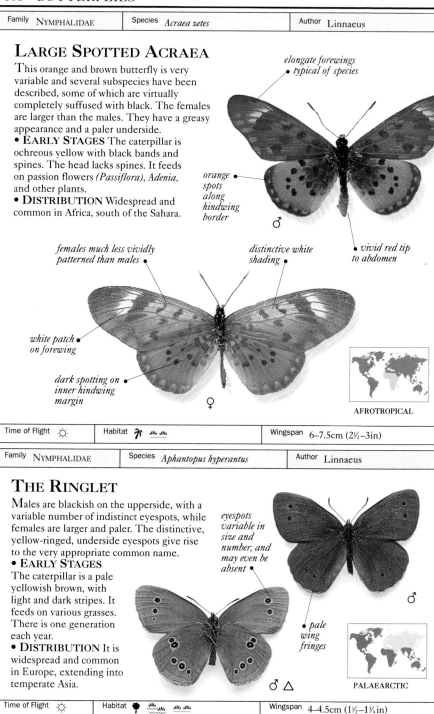

| Family | NYMPHALIDAE | Species | *Acraea zetes* | Author | Linnaeus |

LARGE SPOTTED ACRAEA

This orange and brown butterfly is very variable and several subspecies have been described, some of which are virtually completely suffused with black. The females are larger than the males. They have a greasy appearance and a paler underside.
• **EARLY STAGES** The caterpillar is ochreous yellow with black bands and spines. The head lacks spines. It feeds on passion flowers *(Passiflora)*, *Adenia*, and other plants.
• **DISTRIBUTION** Widespread and common in Africa, south of the Sahara.

elongate forewings typical of species

orange spots along hindwing border

♂

females much less vividly patterned than males

distinctive white shading

vivid red tip to abdomen

white patch on forewing

dark spotting on inner hindwing margin

♀

AFROTROPICAL

| Time of Flight | ☀ | Habitat | 🦋 〰 〰 | Wingspan | 6–7.5cm (2½–3in) |

| Family | NYMPHALIDAE | Species | *Aphantopus hyperantus* | Author | Linnaeus |

THE RINGLET

Males are blackish on the upperside, with a variable number of indistinct eyespots, while females are larger and paler. The distinctive, yellow-ringed, underside eyespots give rise to the very appropriate common name.
• **EARLY STAGES**
The caterpillar is a pale yellowish brown, with light and dark stripes. It feeds on various grasses. There is one generation each year.
• **DISTRIBUTION** It is widespread and common in Europe, extending into temperate Asia.

eyespots variable in size and number, and may even be absent

♂

pale wing fringes

♂ △

PALAEARCTIC

| Time of Flight | ☀ | Habitat | 🌳 〰 〰 | Wingspan | 4–4.5cm (1½–1¾in) |

Family NYMPHALIDAE	Species *Actinote pellenea*	Author Hübner

SMALL LACE-WING

This butterfly is quite closely related to the *Acraea* butterflies of Africa. The combination of black and orange markings indicates that it is distasteful to birds.
• **EARLY STAGES** The life cycle is unknown, but caterpillars of related species have spiny bodies and smooth heads.
• **DISTRIBUTION** South America from Argentina to Venezuela, and the West Indies.

NEOTROPICAL

unusual, flattened clubs on antennae

elongate, rounded forewings

♂

Time of Flight ☼	Habitat 🌾	Wingspan 4.5–5cm (1¾–2in)

Family NYMPHALIDAE	Species *Bematistes aganice*	Author Hewitson

THE WANDERER

Males are black and orange, while the larger females are black and white and have more rounded forewings. The undersides are similar but have distinctive reddish brown, black-spotted hindwing bases. The butterflies have a relatively slow flight, and are attracted to flowers. This is a poisonous species that is mimicked by a number of more palatable African butterflies such as *Pseudacraea eurytus*.
• **EARLY STAGES**
The caterpillar is white, with purplish red spots and stripes, and yellow spines. It feeds on *Adenia gummifera* and passion flowers *(Passiflora)*.
• **DISTRIBUTION**
This species occurs from Ethiopia and Sudan down to South Africa.

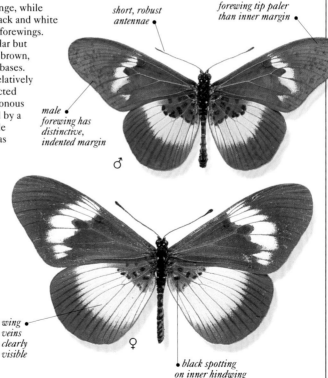

short, robust antennae

forewing tip paler than inner margin

male forewing has distinctive, indented margin

♂

wing veins clearly visible

♀

• black spotting on inner hindwing

AFROTROPICAL

Time of Flight ☼	Habitat 🌾	Wingspan 5.5–8cm (2¼–3¼in)

| Family NYMPHALIDAE | Species *Cepheuptychia cephus* | Author Fabricius |

BLUE NIGHT BUTTERFLY

The iridescent blue of males of this species is most unusual in a group of predominantly brown butterflies. The underside is even more striking, with its distinctive black banding. By contrast, females are brown, with a narrow, blue, marginal line on the upperside and blue below, with dark bands and eyespots.

• **EARLY STAGES** Nothing is known of the early stages of this species.

• **DISTRIBUTION** Found from Surinam and Colombia to southern Brazil and the West Indies.

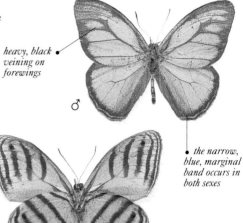

heavy, black veining on forewings

♂

the narrow, blue, marginal band occurs in both sexes

two very small eyespots on the hindwing

♂ △

NEOTROPICAL

| Time of Flight ☼ | Habitat 🌴 | Wingspan 4cm (1½in) |

| Family NYMPHALIDAE | Species *Cithaerias esmeralda* | Author Doubleday |

THE ESMERALDA

This unusual and attractive butterfly belongs to a group in which the wings are almost entirely transparent. They are lightly scaled, and have veins and margins that appear dark brown. On the hindwing there is a pinkish patch that can vary in colour, and a yellow-rimmed eyespot. This butterfly becomes almost invisible when flying close to the ground in the dense rainforest where the light is poor.

• **EARLY STAGES** Nothing is known about the early stages of this species or its foodplant.

• **DISTRIBUTION** Found in Brazil and Peru.

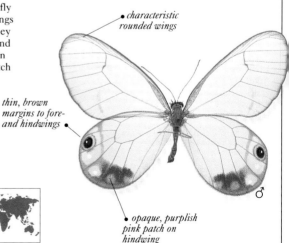

characteristic rounded wings

thin, brown margins to fore- and hindwings

♂

opaque, purplish pink patch on hindwing

NEOTROPICAL

| Time of Flight ☼ | Habitat 🌴 | Wingspan 5cm (2in) |

Family NYMPHALIDAE	Species *Cercyonis pegala*	Author Fabricius

LARGE WOOD NYMPH

This is a variable species, ranging from light brown to blackish brown in colour. The underside is dark, brownish grey with white-centred, orange-rimmed, black eyespots, which are variable in number. The sexes are similar. It is often called the blue-eyed greyling, due to the bluish colour of the centre of the eyespots. Butterflies are on the wing from early summer to early autumn.

• **EARLY STAGES** The caterpillar is green, with longitudinal yellow lines, and two red tails.

• **DISTRIBUTION** In woodlands and meadows in the USA from central Canada to Florida.

small antennae relative to wing area

blue centre to eyespots

♂

NEARCTIC

scalloped hindwing margin

Time of Flight ☀	Habitat ⸲⸲, ⸲⸲,	Wingspan 5–7.5cm (2–3in)

Family Nymphalidae	Species *Coenonympha inornata*	Author Edwards

PLAIN RINGLET

This butterfly is almost indistinguishable from some of the other *Coenonympha* species. The underside of the forewing is orange-brown with a grey tip, and sometimes a single, small eyespot. The hindwing is olive-grey with a broken white band, and occasionally a few minute eyespots. Another common name for the butterfly is the prairie ringlet.

• **EARLY STAGES** The caterpillar is reddish brown, or olive-brown, with two tails. It feeds on various grasses.

• **DISTRIBUTION** Found in prairies, meadows, and woodland clearings from Canada to South Dakota and New York.

the upperside is very simple in pattern

♂

roughly scaled wing fringes give a rather furry appearance

NEARCTIC

Time of Flight ☀	Habitat 🌳 ⸲⸲, ⸲⸲,	Wingspan 2.5–4.5cm (1–1¾in)

Family NYMPHALIDAE	Species *Coenonympha tullia*	Author Müller

LARGE HEATH

This is a very variable species with many described subspecies. The ground colour and the spots can vary. Males are usually brighter.
• **EARLY STAGES** The caterpillar is green, with a dark green line along the back, and white bands along each side. It feeds on sedge *(Carex)* and cotton grass *(Eriophorum)*.
• **DISTRIBUTION** Occurs in central and northern Europe.

eyespots less distinct on upper surface

♀

broken, white band on hindwing

♂ △

PALAEARCTIC

Time of Flight ☼	Habitat 〰 ▲ 〰	Wingspan 3–4cm (1¼–1½in)

Family NYMPHALIDAE	Species *Enodia portlandia*	Author Fabricius

PEARLY EYE

The underside of this distinctively spotted butterfly is greyish brown, with dark brown and white bands and lines. The yellow-ringed eyespots are much more prominent on the underside. The hindwing eyespots have pearly white centres.
• **EARLY STAGES** The caterpillar is yellowish green with red-tipped horns on the head and tail. It feeds on giant cane *(Arundinaria gigantea)*.
• **DISTRIBUTION** The USA; from Illinois, south to Florida.

sharply triangular forewings

♂

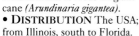

NEARCTIC

Time of Flight ◑ ☼	Habitat ♦	Wingspan 4.5–5cm (1¾–2in)

Family NYMPHALIDAE	Species *Euptychia cymela*	Author Cramer

LITTLE WOOD SATYR

The orange-ringed eyespots of this dark brown butterfly each have two or more minute, metallic, silvery blue spots. Similar eyespots occur on the underside, but there is a series of rounded, metallic-silver spots between them.
• **EARLY STAGES** The caterpillar is brown, sprinkled with tiny, white, raised spots. It feeds on grasses. There is one brood a year in the north of its range, and two in the south.
• **DISTRIBUTION** Common in woodland clearings from southern Canada to northern Mexico.

rounded forewings

♂

two distinctive, dark, marginal lines

NEARCTIC

Time of Flight ☼	Habitat ♦ 〰 〰	Wingspan 4.5–5cm (1¾–2in)

| Family NYMPHALIDAE | Species *Elymnias agondas* | Author Boisduval |

PALMFLY

The male's pale, blue-tinged wing margins are more strongly developed in some forms. The underside has an orange patch, enclosing two eyespots, on each hindwing. The females have the same striking, black and white pattern on each surface.
• **EARLY STAGES** The caterpillar is not described, but is known to feed on palms (Palmae).
• **DISTRIBUTION** From Papua New Guinea to northern Australia.

INDO-AUSTRALIAN

striking, plain black forewings

long, slender antennae

blue tinge to wing margins

brown leading edge to forewings

♂

scalloped wing margins

thin, white wing margins

hindwing eyespots are much smaller than those on underside

♀

| Time of Flight ☼ | Habitat 🌴 | Wingspan 7–9cm (2¾–3½ in) |

| Family NYMPHALIDAE | Species *Heteronympha merope* | Author Fabricius |

COMMON BROWN

The sexes of this butterfly are very different. The male underside is similar to the upper surface, but has fewer dark markings and smaller eyespots. The underside of the female forewing is similar to the upperside, but the hindwing is mottled with reddish brown and greyish brown, and has a few eyespots.
• **EARLY STAGES** The caterpillar is very variable in colour, ranging from green to grey, or light brown, with darker mottling and two short tails. It feeds on grasses. There are one or two generations a year depending on locality.
• **DISTRIBUTION** Found in south-western and south-eastern Australia, including Tasmania.

female forewing is much broader, and less pointed at the tip

♂

scalloped hindwing margin similar on both sexes

INDO-AUSTRALIAN

♀

| Time of Flight ☼ | Habitat ⚶ ⚶ | Wingspan 5–6cm (2–2½in) |

| Family NYMPHALIDAE | Species *Maniola jurtina* | Author Linnaeus |

MEADOW BROWN

This extremely common species has many described subspecies and forms. Males are generally smaller and darker. The undersides of both sexes are similar with orange forewings and brown hindwings, but females have more clearly defined light and dark regions.
• **EARLY STAGES** The caterpillar is green with long, white hairs and yellow lines along the sides. It feeds on grasses, particularly *Poa* and *Agrostis*.
• **DISTRIBUTION** Europe to North Africa, across to Iran.

♀

eyespot diverts birds from the delicate body

scalloped hindwing margins

irregular, dividing line of colours on the hindwing underside

PALAEARCTIC

♀ △

| Time of Flight ☼ | Habitat ♣ ⚶ ⚶ | Wingspan 4–5.5cm (1½–2¼in) |

Family NYMPHALIDAE	Species *Hypocysta adiante*	Author Hübner

ORANGE RINGLET

This butterfly has golden-brown fore- and hindwings. The underside of the forewing is similar to the upperside but paler, and the hindwing eyespots are encircled by pale, greyish brown outer rings.
• **EARLY STAGES** The caterpillar is pinkish brown, with darker lines. The head is hairy, with a pair of pointed horns. It feeds on grasses.
• **DISTRIBUTION** Can be found in northern and eastern Australia with two described subspecies.

brown forewing border

brown spot in hindwing corner

♂

hindwing eyespots

⊕

INDO-AUSTRALIAN

Time of Flight ☼	Habitat ⸹⸹, ⸹⸹	Wingspan 3–4cm (1¼–1½in)

Family NYMPHALIDAE	Species *Hipparchia fagi*	Author Scopoli

WOODLAND GRAYLING

Males tend to have the forewing band suffused with greyish brown and the eyespots are usually less well developed than those of the female. The undersides of the sexes are similar. Butterflies are on the wing in the summer.
• **EARLY STAGES** The caterpillar is pale, greyish brown to yellowish brown, with darker lines and stripes. It feeds chiefly on soft-grasses *(Holeus).* There is one generation a year.
• **DISTRIBUTION** It is widespread in open woodland in central and southern Europe.

♀

jagged white band to forewing

underside hindwing pattern provides good camouflage when species is at rest

scalloped hindwings

♀ △

PALAEARCTIC

Time of Flight ☼	Habitat ♠	Wingspan 7–7.5cm (2¾–3in)

Family NYMPHALIDAE	Species *Melanargia galathea*	Author Linnaeus

MARBLED WHITE

Although quite variable in pattern, this is a very distinctive black and white butterfly. In some forms, the ground colour is a strong yellow. The sexes are alike, although females tend to be larger and paler. Butterflies are on the wing in summer, and are attracted to the flowers of thistles *(Carduus)*, and knapweeds *(Centaurea)*.

• **EARLY STAGES** The caterpillar is yellowish green or pale brown, with dark lines along the back. It feeds on fescues *(Festuca)*.

• **DISTRIBUTION** It is widespread in Europe, extending to North Africa and western temperate Asia.

distinctive chequered pattern distinguishes this from other species

♂

broken marginal band on underside of hindwing •

♂ △

PALAEARCTIC

Time of Flight ☼	Habitat ⚞ ⚞	Wingspan 4.5–5.5cm (1¾–2¼in)

Family NYMPHALIDAE	Species *Melanitis leda*	Author Linnaeus

EVENING BROWN

This butterfly has a very distinctive shape. The underside is mottled dark brown with very narrow, blackish brown margins, and resembles a dead leaf when the butterfly is resting with its wings closed. These butterflies are usually active at dawn, and just before dusk.

• **EARLY STAGES** The caterpillar is yellowish green, and densely covered with short hairs. It feeds on rice *(Oryza)*, sugar cane *(Saccharum)*, *Sorghum*, and various grasses.

• **DISTRIBUTION** Common from Africa to South-east Asia, and Australia.

"square" eyespots on forewing •

slightly scalloped hindwings with small tails •

♂

AFROTROPICAL
INDO-AUSTRALIAN

Time of Flight ☼	Habitat ⚞ ⚞ ⚞	Wingspan 6–8cm (2½–3¼in)

Family NYMPHALIDAE	Species *Minois dryas*	Author Scopoli

DRYAD BUTTERFLY

Males of this distinctive butterfly are smaller and darker than females, and tend to have smaller eyespots. The underside is paler, and there are sometimes grey bands on the hindwing. The butterflies are on the wing from early summer to early autumn.

• **EARLY STAGES** The caterpillar is dirty white, with dark markings, and two blackish brown stripes extending to the forked tail. It feeds on various grasses, especially purple moor-grass *(Molinia)*.

• **DISTRIBUTION** Can be found in open woodland and on grassy slopes in central and southern Europe, extending across temperate Asia to Japan.

blue centres to eyespots distinguish this from similar species
scalloped hindwing margins are most noticeable in females
♀

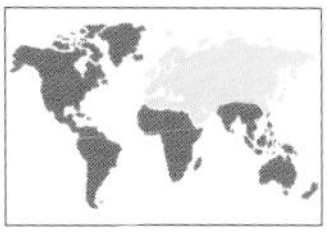

PALAEARCTIC

Time of Flight	Habitat	Wingspan 5–7cm (2–2¾in)

Family NYMPHALIDAE	Species *Pararge aegeria*	Author Linnaeus

SPECKLED WOOD

The sexes of this dappled woodland butterfly are very similar. Females have more rounded forewings. The eyespots on the upperside are much more developed than on the underside. The spots vary from creamy white to deep orange. Speckled wood butterflies often feed from the blossoms of bramble *(Rubus)*.

• **EARLY STAGES** The caterpillar is yellowish green with a dark green stripe down the back, and light and dark lines along the sides. It feeds on couch *(Agropyron)* and other grasses.

• **DISTRIBUTION** Widespread in Europe, extending through to central Asia.

pale scalloping to wing edges
♂
scalloped hindwing margins

weakly developed eyespots
♂ △

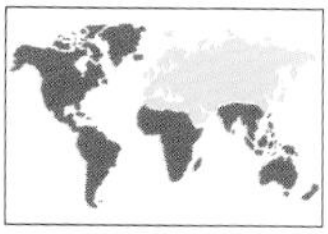

PALAEARCTIC

Time of Flight	Habitat	Wingspan 4–4.5cm (1½–1¾in)

Family NYMPHALIDAE	Species *Pararge schakra*	Author Kollar

COMMON WALL BUTTERFLY

Although the upperside of this butterfly is not particularly distinctive, with its black and white eyespots set in orange patches on a brown background, the underside is more easily recognized, with its attractive hindwing row of multi-ringed eyespots, and its "scorched" forewings. These butterflies are active fliers, usually keeping close to the ground. They occur at most times of the year, on sunny hillsides above 2,000m (6,560ft).

• **EARLY STAGES** Although little seems to be known of the early stages, it is almost certain that the caterpillar feeds on grasses.

• **DISTRIBUTION** Occurs from Iran throughout northern India to western China.

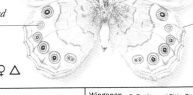

♂

PALAEARCTIC
INDO-AUSTRALIAN

marginal row of double-ringed eyespots •

• *distinctive light and dark wing fringes*

♀ △

Time of Flight ☼	Habitat ⛰	Wingspan 5.5–6cm (2¼–2½in)

Family NYMPHALIDAE	Species *Taygetis echo*	Author Cramer

NIGHT BUTTERFLY

This brown butterfly has a velvety black centre to the forewing. The underside is similar in coloration to the upperside, and has a marginal band of minute, yellowish white spots on the forewing, becoming larger on the hindwing. The sexes are similar.

• **EARLY STAGES** Little is known of the early stages although other members of the genus have smooth caterpillars that feed on grasses, and bamboos *(Chusquea)*.

• **DISTRIBUTION** Found in tropical South America, from Surinam to Brazil. Also occurs in Trinidad.

forewing tip is suffused • *with golden brown*

♂

NEOTROPICAL

irregular scalloping of • *the hindwing margin*

dark colour makes • *this butterfly difficult to see when it flies at night*

Time of Flight ◐ ☼	Habitat 🌿	Wingspan 5.7–6cm (2¼–2½in)

Family NYMPHALIDAE	Species *Pierella hyceta*	Author Hewitson

HEWITSON'S PIERELLA

This distinctive angular-shaped butterfly, with its orange-tipped hindwings, belongs to a South American genus of about 50 species. The underside lacks the bright hindwing patch and so is better camouflaged when the butterfly closes its wings. The vertical lines crossing the wing veins are very noticeable. The sexes are similar.
• **EARLY STAGES** Little is known of the early stages, although related species have dull brown caterpillars with short, double tails, and feed on the foliage of various Heliconiaceae and Marantaceae.
• **DISTRIBUTION** Widespread in South America from Brazil to Guyana.

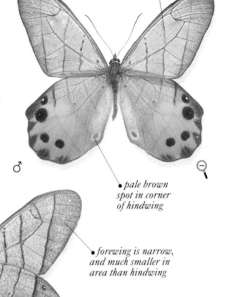

yellow shading on forewings

♂

pale brown spot in corner of hindwing

forewing is narrow, and much smaller in area than hindwing

tiny white spots on forewing

margins of hindwing are strangely angular

♀ △

NEOTROPICAL

Time of Flight ☼	Habitat 🌴	Wingspan 7–7.5cm (2¾–3in)

Family NYMPHALIDAE	Species *Chazara briseis*	Author Linnaeus

THE HERMIT

Females of this butterfly are larger than males, but are otherwise similar. The underside of the forewing is similar to the upperside, but the hindwing is mottled with brown and does not have the pale central band.
• **EARLY STAGES** The caterpillar is greyish white. It feeds mainly at night on blue moor grass (*Sesleria caerulea*).
• **DISTRIBUTION** Widespread in central and southern Europe, Turkey, and Iran.

pale brown leading edge of forewing

♀

distinctively scalloped hindwings

PALAEARCTIC

Time of Flight ☼	Habitat ▲ 🌾 🌾	Wingspan 4–7cm (1½–2¾in)

| Family NYMPHALIDAE | Species *Tisiphone abeone* | Author Donovan |

SWORD-GRASS BROWN

The orange forewing markings are an unusual shape, and the prominent hindwing eyespots divert predators from the vulnerable head and body. The underside is lighter, with a yellowish white band across the hindwings, and more strongly developed hindwing eyespots. Females are similar to males, but have paler markings.
• **EARLY STAGES**
The caterpillar is green and hairy. It feeds on sword-grass *(Gahnia)*.
• **DISTRIBUTION**
Occurs in south-eastern Australia.

all eyespots have blue and white centres

INDO-AUSTRALIAN

♂

| Time of Flight ☼ | Habitat 〰, 〰 | Wingspan 5–5.5cm (2–2¼in) |

| Family NYMPHALIDAE | Species *Ypthima asterope* | Author Klug |

AFRICAN RINGLET

This common butterfly is one of a group of very similar species that are difficult to distinguish. The underside is characteristically patterned with fine white lines. The sexes are alike.
• **EARLY STAGES** The caterpillar is undescribed. It feeds on grasses.
• **DISTRIBUTION**
Occurs in dry bush country throughout Africa, south of the Sahara, and south-western Asia.

white dots in centre of yellow-ringed forewing eyespots

pale hindwing fringes

♂

AFROTROPICAL

| Time of Flight ☼ | Habitat 〰, 〰 | Wingspan 3–4cm (1¼–1½in) |

| Family NYMPHALIDAE | Species *Ypthima baldus* | Author Fabricius |

COMMON FIVE RING BUTTERFLY

This species has five yellow-ringed eyespots on the fore- and hindwings. The upperside is brown, and is suffused with a pattern of small whitish lines. The sexes are similar. Adult butterflies are on the wing all year in the south, and in spring and summer in the north.
• **EARLY STAGES**
The green caterpillar feeds on grasses.
• **DISTRIBUTION**
This species occurs from India, to Pakistan, and Burma.

prominent forewing eyespots

variation in size of hindwing eyespots

♀

INDO-AUSTRALIAN

| Time of Flight ☼ | Habitat ▲ 🌴 〰, 〰 | Wingspan 3–4.5cm (1¼–1¾in) |

Family NYMPHALIDAE	Species *Zipaetis scylax*	Author Hewitson

DARK CATSEYE BUTTERFLY

This is one of only three known species in the genus occurring in the region extending from India to China. The brown upperside of both sexes is virtually unmarked, but the underside bears distinctive, yellow-ringed eyespots, which give the species its common name. Butterflies have a weak flight, and mostly stay in areas of dense bush.

brown and yellow marginal lines are
• present on both surfaces

rudiments of • an eyespot

• **EARLY STAGES**
Nothing seems to be known of the early stages of this species, although the caterpillar probably feeds on grasses.

upperside much • plainer than the underside

♂

• **DISTRIBUTION** It is common in the hill ranges of northern India, Pakistan, and Burma.

• slightly scalloped hindwing

• white hindwing fringe

paler brown to wing margins •

varying sizes of eyespots •

♂ △

• small, white-framed eyespot

striking, silvery-white band • surrounding hindwing eyespots

INDO-AUSTRALIAN

Time of Flight ☼	Habitat 🦗	Wingspan 5.7–6cm (2¼–2⅜in)

Family NYMPHALIDAE	Species *Tellervo zoilus*	Author Fabricius

CAIRNS HAMADRYAS

The underside of this black and white species is similar to the upperside, but has white spots in the black margins. The sexes are similar.

white spotting varies between
• different subspecies

• **EARLY STAGES** The caterpillar is dark grey coloured. It is known to feed on parsonsia *(P. velutina)*.

• **DISTRIBUTION**
Found from Sulawesi to Papua New Guinea, as well as the Solomon Islands, and northern regions of Australia.

♂

• long, slender body

INDO-AUSTRALIAN

Time of Flight ☼	Habitat 🦗	Wingspan 4–4.5cm (1½–1¾in)

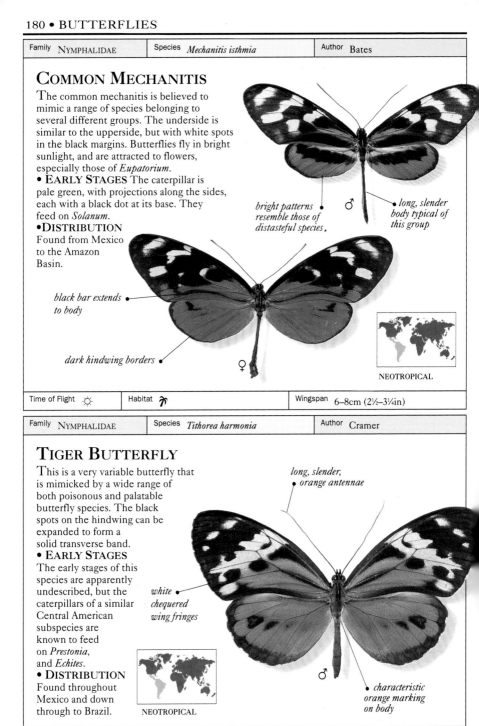

Family NYMPHALIDAE	Species *Mechanitis isthmia*	Author Bates

COMMON MECHANITIS

The common mechanitis is believed to mimic a range of species belonging to several different groups. The underside is similar to the upperside, but with white spots in the black margins. Butterflies fly in bright sunlight, and are attracted to flowers, especially those of *Eupatorium*.
• **EARLY STAGES** The caterpillar is pale green, with projections along the sides, each with a black dot at its base. They feed on *Solanum*.
•**DISTRIBUTION** Found from Mexico to the Amazon Basin.

bright patterns resemble those of distasteful species

♂

long, slender body typical of this group

black bar extends to body

dark hindwing borders

♀

NEOTROPICAL

Time of Flight ☼	Habitat 🌳	Wingspan 6–8cm (2½–3¼in)

Family NYMPHALIDAE	Species *Tithorea harmonia*	Author Cramer

TIGER BUTTERFLY

This is a very variable butterfly that is mimicked by a wide range of both poisonous and palatable butterfly species. The black spots on the hindwing can be expanded to form a solid transverse band.
• **EARLY STAGES** The early stages of this species are apparently undescribed, but the caterpillars of a similar Central American subspecies are known to feed on *Prestonia*, and *Echites*.
• **DISTRIBUTION** Found throughout Mexico and down through to Brazil.

long, slender, orange antennae

white chequered wing fringes

♂

characteristic orange marking on body

NEOTROPICAL

Time of Flight ☼	Habitat 🌿	Wingspan 5.5–7.5cm (2¼–3in)

Family NYMPHALIDAE	Species *Thyridia themisto*	Author Hübner

SMALL THYRIDIA

Belonging to a group of about seven described species from South America, this impressive butterfly has transparent wings, and strong black veins, bands, and margins. They are mimicked by several other species of butterfly and moth, including the day-flying Castniid moth, *Gazera linus*.
• **EARLY STAGES** The caterpillar is black with bright yellow rings, indicating that the species is almost certainly poisonous. It feeds on manaca *(Brunfelsia)* shrubs.
• **DISTRIBUTION** Found widely in Argentina and Brazil, where it is often seen in towns.

long, slender antennae with white clubs

NEOTROPICAL

transparent patches where wing-scales are modified to form slender hairs

forewings of this species have a distinctive, bulbous outline

♀

Time of Flight ☼	Habitat 🌴 ⏜ ⏜	Wingspan 7–8cm (2¾–3¼in)

Family NYMPHALIDAE	Species *Melinaea lilis*	Author Bates

MECHANITIS MIMIC

This highly variable butterfly mimics many different species belonging to various groups. It can be distinguished from similar species by its long, yellow antennae, and its relatively small head. The underside is similar in appearance to the upperside, but with white spots along the dark brown margins. They are on the wing for most of the year. Both sexes visit flowers.
• **EARLY STAGES** The caterpillar is conspicuously ringed. The area behind the head is red and pale orange-pink, and there are two whip-like, black and white filaments that twitch. It feeds on *Markea neurantha*.
• **DISTRIBUTION** Found from Mexico to the Amazon Basin.

the striking caterpillar is probably distasteful

CATERPILLAR OF *MELINAEA LILIS*

NEOTROPICAL

black and orange pattern warns that this species may be poisonous

♂

Time of Flight ☼	Habitat 🌴	Wingspan 7–7.5cm (2¾–3in)

Family NYMPHALIDAE	Species *Amauris echeria*	Author Stoll

CHIEF BUTTERFLY

One of a group of very similar species, the chief butterfly varies geographically and has several described subspecies. Identification is further complicated due to the fact that this species is mimicked by certain Papilio species. The underside is very similar to the upperside, but has more small, white spots in the margins. The sexes are alike. These butterflies are on the wing at most times of the year.

• **EARLY STAGES** The caterpillar is black with yellow dots. It has five pairs of tapered, black filaments along its back. The head is smooth and black. It feeds on *Tylophora, Secamone, Marsdenia,* and other plants.

• **DISTRIBUTION** Tropical central Africa to South Africa.

pointed forewings

irregular, white spotting on forewings

orange-yellow hindwing traversed by black veins

♂

AFROTROPICAL

Time of Flight ☼	Habitat 🌳	Wingspan 6–8cm (2½–3¼in)

Family NYMPHALIDAE	Species *Danaus chrysippus*	Author Linnaeus

PLAIN TIGER

This very common and distinctive butterfly displays warning colours of black and orange. There are many minor variations in pattern, and some forms lack the dark forewing tip with white spots. The underside is similar to the upperside, but is paler. Several other butterfly species are convincing mimics of the plain tiger. Also commonly known as the African monarch, and the lesser wanderer, this species can be seen on the wing at most times of the year.

• **EARLY STAGES** The caterpillar is banded with orange-black and bluish white. It feeds on milkweeds *(Asclepias),* and other related plants.

• **DISTRIBUTION** From Africa, to India, Malaysia, Japan, and Australasia.

dark brown leading edge to forewing

black and white wing fringes occur on all forms

♂

size and distribution of hindwing spots distinguishes various forms

AFROTROPICAL
INDO-AUSTRALIAN
PALAEARCTIC

Time of Flight ☼	Habitat 🌾🌾	Wingspan 7–8cm (2¾–3¼in)

Family NYMPHALIDAE	Species *Euploe core*	Author Cramer

COMMON INDIAN CROW

One of a group of rather similar butterflies, this is the commonest. It has a number of described races and forms which vary greatly in the degree of spotting. The underside is similar to the upperside, but is paler. The sexes are similar.

- **EARLY STAGES** The caterpillar is white, strongly ringed with dark brown. It has yellow and white stripes along the side, and four pairs of purplish brown filaments along the back. It feeds on a wide range of plants including oleander *(Nerium oleander)* and milkweeds *(Asclepias).*
- **DISTRIBUTION** Found from India to China, Sumatra, and Java, and also in northern and eastern Australia.

forewings much darker than hindwings

relatively short antennae, a feature of the group

♂

white spotting along wing margins

INDO-AUSTRALIAN

Time of Flight ☼	Habitat 🌿🌿	Wingspan 8–9.5cm (3¼–3¾in)

Family NYMPHALIDAE	Species *Danaus gilippus*	Author Cramer

QUEEN BUTTERFLY

This handsome butterfly is dark, orange-brown, with black borders and white spots. The underside is paler, and the hindwings have more prominent black veining.

- **EARLY STAGES** The caterpillar is pale, bluish grey, with transverse black rings, and bands spotted with reddish orange. The caterpillar feeds on milkweeds *(Asclepias).*
- **DISTRIBUTION** Widely distributed from Argentina to Central America and southern parts of North America. This is not a migrant species, unlike most of its relatives.

darker leading edge to forewings

distinctive white spotting

♂

scent scales on hindwing

gently scalloped, hindwing margin

NEOTROPICAL
NEARCTIC

Time of Flight ☼	Habitat 🌿🌿	Wingspan 7–7.5cm (2¾–3in)

Family NYMPHALIDAE	Species *Danaus plexippus*	Author Linnaeus

MONARCH BUTTERFLY

With its bold pattern of black and orange, and wing veins
enhanced by dark borders, this is one of the best-known
butterflies. The sexes are alike.

• **EARLY STAGES** The caterpillar is banded with black,
yellow, and cream, and has tentacles behind the head. It
feeds on milkweeds *(Asclepias)* and related plants.

• **DISTRIBUTION** This butterfly is a well-known
migrant. It has spread from its home in the Americas to
Indonesia, Australasia, and the Canary Islands, and has
recently established colonies in Mediterranean countries.

WORLDWIDE

*three orange
patches at
forewing tip*

*robust structure
makes this species
a strong flier*

*hindwings
much more
rounded
than
forewings*

*orange and
black pattern
indicates these
butterflies are
poisonous*

♀

*white patches on
outer margins of
forewings and
hindwings*

♀ △

*hindwing
undersides are
paler than
uppersides*

Time of Flight ☀	Habitat ⸱ılı. ⸱ılı.	Wingspan 7.5–10cm (3–4in)

Family NYMPHALIDAE	Species *Euploea mulciber*	Author Cramer

STRIPED BLUE CROW

The uppersides on the forewings of both sexes of this large butterfly are shot with iridescent purple, although it is most evident in the darker male. The female has brown hindwings shot with white lines. The undersides are similar, but lack the iridescence. This species belongs to a large Indo-Australian genus known as crow butterflies because of their iridescent dark colours. Both caterpillars and adults are poisonous.
• **EARLY STAGES** The caterpillar is yellowish brown, with paler and darker bands, and four pairs of black-tipped, red filaments. It feeds on oleander *(Nerium)*, fig *(Ficus)*, and various pipevines *(Aristolochia)*.
• **DISTRIBUTION** India to southern China, Malaysia, and the Philippines.

INDO-AUSTRALIAN

white spots ringed with paler blue

darker brown to forewing base

some spots lack the white centre

white-spotted fringes to hindwings

paler triangle at base of hindwings

♂

purple colour less distinct than in male

female hindwings rayed with white

♀

Time of Flight ☼	Habitat 🌴	Wingspan 9 –10cm (3½–4in)

Family NYMPHALIDAE	Species *Idea leuconoe*	Author Erichson

LARGE TREE NYMPH

The large wings of this delicate butterfly are translucent greyish white, with distinctive black markings. The wings are often suffused with yellow towards the base. Large tree nymphs have a slow, gliding flight, and prefer to remain just below the forest canopy.
• **EARLY STAGES** The caterpillar is velvety black, with narrow, pale yellow rings, and red spots. There are four pairs of black filaments running along its back. It feeds on *Parsonsia*, *Cynanchum*, and *Tylophora*.
• **DISTRIBUTION** From Thailand to Malaysia, the Philippines, and Taiwan. In Malaysia it is largely coastal, in mangrove swamps.

distinctive, red and black
• patterning

CATERPILLAR OF
IDEA LEUCONOE

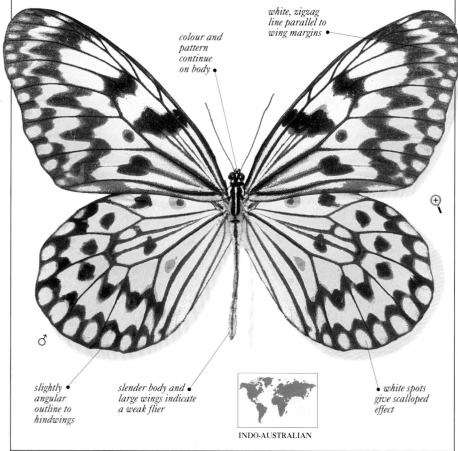

white, zigzag line parallel to wing margins •

colour and pattern continue on body •

♂

slightly •
angular
outline to
hindwings

slender body and •
large wings indicate
a weak flier

• white spots
give scalloped
effect

INDO-AUSTRALIAN

Time of Flight ☼	Habitat 🌴	Wingspan 9.5–10.8cm (3¾–4½ in)

| Family NYMPHALIDAE | Species *Ideopsis vitrea* | Author Blanchard |

BLANCHARD'S IDEOPSIS

This beautiful species is very variable with several described subspecies, ranging in colour from white to green. The darker male's forewings are more slender and pointed than those of the female.
• **EARLY STAGES** The caterpillar and its foodplants are unknown. Other *Ideopsis* species have pale, spotted bodies with one pair of tentacles near the head, and a second pair close to the tail.
• **DISTRIBUTION** Found in woodlands, from Sulawesi, through the Moluccas, to Papua New Guinea.

prominent brown wing veins

antennae with rounded clubs

dark markings uniform in both sexes

long, slender abdomen

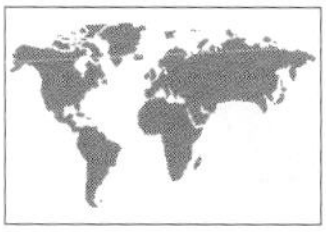

♂

INDO-AUSTRALIAN

| Time of Flight ☼ | Habitat 🌴 | Wingspan 7–9.5cm (2¾–3¾ in) |

| Family NYMPHALIDAE | Species *Lycorea cleobaea* | Author Godart |

LARGE TIGER

This extremely variable butterfly resembles certain *Heliconius* species, but actually belongs to a sub-family of its own.
• **EARLY STAGES** The caterpillar is white with black rings, and a pair of black, flexible tentacles. It feeds on plants including fig *(Ficus)* and pawpaw *(Carica papaya)*.
• **DISTRIBUTION** Mexico to Brazil. Occasionally strays into southern USA.

yellow-clubbed antennae

black and orange colours warn birds that butterfly is distasteful

marginal row of white spots on hindwing

dark brown ground colour

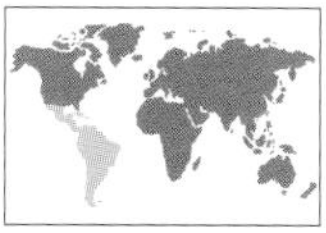

♂

NEOTROPICAL

| Time of Flight ☼ | Habitat 🌴 | Wingspan 7–8cm (2¾–3¼ in) |

MOTHS

THYATIRIDAE

T HE MOTHS BELONGING to this fairly small family, containing about 100 species, occur in many parts of the world. They are, however absent from the Afrotropical and Indo-Australian regions. Sometimes referred to collectively as the lutestrings, these medium-sized moths are generally fairly dull in colour. Nevertheless, there are some exceptions that are quite distinctively and attractively marked with pink spots or pale lines.

———— • ————

The smooth caterpillars either live openly on foliage, or else conceal themselves between leaves woven together with silk, where the pupae are formed in their silken cocoons.

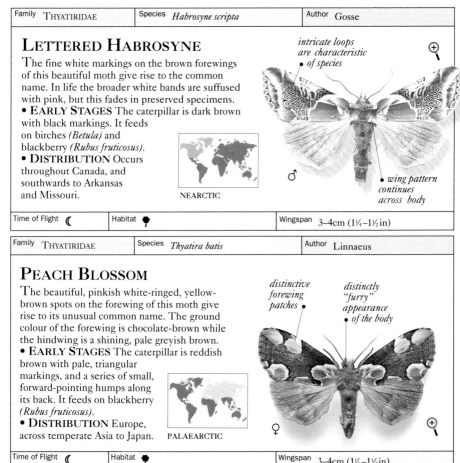

Family THYATIRIDAE	Species *Habrosyne scripta*	Author Gosse

LETTERED HABROSYNE

The fine white markings on the brown forewings of this beautiful moth give rise to the common name. In life the broader white bands are suffused with pink, but this fades in preserved specimens.
• **EARLY STAGES** The caterpillar is dark brown with black markings. It feeds on birches *(Betula)* and blackberry *(Rubus fruticosus)*.
• **DISTRIBUTION** Occurs throughout Canada, and southwards to Arkansas and Missouri.

NEARCTIC

♂

intricate loops are characteristic of species

wing pattern continues across body

Time of Flight ☾	Habitat ♣	Wingspan 3–4cm (1¼–1½ in)

Family THYATIRIDAE	Species *Thyatira batis*	Author Linnaeus

PEACH BLOSSOM

The beautiful, pinkish white-ringed, yellow-brown spots on the forewing of this moth give rise to its unusual common name. The ground colour of the forewing is chocolate-brown while the hindwing is a shining, pale greyish brown.
• **EARLY STAGES** The caterpillar is reddish brown with pale, triangular markings, and a series of small, forward-pointing humps along its back. It feeds on blackberry *(Rubus fruticosus)*.
• **DISTRIBUTION** Europe, across temperate Asia to Japan.

PALAEARCTIC

♀

distinctive forewing patches

distinctly "furry" appearance of the body

Time of Flight ☾	Habitat ♣	Wingspan 3–4cm (1¼–1½ in)

DREPANIDAE

THIS GROUP OF about 800 species occurs throughout the world, with the exception of Central and South America. The most distinctive characteristic of the Drepanidae is the strongly curved forewing tip that is present in many species. This gives rise to the name hook-tips which is popularly applied to this group. Moths have very poorly formed tongues or no tongue at all, and so are unable to feed in this stage. The caterpillars of this group are distinctive as they lack the pair of claspers at the end of the body that are common in other families. In many species the body tapers to a distinctive pointed tail instead.

•

Caterpillars usually feed on the foliage of broad-leaved trees and shrubs. The pupae are sometimes covered with an unusual bluish, waxy coating.

Family DREPANIDAE	Species *Drepana arcuata*	Author Walker

ARCHED HOOK-TIP

This distinctive moth has a particularly sharply pointed hook to the wing-tip that distinguishes it from all other North American moths of this group. The ground colour ranges from pale yellowish white to orange-yellow, and the reddish brown markings vary in distinctness. The hindwing is similar to the forewing, but is paler. The sexes are alike. Moths are on the wing from mid-spring to early autumn.
• **EARLY STAGES** The caterpillar feeds on alders *(Alnus)* and birches *(Betula)*. It is green and brown with yellow markings.
• **DISTRIBUTION** From Canada to South Carolina.

feathered antennae of males

distinctive, dark forewing band extends into "hook-tip"

dark brown marginal line extends round the hindwings

NEARCTIC

Time of Flight	Habitat	Wingspan 2.5–5cm (1–2in)

Family DREPANIDAE	Species *Oreta erminea*	Author Warren

WARREN'S HOOK-TIP

This genus of about 40 species is mostly found in eastern and south-eastern Asia. The male moths of this group are unusual in that they lack the wing-coupling bristle typical of moths. The upperside of Warren's hook-tip has a glossy sheen, and varies in colour from yellowish to dark purplish brown.
• **EARLY STAGES** Nothing is known about the early stages of this species.
• **DISTRIBUTION** Common in north-east Queensland, in Australia, also can be found in Papua New Guinea.

base of forewing has distinctive patch of silvery white scales

hairy appearance of inner hindwing margin

INDO-AUSTRALIAN

Time of Flight	Habitat	Wingspan 2.5–4.5cm (1–1¾in)

URANIIDAE

ALTHOUGH THIS is a fairly small family of moths, it contains some of the most striking species to be found in the world, including the stunning Madagascan sunset moth (see opposite). They are found in the tropics of America, Africa, and Indo-Australia. The day-flying species are more vivid and beautifully coloured than the night fliers; many have iridescent scaling and very well-developed tails to their wings, so that they are often mistaken for butterflies. Those species that fly at night are mostly rather flimsy insects that have white or pale-coloured wings, with darker stripes. Uraniidae are similar to the Geometer moths (Geometridae), to which they are related, but they differ in the arrangement of their wing veins.

Family URANIIDAE	Species *Alcides zodiaca*	Author Butler

ZODIAC MOTH

This is the only member of this genus of eleven day-flying species to occur in Australia. The wings are black with coppery green tones and purplish pink iridescent bands. The hindwing margins are strongly scalloped and have short but distinct, pale bluish green tails. The underside is pale, iridescent bluish green with black bands. The moths commonly visit flowers by day, and in the evening fly high in the forest canopy.

• **EARLY STAGES** The caterpillar is black with white bands and an area of bright red on the back, behind the head. It feeds on the foliage of a large vine, *Omphalea queenslandiae* and also on *Endospermum*.

• **DISTRIBUTION** Papua New Guinea and north-eastern Australia.

striped leading edge of forewing

long, slender antennae

black and white chequered forewing edge

♀

silvery fringe to hindwing edge

iridescent colour of wings is matched on body

INDO-AUSTRALIAN

Time of Flight ☼	Habitat 🌴	Wingspan 8–10cm (3¼–4in)

| Family URANIIDAE | Species *Chrysiridia riphearia* | Author Hübner |

MADAGASCAN SUNSET MOTH

This is often regarded as the most spectacular and distinctive of all moths. Its colours made it popular with the Victorians, who used its wings to make jewellery. The hindwings have numerous short and slender tails.
• **EARLY STAGES** The caterpillar is yellow and black with long, club-tipped hairs. It feeds on the foliage of *Omphalea*. The poisonous foodplant and bright colours of the moth suggest that it is distasteful to birds and animals.
• **DISTRIBUTION** Confined to Madagascar.

pointed forewings resemble those of Papilio butterflies

hindwing spotting distinguishes this from similar species

AFROTROPICAL

♀

| Time of Flight ☀ | Habitat 🌴 | Wingspan 8–10cm (3¼–4in) |

| Family URANIIDAE | Species *Uranus sloanus* | Author Cramer |

SLOANE'S URANIA

One of the most spectacular Caribbean day-flying moths, Sloane's urania has hindwings marked with multicoloured, iridescent scales. The underside is pale, metallic-bluish green with narrow black bands. This is the South American counterpart of the Madagascan sunset moth (see above).
• **EARLY STAGES** The caterpillars are marked black, blue, and white, indicating that they are probably poisonous. They have distinctive clubbed hairs and feed on the foliage of *Omphalea*.
• **DISTRIBUTION** Confined to Jamaica.

coppery green bands become pinkish orange closer to the body

these moths are distinguished by their long hindwing tails

striped pattern continues on body

NEOTROPICAL

♀

| Time of Flight ☀ | Habitat 🌴 | Wingspan 5–7cm (2–2¾in) |

GEOMETRIDAE

T HIS IS the second largest family of moths, containing approximately 15,000 described species. Geometridae or "Geometers" typically have fairly large, rounded wings and slender bodies, and their flight is weak and fluttering. In such a large group, however, there are many deviants. In a number of species, the wings of the females are reduced to tiny vestiges so that they are unable to fly. Although most species are rather dull in colour and will frequently display camouflage patterns, there are a few tropical groups that are actually very brightly coloured. The name Geometridae refers to the looper caterpillars of this family, which are so-called because of their wholly characteristic, ungainly walk. They are also known in the USA as inchworms.

Family GEOMETRIDAE	Species *Archiearis infans*	Author Möschler

THE INFANT

The infant is a distinctive, little moth with a hairy appearance, caused by its long, coarse wing fringes. The forewings are blackish brown, sprinkled with white scales, while the hindwings are orange, making this an easy species to recognize. The sexes are similar. These moths are on the wing from early to late spring and may be seen flying on warm afternoons.
• **EARLY STAGES** The caterpillar is green to reddish brown, with fine yellowish white lines along the body. It feeds on the foliage of birch *(Betula)*.
• **DISTRIBUTION** Occurs in birch woodlands from Canada to northern USA.

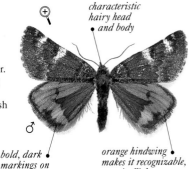

characteristic hairy head and body

♂

bold, dark markings on hindwing

orange hindwing makes it recognizable, even in flight

NEARCTIC

Time of Flight ☼	Habitat ♠	Wingspan 3–4cm (1¼–1½in)

Family GEOMETRIDAE	Species *Alsophila pometaria*	Author Harris

FALL CANKERWORM MOTH

The males of this species are pale greyish brown with a greyish white, serrated line crossing both pairs of wings. Females are totally flightless, their wings having been reduced to tiny vestiges. The moths fly in early winter.
• **EARLY STAGES** The brown and white, or green and white, striped caterpillar is a pest of apple *(Malus domestica)* and other fruit trees, broad-leaved trees such as maple *(Acer)* and oak *(Quercus)*.
• **DISTRIBUTION** Widespread in northern USA and southern Canada. A similar species, the March moth *(Alsophila aescularia)*, occurs in Europe.

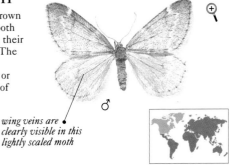

♂

wing veins are clearly visible in this lightly scaled moth

NEARCTIC

Time of Flight ☾	Habitat ♠	Wingspan (males) 2.5–3cm (1–1¼in)

| Family GEOMETRIDAE | Species *Oenochroma vinaria* | Author Guenée |

HAKEA MOTH

This moth varies in colour from grey, to purplish red and lobster-pink. The sexes are alike, although females are generally larger. Hakea moths are on the wing throughout the year.

• **EARLY STAGES** The caterpillar is green, to reddish brown or purplish red, with a pair of small warts in the middle of its back. It feeds on *Grevillea* and *Hakea*, resting stretched out on twigs by day.

• **DISTRIBUTION** Widespread in eastern and southern Australia, including Tasmania.

caterpillar is in a typical resting position

CATERPILLAR OF
OENOCHROMA VINARIA

hooked tip to forewings

dark bands are present in all colour forms

♂

characteristic dark purple spot on underside of forewing

♂ △

INDO-AUSTRALIAN

| Time of Flight ☾ | Habitat 🌳 | Wingspan 4.5–5.5cm (1¾–2¼in) |

| Family GEOMETRIDAE | Species *Chlorocoma dichloraria* | Author Guenée |

GUENÉE'S EMERALD

Guenée's emerald is the largest of about 20 species of this genus occurring in southern Australia, many of which are bluish green in colour. The females are unusual in that they lack the wing-coupling bristles. The underside is similar to, but paler than, the upperside. The sexes are similar but only males have feathered antennae.

• **EARLY STAGES** The looper caterpillar feeds on foliage of acacia.

• **DISTRIBUTION** Widespread in eastern and southern Australia, including Tasmania.

characteristic zigzag white lines

⊕

♂

striking red wing fringes

INDO-AUSTRALIAN

| Time of Flight ☾ | Habitat 🌷 | Wingspan 2.5–3cm (1–1¼in) |

Family GEOMETRIDAE	Species *Aporandria specularia*	Author Guenée

LARGE GREEN APORANDRIA

This large, green moth has brown markings on the hindwing. The underside is a pale, slightly iridescent green. The sexes are similar, although males have more strongly feathered antennae.
• **EARLY STAGES** The caterpillar is undescribed. It feeds on mango *(Mangifera indica)*.
• **DISTRIBUTION** Widespread from India and Sri Lanka to Malaysia, Sumatra, the Philippines, and Sulawesi.

INDO-AUSTRALIAN

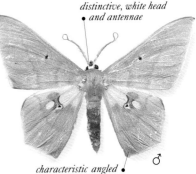
distinctive, white head and antennae

characteristic angled shape of hindwing

♂

Time of Flight ☾	Habitat 🦋	Wingspan 4.5–6cm (1¾–2½in)

Family GEOMETRIDAE	Species *Geometra papilionaria*	Author Linnaeus

LARGE EMERALD

This bluish green moth is large and distinctively shaped. The wings are patterned with inconspicuous broken white lines. The sexes are similar, except that males have feathered antennae.
• **EARLY STAGES** The yellowish green caterpillar feeds on birch *(Betula)*, beech *(Fagus sylvatica)*, alder *(Alnus)*, and hazel *(Corylus)*.
• **DISTRIBUTION** Widespread in Europe, extending across temperate Asia to Japan.

PALAEARCTIC

♂

hindwings characteristically scalloped at margins

broad, rather rounded wings

Time of Flight ☾	Habitat 〰️🌳 〰️	Wingspan 4.5–6cm (1¾–2½in)

Family GEOMETRIDAE	Species *Omphax plantaria*	Author Guenée

SMOOTH EMERALD

This moth belongs to a large group of African species, many of which are bright green or blue-green. This species is a uniform green with purplish red and cream lines around the margins. There is a line of purplish red along the body towards the tail. The sexes are similar.
• **EARLY STAGES** Little is known about the early stages, except that it has a looper caterpillar which feeds on the foliage of *Vangueria*.
• **DISTRIBUTION** Extends through southern Africa from Zimbabwe and Mozambique to Transvaal and Natal.

characteristically short, stout antennae

brightly coloured wing margins

AFROTROPICAL

♂

Time of Flight ☾	Habitat 🌴 〰️	Wingspan 3–4cm (1¼–1½in)

Family GEOMETRIDAE	Species *Crypsiphona ocultaria*	Author Donovan

RED-LINED GEOMETRID

The distinctive feature of this grey and white moth is its strikingly coloured underside, which has bold, red and black bands on the white, scalloped hindwings. The upperside's grey wing patterning is continued on the body. The sexes of this moth are similar. These moths are on the wing at most times of year, and are commonly found in the dry sclerophyll forests in southern Australia.

• EARLY STAGES The caterpillar is bluish green with a yellowish white line along the sides, making it well camouflaged when it feeds on young or mature foliage of eucalyptus.

• DISTRIBUTION
This species is found in Eastern and southern Australia, from Queensland to Victoria and Tasmania.

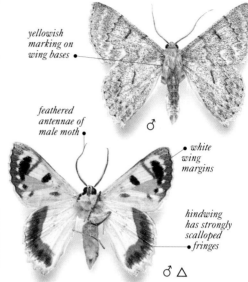

yellowish marking on wing bases •

feathered antennae of male moth •

♂

• white wing margins

hindwing has strongly scalloped • fringes

♂ △

INDO-AUSTRALIAN

Time of Flight ☾	Habitat 🌿	Wingspan 4–5cm (1½–2in)

Family GEOMETRIDAE	Species *Dysphania cuprina*	Author Felder

COPPERY DYSPHANIA

This species is one of a large group of brightly coloured, mainly day-flying, tropical moths. They are generally regarded to be distasteful to birds and are distinctively patterned in the warning colours of orange, black, and white. They often fly in company with similarly coloured butterflies. The underside is similar to the upperside, with the orange coloration being even brighter. The sexes are similar.

• EARLY STAGES Although little is known of the biology of this species, caterpillars of *dysphania* moths are generally yellow with a distinctive pattern of black or bluish black markings. Some species are known to feed on the foliage of species of *Carallia*.

• DISTRIBUTION
Widespread from India and Pakistan to Indonesia, the Philippines, and Papua New Guinea.

INDO-AUSTRALIAN

bright colours of wings indicate moth is probably • poisonous

distinctively • shaped, angular hindwing

♀

Time of Flight ☾ ☀	Habitat 🌿	Wingspan 7–7.5cm (2¾–3in)

Family GEOMETRIDAE	Species *Rhodometra sacraria*	Author Linnaeus

THE VESTAL

The colour of the forewings varies from pale yellow to deep straw-coloured, with the diagonal band ranging from pinkish red to brown. Bright red forms may occur if the pupae are exposed to extremes of temperature.
• **EARLY STAGES** The long, thin caterpillar is pale brown or green. It feeds on knotgrass *(Polygonum)*, camomile *(Anthemis)*, and other plants.
• **DISTRIBUTION** A migrant species occurring throughout Europe, and ranging to North Africa and northern India.

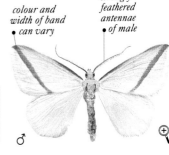

colour and width of band can vary

strongly feathered antennae of male

♂

PALAEARCTIC

Time of Flight ☾	Habitat ⁂	Wingspan 2.5–3cm (1–1¼in)

Family GEOMETRIDAE	Species *Erateina staudingeri*	Author Snellen

STAUDINGER'S LONGTAIL

This unusual moth belongs to a large, tropical American group of species with the hindwings ranging from rounded to extremely elongate. This species is one of the most striking examples of its group. The black and orange pattern suggest it is poisonous. The underside is a rich reddish brown to orange, banded and lined with lemon-yellow.
• **EARLY STAGES** Nothing seems to be known of the early stages.
• **DISTRIBUTION** Found in the tropical forests of Venezuela.

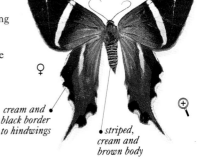

♀

cream and black border to hindwings

striped, cream and brown body

NEOTROPICAL

Time of Flight ☼	Habitat 🌴	Wingspan 3–4cm (1¼–1½in)

Family GEOMETRIDAE	Species *Operophtera brumata*	Author Linnaeus

WINTER MOTH

While males have normally developed wings, patterned with greyish brown, the wings of the female are reduced to short stubs.
• **EARLY STAGES** The caterpillar is green, usually with a dark line along the back. It feeds on the foliage of broad-leaved trees, including fruit trees such as apple *(Malus domestica)* and pear *(Pyrus communis)*. It will also feed on heather *(Calluna vulgaris)*.
• **DISTRIBUTION** Widespread and common throughout Europe, ranging across temperate Asia to Japan. Also occurs in Canada.

♂

dark dots around margin of glossy hindwings

HOLARCTIC

Time of Flight ☾	Habitat 🌳 ⁂	Wingspan (male) 2.5–3cm (1–1¼in)

| Family GEOMETRIDAE | Species *Rheumaptera hastata* | Author Linnaeus |

ARGENT AND SABLE

This striking, black and white patterned moth has an appropriate common name. The sexes are alike. In North America it is also called the spear-marked black.
• **EARLY STAGES** The caterpillar is olive-green to brown with a dark line along the back. In Europe it feeds on birches *(Betula)* and bog myrtle *(Myrica gale)*, but in North America it feeds on a wide range of trees and shrubs.
• **DISTRIBUTION** Found in Europe, extending to temperate Asia and North America.

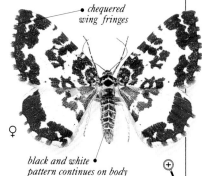

chequered wing fringes

♀

black and white pattern continues on body

HOLARCTIC

| Time of Flight ☼ | Habitat | Wingspan 2.5–4cm (1–1½in) |

| Family GEOMETRIDAE | Species *Venusia cambrica* | Author Curtis |

WELSH WAVE

The forewings of this pale coloured moth are characteristically patterned with greyish brown. The hindwings are plain cream.The sexes are similar.
• **EARLY STAGES** The caterpillar is yellowish green and variably marked with patches of reddish brown. It feeds on rowan *(Sorbus aucuparia)*, and a wide range of other trees such as alder *(Alnus)* and apple *(Malus domestica)* in North America.
• **DISTRIBUTION** Widespread in Europe, ranging across temperate Asia to Japan. Also occurs in Canada and northern USA.

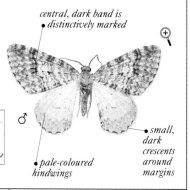

central, dark band is distinctively marked

♂

small, dark crescents around margins

pale-coloured hindwings

HOLARCTIC

| Time of Flight ☾ | Habitat | Wingspan 2.5–3cm (1–1¼in) |

| Family GEOMETRIDAE | Species *Xanthorhoe fluctuata* | Author Linnaeus |

GARDEN CARPET

This is a very common and variable species with both pale forms and melanic forms that are almost black. It can usually be recognized by the square black markings on the mid-frontal area of the forewings. They are to be seen on the wing from mid-spring to mid-autumn.
• **EARLY STAGES** The caterpillar is coloured grey, brown, or green. It feeds on cabbage *(Brassica)* and related plants, and curls up when resting.
• **DISTRIBUTION** Very common in gardens and hedgerows throughout Europe, ranging to North Africa and Japan.

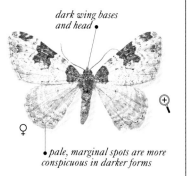

dark wing bases and head

♀

pale, marginal spots are more conspicuous in darker forms

PALAEARCTIC

| Time of Flight ☾ | Habitat | Wingspan 2.5–3cm (1–1¼in) |

Family GEOMETRIDAE	Species *Abraxas grossulariata*	Author Linnaeus

MAGPIE MOTH

This is a very variable moth ranging from white with narrow, yellow and black bands, to black with white wing bases. The typical form is illustrated.
• **EARLY STAGES** The caterpillar is yellowish white with black spots and an orange-red line along the side. It feeds on the foliage of a wide range of shrubs and it is sometimes a pest of gooseberry *(Ribes grossularia)*.
• **DISTRIBUTION** Widespread in Europe, extending across temperate Asia to Japan.

PALAEARCTIC

bright pattern shows that this species is distasteful to birds

colour pattern of body is the same in all forms

Time of Flight ☾	Habitat ♥ ⁓ ⁓	Wingspan 4–5cm (1½–2in)

Family GEOMETRIDAE	Species *Angerona prunaria*	Author Linnaeus

ORANGE MOTH

This moth has several different colour forms, ranging from pale yellow with minute, brown flecks, to dark brown with orange markings. Females are similar to males, but do not have feathered antennae.
• **EARLY STAGES** The caterpillar is yellowish brown with a pair of conical projections on the back near the tail. It feeds on blackthorn *(Prunus spinosa)*, hawthorn *(Crataegus)*, and many other trees and shrubs.
• **DISTRIBUTION** Europe, extending to temperate western Asia.

PALAEARCTIC

feathered antennae of male moth

chequered brown and yellow wing fringes

Time of Flight ☾	Habitat ♥ ⁓ ⁓	Wingspan 4–5.5cm (1½–2¼in)

Family GEOMETRIDAE	Species *Biston betularia*	Author Linnaeus

PEPPERED MOTH

The common name of this moth derives from the typical form that is white, peppered with black scales. A black form has evolved in industrial regions, where tree trunks on which the moth may settle are polluted with soot.
• **EARLY STAGES** The twig-like caterpillar is green or brown. It feeds on oak *(Quercus)* and other broad-leaved trees and shrubs.
• **DISTRIBUTION** Widespread in Europe, ranging across temperate Asia to Japan.

PALAEARCTIC

pattern provides good camouflage on lichen-covered trees

Time of Flight ☾	Habitat ♥	Wingspan 4.5–6cm (1¾–2½in)

Family GEOMETRIDAE	Species *Boarmia roboraria*	Author Denis & Schiffermüller

GREAT OAK BEAUTY

This large and attractive species is very variable and many forms occur that are darker than the one shown here.
• **EARLY STAGES** The caterpillar is brownish with greyish brown swellings on the back which make it resemble a twig. It feeds on the foliage of oak *(Quercus)*.
• **DISTRIBUTION** Occurs in Europe, and extends across temperate Asia to Japan.

PALAEARCTIC

feathered antennae

♂

Time of Flight ☾	Habitat 🌳	Wingspan 6–7cm (2½–2¾in)

Family GEOMETRIDAE	Species *Callioratis millari*	Author Hampson

MILLAR'S TIGER

Millar's tiger is one of several species in the genus, all having similar patterns of orange, grey, and black. They resemble distasteful *Hypsid* moths and may also be poisonous themselves. The underside is similar to the upperside.
• **EARLY STAGES** Nothing seems to be known about the early stages of this moth, or its foodplants.
• **DISTRIBUTION** Occurs in South Africa.

AFROTROPICAL

silvery grey scales on black bands

♂

black and orange chequered wing fringes

Time of Flight ☼	Habitat 🌾 🌾	Wingspan 5.5–6cm (2¼–2½in)

Family GEOMETRIDAE	Species *Ennomos subsignaria*	Author Hübner

ELM SPANWORM MOTH

This pure white moth is easily distinguished from other white species by the unusually angled outer edge of the forewing. Another common name for the adult moth is the snow-white linden.
• **EARLY STAGES** The looper caterpillar feeds on the foliage of apple *(Malus domestica)*, elm *(Ulmus)*, and many other broad-leaved trees and shrubs. It can be a pest.
• **DISTRIBUTION** Widespread in Canada and the USA.

robust male antennae

triangular shape of forewing

⊕

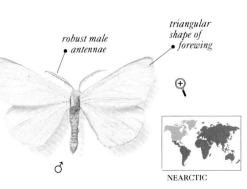

♂

NEARCTIC

Time of Flight ☾	Habitat 🌳	Wingspan 3–4cm (1¼–1½in)

Family GEOMETRIDAE	Species *Epimecis hortaria*	Author Fabricius

TULIP-TREE BEAUTY

A large and beautiful moth, the tulip-tree beauty is very variable, with some forms strongly banded and others almost black. Females are larger than males and have thread-like antennae. These moths can be seen on the wing from spring to autumn.
• **EARLY STAGES** The looper caterpillar feeds on the foliage of poplars *(Populus)*, tulip-tree *(Liriodendron tulipifera)*, and pawpaw *(Carica papaya)*.
• **DISTRIBUTION** Widespread from southern Canada to Florida.

males have feathered antennae •

• strongly scalloped edge to hindwings

NEARCTIC

Time of Flight ☾	Habitat ♣	Wingspan 4.5–5.5cm (1¾–2¼in)

Family GEOMETRIDAE	Species *Erannis defoliaria*	Author Clerck

MOTTLED UMBER

Males of this common moth are very variable, ranging from pale straw with brown bands to almost black. The wingless females also have a black form in industrial regions, where they have had to adapt to the surroundings.
• **EARLY STAGES** The caterpillar is brown with patches of yellow and reddish brown along the sides. It feeds on oak *(Quercus)*, birch *(Betula)*, and many other broad-leaved trees and shrubs, and can sometimes be a pest.
• **DISTRIBUTION** Widespread in Europe, extending into regions of temperate Asia.

triangular forewing shapes •

♂

• dark speckling on hindwings

PALAEARCTIC

Time of Flight ☾	Habitat ♣	Wingspan (male) 3–4.5cm (1¼–1¾in)

Family GEOMETRIDAE	Species *Lycia hirtaria*	Author Clerck

BRINDLED BEAUTY

The brown and white pattern of this furry-looking moth provides effective camouflage when it rests on tree trunks. A black form has evolved in sooty industrial regions. They are on the wing in spring.
• **EARLY STAGES** The caterpillar is brown to greenish grey, speckled with black, and spotted with yellow. It feeds on the foliage of most broad-leaved trees.
• **DISTRIBUTION** Widespread throughout Europe.

leading edge of forewings paler in females •

♂

wings of • female suffused with pale yellowish brown

♀

PALAEARCTIC

Time of Flight ☾	Habitat ♣	Wingspan 4–5cm (1½–2in)

Family GEOMETRIDAE	Species *Milionia isodoxa*	Author Prout

HOOP PINE MOTH

This is one of a genus of about 40 species, all with bright metallic colours that are quite unlike any other Geometer moths. The sexes are alike, although females tend to drink nectar from flowers while males feed on rotting animal and vegetable material found on the ground.
• **EARLY STAGES** The caterpillar is yellowish white with brown stripes. It feeds on hoop pine *(Araucaria cunninghami)*, causing extensive damage in plantations.
• **DISTRIBUTION** Found in the highlands of Papua New Guinea.

long, slender
• antennae

♂

• metallic-blue wing bases
characteristic of this species

INDO-AUSTRALIAN

Time of Flight ☼	Habitat 🎋	Wingspan 4–5cm (1½–2in)

Family GEOMETRIDAE	Species *Ourapteryx sambucaria*	Author Linnaeus

SWALLOW-TAILED MOTH

This striking, pale yellow moth is often mistaken for a butterfly when disturbed by day. As its name suggests, it has a small tail-like extension on the hindwings. The sexes of this moth are similar.
• **EARLY STAGES** The long and slender looper caterpillar is brown with pale stripes along the sides. It feeds on the foliage of hawthorns *(Crataegus)*, privet *(Ligustrum vulgare)*, ivy *(Hedera)*, and many other trees and shrubs.
• **DISTRIBUTION** Widespread in Europe, extending into temperate Asia.

two dark yellow
• lines on forewings

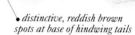

♀

• distinctive, reddish brown
spots at base of hindwing tails

PALAEARCTIC

Time of Flight ☾	Habitat 🌳 ᵢₗₗ ᵢₗₗ	Wingspan 4.5–6cm (1¾–2½in)

Family GEOMETRIDAE	Species *Plagodis dolabraria*	Author Linnaeus

SCORCHED WING

The unusual wing shape of this moth, coupled with the dark brown lines and patches on the wings, give it the appearance of having been scorched by fire. In fact, it is well camouflaged in the woodland localities it frequents. The sexes are alike. These moths can be seen on the wing in late spring and early summer.
• **EARLY STAGES** The twig-like, brown looper caterpillar feeds on oaks *(Quercus)*, willows *(Salix)*, and birches *(Betula)*.
• **DISTRIBUTION** Widespread in Europe, extending across temperate regions of Asia to Japan.

unusual pattern of
• fine, dark lines

⊕

♂

indented margin of •
forewings and hindwings

PALAEARCTIC

Time of Flight ☾	Habitat 🌳	Wingspan 3–4cm (1¼–1½in)

Family GEOMETRIDAE	Species *Prochoerodes transversata*	Author Drury

LARGE MAPLE SPANWORM MOTH

This large, pale yellowish brown moth with dark brown lines can be distinguished from other species by the small, tail-like projections on the hindwings. The sexes are similar.

angled forewing margins

sharply pointed forewing tips

• **EARLY STAGES** The looper caterpillar feeds on maples *(Acer)*, apple *(Malus domestica)*, and other plants, including grasses.

• **DISTRIBUTION** Widespread from Canada to the eastern USA.

♂

NEARCTIC

Time of Flight ☾	Habitat	Wingspan 3–5cm (1¼–2in)

Family GEOMETRIDAE	Species *Selenia tetralunaria*	Author Hufnagel

PURPLE THORN

The purple thorn belongs to a group of moths with distinctively ragged wing margins. The banding and marking are characteristic, but there is some seasonal variation with spring broods having more white markings.

thread-like antennae of females

• **EARLY STAGES** The caterpillar is brown and twig-like. It feeds on the foliage of birches *(Betula)*, alders *(Alnus)*, oaks *(Quercus)*, and other deciduous trees.

• **DISTRIBUTION** Occurs in Europe, extending across temperate Asia to Japan.

PALAEARCTIC

♀

dark spot on hindwings characteristic of this species

Time of Flight ☾	Habitat ♣	Wingspan 4–5cm (1½–2in)

Family GEOMETRIDAE	Species *Semiothisa bisignata*	Author Walker

RED-HEADED INCHWORM MOTH

The wings of this small Geometer are dirty pinkish white, powdered with brown scales, and with distinctive, chocolate-brown patches on the forewings. The head is a vivid, reddish brown. The sexes are alike. These moths can be seen on the wing from late spring to late summer.

distinctively shaped, dark marking on forewings

• **EARLY STAGES** The green looper caterpillar feeds on eastern white pine *(Pinus strobus)* and other *Pinus* species.

• **DISTRIBUTION** Widespread in Canada and the northern USA.

♂

⊕

unusual angled margin to hindwings

NEARCTIC

Time of Flight ☾	Habitat ♣	Wingspan 2–3cm (¾–1¼in)

Family GEOMETRIDAE | Species *Thalaina clara* | Author Walker

CLARA SATIN MOTH

This is one of a group of about ten species, mostly with satin-white wings, occurring in Australia. It has a characteristic pattern of bright orange-brown, angled lines on the forewings.

• **EARLY STAGES** The caterpillar is green with a pattern of fine, yellowish white lines. It feeds on wattle *(Acacia decurrens)*.

• **DISTRIBUTION** Found in eastern and south-eastern Australia, and northern Tasmania.

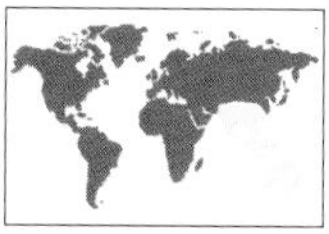

INDO-AUSTRALIAN

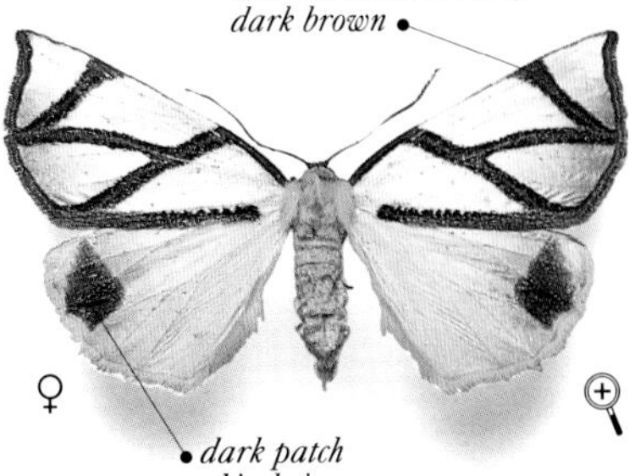
characteristic, angled lines are bordered with dark brown
♀
dark patch on hindwings

Time of Flight ☾ | Habitat | Wingspan 4–4.5cm (1½–1¾in)

Family GEOMETRIDAE | Species *Thinopteryx crocopterata* | Author Kollar

ORANGE SWALLOW-TAILED MOTH

The wings are orange-yellow, except for the forewings' leading edges, which are spotted with greyish brown. The sexes are similar.

• **EARLY STAGES** The caterpillar is reddish brown with paler lines and a pale brown head.

• **DISTRIBUTION** Occurs from India and Sri Lanka to China, Japan, Malaysia, and Java.

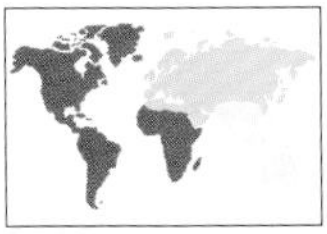

INDO-AUSTRALIAN
PALAEARCTIC

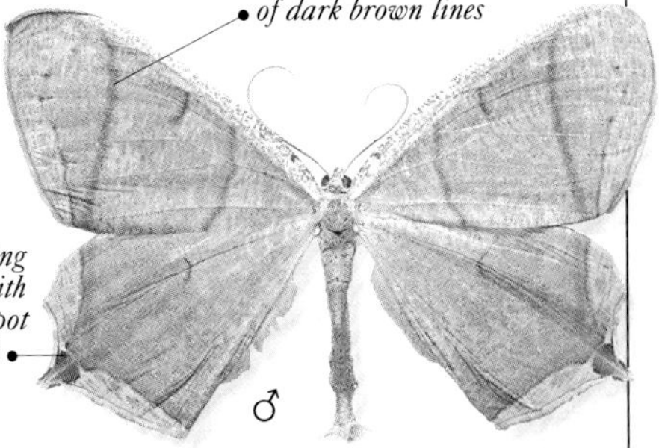
characteristic pattern of dark brown lines
short hindwing tails with dark spot at base
♂

Time of Flight ☾ | Habitat | Wingspan 5.5–6cm (2¼–2½in)

Family GEOMETRIDAE | Species *Xanthisthisa niveifrons* | Author Prout

WHITE-HEADED THORN

Males are pale yellow to orange-brown and are finely speckled with darker brown. Females are similar except that the tips of the forewings are more strongly hooked and the wings are more heavily speckled with reddish brown or grey.

• **EARLY STAGES** The caterpillar is apparently undescribed, but is known to feed on pine *(Pinus)* and cypress *(Cupressus)*.

• **DISTRIBUTION** From Angola, Zambia, and Malawi, to Mozambique and the Transvaal.

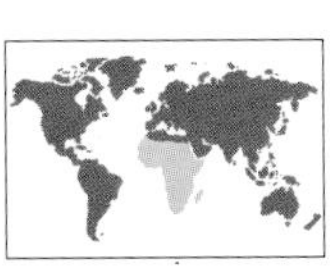

AFROTROPICAL

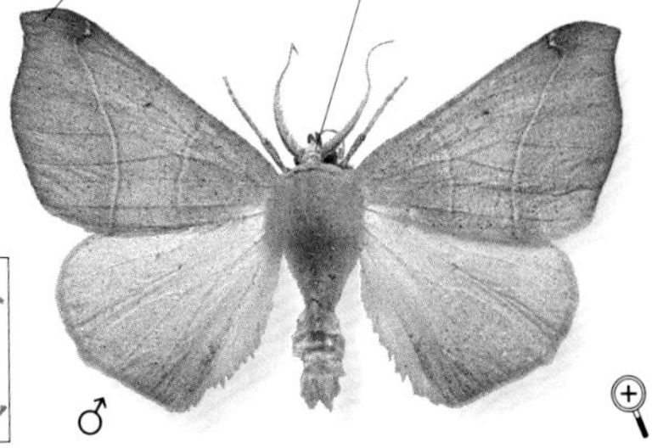
forewings are hooked at the tips
distinctive white head gives rise to its common name
♂

Time of Flight ☾ | Habitat | Wingspan 3–4.5cm (1¼–1¾in)

LASIOCAMPIDAE

T HIS IS A FAMILY of about 1,000 species of medium- to large-sized moths occurring around the world. They are generally rather dull in colour, mostly banded with various shades of brown. Lasiocampidae have two unusual characteristics: they lack the typical wing-coupling device of most moths, and the tongue is reduced and non-functional. Caterpillars of this group are particularly hairy; some have long-haired lobes or lappets along their sides, giving rise to their common name of lappet moth.

Pupae are formed in robust cocoons. The egg-like shape of these cocoons provides the origin of the name "eggar", which is applied to many moths in this family.

Family LASIOCAMPIDAE	Species *Gastropacha quercifolia*	Author Linnaeus

LAPPET MOTH

The reddish brown wings of this robust moth have a purplish brown sheen. The sexes are similar. When a lappet moth rests, the wings are folded in a curious way over the body, to resemble a bunch of dead leaves.
• **EARLY STAGES** The grey caterpillar has fleshy lappets, covered with long, brown hairs, on its body. It feeds on blackthorn *(Prunus spinosa)*, hawthorn *(Crataegus)*, and other plants.
• **DISTRIBUTION** Occurs in Europe, across temperate Asia to China and Japan.

distinctive, scalloped wing margins

♀

hindwings smaller and more rounded than forewings

PALAEARCTIC

Time of Flight ☾	Habitat ⚘	Wingspan 4–7.5cm (1½–3in)

Family LASIOCAMPIDAE	Species *Dendrolimus pini*	Author Linnaeus

PINE-TREE LAPPET

This is a very variable moth, ranging in colour from greyish white to almost any shade of grey or brown. The forewings are distinctively banded.
• **EARLY STAGES** The hairy caterpillar is brown or greyish brown with bands of white, scale-like hairs along the back. It feeds on pine *(Pinus)*, spruce *(Picea)*, fir *(Abies)*, and various other conifers.
• **DISTRIBUTION** Europe, excluding the British Isles, to North Africa and central Asia.

white spot present on forewing of both sexes

♂

short, furry body

PALAEARCTIC

Time of Flight ☾	Habitat ⚘	Wingspan 5–8cm (2–3¼in)

Family LASIOCAMPIDAE	Species *Eucraera gemmata*	Author Distant

BUDDED LAPPET

This robust species of moth is a pale yellowish
brown to olive-brown with three white bands
on the fore- and hindwings.
• **EARLY STAGES** The caterpillar is brown,
patterned with yellow and red lines and dots,
and covered with long, dark brown hairs. It
feeds on the foliage of
Lannea, *Brachystegia*,
and *Julbernardia*.
• **DISTRIBUTION**
Occurs from Angola,
westwards as far as
Mozambique.

AFROTROPICAL

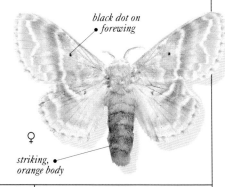

black dot on
forewing

♀

striking,
orange body

Time of Flight ☾	Habitat 🦅 ⚘ ⚘	Wingspan 3–5cm (1¼–2in)

Family LASIOCAMPIDAE	Species *Digglesia australasiae*	Author Fabricius

WATTLE SNOUT MOTH

The colour of this moth varies from yellow to reddish
brown with a distinctive pattern of dark lines and spots.
Females are larger than males and have more elongate
wings. Males have strongly feathered antennae.
• **EARLY STAGES** The hairy caterpillar of this
species is greenish grey
in colour. It feeds on
acacia and *Exocarpos*.
• **DISTRIBUTION**
This species occurs
in eastern and
southern Australia.

INDO-AUSTRALIAN

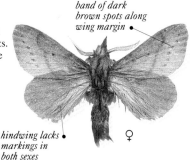

band of dark
brown spots along
wing margin

hindwing lacks
markings in
both sexes

♀

Time of Flight ☾	Habitat 🌿 ⚘ ⚘	Wingspan 2.5–5cm (1–2in)

Family LASIOCAMPIDAE	Species *Bombycopsis indecora*	Author Walker

INDECOROUS EGGAR

This is a very variable species of moth. The
forewings range in colour from greenish brown
to reddish brown, and have darker tips. The
hindwings range from cream to brown.
• **EARLY STAGES** The caterpillar is reddish
brown with tufts of hairs along the sides of the
body, especially towards
the head. It feeds on
Eriosema and *Protea*.
• **DISTRIBUTION**
From equatorial western
Africa to Zambia, and the
Transvaal in South Africa.

AFROTROPICAL

parallel, diagonal
lines along wing
margin

pale base to
hindwing

♀

Time of Flight ☾	Habitat 🦅	Wingspan 2.5–6cm (1–2½in)

Family LASIOCAMPIDAE	Species *Gonometa postica*	Author Walker

DARK CHOPPER

Moths of this group are called choppers because of the razor-edged appearance to the male hindwing. Females are much larger than males and have a different wing shape.
• **EARLY STAGES** The hairy caterpillar is black with orange, yellow, or white tufts along the sides of the body. The body hairs are irritant. The caterpillar feeds on the foliage of acacia, *Brachystegia*, and *Elephantorrhiza*, and various other plants.
• **DISTRIBUTION** Ranges from Zimbabwe to Mozambique, the Transvaal in South Africa, Botswana, and Namibia.

diffuse, transverse, greyish brown bands on forewings

AFROTROPICAL

cream-coloured base to female hindwing

abdomen clothed with pale, hair-like scales

Time of Flight ☾	Habitat 〜 〜	Wingspan 4–9cm (1½–3½in)

Family LASIOCAMPIDAE	Species *Grammodora nigrolineata*	Author Aurivillius

BLACK-LINED EGGAR

This distinctive moth has cream-coloured forewings with four orange-red streaks and double, blackish brown lines along the veins. Males have pale cream hindwings while the larger females have greyish brown hindwings with cream-coloured fringes.
• **EARLY STAGES** The hairy caterpillar is pale yellowish brown with brown and orange speckling and oblique, white streaks. It feeds on the foliage of *Cassia* and *Albizia*.
• **DISTRIBUTION** Range extends from Tanzania, Zambia, Zimbabwe, and Malawi to Transvaal.

female antennae are short

deep cream coloured wing fringes on female moth

red forewing streaks present in both sexes

AFROTROPICAL

Time of Flight ☾	Habitat 〜 〜	Wingspan 4–6cm (1½–2½in)

Family LASIOCAMPIDAE	Species *Lasiocampa quercus*	Author Linnaeus

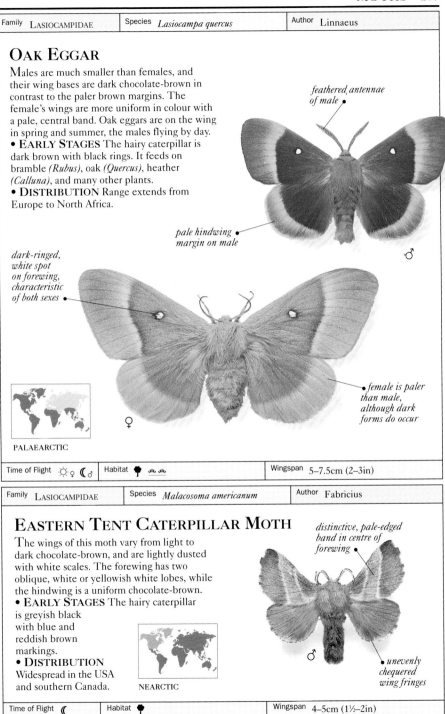

OAK EGGAR

Males are much smaller than females, and their wing bases are dark chocolate-brown in contrast to the paler brown margins. The female's wings are more uniform in colour with a pale, central band. Oak eggars are on the wing in spring and summer, the males flying by day.
• **EARLY STAGES** The hairy caterpillar is dark brown with black rings. It feeds on bramble *(Rubus)*, oak *(Quercus)*, heather *(Calluna)*, and many other plants.
• **DISTRIBUTION** Range extends from Europe to North Africa.

feathered antennae of male

pale hindwing margin on male

♂

dark-ringed, white spot on forewing, characteristic of both sexes

female is paler than male, although dark forms do occur

♀

PALAEARCTIC

Time of Flight ☼♀ ☾♂	Habitat 🌳 ⚘ ⚘	Wingspan 5–7.5cm (2–3in)

Family LASIOCAMPIDAE	Species *Malacosoma americanum*	Author Fabricius

EASTERN TENT CATERPILLAR MOTH

The wings of this moth vary from light to dark chocolate-brown, and are lightly dusted with white scales. The forewing has two oblique, white or yellowish white lobes, while the hindwing is a uniform chocolate-brown.
• **EARLY STAGES** The hairy caterpillar is greyish black with blue and reddish brown markings.
• **DISTRIBUTION** Widespread in the USA and southern Canada.

distinctive, pale-edged band in centre of forewing

♂

unevenly chequered wing fringes

NEARCTIC

Time of Flight ☾	Habitat ⚘	Wingspan 4–5cm (1½–2in)

Family Lasiocampidae	Species *Trabala viridana*	Author Joicey & Talbot

Moss-green Lappet

This beautiful moth belongs to a large complex of similar species, many occurring in South-east Asia. The female is much larger than the male and has strongly triangular forewings with large, pale brown patches towards the base. In museum specimens the beautiful, green colour of these moths will often fade quite badly.

• **Early Stages** Little is known of the life-cycle but caterpillars of related species are hairy and have two forward-pointing tufts of bristles situated just behind head. They are known to feed on *Barringtonia*, *Eugenia*, *Rubus*, and *Shorea robusta*.

• **Distribution** Range extends from Malaysia to Sumatra, Java, and Borneo.

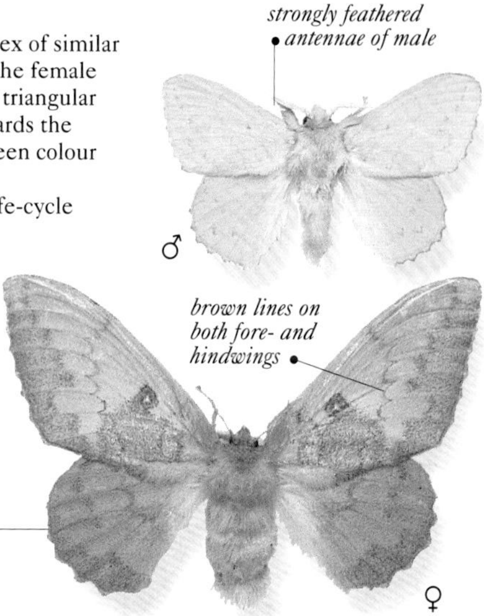
strongly feathered antennae of male
♂
brown lines on both fore- and hindwings
distinctively scalloped hindwings
♀

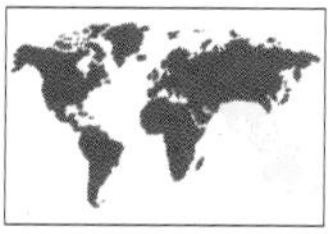

INDO-AUSTRALIAN

Time of Flight	Habitat	Wingspan 4–6cm (1½–2½in)

Family Lasiocampidae	Species *Pinara fervens*	Author Walker

Gum Snout Moth

The forewings of this robust moth are brownish grey with darker grey lines and spots. The hindwings are brownish yellow without markings. The sexes are similar but females are larger than males. Gum snout moths are on the wing in summer.

• **Early Stages** The hairy caterpillar is grey and has a single knob-like projection on the back near to the tail. If threatened, it arches its body to display two black patches behind the head. It feeds at night on the foliage of eucalyptus, resting by day on the bark where it is very well camouflaged.

• **Distribution** Occurs in southern parts of Australia, including Tasmania.

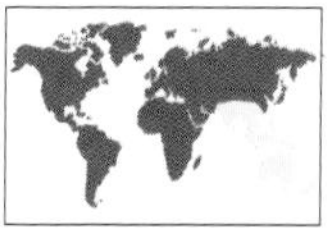

INDO-AUSTRALIAN

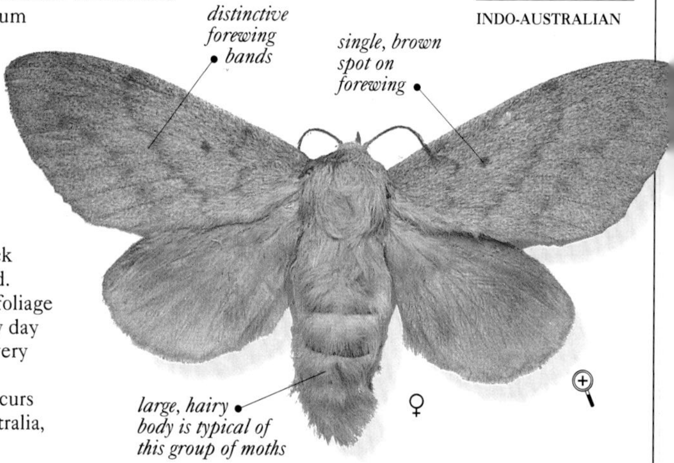
distinctive forewing bands
single, brown spot on forewing
large, hairy body is typical of this group of moths
♀

Time of Flight	Habitat	Wingspan 4.5–7.5cm (1¾–3in)

Family Lasiocampidae	Species *Porela vetusta*	Author Walker

EUCALYPTUS LAPPET

This furry-looking moth is greyish brown with chocolate-brown and white markings on the forewing. The fringes are chequered with dark brown and white. Males have a tuft on the tail.
• **EARLY STAGES** The hairy caterpillar feeds on the foliage of eucalyptus, as well as *Leptospermum flavescens*.
• **DISTRIBUTION** South Queensland to Victoria and South Australia.

INDO-AUSTRALIAN

long, white, hair-like scales on head and thorax •

♀

• chequered wing fringes

Time of Flight ☾	Habitat ♣	Wingspan 2.5–4.5cm (1–1¾in)

Family Lasiocampidae	Species *Tolype velleda*	Author Stol

LARGE TOLYPE

This beautiful, grey and white moth is very distinctively patterned, and the body is particularly hairy. Males are smaller than females and have strongly feathered antennae. These moths are on the wing in autumn.
• **EARLY STAGES** The caterpillar feeds on the foliage of birch *(Betula)*, oak *(Quercus)*, and other trees.
• **DISTRIBUTION** Widespread from southern Canada to the USA.

NEARCTIC

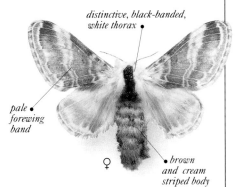

distinctive, black-banded, white thorax •

pale • forewing band

♀

• brown and cream striped body

Time of Flight ☾	Habitat ♣	Wingspan 3–5.5cm (1¼–2¼in)

Family Lasiocampidae	Species *Pachypasa bilinea*	Author Walker

TWIN-LINE LAPPET

The distinctive "twin-line" pattern occurs on the forewing of the female. The much smaller males have an additional irregular, marginal line on the forewing. The hindwings lack any markings or patterning at all.
• **EARLY STAGES** The caterpillar feeds on the foliage of *Annona* and *Bauhinia* species.
• **DISTRIBUTION** Range extends from equatorial East and West Africa south to Zambia, Malawi, and Zimbabwe.

AFROTROPICAL

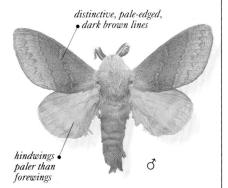

distinctive, pale-edged, • dark brown lines

hindwings • paler than forewings

♂

Time of Flight ☾	Habitat ⸬⸬	Wingspan 5–10cm (2–4in)

EUPTEROTIDAE

A SMALL FAMILY of just over 300 species of medium- to large-sized moths, the Eupterotidae are related to the emperor moths (Saturniidae). They are found in the tropical parts of Africa and Indo-Australia. They are mostly fairly dull-coloured with shades of brown and grey predominating. Because of their hairy appearance, they are often known as "monkeys". The caterpillars are covered in long hairs, which are often highly irritant and cause rashes.

———— • ————

Many of the caterpillars belonging to this family are gregarious and live in communal webs. Some species are known to be pests of certain trees, including the eucalyptus, and cause serious damage to them.

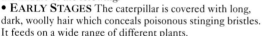

| Family EUPTEROTIDAE | Species *Tagora pallida* | Author Walker |

PALLID MONKEY MOTH

This large, brownish white moth is delicately patterned and lined with darker brown. Females are larger than males and have darker markings and a translucent, white spot in the middle of the forewing.
• **EARLY STAGES** The caterpillar is covered with long, dark, woolly hair which conceals poisonous stinging bristles. It feeds on a wide range of different plants.
• **DISTRIBUTION** Widespread from India to Malaysia, Sumatra, and Borneo.

INDO-AUSTRALIAN

distinctively curved wing-tips

single pale spot on forewing

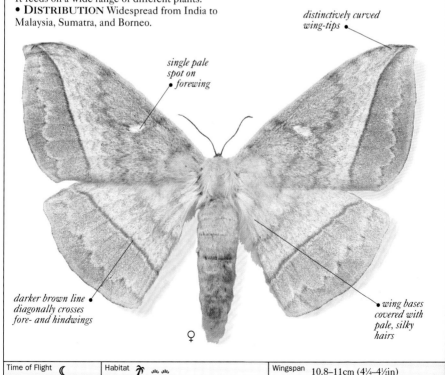

darker brown line diagonally crosses fore- and hindwings

wing bases covered with pale, silky hairs

♀

| Time of Flight ☾ | Habitat 🐾 ⸱⸱⸱ ⸱⸱⸱ | Wingspan 10.8–11cm (4¼–4½in) |

Family EUPTEROTIDAE	Species *Janomima westwoodi*	Author Aurivillius

INQUISITIVE MONKEY

This large and handsome moth has a distinctly furry appearance. It varies in colour from pale fawn to brownish yellow with a pattern of dark brown lines on both the fore- and hindwing. The hindwing has a black spot at the base.
• **EARLY STAGES** The large caterpillar is densely covered with long, back-swept, black and white hairs which have irritant properties. It feeds on *Bauhinia*.
• **DISTRIBUTION** Range extends from Zimbabwe to Zambia and Zaire.

AFROTROPICAL

characteristic, sinuous lines on forewing

furry appearance continues on thorax

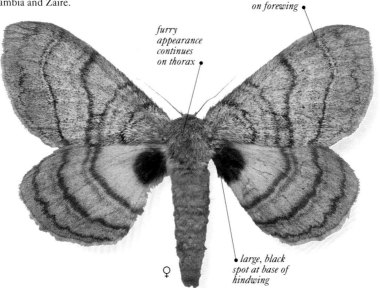

♀

large, black spot at base of hindwing

Time of Flight ☾	Habitat	Wingspan 7.5–10cm (3–4in)

Family EUPTEROTIDAE	Species *Panacela lewinae*	Author Lewin

LEWIN'S BAG-SHELTER MOTH

Males of this species have dark, banded, reddish brown forewings that are hooked towards the tips. Females have reddish to purplish brown wings
• **EARLY STAGES** The hairy caterpillar feeds at night on eucalyptus, *Lophostemon*, *Angophora*, and *Syncarpia*. It lives in a silken bag spun among twigs of the tree on which it feeds.
• **DISTRIBUTION** Range in Australia extends from southern Queensland to southern NSW.

hooked tip to forewing

characteristic, dark brown forewing band

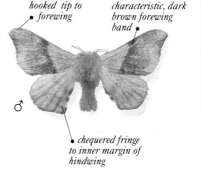

♂

chequered fringe to inner margin of hindwing

INDO-AUSTRALIAN

Time of Flight ☾	Habitat	Wingspan 2.5–4cm (1–1½in)

ANTHELIDAE

T HIS SMALL FAMILY of less than 100 species of moth is confined to Australia and Papua New Guinea, and is closely related to the families Eupterotidae and Lasiocampidae. Many of the species are distinctively patterned with lines and bands of brown, yellow, and red. The greatly reduced tongues of these moths means that they are unable to feed in the adult stage. The caterpillars of most species are covered with tufts of hair, which are sometimes irritant. Many feed on eucalyptus or acacia species.

Family ANTHELIDAE	Species *Chelepteryx collesi*	Author Gray

GIANT ANTHELID

The large, bat-like female of this species can attain a wingspan of 16cm (6¼in). The blackish brown forewings of both sexes are banded and heavily dusted with white and brownish yellow scales. The dark hindwings have a straight inner line of white and a scalloped outer line of orange-yellow. If alarmed, the male rears up to reveal its white underside and dark forelegs, and resembles a large spider.
• **EARLY STAGES** The caterpillar is greyish white with black, transverse bands across the back, and tufts of stout, irritant hairs. It feeds on eucalyptus species.
    • **DISTRIBUTION** Range extends from southern Queensland to NSW and Victoria in Australia.

vivid, black stripes along body

INDO-AUSTRALIAN

CATERPILLAR OF
CHELEPTERYX COLLESI

scalloped, marginal line on hindwing

♂

unusual pointed tips to hindwing

Time of Flight ☾	Habitat ⚘	Wingspan 12–16cm (4¾–6¼in)

Family ANTHELIDAE	Species *Anthela ocellata*	Author Walker

EYESPOT ANTHELID

This brownish white moth has distinctive, dark brown forewing bands and black eyespots which are more strongly developed in females. The pale hindwings have a marginal band of dark spots and a large, inner, black spot. Females are larger than males and have thread-like antennae. Eyespot anthelids are on the wing in the summer months. They are rather inactive and readily feign death if threatened. Moths are on the wing throughout the summer months, and there are thought to be two generations a year.

• **EARLY STAGES** The caterpillar is undescribed, but is known to feed on various native and introduced grasses. When fully grown, it forms its pupa within a double-walled, grey cocoon incorporating caterpillar hairs.

• **DISTRIBUTION** Widely distributed throughout eastern and southern Australia, including Tasmania.

characteristic feathered antennae of male moth

two comma-shaped markings on forewing

♂

curved, pale forewing band present in both sexes

hindwings much paler than forewings

♀

large, heavy body of female moth

INDO-AUSTRALIAN

Time of Flight ☽	Habitat 〽〽	Wingspan 4.5–5cm (1¾–2in)

Family ANTHELIDAE	Species *Nataxa flavescens*	Author Walker

YELLOW-HEADED ANTHELID

Males of this species are brownish red in colour with pale yellow bands on both the fore- and hindwings. The larger females are greyish brown in colour with a large, white patch on the forewing, in the middle of which is a black spot. In contrast with the male, the female body is long and heavy, with a whitish band near the end.

• **EARLY STAGES** The pale-coloured, hairy caterpillar has two dark patches on the back behind the head, and a small, black hump towards the tail. It is known to feed on the foliage of acacia.

• **DISTRIBUTION** Range extends from southern Queensland to Victoria and Tasmania in Australia.

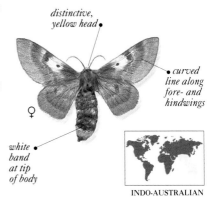

distinctive, yellow head

curved line along fore- and hindwings

♀

white band at tip of body

INDO-AUSTRALIAN

Time of Flight ☽	Habitat ❦	Wingspan 3–4cm (1¼–1½in)

BOMBYCIDAE

ALTHOUGH THIS IS a relatively small family of some 300 species, mostly confined to the oriental region, it contains some of the most famous of all moths – the silkmoths.

———— • ————

Moths of this family have rounded, furry bodies. Many species have slightly hooked forewing tips. Their mouthparts are not developed so they are unable to feed as adults. The caterpillars are usually rather swollen at the front and have a single, fleshy horn at the tail. Although they often appear smooth, the caterpillars are, in fact, covered with numerous minute hairs. Many species of this family feed on the foliage of plants of the nettle family (Urticaceae). They form their pupae within silken cocoons.

Family BOMBYCIDAE	Species *Bombyx mori*	Author Linnaeus

SILKMOTH

This moth has been bred in captivity for thousands of years. The wings are usually white, although some strains occasionally produce brown forms. These moths have attractive white wings, but they cannot fly.
• **EARLY STAGES** The caterpillar is usually white, variably marked with brown, and has pinkish eyespots on the back. It is reared commercially on trays of white mulberry *(Morus alba)*.
• **DISTRIBUTION** No wild colonies remain, but it is believed that its origins are in China where the silkmoth industry was founded around 2,640 BC.

PALAEARCTIC

characteristically hooked
• forewing tips

♀

• distinctly
visible wing veins

Flightless	Habitat	Wingspan 4–6cm (1½–2½in)

Family BOMBYCIDAE	Species *Ocinara ficicola*	Author Westwood & Ormerod

SMALL SILKMOTH

Males of this moth are quite variable, the forewings ranging in colour from grey to brownish grey with fine, dark lines and spots. These moths rest with the forewings held at right angles to the body and the hindwings beneath. The females are pale brown.
• **EARLY STAGES** The caterpilllar is brown beneath and white above, with two pairs of red markings on the back, and a fleshy horn on the tail. It feeds on the foliage of figs *(Ficus)* and various other plants.
• **DISTRIBUTION** Ranges from Zimbabwe to Transvaal.

AFROTROPICAL

this species
has rounded
• wing-tips

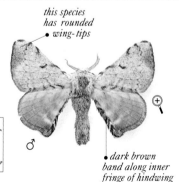

♂

• dark brown
band along inner
fringe of hindwing

Time of Flight ☾	Habitat	Wingspan 2–3cm (¾–1¼in)

Family BOMBYCIDAE	Species *Theophila religiosae*	Author Helfer

INDIAN SILKMOTH

This moth is quite closely related to the cultivated silkmoth. It has distinctly curved forewing tips marked with dark chocolate-brown. Both fore- and hindwings have characteristic sinuous pale lines. This species is bred commercially for its silk.
• EARLY STAGES The caterpillar is mottled and streaked with yellow, brown, and black. It is known to feed on mulberry *(Morus)*.
• DISTRIBUTION Northern India to Malaysia.

unusual straight inner line on forewing

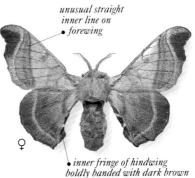

INDO-AUSTRALIAN

♀

inner fringe of hindwing boldly banded with dark brown

Time of Flight ☾	Habitat ꕔ ⚘	Wingspan 4–5cm (1½–2in)

Family BOMBYCIDAE	Species *Penicillifera apicalis*	Author Walker

MUSLIN BOMBYX

Males have white, semi-translucent wings, marked with grey and black. The leading edge of the forewing is usually streaked with black and there is a strong black spot above the centre of the wing. Females are coloured white.
• EARLY STAGES The caterpillar is brown with humps along the back and a horn at the tail. It feeds on fig *(Ficus)*.
• DISTRIBUTION From the Himalayas to Burma, Malaysia, and the Philippines.

black spots on forewings of both sexes, are much fainter in females.

INDO-AUSTRALIAN

♂

distinctive, black markings on inner edge of hindwing

Time of Flight ☾	Habitat ⚘	Wingspan 2.5–5cm (1–2in)

Family BOMBYCIDAE	Species *Gunda ochracea*	Author Walker

OCHRACEOUS BOMBYX

This species is among the most brightly coloured and attractive in a family of rather dull-coloured moths. The ground colour has various shades of reddish brown, and the forewings have a central area shaded with grey. The larger females have golden-yellow to brownish yellow forewings, and lighter hindwings.
• EARLY STAGES Little is known of the early stages.
• DISTRIBUTION From northern India to Malaysia, Sumatra, and the Philippines.

two distinctive white spots present on the forewing

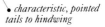

INDO-AUSTRALIAN

♂

characteristic, pointed tails to hindwing

Time of Flight ☾	Habitat ⚘	Wingspan 4–6cm (1½–2½in)

BRAHMAEIDAE

T HIS is a very small family of only 20 or so described species of moth, confined to Africa, Asia, and Europe. These are medium- to large-sized, and are rather like emperor moths (Saturniidae, p.218) in appearance, but have such a distinctive pattern of their own that they are always easy to recognize. The Brahmaeid moths have well-developed eyespots, earning for some species the common name of owl moth, although this is a term generally reserved for the family Noctuidae (see p.252). Unlike moths of many related families, adults of this group have well-developed tongues, so they can feed. The caterpillars have long projections on the body in the early stages but these are lost in the final stage.

Family Brahmaeidae	Species *Brahmaea wallichii*	Author Gray

OWL MOTH

One of the largest and most handsome species in the Brahmaeidae family, the owl moth has very well-developed eyespots at the base of the forewings and a characteristic pattern of blackish brown lines. The robust body is coloured blackish brown with a distinctive pattern of orange-brown stripes. The males of this species are smaller than females. Although owl moths are active in the evening, they tend to remain resting on tree trunks or on the ground with wings outspread by day. If this moth is disturbed, it rocks back and forth rather than flying off.
• **EARLY STAGES** In captivity the caterpillar will eat privet *(Ligustrum)*, lilac *(Syringa)*, and elder *(Sambucus)*.
• **DISTRIBUTION** Occurs from northern India to Nepal, Burma, China, Taiwan, and Japan.

PALAEARCTIC
INDO-AUSTRALIAN

characteristic, marginal pattern of black and orange lines

large eyespot at base of forewing

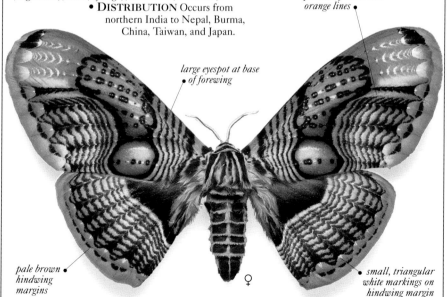

pale brown hindwing margins

♀

small, triangular white markings on hindwing margin

Time of Flight ☾	Habitat 🌿 🍂	Wingspan 9–16cm (3½–6¼in)

Family Brahmaeidae	Species *Acanthobrahmaea europaea*	Author Hartig

HARTIG'S BRAHMAEA

This distinctive European moth was discovered less than 30 years ago.
• **EARLY STAGES** The caterpillar is shiny black with white lines and spots on the back and sides, except for the front segments which are patterned with yellow. It feeds on the foliage of ash *(Fraxinus excelsior).*
• **DISTRIBUTION** In woodlands, on the shores of a volcanic lake in Lucania, Italy. It is now protected by law.

PALAEARCTIC

characteristic dark spot at the wing-tip•

•wing veins visible through the translucent scales

♂

Time of Flight ☾	Habitat ⚘	Wingspan 5–7cm (2–2¾in)

Family Brahmaeidae	Species *Dactylocerus swanzii*	Author Butler

BUTLER'S BRAHMIN

This particular moth is distinguishable from other Brahmaeid moths by its more elongate, curved forewings. The forewing eyespot is poorly developed in this species, being represented by a tear-shaped, dark brown spot. The marginal band along the fore-and hindwings is lined with black and orange-brown.
• **EARLY STAGES** Surprisingly, very little seems to be known about the biology of this large and attractive African moth. The caterpillar is said to have paired, conical, hairy spines on each body segment, and it is believed to feed on the foliage of plants of the family Oleaceae.
• **DISTRIBUTION** Occurs in tropical forests of Africa.

AFROTROPICAL

distinctively curved forewing edge •

characteristically • short antennae

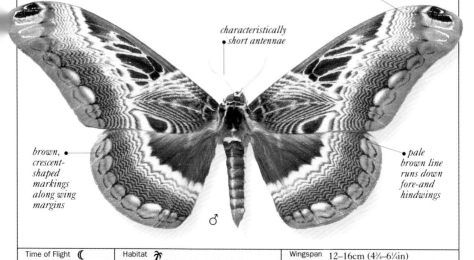

brown, • crescent-shaped markings along wing margins

•pale brown line runs down fore-and hindwings

♂

Time of Flight ☾	Habitat 🌴	Wingspan 12–16cm (4¾–6¼in)

SATURNIIDAE

T HIS VAST, worldwide family of over 1,000 species includes many of the world's largest and most spectacular moths. Because of their size and handsome colours, Saturniid moths are often referred to as emperor moths. Many species have well-developed eyespots or transparent patches on both the fore- and hindwings. A number of species have long tails on the hindwings. Male and female wing patterns can often be totally different. In adult Saturniid moths the tongue is reduced, or absent so that they are unable to feed.

———— • ————

When fully grown, the caterpillars spin large cocoons to protect their pupae. These cocoons are sometimes used in the manufacture of coarse silks.

Family SATURNIIDAE	Species *Citheronia regalis*	Author Fabricius

REGAL MOTH

The forewings of this moth are grey with deep orange veins and pale yellow, oval spots. The hindwings are orange-brown. The sexes are similar, although females are larger than males. Another common name for the adult moth is the royal walnut moth.
• **EARLY STAGES** The striking caterpillar is green with a group of large, branched horns behind the head. It feeds on a wide range of trees, including walnut *(Juglans)* and hickory *(Carya)*, and is known as the hickory horned devil.
• **DISTRIBUTION** Range extends throughout south-eastern USA.

NEARCTIC

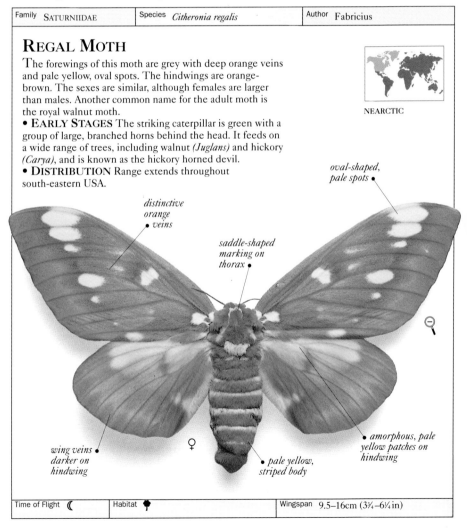

oval-shaped, pale spots

distinctive orange • veins

saddle-shaped marking on thorax •

wing veins • darker on hindwing

♀

pale yellow, striped body

amorphous, pale yellow patches on hindwing

Time of Flight ☾	Habitat ⚘		Wingspan 9.5–16cm (3¾–6¼in)

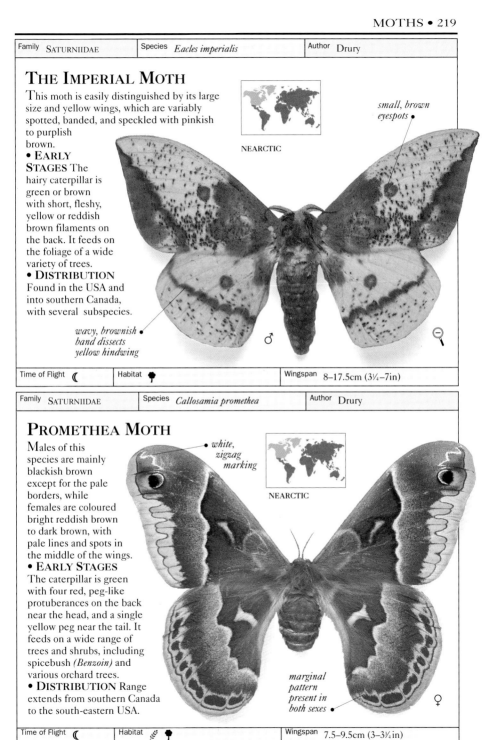

Family SATURNIIDAE	Species *Eacles imperialis*	Author Drury

THE IMPERIAL MOTH

This moth is easily distinguished by its large size and yellow wings, which are variably spotted, banded, and speckled with pinkish to purplish brown.

- **EARLY STAGES** The hairy caterpillar is green or brown with short, fleshy, yellow or reddish brown filaments on the back. It feeds on the foliage of a wide variety of trees.
- **DISTRIBUTION** Found in the USA and into southern Canada, with several subspecies.

NEARCTIC

small, brown eyespots

wavy, brownish band dissects yellow hindwing

♂

Time of Flight ☾	Habitat 🌳	Wingspan 8–17.5cm (3¼–7in)

Family SATURNIIDAE	Species *Callosamia promethea*	Author Drury

PROMETHEA MOTH

Males of this species are mainly blackish brown except for the pale borders, while females are coloured bright reddish brown to dark brown, with pale lines and spots in the middle of the wings.

- **EARLY STAGES** The caterpillar is green with four red, peg-like protuberances on the back near the head, and a single yellow peg near the tail. It feeds on a wide range of trees and shrubs, including spicebush *(Benzoin)* and various orchard trees.
- **DISTRIBUTION** Range extends from southern Canada to the south-eastern USA.

white, zigzag marking

NEARCTIC

marginal pattern present in both sexes

♀

Time of Flight ☾	Habitat 🌿 🌳	Wingspan 7.5–9.5cm (3–3¾in)

Family SATURNIIDAE	Species *Automeris io*	Author Fabricius

Io Moth

Males of this species have yellow
forewings, while those of the females are
reddish to purplish brown. The females
are larger than the males. The markings
are variable in both sexes, and there
are many named races.
• **EARLY STAGES** The caterpillar is
pale green, with branched, stinging spines
along the back, and red and white lines along
the sides. It is known to feed on a wide range
of plant species, which include birch *(Betula)*,
maize *(Zea mays)*, and clover *(Trifolium)*.
• **DISTRIBUTION** Range
extends from southern Canada, through to the USA
and south to Mexico.

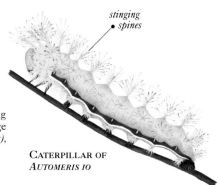

stinging
spines

CATERPILLAR OF
AUTOMERIS IO

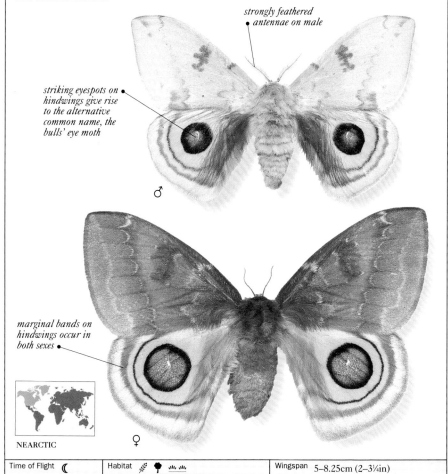

strongly feathered
antennae on male

striking eyespots on
hindwings give rise
to the alternative
common name, the
bulls' eye moth

♂

marginal bands on
hindwings occur in
both sexes

NEARCTIC

♀

Time of Flight ☾	Habitat	Wingspan 5–8.25cm (2–3¼in)

| Family SATURNIIDAE | Species *Attacus atlas* | Author Linnaeus |

ATLAS MOTH

This is the world's largest moth in overall size, although the owlet moth (*Thysania agrippina*, see p.265) has a greater wingspan. Distinctively shaped, its wings are richly patterned in various shades of brown. The sexes are similar.
• **EARLY STAGES** The caterpillar is pale yellowish green with long, fleshy spines, which are heavily powdered with a white, waxy substance. It can grow up to 10cm (4in) long. It feeds on a wide range of plants, and in captivity will eat willow *(Salix)*, poplar *(Populus)*, and privet *(Ligustrum)*.
• **DISTRIBUTION** Occurs from India and Sri Lanka to China, Malaysia, and Indonesia.

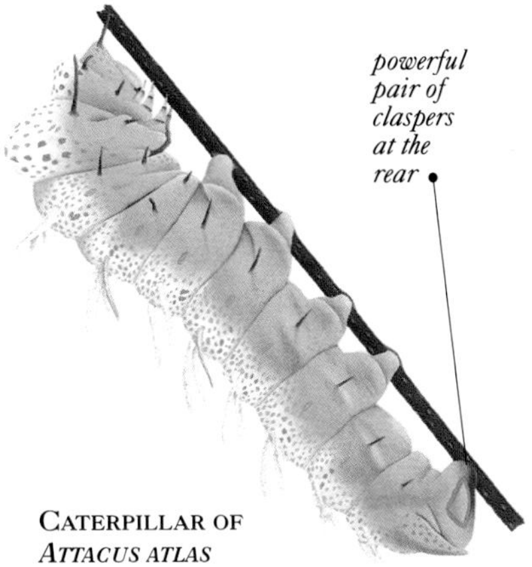

powerful pair of claspers at the rear

CATERPILLAR OF
ATTACUS ATLAS

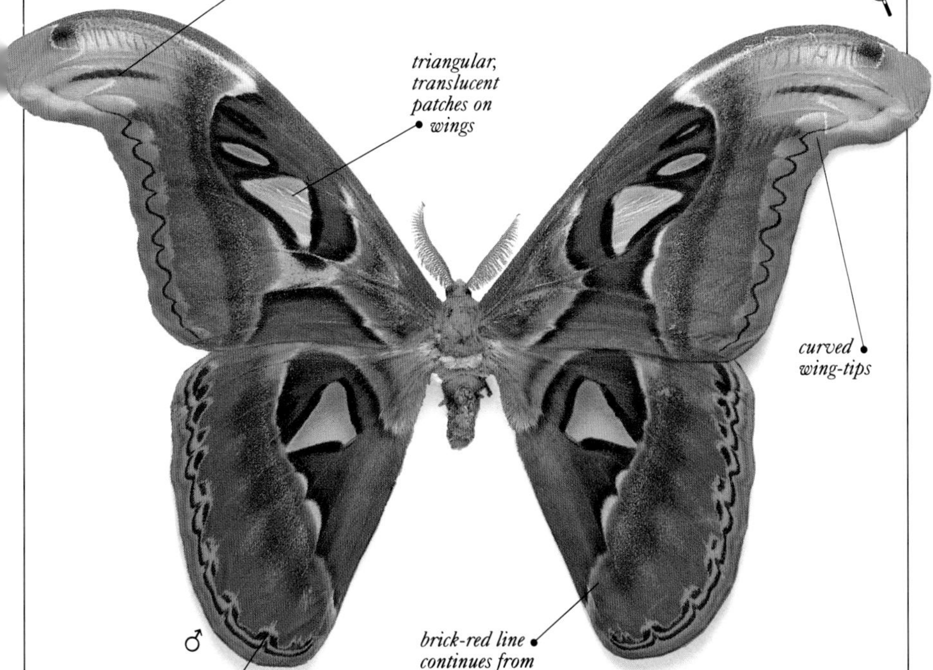

red flash on curved tip of forewings

triangular, translucent patches on wings

curved wing-tips

♂

brick-red line continues from fore- to hindwings

pale-edged brown spots along wing margins

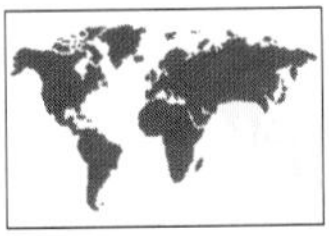

INDO-AUSTRALIAN

| Time of Flight ☾ | Habitat 🌴 ⬚ ⬚ | Wingspan 15.9–30cm (6¼–12in) |

| Family SATURNIIDAE | Species *Actias luna* | Author Linnaeus |

AMERICAN MOON MOTH

This beautiful and distinctive species with long hindwing tails varies in colour from yellowish green to pale bluish green, depending on location and season. The sexes are similar, but males have more strongly feathered antennae.

• **EARLY STAGES** The plump, green caterpillar has dark, pinkish red, raised spots. It feeds on the foliage of many broad-leaved trees, including birch *(Betula)* and alder *(Alnus)*.

• **DISTRIBUTION** Widespread from the USA south to Mexico. This species occurs, but is scarce in southern Canada.

forewing eyespots at leading edges of wings

dark forewing borders extend across body

red border to fore- and hindwings

♀

plump, furry body

pale yellow inner border to hindwing tails

NEARCTIC

| Time of Flight ☾ | Habitat ♣ | Wingspan 7.5–10.8cm (3–4¼in) |

| Family SATURNIIDAE | Species *Aglia tau* | Author Linnaeus |

TAU EMPEROR

Males of this very attractive, tan-coloured species are smaller and darker than females. They fly in the morning, while females are active at night. They rest with their wings folded back, in the manner of butterflies.

• **EARLY STAGES** The hump-backed caterpillar has reddish yellow spines. It feeds on broad-leaved trees.

• **DISTRIBUTION** Occurs in Europe, across temperate Asia to Japan.

markings resemble Greek letter "tau", hence the common name

PALAEARCTIC

♂

| Time of Flight ☀ ♂ ☾ ♀ | Habitat ♣ | Wingspan 5.5–9cm (2¼–3½in) |

Family SATURNIIDAE	Species *Actias selene*	Author Hübner

INDIAN MOON MOTH

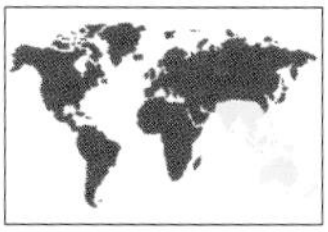

This great favourite of moth breeders is coloured a
beautiful, pale bluish green, while its long hindwing tails
are suffused with yellow and pink. The sexes are similar,
but males have more strongly feathered antennae. There
are numerous described races.
• **EARLY STAGES** The plump caterpillar is bright
yellowish green with dark yellow or orange, raised warts.
It feeds on a wide range of broad-leaved trees and shrubs.
• **DISTRIBUTION** Occurs from India and Sri Lanka, to
China, Malaysia, and Indonesia.

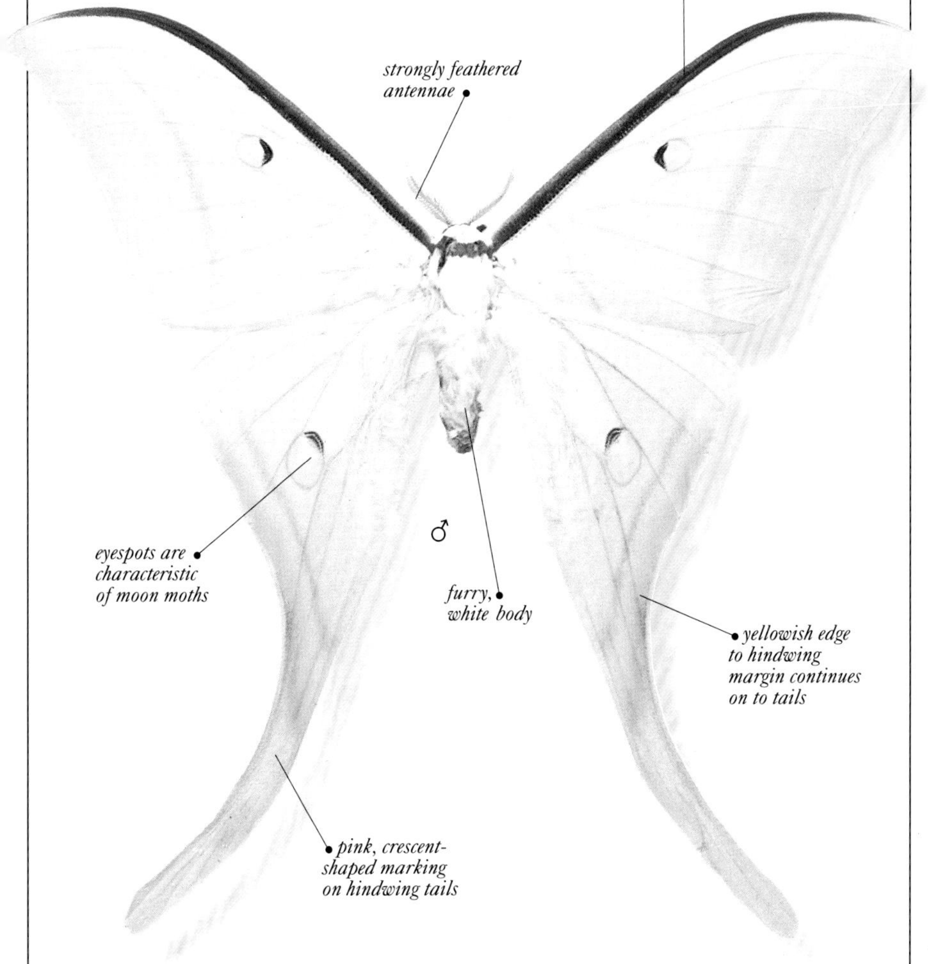

INDO-AUSTRALIAN

*purplish brown
leading edge to
forewings*

*strongly feathered
antennae*

*eyespots are
characteristic
of moon moths*

♂

*furry,
white body*

*yellowish edge
to hindwing
margin continues
on to tails*

*pink, crescent-
shaped marking
on hindwing tails*

Time of Flight ☾	Habitat 🌿 🌷	Wingspan 8–12cm (3¼–4¾in)

Family SATURNIIDAE	Species *Argema mimosae*	Author Boisduval

AFRICAN MOON MOTH

This moth is very similar to the Indian moon moth (*Actias selene*, see p.223), although it belongs to a different genus. Its beautiful colour tends to fade in museum specimens. Females can be recognized by their more curved tails.
• **EARLY STAGES** The caterpillar is green with green or yellow warts on the back, which bear short, black and yellow bristles. It feeds on the leaves of maroda plum *(Sclerocarya caffra)*, but in captivity will eat walnut *(Juglans)*.
• **DISTRIBUTION** Ranges from Kenya and Zaire to subtropical South Africa.

CATERPILLAR OF
ARGEMA MIMOSAE

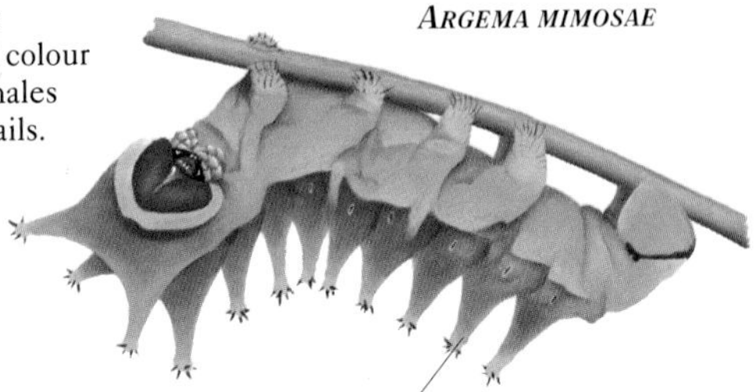

distinctive fleshy
projections
along back

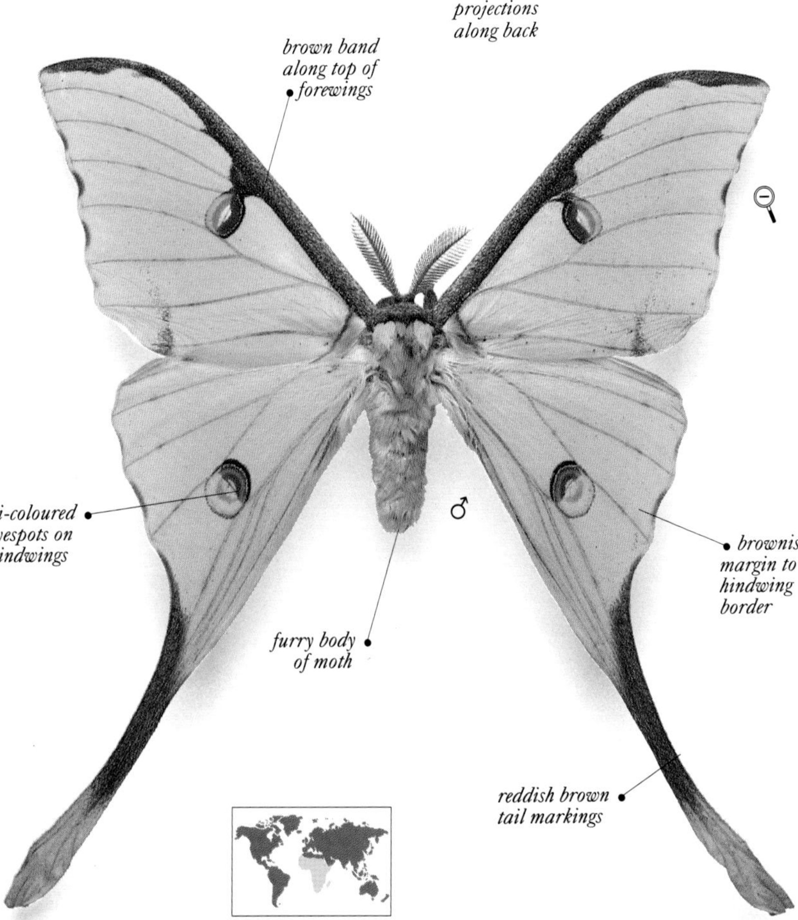

brown band
along top of
forewings

bi-coloured
eyespots on
hindwings

♂

brownish
margin to
hindwing
border

furry body
of moth

reddish brown
tail markings

AFROTROPICAL

Time of Flight ☾	Habitat 🜊	Wingspan 12–13cm (4¼–5in)

Family SATURNIIDAE	Species *Antheraea polyphemus*	Author Cramer

POLYPHEMUS MOTH

The ground colour of this moth's wings varies from yellow to reddish brown, but the distinctive pattern of bands and eyespots makes it an easy species to recognize. The sexes are similar. There are one or two broods a year, with moths on the wing in summer.
• **EARLY STAGES** The plump, bright yellow-green caterpillar is humped along the back and has raised, red spots. It feeds on the foliage of many broad-leaved trees and shrubs, especially that of apple *(Malus domestica)*.
• **DISTRIBUTION** Common and widespread in the USA and southern Canada.

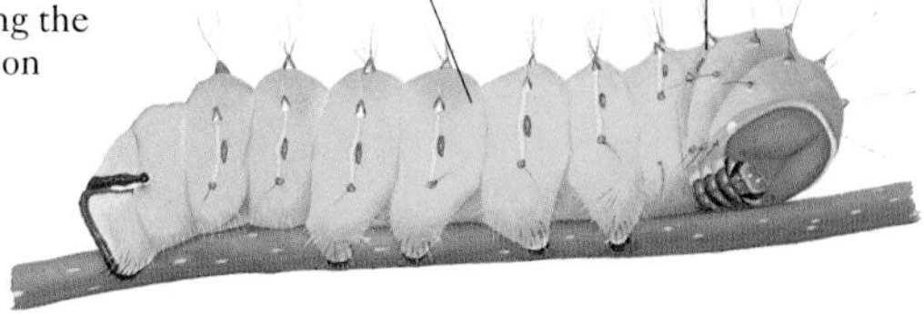

green caterpillar is well camouflaged among foliage

hairs growing from red spots

**CATERPILLAR OF
ANTHERAEA POLYPHEMUS**

red-margined line near base of forewings

two dark patches at forewing tip

feathered antennae characteristic of males

lemon-shaped patch within large, grey eyespots on hindwings

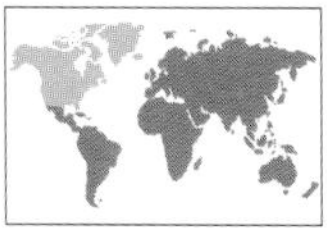

♂

NEARCTIC

Time of Flight ☾	Habitat ♦	Wingspan 10–13cm (4–5in)

Family	Species	Author
SATURNIIDAE	*Eupackardia calleta*	Westwood

CALLETA SILKMOTH

The blackish brown wings of this moth are banded with white, and each wing has a white V-shaped mark at its centre. Females are larger than males, and their wings are more rounded.

• **EARLY STAGES** The caterpillar is green with blue and black, spiny warts on red bases. It feeds on *Leucophyllum*, *Fouquieria*, *Prosopis*, and acacia, and in captivity will eat the foliage of ash *(Fraxinus)*, privet *(Ligustrum)*, and other trees.

• **DISTRIBUTION** Range extends from southern USA to central Mexico.

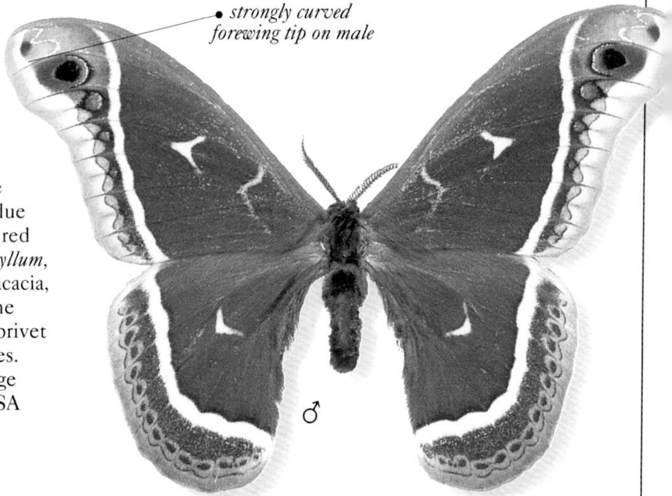
strongly curved forewing tip on male
♂

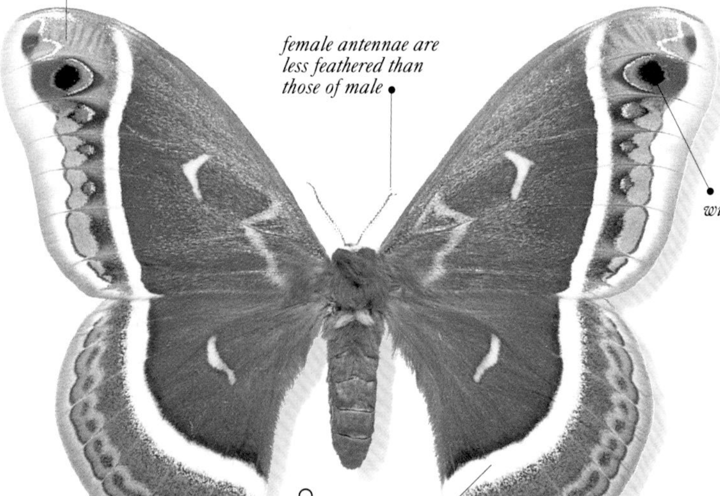
whitish sheen to forewing tip
female antennae are less feathered than those of male
eyespots on wing-tips
♀
white band continues down from forewings

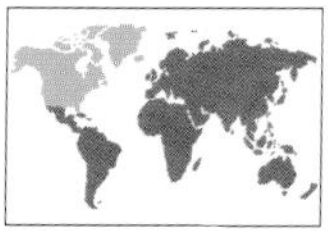

NEARCTIC

Time of Flight	Habitat	Wingspan
☾		8.25–11cm (3¼–4½in)

Family SATURNIIDAE	Species *Hyalophora cecropia*	Author Linnaeus

ROBIN MOTH

This easily recognized species gained its name from its red body, distinctively banded with white. The dark brown wings are banded with white and pinkish red. The sexes are similar, but males have smaller bodies. Another common name is the cecropia moth.

- **EARLY STAGES** The caterpillar is green with bright yellow, club-shaped protuberances along the back and blue protuberances below. It feeds on a wide range of broad-leaved trees and shrubs.
- **DISTRIBUTION** Widely distributed in forests, arable land, and gardens, from southern Canada through the USA to Mexico.

silvery patch to forewing tip •

dark eyespots
• near wing-tips

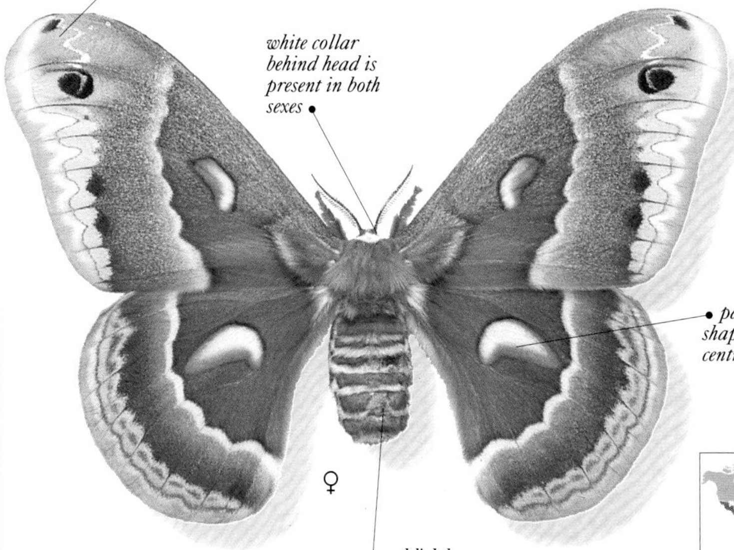

♂

small, reddish
marking on
• wing-tip

white collar
behind head is
present in both
sexes •

• pale, crescent-
shaped spots in
centre of hindwings

♀

• reddish brown
and pale brown
striped body

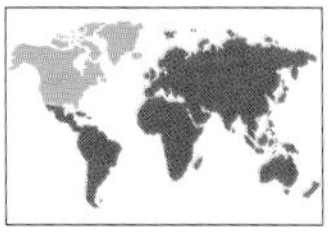

NEARCTIC

Time of Flight ☾ ☀	Habitat 🌾 🌳	Wingspan 11–15cm (4½–6in)

Family SATURNIIDAE	Species *Coscinocera hercules*	Author Miskin

HERCULES MOTH

The common name of this moth refers to its size. Males
have distinctive, long tails, while the paler females have
broad hindwings with a double lobe in place of a tail.
• **EARLY STAGES** The caterpillar is pale bluish green
with yellow spikes on the back, and can grow up to 17cm
(6¾in) long. It feeds on the foliage of bleeding heart tree
(Homalanthus populifolia), *Dysoxylum*, and *Panax*.
• **DISTRIBUTION** Range extends from Papua New
Guinea to northern Australia.

INDO-AUSTRALIAN

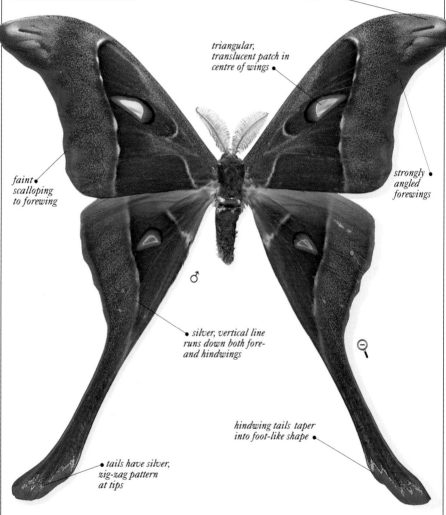

misty white
wing tips •

triangular,
translucent patch in
centre of wings •

faint •
scalloping
to forewing

strongly •
angled
forewings

♂

silver, vertical line
runs down both fore-
and hindwings

hindwing tails taper
into foot-like shape •

tails have silver,
zig-zag pattern
at tips

Time of Flight ☾	Habitat 🌴	Wingspan 16.5–25cm (6½–10in)

| Family SATURNIIDAE | Species *Graellsia isabellae* | Author Graëlls |

SPANISH MOON MOTH

The Spanish moon moth is considered by many to be the most beautiful of all European moths. The veins on the wings are strongly marked with reddish brown, and outlined with dark brown. Each wing bears a white-centred eyespot, half of which is yellow, and half of which is purplish blue with a reddish brown bar. Males have long, curved hindwing tails; those of females are shorter and broader.

• **EARLY STAGES** The caterpillar is yellowish green, finely spotted with white, and banded with chestnut-brown and white. It is covered with long, fine, brown hairs. It feeds on pines, particularly *Pinus sylvestris* and *Pinus laricio*.

• **DISTRIBUTION** Forests in the mountainous regions of central Spain and the Pyrenees.

male forewings are more sharply angular in shape than female forewings

♂

pale brown leading edge to forewings

outer wing margins have distinct yellowish green suffusion

hindwing tails reduced to pointed lobes in female moth

♀

yellow and brown banded female body is larger than that of male

PALAEARCTIC

| Time of Flight ☾ | Habitat 🔺 🌳 | Wingspan 6–10cm (2½–4in) |

| Family SATURNIIDAE | Species *Loepa katinka* | Author Westwood |

GOLDEN EMPEROR

This attractive yellow moth has a streak of dark brown along the leading edge of the forewings. Each wing has a reddish brown ringed eyespot at its centre. The wings are also patterned with fine wavy lines of reddish brown. The sexes are alike.

• **EARLY STAGES** Caterpillar is dark brown marbled with light brown and black, and has metallic blue warts. Along the sides are triangular yellow patches. The caterpillar feeds on vines *(Vitis and Parthenocisssus)*.

• **DISTRIBUTION** Widespread from North India to China.

CATERPILLAR OF
LOEPA KATINKA

warts each bear brown hairs

slender, elongated forewings of male moth

forewings of male more angular than those of female

♂

black eyespot marking at forewing tips

pale brown leading edge to forewing

white, crescent-shaped marking at forewing tips

fine, white, wavy line along wing margins

♀

INDO-AUSTRALIAN

| Time of Flight ☾ | Habitat 🌴 | Wingspan 9–10cm (3½–4in) |

Family SATURNIIDAE	Species *Bunaea alcinoe*	Author Stoll

COMMON EMPEROR

The common emperor varies in colour from reddish brown to dark purplish brown, with striking, pale bands on the fore- and hindwings.
• **EARLY STAGES** The dull black caterpillar has long, black spines behind the head, and yellowish white coloured protuberances along the rest of the body. It feeds on many types of plant, including *Celtis* and *Terminalia*.
• **DISTRIBUTION** Widespread throughout Africa, south of the Sahara, and also in Madagascar.

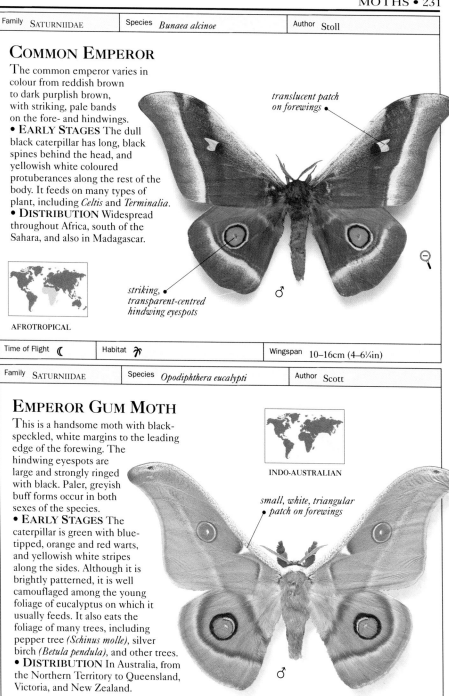

translucent patch on forewings

♂

striking, transparent-centred hindwing eyespots

AFROTROPICAL

Time of Flight ☾	Habitat 🌱	Wingspan 10–16cm (4–6¼in)

Family SATURNIIDAE	Species *Opodiphthera eucalypti*	Author Scott

EMPEROR GUM MOTH

This is a handsome moth with black-speckled, white margins to the leading edge of the forewing. The hindwing eyespots are large and strongly ringed with black. Paler, greyish buff forms occur in both sexes of the species.
• **EARLY STAGES** The caterpillar is green with blue-tipped, orange and red warts, and yellowish white stripes along the sides. Although it is brightly patterned, it is well camouflaged among the young foliage of eucalyptus on which it usually feeds. It also eats the foliage of many trees, including pepper tree *(Schinus molle)*, silver birch *(Betula pendula)*, and other trees.
• **DISTRIBUTION** In Australia, from the Northern Territory to Queensland, Victoria, and New Zealand.

INDO-AUSTRALIAN

small, white, triangular patch on forewings

♂

Time of Flight ☾	Habitat 🌱 🌷	Wingspan 8–13cm (3¼ – 5in)

| Family SATURNIIDAE | Species *Nudaurelia cytherea* | Author Fabricius |

PINE EMPEROR

This moth is banded and shaded with reddish, yellowish, and purplish brown. The forewing eyespots are ringed with black and orange, and have translucent, oval centres. The hindwing eyespots are broadly ringed with black and orange, and have minute, rounded, transparent centres.

• **EARLY STAGES** The caterpillar is strikingly beautiful with its black body speckled with green, yellow, and silver. There are also striking, broad bands of brownish red across the back. This species is a particularly notorious pest of pine trees *(Pinus)*, but also feeds on the foliage of cypress *(Cupressus)* and acacia, apple *(Malus domestica)*, guava *(Psidium guajava)*, and other wild and cultivated trees and shrubs.

• **DISTRIBUTION** Widespread and common in South Africa.

AFROTROPICAL

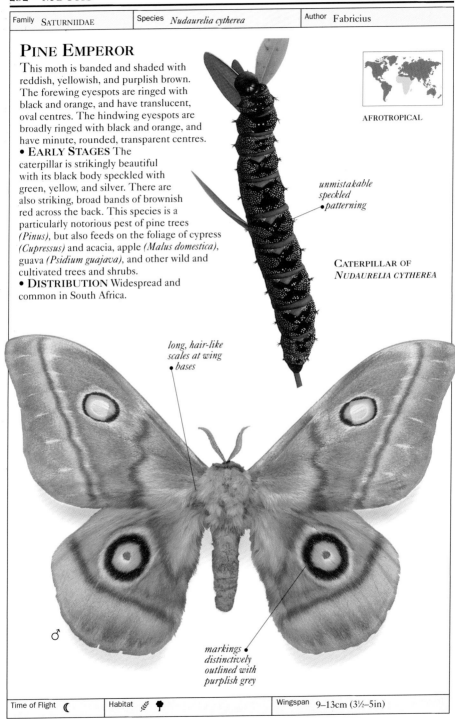

unmistakable speckled • patterning

CATERPILLAR OF
NUDAURELIA CYTHEREA

long, hair-like scales at wing • bases

♂

markings • distinctively outlined with purplish grey

| Time of Flight ☾ | Habitat 🌾 🌳 | Wingspan 9–13cm (3½–5in) |

Family SATURNIIDAE	Species *Rothschildia orizaba*	Author Westwood

ORIZABA SILKMOTH

A handsome and distinctive moth, this silkmoth belongs to a largely South American genus of moths which are characterized by the presence of large, translucent, window-like patches on both fore- and hindwings. The reddish brown wings are lined and patterned with white, black, and various shades of brown. Females have more rounded hindwings.

• **EARLY STAGES** The caterpillar is yellowish green above and bluish green below. The foodplants of this moth are apparently unknown. It has been successfully reared in captivity on the foliage of privet *(Ligustrum).*

• **DISTRIBUTION** Central and tropical South America, and can occur in southern Texas, USA.

caterpillar in resting position

CATERPILLAR OF
ROTHSCHILDIA ORIZABA

small, black rudiments of an eyespot near forewing tips

antennae of male moth more feathered than female

♂

pale-ringed brown spots along hindwing margins

purple-brown wavy marking on hindwings

NEOTROPICAL

Time of Flight ☾	Habitat 🌴	Wingspan 11–14.5cm (4½–5¼in)

Family SATURNIIDAE	Species *Samia cynthia*	Author Drury

AILANTHUS SILKMOTH

The ground colour of this large moth varies from khaki-brown to an olive-green or orange-brown. The broad, pale band that traverses both fore- and hindwings is characteristic, as are the narrow, crescent-shaped, translucent patches in the centre of each wing. Males have more elongate forewings than the females, and their antennae are more strongly feathered. Another common name for the adult is the eri silkmoth.

• **EARLY STAGES** The fleshy, spined caterpillar is bluish green, overlaid with a white, waxy powder. As its common name suggests, it feeds on the foliage of tree of heaven *(Ailanthus altissima)*, although in captivity it eats privet *(Ligustrum)* or lilac *(Syringa)*. The caterpillars are reared for the silk of their cocoons.

• **DISTRIBUTION** Originating from Asia, this species has been introduced into North America and is now established in parts of Europe.

caterpillar appears white because it is covered with waxy powder

CATERPILLAR OF SAMIA CYNTHIA

white spots on hairy thorax

♂

narrow, crescent-shaped markings, characteristic of this species

vertical, black line runs down length of wings

HOLARCTIC

Time of Flight ☾	Habitat	Wingspan 9–14cm (3½–5½in)

Family SATURNIIDAE	Species *Saturnia pyri*	Authors Denis & Schiffermüller

GREAT PEACOCK MOTH

The great peacock moth is Europe's largest native moth, and as such is easy to recognize. It has red, black, and brown ringed eyespots on all wings. The wings are brown with light and dark bands, and the leading edge of the forewing is extensively suffused with silvery white. The sexes are similar. Other common names for the adult moth are the giant emperor and the Viennese emperor.

• **EARLY STAGES** The caterpillar is bright yellowish green with raised, blue warts bearing tufts of black hairs. It feeds on the foliage of apple *(Malus domestica)*, pear *(Pyrus communis)*, and other broad-leaved trees, and it is occasionally a minor orchard pest.

• **DISTRIBUTION** Widespread in central and southern Europe, extending to north Africa and western Asia.

CATERPILLAR OF
SATURNIA PYRI

caterpillar is yellowish • green with white line along its side

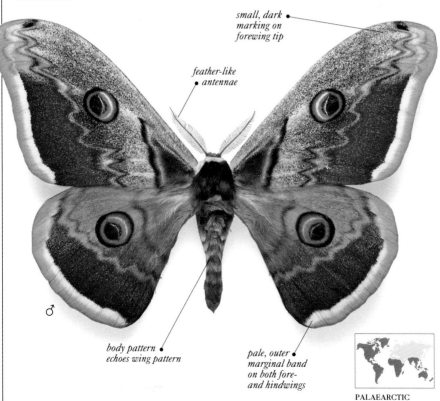

small, dark • marking on forewing tip

feather-like • antennae

♂

body pattern • echoes wing pattern

pale, outer • marginal band on both fore- and hindwings

PALAEARCTIC

Time of Flight ☾	Habitat 🌿🌳	Wingspan 10–15cm (4–6in)

SPHINGIDAE

T HIS IS a worldwide family of about 1,000 medium- to large-sized moths. Their very distinctive, streamlined wing shapes and robust bodies set them apart from other moths, making them one of the easiest groups to recognize. Because of their structure, they are extremely powerful fliers, some even reaching speeds of up to 50km (30 miles) per hour. It is probably owing to their speed in flight that they have earned their common name of hawk-moths.

———— • ————

Moths from this family usually have well-developed tongues enabling them to take nectar from even the most deep-throated, tubular flowers. Some species are day-fliers, and may be seen hovering over flower beds in gardens.

Family SPHINGIDAE	Species *Acherontia atropos*	Author Linnaeus

DEATH'S HEAD HAWK-MOTH

Many superstitions were at one time based around this distinctive moth, and it was generally considered to be a portent of death or grave misfortune. The moths have a very stout, strong tongue, which they use to pierce the wax cells of beehives so that they can feed on the honey inside.
• **EARLY STAGES** The caterpillar ranges from yellow to green or brown. It feeds on the foliage of potato *(Solanum)*, deadly nightshade *(Atropa)* and related plants.
• **DISTRIBUTION** Mediterranean, North Africa. It migrates northwards into Europe.

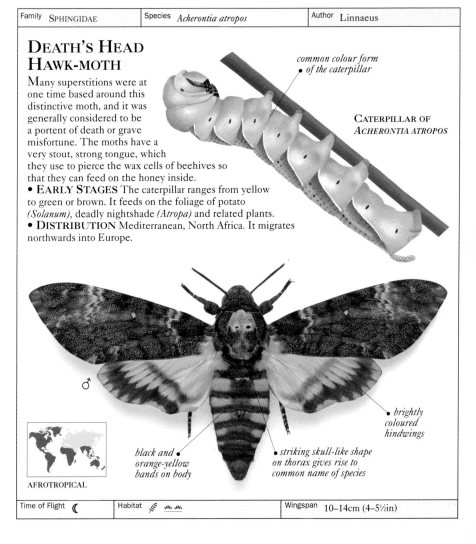

common colour form • of the caterpillar

CATERPILLAR OF
ACHERONTIA ATROPOS

♂

AFROTROPICAL

• brightly coloured hindwings

black and • orange-yellow bands on body

• striking skull-like shape on thorax gives rise to common name of species

Time of Flight ☾	Habitat 🌿 ⚘ ⚘	Wingspan 10–14cm (4–5½in)

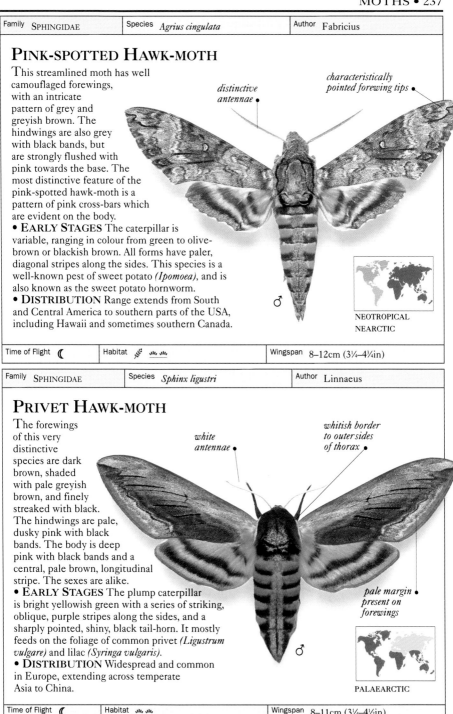

| Family SPHINGIDAE | Species *Agrius cingulata* | Author Fabricius |

PINK-SPOTTED HAWK-MOTH

This streamlined moth has well camouflaged forewings, with an intricate pattern of grey and greyish brown. The hindwings are also grey with black bands, but are strongly flushed with pink towards the base. The most distinctive feature of the pink-spotted hawk-moth is a pattern of pink cross-bars which are evident on the body.

distinctive antennae

characteristically pointed forewing tips

• **EARLY STAGES** The caterpillar is variable, ranging in colour from green to olive-brown or blackish brown. All forms have paler, diagonal stripes along the sides. This species is a well-known pest of sweet potato *(Ipomoea)*, and is also known as the sweet potato hornworm.
• **DISTRIBUTION** Range extends from South and Central America to southern parts of the USA, including Hawaii and sometimes southern Canada.

NEOTROPICAL
NEARCTIC

| Time of Flight ☾ | Habitat | Wingspan 8–12cm (3¼–4¾in) |

| Family SPHINGIDAE | Species *Sphinx ligustri* | Author Linnaeus |

PRIVET HAWK-MOTH

The forewings of this very distinctive species are dark brown, shaded with pale greyish brown, and finely streaked with black. The hindwings are pale, dusky pink with black bands. The body is deep pink with black bands and a central, pale brown, longitudinal stripe. The sexes are alike.

white antennae

whitish border to outer sides of thorax

pale margin present on forewings

• **EARLY STAGES** The plump caterpillar is bright yellowish green with a series of striking, oblique, purple stripes along the sides, and a sharply pointed, shiny, black tail-horn. It mostly feeds on the foliage of common privet *(Ligustrum vulgare)* and lilac *(Syringa vulgaris)*.
• **DISTRIBUTION** Widespread and common in Europe, extending across temperate Asia to China.

PALAEARCTIC

| Time of Flight ☾ | Habitat | Wingspan 8–11cm (3¼–4⅓in) |

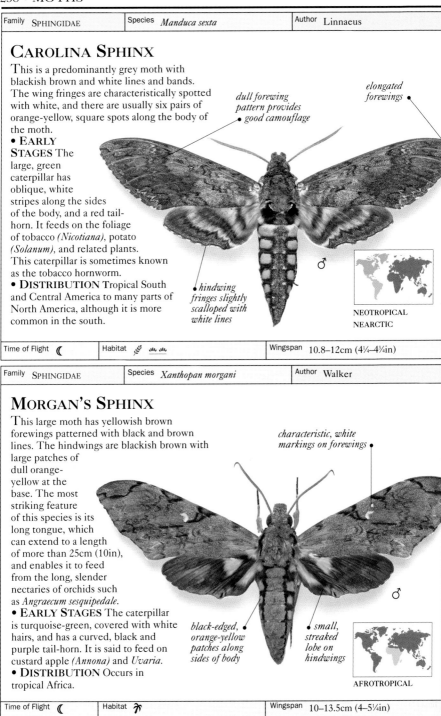

Family SPHINGIDAE	Species *Manduca sexta*	Author Linnaeus

CAROLINA SPHINX

This is a predominantly grey moth with blackish brown and white lines and bands. The wing fringes are characteristically spotted with white, and there are usually six pairs of orange-yellow, square spots along the body of the moth.

dull forewing pattern provides good camouflage

elongated forewings

• **EARLY STAGES** The large, green caterpillar has oblique, white stripes along the sides of the body, and a red tail-horn. It feeds on the foliage of tobacco *(Nicotiana)*, potato *(Solanum)*, and related plants. This caterpillar is sometimes known as the tobacco hornworm.

• **DISTRIBUTION** Tropical South and Central America to many parts of North America, although it is more common in the south.

hindwing fringes slightly scalloped with white lines

♂

NEOTROPICAL
NEARCTIC

Time of Flight ☾	Habitat	Wingspan 10.8–12cm (4¼–4¾in)

Family SPHINGIDAE	Species *Xanthopan morgani*	Author Walker

MORGAN'S SPHINX

This large moth has yellowish brown forewings patterned with black and brown lines. The hindwings are blackish brown with large patches of dull orange-yellow at the base. The most striking feature of this species is its long tongue, which can extend to a length of more than 25cm (10in), and enables it to feed from the long, slender nectaries of orchids such as *Angraecum sesquipedale*.

characteristic, white markings on forewings

• **EARLY STAGES** The caterpillar is turquoise-green, covered with white hairs, and has a curved, black and purple tail-horn. It is said to feed on custard apple *(Annona)* and *Uvaria*.

• **DISTRIBUTION** Occurs in tropical Africa.

black-edged, orange-yellow patches along sides of body

small, streaked lobe on hindwings

♂

AFROTROPICAL

Time of Flight ☾	Habitat	Wingspan 10–13.5cm (4–5¼in)

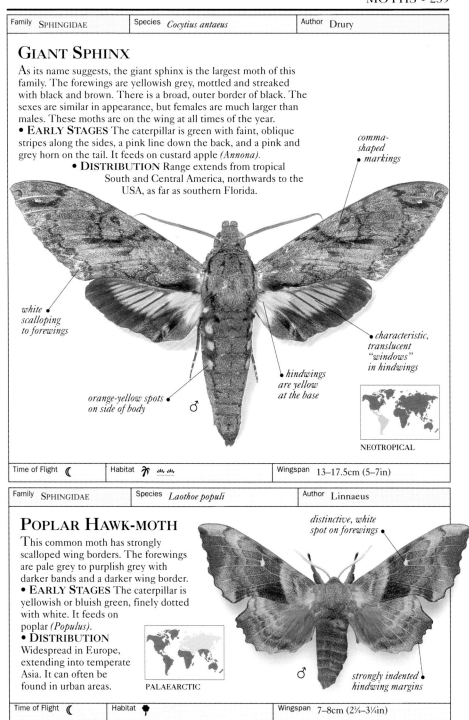

Family SPHINGIDAE	Species *Cocytius antaeus*	Author Drury

GIANT SPHINX

As its name suggests, the giant sphinx is the largest moth of this family. The forewings are yellowish grey, mottled and streaked with black and brown. There is a broad, outer border of black. The sexes are similar in appearance, but females are much larger than males. These moths are on the wing at all times of the year.
• **EARLY STAGES** The caterpillar is green with faint, oblique stripes along the sides, a pink line down the back, and a pink and grey horn on the tail. It feeds on custard apple *(Annona)*.
• **DISTRIBUTION** Range extends from tropical South and Central America, northwards to the USA, as far as southern Florida.

comma-shaped markings

white scalloping to forewings

characteristic, translucent "windows" in hindwings

orange-yellow spots on side of body ♂

hindwings are yellow at the base

NEOTROPICAL

Time of Flight ☾	Habitat	Wingspan 13–17.5cm (5–7in)

Family SPHINGIDAE	Species *Laothoe populi*	Author Linnaeus

POPLAR HAWK-MOTH

This common moth has strongly scalloped wing borders. The forewings are pale grey to purplish grey with darker bands and a darker wing border.
• **EARLY STAGES** The caterpillar is yellowish or bluish green, finely dotted with white. It feeds on poplar *(Populus)*.
• **DISTRIBUTION** Widespread in Europe, extending into temperate Asia. It can often be found in urban areas.

distinctive, white spot on forewings

PALAEARCTIC

♂

strongly indented hindwing margins

Time of Flight ☾	Habitat	Wingspan 7–8cm (2¾–3¼in)

Family SPHINGIDAE	Species *Coequosa triangularis*	Author Donovan

DOUBLE-HEADED HAWK-MOTH

This spectacularly large hawk-moth has distinctively shaped, brown forewings with a large and prominent, dark brown, triangular marking on the leading edge.
- **EARLY STAGES** The unusual-looking caterpillar is green but covered with small, white-tipped, yellow warts. It has a raised, white-centred, black "eye" on the hind claspers, creating the appearance of a lizard's head. It feeds on *Banksia*, *Grevillea*, and *Macadamia*, and other plants belonging to the family Proteaceae.
- **DISTRIBUTION** Eastern Australia, particularly NSW.

silvery grey edge to marking

triangular shaped marking

slightly indented forewing margins

♂

narrow, dark line along middle of body

orange-yellow base to hindwings

INDO-AUSTRALIAN

Time of Flight ☾	Habitat ♣	Wingspan 15–16cm (6–6 ¼in)

Family SPHINGIDAE	Species *Mimas tiliae*	Author Linnaeus

LIME HAWK-MOTH

distinctively shaped patch near forewing tips

variable camouflage pattern on forewings

This moth ranges from dusky pink to reddish or yellowish brown with olive-green markings on the forewing.
- **EARLY STAGES** The caterpillar is green, speckled with yellowish white dots and has yellow stripes along the sides. It feeds on the foliage of lime *(Tilia)* and other broad-leaved trees.
- **DISTRIBUTION** Commonly found across Europe through to Siberia and also in Japan.

PALAEARCTIC

yellowish brown hindwings with darker patch

♀

ragged wing margins

Time of Flight ☾	Habitat ♣	Wingspan 6–7.5cm (2½–3in)

| Family | SPHINGIDAE | Species | *Smerinthus jamaicensis* | Author | Drury |

TWIN-SPOTTED SPHINX

While the forewings of this hawk-moth are light and dark greyish brown, the hindwings are deep pink with striking, black-ringed, blue eyespots.
• **EARLY STAGES** The caterpillar is green with white, diagonal stripes along the sides of the body and a straight, purplish pink or blue tail-horn. It feeds on the foliage of apple (*Malus domestica*).
• **DISTRIBUTION** Canada and the USA.

camouflage pattern to forewings

notched tips to forewing

broad, pale border to hindwings

black bar through eyespots

NEARCTIC

♀

| Time of Flight ☾ | Habitat 🌴 | Wingspan 5–8cm (2–3¼in) |

| Family | SPHINGIDAE | Species | *Protambulyx strigilis* | Author | Linnaeus |

STREAKED SPHINX

The streaked sphinx belongs to a genus of Central and South American species characterized by their long, narrow forewings. It can be distinguished from similar species by a dark brown line along the outer margin of the forewings.
• **EARLY STAGES** The caterpillar is yellowish green with greenish white or yellowish green, oblique bands along the sides, and a distinct horn on the tail. It feeds on the foliage of *Anacardium spondias* and other related plants.
• **DISTRIBUTION** From Argentina to Florida, USA.

CATERPILLAR OF
PROTAMBULYX STRIGILIS

green and spotted, with diagonal stripes along its sides

distinctive notch at tip of forewings

pale, oblique markings on body

blackish brown spots on hind margin of forewings

♂

NEOTROPICAL

| Time of Flight ☾ | Habitat 🎋 | Wingspan 9.5–12cm (3¾–4¾in) |

| Family SPHINGIDAE | Species *Cephonodes kingi* | Author Macleay |

KING'S BEE-HAWK

This bee-hawk has a distinctive, olive-green colour. On emergence from the pupa, the wings are completely covered with scales, but most of these are lost in flight, leaving clear patches with dark veins.
• **EARLY STAGES** The caterpillar varies in colour from green to greenish black and has an S-shaped horn at the tail. It feeds on the foliage of *Canthium*.
• **DISTRIBUTION** From Western Australia and Queensland to NSW.

finely pointed tips to antennae

patch of olive-green scales on forewings

♂

broad, dark, scaled tails

INDO-AUSTRALIAN

| Time of Flight ☼ | Habitat ⚲, ⚲ | Wingspan 4–6.5cm (1½–2½in) |

| Family SPHINGIDAE | Species *Hemaris thysbe* | Author Fabricius |

HUMMINGBIRD CLEARWING

This is one of a group of North American species with large, clear areas on both fore- and hindwings. The clear areas are surrounded by dark reddish brown borders, but the wing bases and front half of the body are olive-green.
• **EARLY STAGES** The plump, yellowish green caterpillar has pale stripes along the back and a yellow and green tail-horn. It feeds on hawthorn *(Crataegus)* and related species.
• **DISTRIBUTION** Common in Canada and the USA.

pale patches on wings give impression of holes

♀

irregular inner margin of reddish brown borders

NEARCTIC

| Time of Flight ☼ | Habitat 🌳 ⚲, ⚲ | Wingspan 4–6cm (1½–2½in) |

| Family SPHINGIDAE | Species *Cizara ardeniae* | Author Lewin |

CIZARA HAWK-MOTH

This remarkable hawk-moth is quite unlike any other species and belongs in a genus of its own. Where the cross-bar reaches the leading edge of the forewings there is a small, white, translucent spot.
• **EARLY STAGES** The caterpillar is undescribed but is known to feed on *Coprosma*.
• **DISTRIBUTION** Queensland to NSW.

bright eyespots near base of forewings

♀

strongly curved outer margin of forewings

distinctive, pale markings on body

INDO-AUSTRALIAN

| Time of Flight ☾ | Habitat 🌴 ⚲, ⚲ | Wingspan 5–7cm (2–2¾in) |

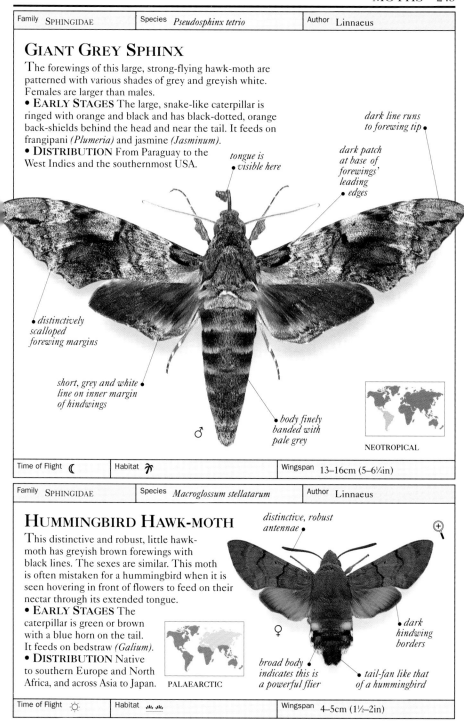

| Family | SPHINGIDAE | Species | *Pseudosphinx tetrio* | Author | Linnaeus |

GIANT GREY SPHINX

The forewings of this large, strong-flying hawk-moth are patterned with various shades of grey and greyish white. Females are larger than males.
• **EARLY STAGES** The large, snake-like caterpillar is ringed with orange and black and has black-dotted, orange back-shields behind the head and near the tail. It feeds on frangipani *(Plumeria)* and jasmine *(Jasminum)*.
• **DISTRIBUTION** From Paraguay to the West Indies and the southernmost USA.

dark line runs to forewing tip

dark patch at base of forewings' leading edges

tongue is visible here

distinctively scalloped forewing margins

short, grey and white line on inner margin of hindwings

♂

body finely banded with pale grey

NEOTROPICAL

| Time of Flight | ☾ | Habitat | 🌴 | Wingspan | 13–16cm (5–6¼in) |

| Family | SPHINGIDAE | Species | *Macroglossum stellatarum* | Author | Linnaeus |

HUMMINGBIRD HAWK-MOTH

This distinctive and robust, little hawk-moth has greyish brown forewings with black lines. The sexes are similar. This moth is often mistaken for a hummingbird when it is seen hovering in front of flowers to feed on their nectar through its extended tongue.
• **EARLY STAGES** The caterpillar is green or brown with a blue horn on the tail. It feeds on bedstraw *(Galium)*.
• **DISTRIBUTION** Native to southern Europe and North Africa, and across Asia to Japan.

distinctive, robust antennae

dark hindwing borders

♀

broad body indicates this is a powerful flier

tail-fan like that of a hummingbird

PALAEARCTIC

| Time of Flight | ☀ | Habitat | 〰〰 | Wingspan | 4–5cm (1½–2in) |

Family SPHINGIDAE	Species *Daphnis nerii*	Author Linnaeus

OLEANDER HAWK-MOTH

Perhaps the most spectacular of all the
hawk-moths, this large species is intricately
patterned with shades of green and purplish
pink. The hindwings are greyish brown. The
body is patterned in a similar way to the
forewings so that the entire
moth is extremely well
camouflaged when it
settles among foliage.
In the tropics,
this moth occurs
throughout the year.
• **EARLY STAGES** The
large caterpillar is olive-green
with two large, blue eyespots on the
body behind the head. The tail-horn
is yellow, tipped with black. It feeds on
oleander *(Nerium oleander)*, periwinkle
(Vinca), and grapevine *(Vitis vinifera)*.
• **DISTRIBUTION** Widespread in Africa
and southern Asia, migrating northwards to
Europe. It has also been recorded in Hawaii.

*strongly curved
• tips to antennae*

AFROTROPICAL
INDO-AUSTRALIAN

*wing •
pattern
extends
across
body*

*• irregular,
greenish grey,
central band*

♀

Time of Flight ☾	Habitat 🦋 ᴧⱼ ᴧⱼ	Wingspan 8–12cm (3¼–4¾ in)

Family SPHINGIDAE	Species *Euchloron megaera*	Author Linnaeus

VERDANT SPHINX

This is arguably the most distinctive of all
hawk-moths. The body and forewings are a
deep shade of green; the hindwings are orange-
yellow with black and reddish brown markings
on the outer margin.
The underside has
varying amounts of
green, but it is also
suffused with pinkish
red or reddish brown.
There are two silvery
patches on the underside
of the body.
• **EARLY STAGES** The
horned caterpillar is reddish pink
with an eyespot on the body some
distance behind the head; there are also
two white stripes along the back. It feeds
on the foliage of grapevine *(Vitis vinifera)*
and Virginia creeper *(Parthenocissus)*.
• **DISTRIBUTION** Widespread in Africa
south of the Sahara, ranging from equatorial
west Africa to Zambia and Natal.

*triangular,
• black markings*

AFROTROPICAL

*• black
and white
markings
at base of
forewing*

♀

*• patch of greyish
white scales on
hindwing margin*

Time of Flight ☾	Habitat 🦋	Wingspan 7–12cm (2¾–4¾ in)

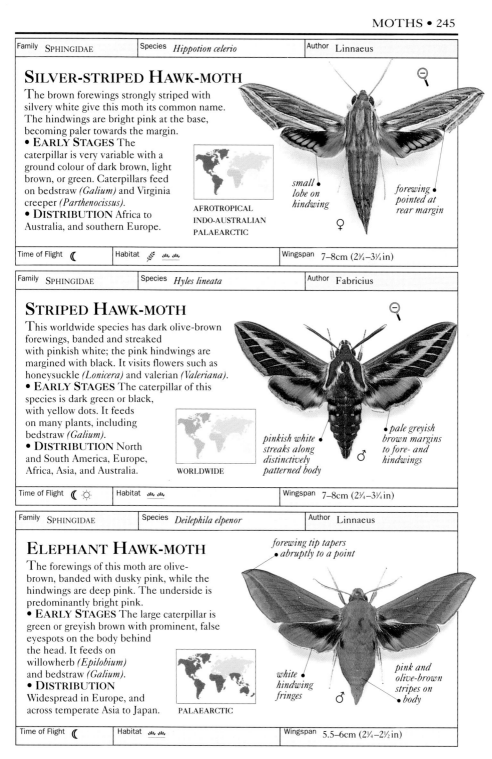

| Family | SPHINGIDAE | Species | *Hippotion celerio* | Author | Linnaeus |

SILVER-STRIPED HAWK-MOTH

The brown forewings strongly striped with silvery white give this moth its common name. The hindwings are bright pink at the base, becoming paler towards the margin.
• **EARLY STAGES** The caterpillar is very variable with a ground colour of dark brown, light brown, or green. Caterpillars feed on bedstraw *(Galium)* and Virginia creeper *(Parthenocissus)*.
• **DISTRIBUTION** Africa to Australia, and southern Europe.

AFROTROPICAL
INDO-AUSTRALIAN
PALAEARCTIC

small lobe on hindwing

forewing pointed at rear margin

♀

| Time of Flight ☾ | Habitat | Wingspan 7–8cm (2¾–3¼ in) |

| Family | SPHINGIDAE | Species | *Hyles lineata* | Author | Fabricius |

STRIPED HAWK-MOTH

This worldwide species has dark olive-brown forewings, banded and streaked with pinkish white; the pink hindwings are margined with black. It visits flowers such as honeysuckle *(Lonicera)* and valerian *(Valeriana)*.
• **EARLY STAGES** The caterpillar of this species is dark green or black, with yellow dots. It feeds on many plants, including bedstraw *(Galium)*.
• **DISTRIBUTION** North and South America, Europe, Africa, Asia, and Australia.

WORLDWIDE

pinkish white streaks along distinctively patterned body

pale greyish brown margins to fore- and hindwings

♂

| Time of Flight ☾ ☼ | Habitat | Wingspan 7–8cm (2¾–3¼ in) |

| Family | SPHINGIDAE | Species | *Deilephila elpenor* | Author | Linnaeus |

ELEPHANT HAWK-MOTH

forewing tip tapers abruptly to a point

The forewings of this moth are olive-brown, banded with dusky pink, while the hindwings are deep pink. The underside is predominantly bright pink.
• **EARLY STAGES** The large caterpillar is green or greyish brown with prominent, false eyespots on the body behind the head. It feeds on willowherb *(Epilobium)* and bedstraw *(Galium)*.
• **DISTRIBUTION** Widespread in Europe, and across temperate Asia to Japan.

PALAEARCTIC

white hindwing fringes

♂

pink and olive-brown stripes on body

| Time of Flight ☾ | Habitat | Wingspan 5.5–6cm (2¼–2½ in) |

NOTODONTIDAE

T HIS IS a large family of more than 2,500 small- to medium-sized species with a worldwide distribution. The moths generally have rather long forewings and a longish body. The predominant wing colours are brown, grey, and green, but some species are more brightly coloured. One of the characteristic features of many of the members in this group is a tuft of scales projecting from the middle of

the hind edge of the forewing. When the wings are folded, these tufts project conspicuously, giving rise to the common name "prominents".

———— • ————

The caterpillars of this family display a great variety of forms, ranging from hairy species that live in communal nests – the "processionary" caterpillars – to smooth species with humps on their backs, or with whip-like tails.

Family NOTODONTIDAE	Species *Cerura vinula*	Author Linnaeus

PUSS MOTH

The white forewings of this distinctive species are patterned with greyish black, zigzag lines. The hindwings lack markings but are heavily suffused with grey and have dark veins. The sexes are alike. These moths are on the wing in spring and summer.
• **EARLY STAGES** The striking caterpillar is bright green with a purple, saddle-shaped marking in the middle of the back and two long tails at the rear end. When the caterpillar is disturbed, these tails are thrust forwards over the head and emit slender, whip-like, pink filaments. The caterpillar can also squirt formic acid from a gland in the throat. It feeds on willow and sallow *(Salix)*, and poplar *(Populus)*.
• **DISTRIBUTION** Widespread in Europe, ranging to North Africa, and across temperate Asia to Japan.

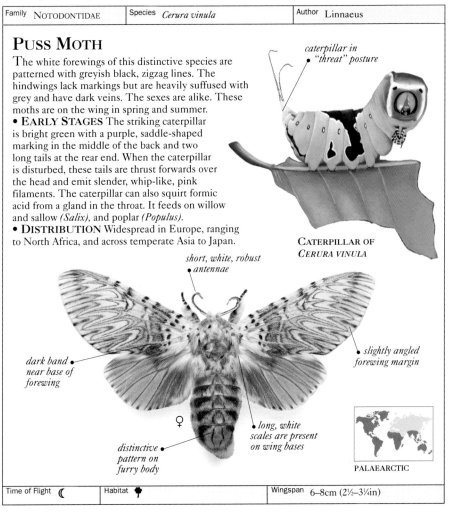

caterpillar in "threat" posture

**CATERPILLAR OF
CERURA VINULA**

short, white, robust antennae

dark band near base of forewing

slightly angled forewing margin

♀

long, white scales are present on wing bases

distinctive pattern on furry body

PALAEARCTIC

Time of Flight ☾	Habitat ♣	Wingspan 6–8cm (2½–3¼in)

Family NOTODONTIDAE	Species *Chliara cresus*	Author Cramer

CROESUS PROMINENT

The family Notodontidae is richly represented in South America but very little is known about the individual species. This beautiful moth belongs to a genus of about ten described species, most of them with metallic markings on the forewing. The forewings of the Croesus prominent are patterned with a network of dark brown lines and suffused with a scattering of golden brown scales – hence the common name, which refers to the wealthy Lydian King Croesus of antiquity. The striking, silver spots are grouped in the centre of the wing and at the base.

• **EARLY STAGES** The caterpillar of this species has not been described and its foodplants are unknown.

• **DISTRIBUTION** Occurs throughout tropical South and Central America.

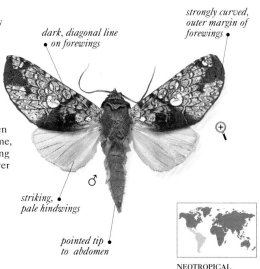

dark, diagonal line on forewings

strongly curved, outer margin of forewings

striking, pale hindwings

♂

pointed tip to abdomen

NEOTROPICAL

Time of Flight ☾	Habitat 🌴	Wingspan 4.5–5.5cm (1¾–2¼in)

Family NOTODONTIDAE	Species *Danima banksiae*	Author Lewin

BANKSIA MOTH

The banksia moth is one of the most distinctive members of this family in Australia. Its grey forewings are patterned with black. The hindwings of the female are a glossy, brownish grey, but those of the smaller male are almost white. The body is orange-yellow. Banksia moths are on the wing at most times of year but are especially common in spring.

• **EARLY STAGES** The caterpillar is a glossy, reddish brown and has white patches and a short, blunt, black horn on the tail. It feeds by day on the foliage of *Banksia marginata* and *Hakea*, and if disturbed it rears up the front part of the body in a threatening posture. The pupae are formed underground.

• **DISTRIBUTION** This species occurs throughout Australia.

sprinkling of white scales on forewings

heavy, white scaling behind the head

orange-yellow tufts along sides of body

♀

black tuft on tails

INDO-AUSTRALIAN

Time of Flight ☾	Habitat ᚚ ᚚ	Wingspan 6–8cm (2½–3¼in)

Family NOTODONTIDAE	Species *Desmeocraera latex*	Author Druce

OLIVE PROMINENT

This is a very variable species of moth, with the forewings ranging in colour from brown with a green suffusion to almost grass-green. The hindwing in both sexes is a pale, shining brown.
• **EARLY STAGES** The caterpillar is brown with white streaks and dark spots along its sides. It feeds on the foliage of fig *(Ficus)* and *Mimusops*.
• **DISTRIBUTION** West Africa to Malawi, Angola and down as far as South Africa.

AFROTROPICAL

slight green coloration sometimes more extensive than shown here •

♀

forewing • pattern extends on to hindwing

Time of Flight ☾	Habitat 🌱 ⚘ ⚘	Wingspan 4–6cm (1½–2½in)

Family NOTODONTIDAE	Species *Nerice bidentata*	Author Walker

DOUBLE-TOOTHED PROMINENT

The "double-tooth" in the common name refers to a white-edged, blackish brown line that extends across the forewings, and the thorax, and divides the brown front portion from the pale grey rear portion.
• **EARLY STAGES** The caterpillar has a series of triangular projections along its back, which resemble the edge of the elm leaf *(Ulmus)* on which it feeds.
• **DISTRIBUTION** Southern Canada and the USA.

NEARCTIC

feathered antennae occur • in both sexes

♀

distinctive • "tooth" marking

• wing pattern continues across body

Time of Flight ☾	Habitat 🌳	Wingspan 3–4cm (1¼–1½in)

Family NOTODONTIDAE	Species *Notodonta dromedarius*	Author Linnaeus

IRON PROMINENT

The forewings of this moth are usually richly coloured with shades of purplish and reddish brown. In northern regions, however, they tend to be darker and suffused with grey.
• **EARLY STAGES** The caterpillar varies from yellowish green to reddish brown. It feeds on the foliage of birch *(Betula)*, oak *(Quercus)*, and other broad-leaves.
• **DISTRIBUTION** Central and northern Europe, extending to Scandinavia.

PALAEARCTIC

reddish brown, inner forewing • margin

scalloped appearance to forewings •

♂

• robust, furry body

Time of Flight ☾	Habitat 🌳	Wingspan 4–5cm (1½–2in)

Family NOTODONTIDAE	Species *Oenosandra boisduvalii*	Author Newman

BOISDUVAL'S AUTUMNAL MOTH

Recently it has been suggested that this distinctive moth belongs in a separate family of its own, the Oenosandridae. Males are smaller than females and have grey forewings speckled with black.
• **EARLY STAGES** The caterpillar is black with a brown head, and has white spots on its back. It feeds on eucalyptus.
• **DISTRIBUTION** Occurs in wooded areas of southern Australia.

INDO-AUSTRALIAN

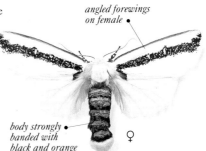
angled forewings on female
body strongly banded with black and orange
♀

Time of Flight ☾	Habitat ⚘	Wingspan 4–5cm (1½–2in)

Family NOTODONTIDAE	Species *Schizura ipomoeae*	Author Doubleday

MORNING-GLORY PROMINENT

This species is very variable, with the greyish brown ground colour either patterned with fine, dark lines and spots, or broadly banded or streaked with black to dark brown. Females are larger than males.
• **EARLY STAGES** The green and brown caterpillar feeds on the foliage of birch *(Betula)*, roses *(Rosa)*, and other plants.
• **DISTRIBUTION** From the USA to southern Canada.

NEARCTIC

pale, triangular spots on forewing margin
♂
pale-ringed, dark spot in middle of forewing

Time of Flight ☾	Habitat ⚘	Wingspan 4–5cm (1½–2in)

Family NOTODONTIDAE	Species *Stauropus fagi*	Author Linnaeus

LOBSTER MOTH

This large, greyish brown species has long, narrow forewings and small, rounded hindwings. Dark forms also occur in which the ground colour is dark grey.
• **EARLY STAGES** The name "lobster" derives from the caterpillar, which has a swollen, lobster-like tail. It feeds on beech *(Fagus sylvatica)*.
• **DISTRIBUTION** Europe across to temperate regions of Asia and Japan.

PALAEARCTIC

distinctive line of dark dots on forewing
♀
furry tip to abdomen

very pale hindwing fringes

Time of Flight ☾	Habitat ⚘	Wingspan 5.5–7cm (2¼–2¾in)

Family NOTODONTIDAE	Species *Clostera albosigma*	Author Fitch

SIGMOID PROMINENT

The pale brown forewings of this moth are patterned with light and dark lines and tipped with dark chocolate-brown. The common name derives from the white, sigma-shaped marking on the forewing.
• **EARLY STAGES** The caterpillar is black, covered with fine, white hairs, and has four orange-yellow lines along the back. It feeds on poplar *(Populus)*.
• **DISTRIBUTION** Found in southern Canada and the USA.

distinctively shaped, dark tip to forewings

slightly concave leading edge to forewings

♂

NEARCTIC

pale hindwings with no patterning

Time of Flight ☾	Habitat 🌳 ⚏ ⚏	Wingspan 3–4cm (1¼–1½in)

Family NOTODONTIDAE	Species *Datana ministra*	Author Drury

YELLOW-NECKED CATERPILLAR MOTH

This fairly large prominent belongs to a group of similar species called hand-maid moths. It can be distinguished from other similar species by the distinctively scalloped outer margin, shaded with black, that gives it an almost scorched appearance.
• **EARLY STAGES** The caterpillar is striped black and yellow. It feeds on the foliage of many broad-leaved trees, including apple *(Malus domestica)*.
• **DISTRIBUTION** Common in southern Canada and USA.

slightly darker, central band to forewings

♀

darker tip to body

distinctive scalloped forewing margins

NEARCTIC

Time of Flight ☾	Habitat ⚘ 🌳	Wingspan 4–5cm (1½–2in)

Family NOTODONTIDAE	Species *Phalera bucephala*	Author Linnaeus

BUFF-TIP

The buff-tip is a very distinctive species with its purplish grey forewings suffused with light silvery grey and lined with black and brown. The common name derives from the forewing that camouflages the moth when it rests.
• **EARLY STAGES** The caterpillar is orange-yellow with black bands. It feeds on the foliage of various broad-leaved trees and shrubs.
• **DISTRIBUTION** Widespread in Europe, and eastwards to Siberia.

buff patch resembles end of a twig

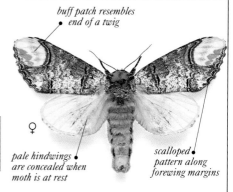

♀

pale hindwings are concealed when moth is at rest

scalloped pattern along forewing margins

PALAEARCTIC

Time of Flight ☾	Habitat ⚘	Wingspan 5.5–7cm (2¼–2¾in)

Family NOTODONTIDAE	Species *Anaphe panda*	Author Boisduval

BANDED BAGNEST

The white forewings of this striking moth are strongly patterned with dark chocolate-brown; the white hindwings lack markings. The sexes are similar.
• **EARLY STAGES** The hairy caterpillar is an off-white colour. It feeds on the foliage of *Diplorhynchus* and *Bridelia*.
• **DISTRIBUTION** Ranges from West Africa through to Kenya, Mozambique, and Natal.

AFROTROPICAL

black, feathered antennae

♀

tuft carries irritant hairs

Time of Flight ☾	Habitat ⸲⸲ ⸲⸲	Wingspan 4–5.5cm (1½–2¼in)

Family NOTODONTIDAE	Species *Epicoma melanosticta*	Author Donovan

COMMON EPICOMA MOTH

This beautiful species has white forewings speckled with black scaling and margined with a chequered pattern of black and yellow. The hindwings are blackish and richly margined with a golden, yellow, toothed pattern.
• **EARLY STAGES** The caterpillar is dark brown in colour and has tufts of short, brown hairs. It tends to feed on the foliage of eucalyptus.
• **DISTRIBUTION** Widespread in eastern and southern Australia.

INDO-AUSTRALIAN

very hairy thorax is characteristic of this species

yellow hindwing margins

♂

bright yellow tail-fans

Time of Flight ☾	Habitat ♣	Wingspan 4–5cm (1½–2in)

Family NOTODONTIDAE	Species *Thaumetopoea pityocampa*	Author Denis & Schiffermüller

PINE PROCESSIONARY MOTH

This is a rather drab species with greyish white forewings banded with dark, greyish brown.
• **EARLY STAGES** The greyish black caterpillar is covered with fine, white hairs along the sides, and has reddish brown warts. Caterpillars move in a head-to-tail procession in search of pine needles on which they feed. They can cause damage to forest plantations.
• **DISTRIBUTION** Found in Mediterranean countries, including those of North Africa.

PALAEARCTIC

darker brown leading edge to forewings

black spot on hindwings is present in both sexes

♀

broken, dark line along margin of forewings

Time of Flight ☾	Habitat ♣	Wingspan 4–5cm (1½–2in)

NOCTUIDAE

T HIS IS ONE OF THE LARGEST and most important of all moth families, with more than 25,000 species occurring worldwide. Noctuid moths are quite robust, and range in size from extremely small to very large. Most are nocturnal and for this reason are often known as owlet moths. The majority of the species are rather drab in colour, ranging from brown to grey, but others are quite bright and may even mimic butterflies. This family contains two important groups of caterpillars that are notorious pests: cutworms that bite through plant stems at ground level; and armyworms that swarm in bands and can devastate entire crops. The pupae of many species of Noctuid moths are formed in the soil at the base of the foodplant.

Family NOCTUIDAE	Species *Agrotis infusa*	Author Boisduval

BOGONG MOTH

The forewings of this moth range in colour from dark brown to greyish black, and are patterned with brown; the hindwings are dark greyish brown.
• **EARLY STAGES** The smooth cutworm caterpillar varies in colour from black to greenish brown or grey. In numbers it can cause serious damage to cultivated crops such as cereals and vegetables.
• **DISTRIBUTION** Can be found throughout temperate regions of southern Australia.

INDO-AUSTRALIAN

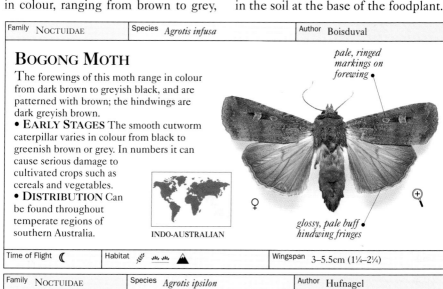

pale, ringed markings on forewing

♀

glossy, pale buff hindwing fringes

Time of Flight ☾	Habitat	Wingspan 3–5.5cm (1¼–2¼)

Family NOCTUIDAE	Species *Agrotis ipsilon*	Author Hufnagel

DARK SWORD-GRASS

The forewings of this species are pale brown with dark brown and black markings. The hindwings are translucent, greyish white with brown veins.
• **EARLY STAGES** The smooth caterpillar is dark purplish or greenish brown with grey lines and grey spots. It feeds on potatoes *(Solanum)*, tobacco *(Nicotiana)*, cabbage *(Brassica)*, and cotton *(Gossypium)*. In many regions it is regarded as a serious pest.
• **DISTRIBUTION** Throughout the world, including the temperate regions of North and South America, Asia, Australia, Africa, and Europe.

WORLDWIDE

black, Y-shaped marking, similar to the Greek letter ipsilon

♂

dark, wavy line at edge of hindwing

Time of Flight ☾	Habitat	Wingspan 4–5.5cm (1½–2¼in)

Family NOCTUIDAE	Species *Heliothis armigera*	Author Hübner

OLD WORLD BOLLWORM

This is a very variable moth. The forewing colour ranges from pale brownish yellow to reddish brown with darker lines or bands. The hindwings are translucent, pale grey with blackish brown veins and marginal bands. It is also known as the scarce bordered straw.
• **EARLY STAGES** The caterpillar has many colour forms ranging from brown to green, with granular skin and yellowish white lines along the back and sides. It feeds on a wide range of low-growing plants, including cultivated crops such as cotton *(Gossypium)*, tomatoes *(Lycopersicon)*, and maize *(Zea mays)*, and is a serious pest.
• **DISTRIBUTION** Range extends from Europe to Africa, Asia, and Australia. It also migrates to the British Isles, where it is called the scarce bordered straw.

highly effective camouflage •

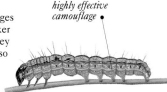

CATERPILLAR OF
HELIOTHIS ARMIGERA

minute, black dots along • forewing margin

PALAEARCTIC
AFROTROPICAL
INDO-AUSTRALIAN

♀

Time of Flight ☾	Habitat	Wingspan 3–4cm (1¼–1½in)

Family NOCTUIDAE	Species *Noctua pronuba*	Author Linnaeus

LARGE YELLOW UNDERWING

This distinctive moth is variable in both sexes. The forewings of the males range in colour from mid-brown to brownish black, while those of the females vary from reddish brown to yellowish or greyish brown. The hindwings of both sexes are deep yellow with a black border.
• **EARLY STAGES** The caterpillar is variable in colour, ranging from greyish brown to bright green, but can be recognized by the two rows of black dashes along the back. It feeds on dock *(Rumex)*, dandelion *(Taraxacum)*, and grasses, and is a minor pest of garden flowers and vegetables.
• **DISTRIBUTION** Europe, ranging to North Africa and western Asia.

♂

distinctive, black marking near forewing tip •

bright yellow • hindwing gives rise to the common name

PALAEARCTIC

• deep, black border to hindwings

♀

Time of Flight ☾	Habitat	Wingspan 5–6cm (2–2½in)

Family NOCTUIDAE	Species *Peridroma saucia*	Author Hübner

PEARLY UNDERWING

This notorious pest has reddish brown or greyish brown forewings, variably patterned with blackish brown. The hindwings are pearly grey, with brown veins and a dark brown suffusion towards the margins.
• **EARLY STAGES** The plump caterpillar is coloured greyish brown tinged with purplish red on its back.
• **DISTRIBUTION** Europe to Turkey, India, North Africa, and the Canary Isles, and North America.

slightly scalloped forewing margin

dark, kidney-shaped mark on forewing

pale hindwing fringes

♂

HOLARCTIC

Time of Flight ☾	Habitat	Wingspan 4–5.5cm (1½–2¼in)

Family NOCTUIDAE	Species *Cerapteryx graminis*	Author Linnaeus

ANTLER MOTH

This distinctive species gets its name from the antler-shaped, yellowish white markings on the brown forewings. These markings are variable and are often interspersed with dark brown streaks. It is attracted to thistles *(Cirsium)* and other flowers.
• **EARLY STAGES** The caterpillar is bronze, and has three pale brown stripes and a wrinkled, glossy skin. It feeds on various grasses.
• **DISTRIBUTION** Europe, across temperate Asia to Siberia, and North America.

blackish brown streaks along forewing margin

♂

pale fringes to hindwings

⊕

PALAEARCTIC

Time of Flight ☾ ☼	Habitat	Wingspan 2.5–3cm (1–1¼in)

Family NOCTUIDAE	Species *Mamestra brassicae*	Author Linnaeus

CABBAGE MOTH

The forewing of this dark brown, mottled moth is distinctively marked with shining, white spots and lines. The hindwing is dark greyish brown, becoming paler towards the base.
• **EARLY STAGES** The caterpillar is green when young, but in the final stage it is brown with a broad, orange band along each side. As its name suggests, this species feeds on cabbage *(Brassica)*, as well as various other plants.
• **DISTRIBUTION** Europe, and Asia, from India to Japan.

white, marginal line

kidney-shaped mark on forewing

pale line around hindwing margin

♀

⊕

PALAEARCTIC

Time of Flight ☾	Habitat	Wingspan 3–5cm (1¼–2in)

| Family NOCTUIDAE | Species *Mythimna unipuncta* | Author Haworth |

WHITE-SPECK

This distinctive, cinnamon-brown moth has a small, white spot in the middle of the forewings, which are often speckled with black and sometimes tinged with orange. The brown-veined hindwings are a glossy, translucent grey suffused with dark brown.
• **EARLY STAGES** The
caterpillar is greyish brown
and has an orange band along
the sides. It feeds on grasses.
• **DISTRIBUTION** North and
South America, Mediterranean
Europe, and parts of Africa.

HOLARCTIC

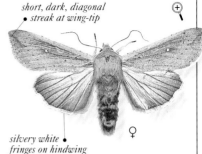

short, dark, diagonal
• *streak at wing-tip*

silvery white •
fringes on hindwing

♀

| Time of Flight ☽ | Habitat | Wingspan 3–4cm (1¼–1½in) |

| Family NOCTUIDAE | Species *Xanthopastis timais* | Author Cramer |

SPANISH MOTH

With its pink forewings marked with black and orange, this species is unmistakable. However, despite its bright colours, this moth is well camouflaged when it rests on tree trunks with folded wings.
• **EARLY STAGES** The
caterpillar is greyish black
spotted with white. It feeds
on the foliage of fig *(Ficus)*
and narcissi *(narcissus)*.
• **DISTRIBUTION** Tropical
South and Central America,
into the USA.

NEOTROPICAL
NEARCTIC

black, double "boomerang"
• *markings on forewing*

♀

furry, •
black body

black •
forewing
fringes

| Time of Flight ☽ | Habitat | Wingspan 4–4.5cm (1½–1¾in) |

| Family NOCTUIDAE | Species *Cucullia convexipennis* | Author Grote & Robinson |

BROWN HOODED OWLET

This moth belongs to a large and distinctive group known collectively as the sharks, presumably because of the streamlined appearance of their folded wings when they are at rest.
• **EARLY STAGES** The caterpillar is striped
with red and black. It feeds on the flowers of
aster, golden rod *(Solidago
virgaurea)*, and various
other low-growing plants.
• **DISTRIBUTION**
Widespread in the USA,
extending northwards
into southern Canada.

NEARCTIC

dark streak on
• *forewing*

♀

raised tufts •
along back
of body

• *pale marginal*
line on both fore-
and hindwing

| Time of Flight ☽ | Habitat | Wingspan 4–5cm (1½–2in) |

Family NOCTUIDAE	Species *Xanthia togata*	Author Esper

PINK-BARRED SALLOW

The common name of this brightly coloured moth
is misleading as it is not pink-barred at all. Its
forewings are yellow to orange-yellow, with a
broad red or purple band. The sexes are alike.
• **EARLY STAGES** The caterpillar is reddish
or purplish brown with dark
speckling. It feeds on sallow
catkins *(Salix)* and low plants.
• **DISTRIBUTION** Occurs
from Europe to temperate
Asia; also in southern Canada
and the northern USA.

sharply pointed
• forewing tips

reddish brown head
• and front of thorax

HOLARCTIC

♂

pale yellowish •
hindwings

Time of Flight ☾	Habitat 🌊 🌳	Wingspan 3–4cm (1¼–1½in)

Family NOCTUIDAE	Species *Acronicta psi*	Author Linnaeus

GREY DAGGER

The forewings of this moth vary in colour from
greyish white to dark grey, but they all have the
distinctive dagger-shaped marking on the margin
that gives rise to the common name. The sexes
are similar, but females have darker hindwings.
• **EARLY STAGES** The caterpillar is dark bluish
grey with a broad band of
yellow along the back and
red spots along the sides. It
feeds on deciduous trees.
• **DISTRIBUTION** Occurs
in Europe, through to North
Africa, and Central Asia.

fine, black, irregular line on
inner margin of forewings •

PALAEARCTIC

♂

• broken, black line
along margin of hindwings

Time of Flight ☾	Habitat 🌳 🌿 🌿	Wingspan 3–4.5cm (1¼–1¾in)

Family NOCTUIDAE	Species *Amphipyra pyramidoides*	Author Guenée

AMERICAN COPPER UNDERWING

This attractive moth is easily recognized by its
coppery brown hindwings. The dark brown
forewings are variably patterned with light and
dark lines. The sexes are similar.
• **EARLY STAGES** The green caterpillar feeds
on a wide range of broad-leaved trees and shrubs,
including apple *(Malus*
domestica) and species of
hawthorn *(Crataegus)*.
• **DISTRIBUTION**
Widespread from southern
Canada through the USA
south to Mexico.

white rings
in centre of
• forewings

NEARCTIC

♂

• finely scalloped, pale,
marginal lines on hindwings

Time of Flight ☾	Habitat 🌳	Wingspan 4–5cm (1½–2in)

Family NOCTUIDAE	Species *Busseola fusca*	Author Fuller

MAIZE STALK-BORER MOTH

This notorious maize and sorghum pest has rather rectangular forewings, varying in colour from reddish brown to dark blackish brown. The hindwings are shining brownish white. The sexes are similar.
• **EARLY STAGES** The caterpillar is dusky, purplish pink with a reddish brown head and greyish brown spots along the sides.
• **DISTRIBUTION** Occurs in wet savanna regions of Africa, south of the Sahara, where cereal crops are grown.

AFROTROPICAL

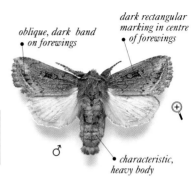

oblique, dark band on forewings

dark rectangular marking in centre of forewings

♂

characteristic, heavy body

Time of Flight ☾	Habitat	Wingspan 2.5–3cm (1–1¼in)

Family NOCTUIDAE	Species *Phlogophora iris*	Author Guenée

OLIVE ANGLE SHADES

This distinctive moth is prettily patterned on the forewings with olive-green and pinkish brown. The hindwings are brownish white, shaded with dark brown at the margin, with pinkish brown, marginal lines. The wing margins are scalloped.
• **EARLY STAGES** The caterpillar is known to feed on various types of low-growing plants, such as dandelion *(Taraxacum)* and docks *(Rumex)*.
• **DISTRIBUTION** Occurs in eastern and central Canada and the northern USA.

NEARCTIC

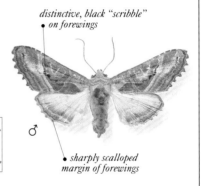

distinctive, black "scribble" on forewings

♂

sharply scalloped margin of forewings

Time of Flight ☾	Habitat	Wingspan 4–4.5cm (1½–1¾in)

Family NOCTUIDAE	Species *Spodoptera litura*	Author Fabricius

ORIENTAL LEAFWORM MOTH

The brown forewings of this widespread pest moth are intricately and variably patterned with pale lines and dark streaks. The hindwings are much paler, with translucent, silvery white and dark veins. The sexes are alike.
• **EARLY STAGES** The caterpillar ranges from greenish brown to dark grey, finely speckled with white. It feeds on a wide range of native and cultivated plants.
• **DISTRIBUTION** Range extends from India to South-east Asia and Australia.

INDO-AUSTRALIAN

black streaks on purplish grey band of forewings

forewing pattern continues on thorax

♂

dark, marginal line around hindwings

Time of Flight ☾	Habitat	Wingspan 3–4cm (1¼–1½in)

Family NOCTUIDAE	Species *Spodoptera exigua*	Author Hübner

SMALL MOTTLED WILLOW MOTH

This greyish brown, mottled moth is a notorious pest species in many parts of the world. It has translucent, pearly white hindwings with dark brown veins.
• **EARLY STAGES** The caterpillar varies in colour from green to dark grey, with black markings on the back and a pinkish brown line along the sides. It feeds on crops such as maize *(Zea mays)* and cotton *(Gossypium)*.
• **DISTRIBUTION** Virtually throughout the world, in both tropical and temperate regions.

WORLDWIDE

grey dots along • forewing border

♂

dark brown outline • to translucent hindwing

Time of Flight ☾	Habitat 🌿 ⏵⏴ ⏵⏴	Wingspan 2.5–3cm (1–1¼in)

Family NOCTUIDAE	Species *Syntheta nigerrima*	Author Guenée

BLACK TURNIP MOTH

One of two species in an exclusively Australian genus, this is a very dark moth with black forewings patterned with intense jet black.
• **EARLY STAGES** The green caterpillar has two white spots on the back near the tail. It feeds on a range of wild and cultivated plants, and is sometimes a serious pest of such field crops as turnip *(Brassica)*, sugar beet *(Beta vulgaris)*, and maize *(Zea mays)*.
• **DISTRIBUTION** From southern Queensland to south-western Australia and Tasmania.

INDO-AUSTRALIAN

front part of body thickly scaled to match black forewings •

♀

white base to • hindwings

• lightly scalloped wing margins

Time of Flight ☾	Habitat 🌿 ⏵⏴ ⏵⏴	Wingspan 4–4.5cm (1½–1¾in)

Family NOCTUIDAE	Species *Earias biplaga*	Author Walker

SPINY BOLLWORM MOTH

This pretty little moth is one of a group of species that are major pests of cultivated cotton in Africa and Asia. This species is very variable, ranging in forewing colour from moss-green to greenish yellow, and is sometimes strongly suffused with purplish red.
• **EARLY STAGES** The small, greyish brown caterpillar is finely banded with white and spotted with red, and has spines along the back and sides. It feeds on cotton *(Gossypium)* and related plants.
• **DISTRIBUTION** Widespread in Africa, south of the Sahara.

AFROTROPICAL

distinctive, squarish • forewings

dark purplish patch on • forewings

♀

⊕

characteristic dark • fringes on hindwings

Time of Flight ☾	Habitat 🌿 ⏵⏴ ⏵⏴	Wingspan 2–2.5cm (¾–1in)

Family NOCTUIDAE	Species *Pseudoips fagana*	Author Fabricius

GREEN SILVER-LINES

This aptly named moth has three silvery white, oblique lines on its green forewings, although a form exists in which there are only two lines. The forewing fringes are sometimes strongly tinged with red. Males have pale greenish yellow hindwings with white bases, whereas those of the female are pure white.
• **EARLY STAGES** The plump, green caterpillar is spotted and patterned with yellowish white. It has broad lines of the same colour along its back. The rear claspers are extra long and striped with red. It feeds on the foliage of many broad-leaved trees, particularly oaks *(Quercus)* and beech *(Fagus sylvatica)*.
• **DISTRIBUTION** Widespread in Europe, extending across temperate Asia to Siberia and Japan.

slender, pinkish red
• *antennae in both sexes*

♂

• *traces of pinkish red markings visible on hindwing*

♀

• *pure white hindwings*

PALAEARCTIC

Time of Flight ☾	Habitat ❦	Wingspan 3–4cm (1¼–1½in)

Family NOCTUIDAE	Species *Achaea janata*	Author Linnaeus

CASTOR SEMI-LOOPER MOTH

The forewings of this large Noctuid moth are variably lined and banded with shades of brown, but it is the distinctively patterned black and white hindwings that make this species easy to recognize.
• **EARLY STAGES** The long, slender caterpillar ranges in colour from black with fine, broken lines of orange-red, to pale pinkish brown with dark bands and pale mottling. It moves in a characteristic "looping" manner, hence the common name. The caterpillar feeds on castor oil plant *(Ricinus communis)*, cowpea *(Vigna ungiculata)*, chilli pepper *(Capsicum annuum)*, rose *(Rosa)*, and many other plants.
• **DISTRIBUTION** From India to Taiwan, Australia, and New Zealand.

characteristic "looping" poise of caterpillar •

CATERPILLAR OF
ACHAEA JANATA

two small, dark spots on forewing are a distinguishing • *feature*

♂

stout body indicates •
that this is a strong-flying species

• *white, marginal patches on hindwing*

INDO-AUSTRALIAN

Time of Flight ☾	Habitat 🌿 ⸱ ⸱	Wingspan 5.5–6cm (2¼–2½in)

Family NOCTUIDAE	Species *Catocala fraxini*	Author Linnaeus

CLIFDEN NONPAREIL

The forewings of this handsome species have a camouflage pattern of greyish white and dark greyish brown. The hindwings are blackish brown with a distinctive band of dusky blue. The sexes are similar.

PALAEARCTIC

• **EARLY STAGES** The long caterpillar is grey, mottled with brown. It is well camouflaged when it rests on a twig. It feeds primarily on ash *(Fraxinus excelsior)*, and aspen *(Populus tremula)*.

• **DISTRIBUTION** Widespread in central and northern Europe. Formerly resident in the British Isles, it now occurs there as an occasional migrant. Ranges across temperate Asia to Japan.

extremely slender antennae

♀

Time of Flight ☾	Habitat 🌳	Wingspan 7.5–9.5cm (3–3¾in)

Family NOCTUIDAE	Species *Catocala ilia*	Author Cramer

ILIA UNDERWING

This is one of a large number of red underwing moths in North America. The camouflaged forewings are quite variable in pattern, ranging from mottled dark greyish brown to almost black. The pinkish red hindwing has two broad, black, irregular bands. This species is also known as the beloved underwing or the wife. The sexes are alike. Moths are on the wing from summer to autumn.

• **EARLY STAGES** The long grey caterpillar has a distinctly rough skin and is well camouflaged when resting pressed to the surface of a twig. It feeds on the foliage of oaks *(Quercus)*.

• **DISTRIBUTION** One of the most widespread and abundant of the underwings in North America, ranging from southern Canada to Florida. A similar species, the dark crimson underwing *(Catocala sponsa)* occurs throughout Europe.

intricate patterning on forewings

pale mark in middle of forewing is sometimes white

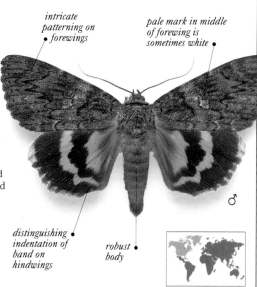

♂

distinguishing indentation of band on hindwings

robust body

NEARCTIC

Time of Flight ☾	Habitat 🌳	Wingspan 7–8cm (2¾–3¼in)

Family NOCTUIDAE	Species *Grammodes stolida*	Author Fabricius

THE GEOMETRICIAN

The forewings are brown banded with cream and dark chocolate brown while the hindwings are brown with white bands and chequered fringes. The sexes are similar.
• **EARLY STAGES** The caterpillar feeds on oaks *(Quercus)*, brambles *(Rubus)*, jujuba *(Zizyphus jujuba)*, and other trees and shrubs.
• **DISTRIBUTION** Mediterranean Europe, Africa, India, and South-east Asia.

PALAEARCTIC
AFROTROPICAL
INDO-AUSTRALIAN

Orange-brown band on forewings

♀

distinctive, white spot on hindwings

Time of Flight ☾	Habitat	Wingspan 2.5–4cm (1–1½in)

Family NOCTUIDAE	Species *Chrysodeixis subsidens*	Author Walker

AUSTRALIAN CABBAGE LOOPER

The forewings of this moth are reddish brown with greyish brown bands and distinctive, silvery white markings. The hindwings are greyish brown with greyish white at the base. The sexes are similar.
• **EARLY STAGES** The semi-looper caterpillar is known to be a pest of field and glasshouse crops.
• **DISTRIBUTION** Found in South and south-eastern Australia and central Queensland. It also occurs in Papua New Guinea, and two other islands, New Caledonia, and Fiji.

INDO-AUSTRALIAN

distinctive silvery white line of forewings

♀

pale brown fringe

Time of Flight ☾	Habitat	Wingspan 2.5–4cm (1–1½in)

Family NOCTUIDAE	Species *Autographa gamma*	Author Linnaeus

SILVER "Y" MOTH

The greyish brown forewing colour is variable. The hindwings are greyish white at the base with broad dark grey margins. The sexes are alike.
• **EARLY STAGES** The caterpillar is bright yellowish to bluish green with a pattern of fine white lines. It eats a variety of plants including clover *(Trifolium)* and lettuce *(Lactuca sativa)*.
• **DISTRIBUTION** Resident in southern Europe, North Africa and western Asia, but migrates northwards as far as the Arctic Circle each year.

PALAEARCTIC

gamma-shaped marking gives rise to the scientific name

♀

scalloped hindwing margin

Time of Flight ☾ ☼	Habitat	Wingspan 3–5cm (1¼–2in)

Family NOCTUIDAE	Species *Trichoplusia ni*	Author Hübner

THE NI MOTH

The forewings are mottled with brown, but they can be distinguished by a silvery white, U-shaped marking and a white spot. The hindwings are dark greyish brown, but paler towards the base.
• **EARLY STAGES** The green caterpillar is lined and spotted with white. It feeds on cabbage *(Brassica)*, maize *(Zea mays)*, and other crops.
• **DISTRIBUTION** Widespread in Europe, North Africa, and the temperate northern hemisphere.

irregular, pale marginal line on forewing

♂

HOLARCTIC

pale fringes with dark spots on hindwing

Time of Flight ☾	Habitat 🌾 🌿 🌿	Wingspan 3–4cm (1¼–1½in)

Family NOCTUIDAE	Species *Hypena proboscidalis*	Author Linnaeus

THE SNOUT

The snout is so-called because of the long, sensory mouthparts called palps that project in front of its head. The brown forewings are distinctively shaped and strongly pointed at the tips. The large, rounded hindwings are greyish brown. The sexes are alike.
• **EARLY STAGES** The long, slender caterpillar is green with yellowish rings and pale lines along the back and sides. It feeds on stinging nettles *(Urtica dioica)*.
• **DISTRIBUTION** Found where nettles abound throughout Europe, into temperate Asia.

distinctively curved forewing margin

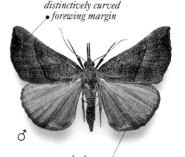

PALAEARCTIC

♂

dark grey hindwing fringes

Time of Flight ◑ ☾	Habitat 🌿 🌿	Wingspan 4–4.5cm (1½–1¾in)

Family NOCTUIDAE	Species *Aedia leucomelas*	Author Linnaeus

EASTERN ALCHYMIST

This species is most easily recognized by the distinctive hindwings, which have pure white bases and white spots on the fringe. The dark brown forewings may be marked with white.
• **EARLY STAGES** The caterpillar is bluish grey with orange-yellow stripes. It is known to feed on sweet potato *(Ipomoea batatas)*, and skeleton weed *(Chondrilla juncea)*.
• **DISTRIBUTION** Widespread in the Indo-Australian region and parts of southern Europe.

slightly scalloped forewing margin

INDO-AUSTRALIAN
PALAEARCTIC

♂

⊕

distinctive pattern on hindwing

Time of Flight ☾	Habitat 🌿 🌿 🌾	Wingspan 3–4cm (1¼–1½in)

Family NOCTUIDAE	Species *Alabama argillacea*	Author Hübner

COTTON MOTH

The forewings of this moth vary from pinkish to olive-brown. The adults can pierce the skins of fruit with their tongues, causing damage.
• **EARLY STAGES** The caterpillar is yellowish green, marked with black, with white lines along the back. It feeds on cotton plants *(Gossypium)*, and is a serious pest of cultivated cotton in the USA.
• **DISTRIBUTION** Tropical South and Central America to the temperate USA and Canada.

NEOTROPICAL
NEARCTIC

pale-centred, dark oval marking in centre of forewing

ringed appearance to body

♂

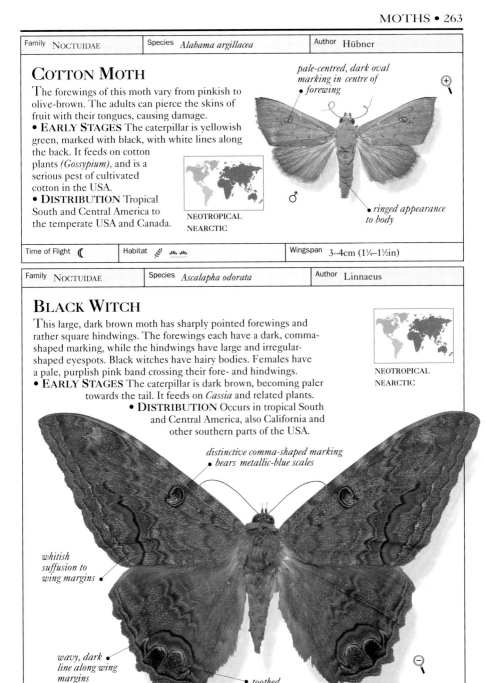

Time of Flight ☾	Habitat	Wingspan 3–4cm (1¼–1½in)

Family NOCTUIDAE	Species *Ascalapha odorata*	Author Linnaeus

BLACK WITCH

This large, dark brown moth has sharply pointed forewings and rather square hindwings. The forewings each have a dark, comma-shaped marking, while the hindwings have large and irregular-shaped eyespots. Black witches have hairy bodies. Females have a pale, purplish pink band crossing their fore- and hindwings.
• **EARLY STAGES** The caterpillar is dark brown, becoming paler towards the tail. It feeds on *Cassia* and related plants.
• **DISTRIBUTION** Occurs in tropical South and Central America, also California and other southern parts of the USA.

NEOTROPICAL
NEARCTIC

distinctive comma-shaped marking bears metallic-blue scales

whitish suffusion to wing margins

wavy, dark line along wing margins

♂

toothed appearance of eyespot

Time of Flight ☾	Habitat	Wingspan 11–15cm (4½–6in)

Family NOCTUIDAE	Species *Calyptra eustrigata*	Author Hampson

VAMPIRE MOTH

The vampire moth belongs to a group of moths noted for their ability to pierce the skin of fruits. This species has a barbed tongue capable of piercing the skin of mammals such as cattle and deer, and feeds on their blood.
• **EARLY STAGES**
Little seems to be known of the caterpillar or its foodplants.
• **DISTRIBUTION**
From India and Sri Lanka to Malaysia.

INDO-AUSTRALIAN

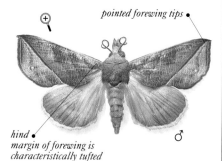

pointed forewing tips

hind margin of forewing is characteristically tufted

♂

Time of Flight ☾	Habitat 🌴 ⁜ ⁜	Wingspan 3–4cm (1¼–1½in)

Family NOCTUIDAE	Species *Scoliopteryx libatrix*	Author Linnaeus

THE HERALD

A very distinctive moth, the herald has reddish brown to purplish brown forewings with pale lines and bright orange scales towards the base.
• **EARLY STAGES** The long, slender caterpillar is velvety green with two fine, yellow lines along its back. It feeds on the foliage of willows *(Salix)*, and poplars *(Populus)*.
• **DISTRIBUTION**
Europe to North Africa; across temperate Asia to Japan; also in North America.

HOLARCTIC

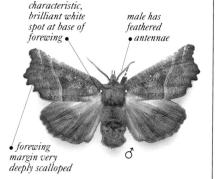

characteristic, brilliant white spot at base of forewing

male has feathered antennae

forewing margin very deeply scalloped

♂

Time of Flight ☾·	Habitat 🌳 ⁜ ⁜	Wingspan 4–5cm (1½–2in)

Family NOCTUIDAE	Species *Diphthera festiva*	Author Fabricius

HIEROGLYPHIC MOTH

This appropriately named moth is quite unmistakable, with yellow forewings distinctively patterned with metallic greyish blue, and three rows of blue-grey spots along the margin.
• **EARLY STAGES** The caterpillar is slate-blue to greenish grey with black stripes. It feeds on the foliage of sweet potato *(Ipomoea batatas)*.
• **DISTRIBUTION**
From tropical South and Central America to Florida and Texas in southern USA.

NEOTROPICAL

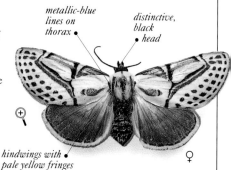

metallic-blue lines on thorax

distinctive, black head

hindwings with pale yellow fringes

♀

Time of Flight ☾	Habitat ⁂ 🌴 ⁜ ⁜	Wingspan 4–5cm (1½–2in)

| Family NOCTUIDAE | Species *Othreis fullonia* | Author Clerck |

TROPICAL FRUIT-PIERCER

This is a very distinctive,
large moth with orange or
orange-yellow hindwings
with black markings.
• **EARLY STAGES** The
long caterpillar varies in
colour from green to black,
and has well developed false
eyespots on the body.
• **DISTRIBUTION**
Tropical Africa, South-
east Asia, to Australia.

AFROTROPICAL
INDO-AUSTRALIAN

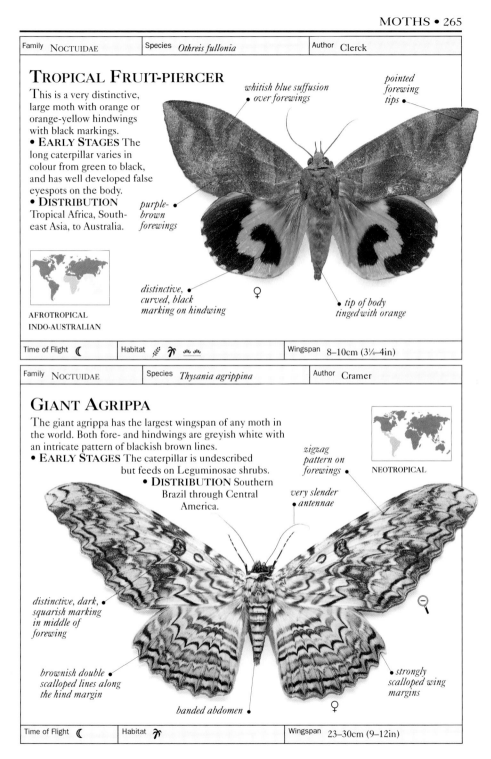

*whitish blue suffusion
over forewings*

*pointed
forewing
tips*

*purple-
brown
forewings*

*distinctive,
curved, black
marking on hindwing*

♀

*tip of body
tinged with orange*

| Time of Flight ☾ | Habitat | Wingspan 8–10cm (3¼–4in) |

| Family NOCTUIDAE | Species *Thysania agrippina* | Author Cramer |

GIANT AGRIPPA

The giant agrippa has the largest wingspan of any moth in
the world. Both fore- and hindwings are greyish white with
an intricate pattern of blackish brown lines.
• **EARLY STAGES** The caterpillar is undescribed
but feeds on Leguminosae shrubs.
    • **DISTRIBUTION** Southern
      Brazil through Central
      America.

NEOTROPICAL

*zigzag
pattern on
forewings*

*very slender
antennae*

*distinctive, dark,
squarish marking
in middle of
forewing*

*brownish double
scalloped lines along
the hind margin*

*strongly
scalloped wing
margins*

banded abdomen

♀

| Time of Flight ☾ | Habitat | Wingspan 23–30cm (9–12in) |

AGARISTIDAE

T HIS RELATIVELY small family of moths is composed of about 300 species that occur throughout the tropical forest regions of the world. They are similar in general appearance to moths of the family Noctuidae, but can usually be distinguished by their distinctive antennae which tend to be thickened towards the tips. Most of the Agaristid moths are day fliers; they have a rapid, powerful flight.

—— • ——

Many species are brightly coloured, and their caterpillars also appear to be avoided by predators, suggesting that they are distasteful to birds.

Family AGARISTIDAE	Species *Agarista agricola*	Author Donovan

LARGE AGARISTA

This striking and distinctive, black moth is variably patterned with bright orange, yellow, red, and metallic greyish blue. Males are generally smaller and darker with less extensive yellow markings at the base of the forewing.
• **EARLY STAGES** The caterpillar is patterned with bands of orange, yellowish white, and black. When fully grown, the white bands turn orange. It is known to feed by day on the foliage of various vines, including grapevine *(Vitis vinifera)*, *Cissus*, and *Cayratia*.
• **DISTRIBUTION** From northern Australia to Queensland and central NSW.

INDO-AUSTRALIAN

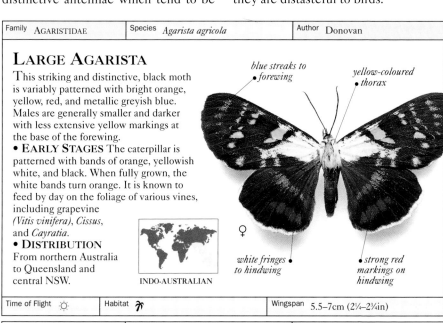

blue streaks to forewing

yellow-coloured thorax

♀

white fringes to hindwing

strong red markings on hindwing

Time of Flight ☼	Habitat 🜪	Wingspan 5.5–7cm (2¼–2¾in)

Family AGARISTIDAE	Species *Alypia octomaculata*	Author Fabricius

EIGHT-SPOTTED FORESTER

The North American representative of a largely tropical group, this species can be recognized by the distinctive wing spots. The forewing spots are pale yellow; the hindwing spots are white.
• **EARLY STAGES** The caterpillar is black with orange stripes and has a black-spotted, orange head. It feeds on grapevine *(Vitis vinifera)* and Virginia creeper *(Parthenocissus)*.
• **DISTRIBUTION** From south-eastern Canada right through the USA as far south as Texas.

NEARCTIC

characteristic pale yellow markings on sides of thorax

♀

both white hindwing spots are variable in size

Time of Flight ☼	Habitat 🌾 ⸬ ⸬	Wingspan 3–4cm (1¼–1½in)

LYMANTRIIDAE

THIS LARGE FAMILY of some 2,500 species occurs worldwide, but is most strongly represented in the tropics of Africa. The moths are similar to those of the family Noctuidae, but they are generally rather hairy in appearance. The wings are usually pale or dull in colour, although some tropical species are more brightly patterned. Some females have greatly reduced wings so they are unable to fly. Lymantriid moths like some other moth families lack functional tongues and cannot feed in the adult stage.

•

The caterpillars are hairy and often brightly coloured. Many species have body hairs grouped in distinctive toothbrush-like tufts, giving rise to the common name of tussock moths. The hairs of many of these caterpillars are irritant, and can cause rashes.

Family LYMANTRIIDAE	Species *Lymantria dispar*	Author Linnaeus

GYPSY MOTH

The sexes of this well-known pest moth are very different from each other. Males are pale yellowish brown with dark brown patterning on the forewings and dark brown borders to the hindwings, while the larger females are predominantly white with distinctive, black markings on the forewings. Gypsy moths are on the wing in summer. Males fly by day, but the sluggish females do not fly at all, and seldom move far from their emergence place.
• **EARLY STAGES** The caterpillar is bluish grey with raised, red and blue, tufted spots on the back. Although showing a preference for oaks *(Quercus)*, they will eat the foliage of most trees and shrubs and are often a serious pest, sometimes stripping the foliage from large areas of forest. There is one generation a year.
• **DISTRIBUTION** Originally a native of Europe and temperate Asia, this moth was introduced into North America in the mid-19th century with a view to using it for silk production. However, moths escaped and the species became established as one of the worst insect pests in North America. It is not regarded as such a serious pest in Europe.

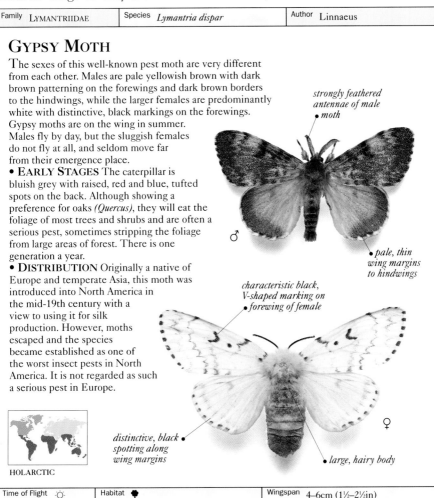

strongly feathered antennae of male moth

♂

pale, thin wing margins to hindwings

characteristic black, V-shaped marking on forewing of female

♀

distinctive, black spotting along wing margins

large, hairy body

HOLARCTIC

Time of Flight ☼	Habitat ♣	Wingspan 4–6cm (1½–2¼in)

Family LYMANTRIIDAE	Species *Calliteara pudibunda*	Author Linnaeus

PALE TUSSOCK

Males of this heavy-bodied moth have pale greyish white forewings with a dark greyish brown, central band. The pale hindwings have a dark brown band. Females are larger with white forewings, suffused and finely lined with greyish brown.
• **EARLY STAGES** The hairy caterpillar is yellow or pale green with two black bands between the body segments, and a bright pink tuft of hairs near the tail. It feeds on the foliage of many broad-leaved trees.
• **DISTRIBUTION** Widespread in Europe, extending across temperate Asia to Japan.

heavily feathered antennae of male

♂

crescent-shaped marking darker than on female

pale crescent-shaped marking on hindwing

♀

dark spotting to forewing margin

PALAEARCTIC

Time of Flight ☾	Habitat ⚘	Wingspan 5–7cm (2–2¾in)

Family LYMANTRIIDAE	Species *Euproctis chrysorrhoea*	Author Linnaeus

BROWN-TAIL MOTH

This distinctive, white moth is appropriately named because of the large tuft of loose brown scales at the tip of the body of the female. The male lacks the distinctive tuft, and has a slender brown "tail". These moths are on the wing in summer. This moth is single brooded.
• **EARLY STAGES** The hairy, brown caterpillar has orange-red markings on its back, and white, scale-like hairs along its sides. It lives in a communal silken nest, and feeds on the foliage of blackthorn *(Prunus spinosa)*, hawthorns *(Crataegus)*, and various fruit and ornamental trees. The caterpillar has barbed hairs, which can cause a painful rash.
• **DISTRIBUTION** Widespread throughout Europe, including the British Isles, south to North Africa and the Canary Islands. It was introduced into North America, but now it is mainly confined to the north-east coast of the USA.

distinctive red spots on back

CATERPILLAR OF
EUPROCTIS CHRYSORRHOEA

pure white wings lack markings

♀

tuft of poisonous hairs provide a protective cover for the eggs

HOLARCTIC

Time of Flight ☾	Habitat ⚘ ⸰⸰ ⸰⸰	Wingspan 3–4.5cm (1¼–1¾in)

Family LYMANTRIIDAE	Species *Euproctis edwardsii*	Author Newman

MISTLETOE BROWNTAIL MOTH

This hairy-looking, greyish brown moth lacks
distinctive markings, but the forewings appear
rather thinly scaled. The hindwing margins
are lightly tinged tinged with yellowish brown.
• EARLY STAGES The hairy caterpillar is dark
reddish brown with a white
band along the back. The hairs
can cause serious skin rashes. It
feeds on mistletoe *(Amyema)*.
• DISTRIBUTION Australia,
from Queensland and NSW to
Victoria and South Australia.

strongly feathered
antennae •

♀

hair-scales at tip •
of body protect eggs

INDO-AUSTRALIAN

Time of Flight ☾	Habitat 🌳	Wingspan 4–5.7cm (1½–2¼in)

Family LYMANTRIIDAE	Species *Dasychira pyrosoma*	Author Hampson

FIERY TUSSOCK

The fiery tussock is a striking white member of
this large genus of moths. The forewings of the
male are patterned with a series of very pale,
brownish yellow lines, which are more suffused
in the otherwise similar female. The abdomen is
patterned with bright orange-red bands and tufts.
• EARLY STAGES The
caterpillar is apparently
undescribed. Its foodplants are
Faurea, Parinari, and *Protea*.
• DISTRIBUTION Range
extends from Zimbabwe to
Transvaal and Natal.

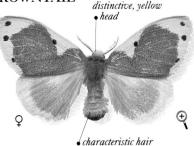

snow-white
• forewings

♂

body colour •
gives rise to the
scientific and common name

AFROTROPICAL

Time of Flight ☾	Habitat 🌿 🌿	Wingspan 4–5cm (1¾–2in)

Family LYMANTRIIDAE	Species *Euproctis hemicyclia*	Author Collenette

COLLENETTE'S VARIEGATED BROWNTAIL

This is one of a large group of South-east Asian
browntails that are variably patterned with
brown and yellow. Collenette's variegated
browntail is characterized by the presence of
black spots in the yellow margin of the forewing.
• EARLY STAGES Nothing is known of the
immature stages of this moth.
Many species in this group feed
on the foliage of tropical fruit,
Cocoa *(Cocao)*, *Lantana*, Acacia
and cultivated trees.
• DISTRIBUTION Found
in tropical forests of Sumatra.

distinctive, yellow
• head

♀

• characteristic hair
tuft on tip of abdomen

INDO-AUSTRALIAN

Time of Flight ☾	Habitat 🐾	Wingspan 3–4.5cm (1¼–1¾in)

Family LYMANTRIIDAE	Species *Orygia leucostigma*	Author Smith

WHITE-MARKED TUSSOCK MOTH

Males of this species have dark brownish grey wings. The forewings are banded with brown. The greyish white females are wingless.
• **EARLY STAGES** The brownish yellow caterpillar has long, plume-like tufts of black and white hairs at the head and tail. It feeds on a wide range of broad-leaved and coniferous trees and is sometimes a pest in forest plantations.
• **DISTRIBUTION** Found in North America and many other parts of the USA.

distinctive, black, marginal line on forewing

NEARCTIC

♂

small white patch gives rise to the common name

Time of Flight ☾	Habitat ♠	Wingspan 2.5–4cm (1–1½in)

Family LYMANTRIIDAE	Species *Leptocneria reducta*	Author Walker

CEDAR TUSSOCK

This rather dull brown moth is one of two species in the genus which is confined to Australia. The forewing has distinctive dark brown markings and an indistinct, brown, marginal line. The hindwings of the male are a pale translucent brown with darker fringes, and a pale brown marking.
• **EARLY STAGES** The hairy caterpillar feeds on the foliage of white cedar *(Melia azedarach)*, and trees that grow in urban areas.
• **DISTRIBUTION** Northern Queensland to southern NSW.

INDO-AUSTRALIAN

faint, dark dots along forewing margin

♂

characteristic, dark marking on hindwing

Time of Flight ☾	Habitat ♠ ⚬⚬⚬	Wingspan 3–7cm (1¼–2¾in)

Family LYMANTRIIDAE	Species *Aroa discalis*	Author Walker

BANDED VAPOURER

The sexes of this moth are completely different. Males are dark reddish brown, with pale orange markings on the forewings and broad orange bands on the hindwings. Females have orange-yellow wings and their forewings are patterned with brown lines. The body is orange and black.
• **EARLY STAGES** The hairy caterpillar is dark brown. It feeds on various grasses.
• **DISTRIBUTION** Range extends from Kenya and Zaire to Angola, Mozambique, and South Africa.

characteristic line of black spots along forewing margin of female

AFROTROPICAL

♂

distinctive, orange and black banded hindwing

Time of Flight ☾ ☀	Habitat ⚬⚬⚬	Wingspan 3–4cm (1¼–1½in)

Family LYMANTRIIDAE	Species *Lymantria monacha*	Author Linnaeus

BLACK ARCHES

This moth is easily recognized by its white forewings with black, zigzag bands, and its greyish brown hindwings with black-spotted, white fringes. The larger females have more elongate forewings.
• **EARLY STAGES** The hairy, grey caterpillar is lined and spotted with black on the back. It is known to feed on the foliage of oak *(Quercus)* and other broadleaves.
• **DISTRIBUTION** Europe, including the British Isles, to temperate Asia and Japan.

male has feathered antennae

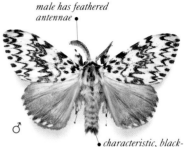

PALAEARCTIC

♂

characteristic, black-banded, pink abdomen

Time of Flight ☾	Habitat ⚘	Wingspan 4–5cm (1½–2in)

Family LYMANTRIIDAE	Species *Teia anartoides*	Author Walker

PAINTED APPLE MOTH

Males of this tussock moth are aptly named due to their orange-marked hindwings. The forewings are banded with shades of brown and black.
• **EARLY STAGES** The hairy caterpillar has a reddish brown head and four long tufts of bristles along the back. The body hairs may cause a rash if handled. The caterpillar feeds on the foliage of various broad-leaved trees and shrubs, and can be a minor pest in orchards.
• **DISTRIBUTION** Australia, from Queensland to South Australia, and Tasmania.

distinctive, brown wing pattern

INDO-AUSTRALIAN

♂

bright orange patches on hindwing

Time of Flight ☾	Habitat 🌿🌳	Wingspan 2.5–3cm (1–1¼in)

Family LYMANTRIIDAE	Species *Orgyia antiqua*	Author Linnaeus

THE VAPOURER MOTH

Males of this species are easily recognized by their rich reddish brown forewings. The females are virtually wingless and unable to fly.
• **EARLY STAGES** The hairy caterpillar is dark grey with red spots, and has four yellow or pale brown "toothbrush" tufts along its back, the hairs of which are irritant. It feeds on the foliage of various trees and shrubs.
• **DISTRIBUTION** Found throughout Europe, temperate Asia, Siberia, and USA.

crescent-shaped white spot

HOLARCTIC

♂

hairy hindwing margin

Time of Flight ☼	Habitat ⚘	Wingspan 2–3cm (¾–1¼in)

Family LYMANTRIIDAE	Species *Palasea albimacula*	Author Wallengren

WHITE BARRED GYPSY

The white barred gipsy moth has a central band of translucent, yellow-white spots on the forewing. The hindwings are a translucent, yellowish brown with brown veins.
• **EARLY STAGES** The hairy, orange-brown caterpillar is darker on the back, and has a black stripe along the sides. It is known to feed on the foliage of *Commiphora*.
• **DISTRIBUTION** Angola, Zambia, and Zimbabwe to Mozambique, Transvaal, Natal, and Cape Province.

characteristic question-mark shape patterning

♂

darker yellow fringes to hindwings

AFROTROPICAL

Time of Flight ☾	Habitat ᴡᴡ ᴡᴡ	Wingspan 2.5–4.5cm (1–1¾in)

Family LYMANTRIIDAE	Species *Psalis africana*	Author Kiriakoff

PENNANT TUSSOCK

The distinctively shaped forewing of this moth is pale yellowish brown with a broad, purplish grey band across the middle. The hindwing is coloured white to yellow-white.
• **EARLY STAGES** The caterpillar is yellow or yellowish brown with black markings, black plumes of hair, and silky white tufts in the middle of the back. It is known to feed on *Hyparrhenia*.
• **DISTRIBUTION** Throughout Africa.

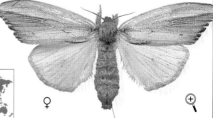

distinctively shaped wing-tips are pronounced in the female

♀

⊕

pale brown body

AFROTROPICAL

Time of Flight ☾	Habitat ᴡᴡ ᴡᴡ	Wingspan 3–4.5cm (1¼–1¾in)

Family LYMANTRIIDAE	Species *Perina nuda*	Author Fabricius

TRANSPARENT TUSSOCK

The transparent forewings and unusually shaped hindwings of the males of this species are quite unlike those of other tussock moths. The females have rounded, pale brown wings with darker brown scales on the forewing.
• **EARLY STAGES** The caterpillar has two tufts of dense, black hairs on the back, and greyish black hair tufts along the sides. It feeds on cultivated fig *(Ficus)*.
• **DISTRIBUTION** From India and Sri Lanka to Burma, China, and Taiwan.

transparent patches present on fore - and hindwings

♂

bright orange hair tuft at tip of abdomen

INDO-AUSTRALIAN

Time of Flight ☾	Habitat ⚘ 🌿	Wingspan 3–4.5cm (1¼–1¾in)

ARCTIIDAE

T HIS IS A LARGE family containing some 10,000 species of moths occurring worldwide, with the greatest numbers present in the tropics. Many are brightly patterned with warning colours, either because they are distasteful, or because they mimic less palatable species. The brightly striped patterns of some species have given rise to the common name of tiger

moths. Arctiidae moths have robust wings and bodies; moths belonging to the sub-family Lithosiinae tend to be generally smaller, with delicate wings and much more slender bodies.

•

The caterpillars of many Arctiids often feed on poisonous plants, storing the toxins in their bodies where they provide protection from predators.

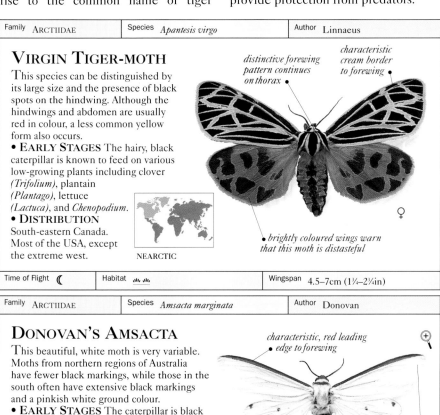

Family ARCTIIDAE	Species *Apantesis virgo*	Author Linnaeus

VIRGIN TIGER-MOTH

This species can be distinguished by its large size and the presence of black spots on the hindwing. Although the hindwings and abdomen are usually red in colour, a less common yellow form also occurs.
• **EARLY STAGES** The hairy, black caterpillar is known to feed on various low-growing plants including clover (*Trifolium*), plantain (*Plantago*), lettuce (*Lactuca*), and *Chenopodium*.
• **DISTRIBUTION** South-eastern Canada. Most of the USA, except the extreme west.

NEARCTIC

distinctive forewing pattern continues on thorax

characteristic cream border to forewing

♀

brightly coloured wings warn that this moth is distasteful

Time of Flight ☾	Habitat	Wingspan 4.5–7cm (1¾–2¾in)

Family ARCTIIDAE	Species *Amsacta marginata*	Author Donovan

DONOVAN'S AMSACTA

This beautiful, white moth is very variable. Moths from northern regions of Australia have fewer black markings, while those in the south often have extensive black markings and a pinkish white ground colour.
• **EARLY STAGES** The caterpillar is black with tufts of long hair. It feeds on capeweed (*Arctotheca calendula*) and other plants.
• **DISTRIBUTION** North-western Australia to South Australia.

INDO-AUSTRALIAN

characteristic, red leading edge to forewing

♂

black-banded abdomen

long, slender forewings with pointed tips

Time of Flight ☾	Habitat	Wingspan 4–4.5cm (1½–1¾in)

| Family ARCTIIDAE | Species *Arctia caja* | Author Linnaeus |

GARDEN TIGER

With its distinctive brown and white forewings and bluish black-spotted, red hindwings, this handsome moth is unmistakable. The markings on both fore- and hindwings are very variable. Rare yellow forms also occur.
• **EARLY STAGES** The black woolly bear caterpillar has rusty red hairs along the lower parts of the body and around the first body segments. It feeds on the foliage of a wide range of low-growing plants and broad-leaved shrubs.
• **DISTRIBUTION** Europe, across temperate Asia to Japan. Occurs less frequently in Canada and the northern USA.

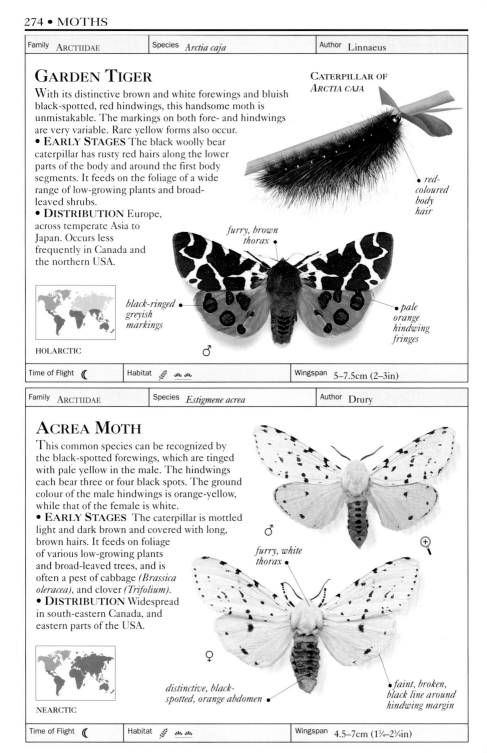

CATERPILLAR OF
ARCTIA CAJA

• *red-coloured body hair*

furry, brown thorax •

black-ringed greyish markings •

• *pale orange hindwing fringes*

HOLARCTIC

♂

| Time of Flight ☾ | Habitat | Wingspan 5–7.5cm (2–3in) |

| Family ARCTIIDAE | Species *Estigmene acrea* | Author Drury |

ACREA MOTH

This common species can be recognized by the black-spotted forewings, which are tinged with pale yellow in the male. The hindwings each bear three or four black spots. The ground colour of the male hindwings is orange-yellow, while that of the female is white.
• **EARLY STAGES** The caterpillar is mottled light and dark brown and covered with long, brown hairs. It feeds on foliage of various low-growing plants and broad-leaved trees, and is often a pest of cabbage *(Brassica oleracea)*, and clover *(Trifolium)*.
• **DISTRIBUTION** Widespread in south-eastern Canada, and eastern parts of the USA.

♂

⊕

furry, white thorax •

♀

distinctive, black-spotted, orange abdomen •

• *faint, broken, black line around hindwing margin*

NEARCTIC

| Time of Flight ☾ | Habitat | Wingspan 4.5–7cm (1¾–2¾in) |

Family ARCTIIDAE	Species *Ecpantheria scribonia*	Author Stoll

GIANT LEOPARD MOTH

This striking species can be recognized quite easily by the distinctive pattern of blackish brown to bluish black, ring-like markings on the forewing.
• **EARLY STAGES** The hairy caterpillar is black with crimson rings between the segments, which are revealed when it curls up in a defensive position. It feeds on a many plants, including cherry *(Prunus)*, and banana *(Musa)*.
• **DISTRIBUTION** South-eastern Canada through eastern USA to Mexico. Common in the southern part of its range.

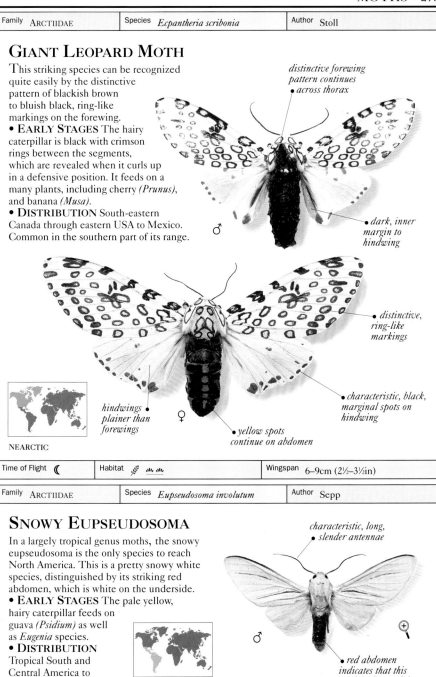

distinctive forewing pattern continues • across thorax

• dark, inner margin to hindwing

♂

• distinctive, ring-like markings

• characteristic, black, marginal spots on hindwing

hindwings • plainer than forewings

♀

• yellow spots continue on abdomen

NEARCTIC

Time of Flight ☾	Habitat	Wingspan 6–9cm (2½–3½in)

Family ARCTIIDAE	Species *Eupseudosoma involutum*	Author Sepp

SNOWY EUPSEUDOSOMA

In a largely tropical genus moths, the snowy eupseudosoma is the only species to reach North America. This is a pretty snowy white species, distinguished by its striking red abdomen, which is white on the underside.
• **EARLY STAGES** The pale yellow, hairy caterpillar feeds on guava *(Psidium)* as well as *Eugenia* species.
• **DISTRIBUTION** Tropical South and Central America to the southern USA.

characteristic, long, • slender antennae

♂

⊕

• red abdomen indicates that this moth is distasteful

NEOTROPICAL

Time of Flight ☾	Habitat	Wingspan 3–4cm (1¼–1½in)

Family ARCTIIDAE	Species *Hyphantria cunea*	Author Drury

FALL WEBWORM MOTH

This moth is sometimes marked with greyish brown spots on the forewing and black spots on the hindwing. The degree of spotting can vary.
• **EARLY STAGES** The caterpillar is green with black spots, and is covered with long, white hair. It feeds on the foliage of various broad-leaved trees and shrubs.
• **DISTRIBUTION** Southern Canada and the USA. Also in central Europe and Japan.

HOLARCTIC

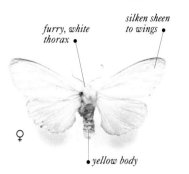

silken sheen to wings •

furry, white thorax •

♀

• *yellow body*

Time of Flight ☾	Habitat ♠	Wingspan 2.5–4cm (1–1½in)

Family ARCTIIDAE	Species *Lophocampa caryae*	Author Harris

HICKORY TUSSOCK MOTH

Also known as the hickory tiger moth, this is a distinctive species with golden-brown forewings patterned with translucent, white spots.
• **EARLY STAGES** The caterpillar is covered with pale grey hairs with a few black tufts on the back. It feeds on the foliage of hickory *(Carya),* walnut *(Juglans),* and other broad-leaved trees.
• **DISTRIBUTION** Southern Canada through the USA to Central America.

NEARCTIC
NEOTROPICAL

elongate, rather pointed forewings •

♀

robust, golden- brown body of female moth •

Time of Flight ☾	Habitat ♠	Wingspan 4–5.5cm (1½–2¼in)

Family ARCTIIDAE	Species *Paracles laboulbeni*	Author Barnes

WATER TIGER

Males of this brown moth tend to have darker brown forewings and pale hindwings; the larger females have yellow-brown fore- and hindwings.
• **EARLY STAGES** The hairy, black, woolly bear caterpillar is capable of living underwater and can swim with ease. Air is trapped between the dense body hairs allowing it to remain underwater. It feeds on water plants of the genus *Mayaca.*
• **DISTRIBUTION** This species is found in tropical South America.

NEOTROPICAL

male forewing is shorter and less triangular than • *female*

feathered antennae • *of male moth*

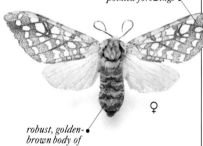

♂

thinly scaled wings •

Time of Flight ☾	Habitat 〰	Wingspan 3–4.5cm (1¼–1¾in)

Family ARCTIIDAE	Species *Premolis semirufa*	Author Walker

SEMIRUFOUS TIGER

A pretty moth, it has yellow-brown patterned forewings. Its hindwings and body are flushed with pink as a warning that it is distasteful.
• **EARLY STAGES** The hairy caterpillar lives around the rubber tree *(Hevea braziliensis)*. It is notorious among rubber tappers as its body hairs are highly irritant if touched.
• **DISTRIBUTION** Occurs in tropical South America.

semi-transparent area towards wing-tip

♂

hindwings plainer than forewings

distinctive concave hindwing

NEOTROPICAL

Time of Flight ☾	Habitat 🌴	Wingspan 4–6cm (1½–2½in)

Family ARCTIIDAE	Species *Phragmatobia fuliginosa*	Author Linnaeus

RUBY TIGER

The ruby tiger is recognizable by its translucent, brownish red forewings and pink or red hindwings with large, black, marginal spots. The forewings can be pale reddish or greyish brown.
• **EARLY STAGES** The brown caterpillar is covered with reddish or yellowish brown hairs. It feeds on a wide range of low-growing plants, including docks *(Rumex)*.
• **DISTRIBUTION** Europe to North Africa and Japan; Canada and northern USA.

characteristic, central black spots on forewing

furry, brown thorax

♀

rows of black spots on red abdomen

hindwings more vivid than forewings

HOLARCTIC

Time of Flight ☾	Habitat 🌸 ⚘ ⚘	Wingspan 3–4cm (1¼–1½in)

Family ARCTIIDAE	Species *Rhodogastria crokeri*	Author Macleay

CROKER'S FROTHER

These moths have elongate, brown forewings with a translucent, pale central region and a yellowish white base. The hindwings are yellowish white.
• **EARLY STAGES** Little is known of this moth. Some related species are known to feed on the native vine *Gymnanthera nitida*, others feed on plants containing heart poisons, so it may be poisonous.
• **DISTRIBUTION** North-western Australia to Queensland and northern NSW.

distinctive, black-spotted thorax

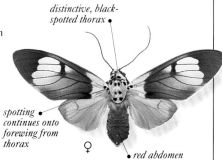

spotting continues onto forewing from thorax

♀

red abdomen suggests that this species is poisonous

INDO-AUSTRALIAN

Time of Flight ☾	Habitat 🌴 ⚘	Wingspan 5.5–7cm (2¼–2¾in)

| Family ARCTIIDAE | Species *Pyrrharctia isabella* | Author Smith |

ISABELLA TIGER MOTH

The forewings of this common moth vary in colour from pale orange-yellow to orange-brown, and are sometimes patterned with faint brown lines. There are a few black spots along the outer margins, particularly towards the wing-tips.
• **EARLY STAGES** The hairy caterpillar is black at either end with a broad, central band of reddish brown. It is known to feed on the foliage of a wide range of low-growing plants and broad-leaved trees.
• **DISTRIBUTION** Widespread in Canada and the USA.

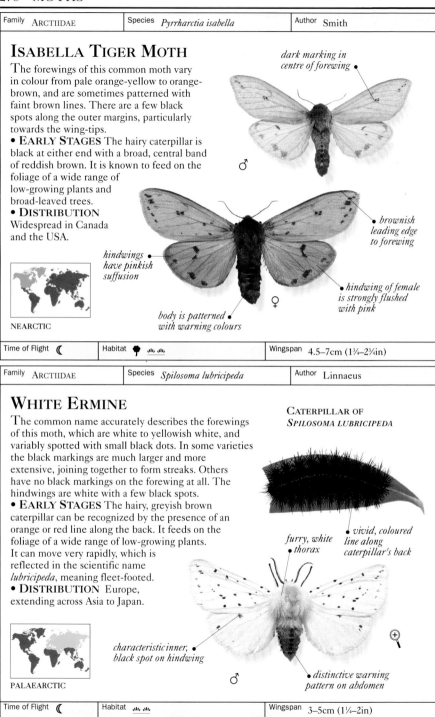

dark marking in centre of forewing

♂

brownish leading edge to forewing

hindwings have pinkish suffusion

hindwing of female is strongly flushed with pink

♀

body is patterned with warning colours

NEARCTIC

| Time of Flight ☾ | Habitat 🌿 ⸲ ⸲ | Wingspan 4.5–7cm (1¾–2¾in) |

| Family ARCTIIDAE | Species *Spilosoma lubricipeda* | Author Linnaeus |

WHITE ERMINE

The common name accurately describes the forewings of this moth, which are white to yellowish white, and variably spotted with small black dots. In some varieties the black markings are much larger and more extensive, joining together to form streaks. Others have no black markings on the forewing at all. The hindwings are white with a few black spots.
• **EARLY STAGES** The hairy, greyish brown caterpillar can be recognized by the presence of an orange or red line along the back. It feeds on the foliage of a wide range of low-growing plants. It can move very rapidly, which is reflected in the scientific name *lubricipeda*, meaning fleet-footed.
• **DISTRIBUTION** Europe, extending across Asia to Japan.

CATERPILLAR OF
SPILOSOMA LUBRICIPEDA

vivid, coloured line along caterpillar's back

furry, white thorax

characteristic inner, black spot on hindwing

♂

distinctive warning pattern on abdomen

PALAEARCTIC

| Time of Flight ☾ | Habitat ⸲ ⸲ | Wingspan 3–5cm (1¼–2in) |

Family ARCTIIDAE	Species *Teracotona euprepia*	Author Hampson

VEINED TIGER

This moth has cream-coloured forewings veined with brown. The transverse, brown bands are variable in width and are sometimes entirely absent. The hindwings are dark pink.
• **EARLY STAGES** Little is known of this species, except that it feeds on tobacco *(Nicotiana tabacum)*.
• **DISTRIBUTION** Angola and Zimbabwe to Zambia and across to Mozambique.

AFROTROPICAL

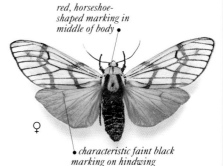

red, horseshoe-shaped marking in middle of body •

♀

• *characteristic faint black marking on hindwing*

Time of Flight ☾	Habitat ⸖⸖ ⸖⸖	Wingspan 4–5.5cm (1½–2¼in)

Family ARCTIIDAE	Species *Utetheisa pulchella*	Author Linnaeus

CRIMSON SPECKLED

This beautiful and distinctive moth has yellowish white forewings patterned with black and red markings. The hindwing is white with irregular, black margins.
• **EARLY STAGES** The hairy, grey caterpillar is marked with transverse, orange bars and longitudinal, white lines. It feeds on borage *(Borago officinalis)* and forget-me-not *(Myosotis)*.
• **DISTRIBUTION** Mediterranean Europe to Africa and Middle East.

PALAEARCTIC

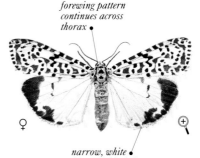

forewing pattern continues across thorax •

♀

⊕

narrow, white • fringe on hindwing

Time of Flight ☼	Habitat ⸖⸖ ⸖⸖	Wingspan 3–4cm (1¼–1½in)

Family ARCTIIDAE	Species *Utetheisa ornatrix*	Author Linnaeus

ORNATE MOTH

This attractive species can be distinguished from the closely related bella moth *(Utetheisa bella)* by the mainly white ground colour of the hindwings. The extent of pink is very variable on the forewing.
• **EARLY STAGES** The hairy caterpillar feeds on the foliage of plants of the pea family (Leguminosae).
• **DISTRIBUTION** Tropical South and Central America, as far north as Florida.

NEOTROPICAL

spotting continues across thorax •

⊕

♀

pale pink, triangular • spot on hindwing tip

Time of Flight ☼	Habitat ⸖⸖ ⸖⸖	Wingspan 3–4.5cm (1¼–1¾in)

Family ARCTIIDAE	Species *Termessa sheperdi*	Author Newman

SHEPERD'S FOOTMAN

This attractively marked moth belongs to a genus of twelve species peculiar to Australia. Most species are boldly marked with patterns of orange and black. The hindwings are a deeper orange-yellow with distinctive black markings on the margins.

• **EARLY STAGES**
Little seems to be known about this moth.

• **DISTRIBUTION**
Occurs in NSW and Victoria in Australia.

INDO-AUSTRALIAN

orange-yellow forewings, banded with black

♂

black marking on hindwing sometimes lacks curved "tail"

Time of Flight ☽	Habitat 🌳	Wingspan 3–4cm (1¼–1½in)

Family ARCTIIDAE	Species *Eilema complana*	Author Linnaeus

SCARCE FOOTMAN

This is one of a group of footman moths with narrow, shiny, grey forewings with a bold, golden yellow stripe along the leading edge. Scarce footman moths visit flowers of thistles, and related plants, at dusk.

• **EARLY STAGES** The hairy, grey caterpillar has rows of alternate orange and white spots along the back, and a yellow stripe along the sides. It feeds on various lichens.

• **DISTRIBUTION**
Europe, across temperate Asia to Siberia, and North America.

orange head and collar

yellow forewing stripe extends onto fringe

HOLARCTIC

♂

yellow tip to abdomen

Time of Flight ☽	Habitat 🌳 ⸲⸲⸲	Wingspan 3–4cm (1¼–1½in)

Family ARCTIIDAE	Species *Lithosia quadra*	Author Linnaeus

FOUR-SPOTTED FOOTMAN

It is the female of this relatively large footman moth that earns the name, four-spotted. Each forewing has two black spots, which vary in size. The forewing of the male is grey, shading to a darker orange-yellow at the base, and over the thorax.

• **EARLY STAGES** The caterpillar has a yellowish band, with red spots. It feeds on *Peltigera canina* and other lichens.

• **DISTRIBUTION**
Widespread in Europe, extending to temperate Asia and to Japan.

forewing fringe suffused with grey

PALAEARCTIC

♂

distinctively shaped, broad hindwing

Time of Flight ☽	Habitat 🌳	Wingspan 3–5.5cm (1¼–2¼in)

Family ARCTIIDAE	Species *Amphicallia bellatrix*	Author Dalman

BEAUTIFUL TIGER

The forewings and hindwings of this moth are bright orange with blue-black, irregular stripes which are outlined with a thin black outline.
• **EARLY STAGES** The red-headed caterpillar is white with grey hairs and black, transverse bands. It feeds on *Crotalaria* and plants of the pea family (Leguminosae).
• **DISTRIBUTION** Found from Kenya to Zambia, Mozambique, and the Cape Province.

AFROTROPICAL

forewing pattern extends onto • thorax

♀

abdomen • characteristically spotted

Time of Flight ☾	Habitat ▲ 🌴	Wingspan 5–7cm (2–2¾in)

Family ARCTIIDAE	Species *Nyctemera amica*	Author White

AUSTRALIAN MAGPIE MOTH

This is an easily recognized species, having black-brown wings with yellowish white spots. The black and orange ringed abdomen suggests that this moth is distasteful. The sexes are similar, but females tend to be smaller than males.
• **EARLY STAGES** The hairy, black caterpillar of this species has red stripes along the back and sides. It feeds on the foliage of *Senecio*.
• **DISTRIBUTION** Widespread throughout most of Australia.

INDO-AUSTRALIAN

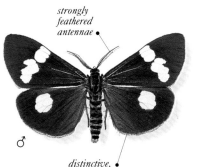
strongly feathered antennae •

♂

distinctive, • orange fringes

Time of Flight ☾ ☀	Habitat 〜 〜	Wingspan 4–4.5cm (1½–1¾in)

Family ARCTIIDAE	Species *Callimorpha dominula*	Author Linnaeus

SCARLET TIGER

This moth has greenish black forewings, spotted with yellowish white, but sometimes these spots are greatly reduced in size.
• **EARLY STAGES** The caterpillar is black with tufts of black and grey hairs, and broken bands of yellowish white along the back and sides. It feeds on comfrey *(Symphytum officinale)*, dock *(Rumex)* and other plants.
• **DISTRIBUTION** Found throughout Europe, and eastwards into temperate Asia.

PALAEARCTIC

forewing pattern continues across thorax •

♂

• abdomen is red with black central stripe

Time of Flight ☀	Habitat 〜 〜	Wingspan 4.5–5.5cm (1¾–2¼in)

Family ARCTIIDAE	Species *Euplagia quadripunctaria*	Author Poda

JERSEY TIGER

This species has black stripes on yellowish white forewings. The black-spotted hindwings are usually red, but a yellow variety also exists.
• **EARLY STAGES** The caterpillar is dark brown, covered with short yellow-brown hair with yellow bands on its back and sides. It feeds on the foliage of a range of low-growing plants.
• **DISTRIBUTION** Europe, extending across temperate Asia.

unusually angled • stripes on forewings

PALAEARCTIC

♀

Time of Flight ☾ ☼	Habitat 🌳 ⚘ ⚘	Wingspan 5–6cm (2–2½in)

Family ARCTIIDAE	Species *Tyria jacobeae*	Author Linnaeus

CINNABAR MOTH

This day-flying moth is often mistaken for a butterfly. It is easily recognized by its forewings, which are distinctively streaked and spotted with red. The hindwings are red, though yellow forms occur occasionally.
• **EARLY STAGES** The orange-yellow caterpillar is boldly ringed with black and feeds openly on ragwort and groundsel *(Senecio)*.
• **DISTRIBUTION** Widespread in Europe and the British Isles.

greenish black • forewings

PALAEARCTIC

♀

glossy black body •

• black hindwing fringes

Time of Flight ☼	Habitat ⚘ ⚘	Wingspan 3–4.5cm (1¼–1¾in)

Family ARCTIIDAE	Species *Antichloris viridis*	Author Druce

BANANA MOTH

This unusual moth has slender, pointed forewings that are metallic blue-green or black. In many specimens, two small tufts of red, hair-like scales are visible behind the head, indicating that it is a poisonous species.
• **EARLY STAGES** The caterpillar is covered with pale yellow hairs. It is known to feed on banana foliage *(Musa)* and is regarded as a pest.
• **DISTRIBUTION** Found in South and Central America.

antennae are strongly feathered at the base, and taper to a slender tip •

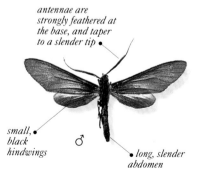

NEOTROPICAL

small, • black hindwings

♂

• long, slender abdomen

Time of Flight ☼	Habitat 🌾	Wingspan 3–4cm (1¼–1½in)

Family ARCTIIDAE	Species *Ctenucha virginica*	Author Esper

VIRGINIAN CTENUCHA

The most distinctive feature of this dark greyish brown moth is its brilliant, metallic-blue abdomen. When feeding from flowers, the Virginian ctenucha resembles a wasp.
• **EARLY STAGES** The variable, grey caterpillar is covered with yellow and black hairs. It feeds mainly on grasses and sedges.
• **DISTRIBUTION** Canada and northern parts of the USA.

metallic blue runs onto forewing base •

• *bright orange head*

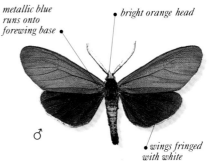

♂

• *wings fringed with white*

NEARCTIC

Time of Flight ☾ ☼	Habitat 〃 〃	Wingspan 4–5cm (1½–2in)

Family ARCTIIDAE	Species *Euchromia lethe*	Author Fabricius

THE BASKER

The wings of this beautiful moth are black with distinctive window-like patches of pale orange-yellow and white. The forewings are marked with small, central flashes of metallic-blue, and the body is ringed with vivid colours.
• **EARLY STAGES** Little is known about this common moth, but the caterpillars are believed to feed on plants of the family Convolvulaceae.
• **DISTRIBUTION** West Africa and the Congo Basin.

head has a blue spot and an orange-red collar •

♂

• *body is ringed with brilliant orange, black, red, white, and dark metallic blue*

AFROTROPICAL

Time of Flight ☼	Habitat 〃 〃	Wingspan 4–5cm (1½–2in)

Family ARCTIIDAE	Species *Syntomis phegea*	Author Linnaeus

NINE-SPOTTED MOTH

This blue-black moth has white spots on the fore- and hindwings. It is also known as the yellow-belted burnet because of the broad, yellow band on the abdomen; it does not belong to the same family as other burnet moths (see Zygaenidae, pp. 288–290).
• **EARLY STAGES** The hairy, grey caterpillar is known to feed on various low-growing plants.
• **DISTRIBUTION** Central and southern Europe, extending to central Asia.

antennae are white at the tips •

six spots on forewing

♂

• *yellow marking at back of thorax*

PALAEARCTIC

Time of Flight ☼	Habitat ▲ 〃 〃	Wingspan 3–4cm (1¼–1½in)

CASTNIIDAE

T HIS IS A RELATIVELY small family of some 200 species of tropical moth occurring mainly in South and Central America. They are generally medium to large, robust, day-flying moths that are often mistaken for butterflies. The forewings are usually dull in colour and provide camouflage when the moths are at rest, but the hindwings are sometimes brilliantly coloured. These bright colours are revealed quite suddenly, with any wing movement if the moth is disturbed, and can startle potential predators, allowing the moth to make an escape.

———— • ————

The caterpillars of Castniid moths are mainly root and stem borers. They feed while they are concealed within the actual plants.

Family CASTNIIDAE	Species *Castnia licus*	Author Fabricius

GIANT SUGARCANE-BORER

This distinctive and very butterfly-like moth can be recognized by the yellowish white, diagonal bands on the brownish black forewings, although other forewing markings are rather variable. The hindwings are banded with white and have a series of square, red spots along the margin.
• **EARLY STAGES** The white, grub-like caterpillar bores into stems of sugarcane *(Saccharum oficinarum)*. Discovered to be a sugarcane pest at the turn of the century, it has subsequently also become a pest of cultivated bananas *(Musa)*, and probably feeds on the roots of related native plants in the wild.
• **DISTRIBUTION** Widespread in tropical South and Central America, particularly where sugarcane and bananas are grown.

NEOTROPICAL

distinctive boring caterpillar •

antennae are thickened and hooked • *at the tips*

♀

• *large wings make this moth a powerful flier*

**CATERPILLAR OF
CASTNIA LICUS**

Time of Flight ☀	Habitat 🌿 🌴	Wingspan 6–10cm (2½–4in)

Family CASTNIIDAE	Species *Divana diva*	Author Butler

DIVA MOTH

This species is confined to Central and South America and is notable for its brilliantly coloured hindwings. The forewings of this moth are well camouflaged with a pattern of dark yellowish brown, with white spots, resembling a dead leaf. The hindwings are an excellent example of flash coloration with deep, metallic violet-blue, bordered with black and orange-red.

NEOTROPICAL

• **EARLY STAGES** Nothing appears to be known about the caterpillar or its foodplants.
• **DISTRIBUTION** Widespread in tropical South and Central America.

characteristic, slightly curved wing-tips •

distinctive white • spotting

• paler orange colour on forewings

black fringes • to hindwing

metallic-blue • bases to hindwings

• orange-red border to hindwing

♀

Time of Flight ☼	Habitat 🌳	Wingspan 6–9.5cm (2½–3¾in)

Family CASTNIIDAE	Species *Synemon parthenoides*	Author Felder

ORANGE-SPOTTED CASTNIID

This is one of a number of species belonging to this solely Australian genus of Castniid moths. The forewings have a dull pattern of greyish brown and white, while the hindwings are brownish black, spotted with orange-yellow.
• **EARLY STAGES** The pinkish white caterpillar feeds in tussocks of sedge *(Lepidosperma carphoides).*
• **DISTRIBUTION** This species occurs from Victoria to South Australia.

distinctive clubbed antennae • with sharply pointed tips

INDO-AUSTRALIAN

♂

• mottled hindwing fringes

Time of Flight ☼	Habitat 🌸	Wingspan 3–4.5cm (1¼–1¾in)

SESIIDAE

T HIS worldwide family of over 1,000 species is notable for containing some of the best wasp mimics among all insects. Most of these small- to medium-sized moths have areas of the wings that are lacking in scales, hence the common name clearwings that is applied to the family as a whole. The hind legs are usually clothed with dense, long hairs. These moths are not only superb wasp mimics in appearance, but also in behaviour, some even producing a buzzing sound when in flight. They are mostly day-flying species and frequently visit flowers. The caterpillars of clearwing moths mostly tunnel in stems of trees, shrubs and other plants, and a number are regarded as pests.

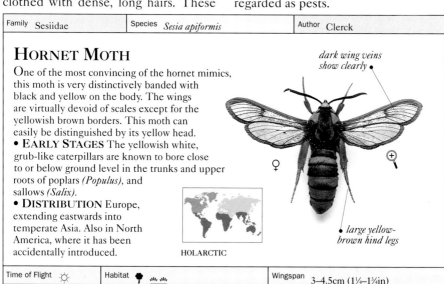

Family Sesiidae	Species *Sesia apiformis*	Author Clerck

HORNET MOTH

dark wing veins show clearly

One of the most convincing of the hornet mimics, this moth is very distinctively banded with black and yellow on the body. The wings are virtually devoid of scales except for the yellowish brown borders. This moth can easily be distinguished by its yellow head.
• **EARLY STAGES** The yellowish white, grub-like caterpillars are known to bore close to or below ground level in the trunks and upper roots of poplars *(Populus)*, and sallows *(Salix)*.
• **DISTRIBUTION** Europe, extending eastwards into temperate Asia. Also in North America, where it has been accidentally introduced.

HOLARCTIC

♀

large yellow-brown hind legs

Time of Flight ☼	Habitat 🌳 ⚘ ⚘	Wingspan 3–4.5cm (1¼–1¾in)

Family Sesiidae	Species *Albuna oberthuri*	Author Le Cerf

GOLDEN CLEARWING

golden-yellow head and antennae

This beautiful little moth is one of only fourteen species of this family known to occur in Australia. It is easily recognized by its brilliant golden forewings margined with black and by the gold bands and tail-tuft on the abdomen. Like most other members of this group it flies rapidly in bright sunlight. Males lack the orange forewing scales of the females.
• **EARLY STAGES** Very little is known about the biology of this moth, and its caterpillar has not been described.
• **DISTRIBUTION** Occurs in Northern Territory, Australia.

INDO-AUSTRALIAN

♀

distinctive yellow bar on clear hindwing

Time of Flight ☼	Habitat 🌴	Wingspan 2.5–3cm (1–1¼in)

LIMACODIDAE

This is a family of about 1,000 species occurring worldwide, but most commonly found in the tropics. They are small- to medium sized and have reduced mouthparts, and rather rounded wings. Some moths are bright green or yellow but most have fairly dull colours and simple patterns. The name Limacodidae, meaning slug-like, derives from the caterpillars of this family. These caterpillars, which look like slugs and move like them, are often very brightly coloured, indicating that they are poisonous. Many of the Limacodid caterpillars have stinging hairs that can cause a very painful reaction and so are known as nettle caterpillars. A number of species feed on cultivated crops and are often regarded as pests.

Family Limacodidae	Species *Sibine stimulea*	Author Clemens

SADDLE-BACK MOTH

The forewings of this moth are deep reddish brown with dark purplish grey and black markings. The hindwings are paler greyish brown. The sexes are similar, but females are larger.

• **EARLY STAGES** The common name of the moth refers to the caterpillar, which is purplish brown with a large central saddle of bright green, edged with white. In the middle of the saddle is a white-edged, dark brown oval marking. At either end of the body is a prominent pair of poisonous horns. The caterpillars are known to feed on the foliage of a wide range plants.

• **DISTRIBUTION** This moth is widespread throughout eastern and southern areas of the USA.

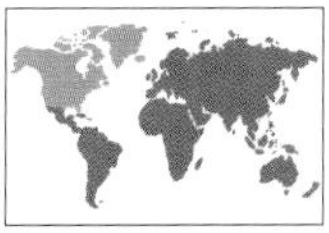

NEARCTIC

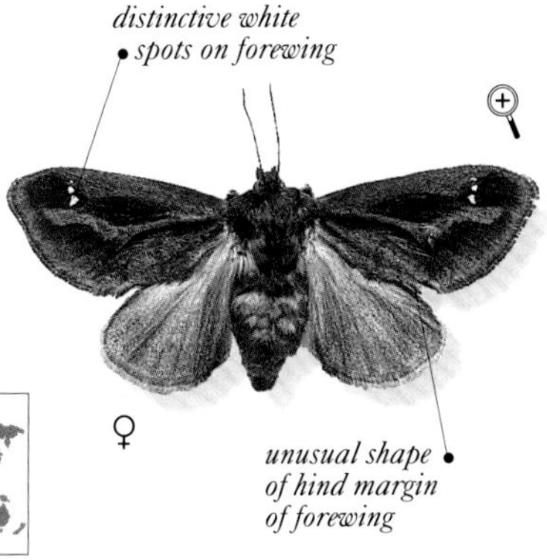
distinctive white spots on forewing
♀
unusual shape of hind margin of forewing

Time of Flight ☾	Habitat	Wingspan 2.5–4cm (1–1½in)

Family Limacodidae	Species *Apoda limacodes*	Author Hufnagel

THE FESTOON

Males of this species are dark yellowish brown with dark brown hindwings while females are predominantly yellow with brown markings. Although mainly nocturnal they will fly around the tops of oak trees in daylight.

• **EARLY STAGES** The unusual flattened caterpillar is pale green with two yellow longitudinal ridges along the back, that are spotted with pinkish red. Festoon caterpillars feed on the foliage of oak *(Quercus)*.

• **DISTRIBUTION** Widely distributed in southern and central Europe, and also occurs in southern parts of the British Isles.

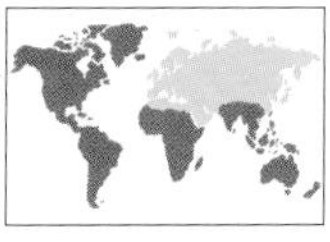

PALAEARCTIC

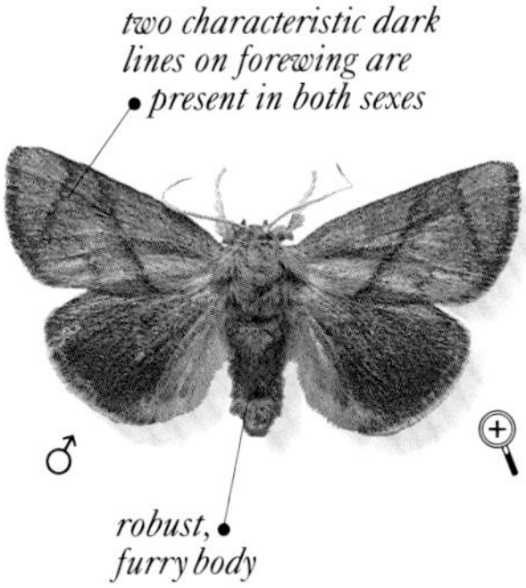
two characteristic dark lines on forewing are present in both sexes
♂
robust, furry body

Time of Flight ☾ ☼	Habitat	Wingspan 2.5–3cm (1–1¼in)

ZYGAENIDAE

T HIS WORLDWIDE FAMILY of some 800 species of small- to medium-sized moth is one of the most distinctive groups of all. Most are day-flying and many are brightly coloured, indicating that they are poisonous.

•

Several of the predominantly red species of the genus *Zygaena* that occur in Europe are known as burnets, while green species of the genus *Adscita* are known as foresters. Most Zygaenid moths have well-developed tongues, and the antennae are usually thickened towards the tips. While most have normally developed wings, the hindwings of one group, (*Himantopterus* see p. 290), are reduced to slender filaments. The poisonous caterpillars are stout and slug-like.

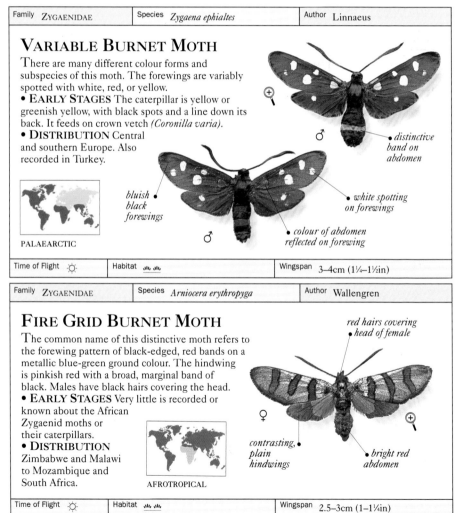

Family ZYGAENIDAE	Species *Zygaena ephialtes*	Author Linnaeus

VARIABLE BURNET MOTH

There are many different colour forms and subspecies of this moth. The forewings are variably spotted with white, red, or yellow.
• **EARLY STAGES** The caterpillar is yellow or greenish yellow, with black spots and a line down its back. It feeds on crown vetch *(Coronilla varia)*.
• **DISTRIBUTION** Central and southern Europe. Also recorded in Turkey.

PALAEARCTIC

♂

distinctive band on abdomen

white spotting on forewings

colour of abdomen reflected on forewing

bluish black forewings

♂

Time of Flight ☼	Habitat	Wingspan 3–4cm (1¼–1½in)

Family ZYGAENIDAE	Species *Arniocera erythropyga*	Author Wallengren

FIRE GRID BURNET MOTH

The common name of this distinctive moth refers to the forewing pattern of black-edged, red bands on a metallic blue-green ground colour. The hindwing is pinkish red with a broad, marginal band of black. Males have black hairs covering the head.
• **EARLY STAGES** Very little is recorded or known about the African Zygaenid moths or their caterpillars.
• **DISTRIBUTION** Zimbabwe and Malawi to Mozambique and South Africa.

AFROTROPICAL

red hairs covering head of female

♀

contrasting, plain hindwings

bright red abdomen

Time of Flight ☼	Habitat	Wingspan 2.5–3cm (1–1¼in)

Family ZYGAENIDAE	Species *Zygaena occitanica*	Author de Villers

PROVENCE BURNET MOTH

The Provence burnet is distinguished by its small size and an all-white, elongate, spot on the outer edge of the forewing. The tip of the abdomen is coloured with a broad band of red.
• **EARLY STAGES** The caterpillar is light green, spotted with yellow, and has black dots on its sides. It feeds on plants of the pea family.
• **DISTRIBUTION** Southern France and Spain. Similar species occur in southern and eastern Europe.

PALAEARCTIC

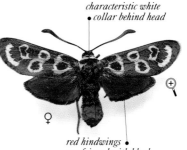

*characteristic white
collar behind head*

♀

*red hindwings
are fringed with black*

Time of Flight ☼	Habitat 〜〜	Wingspan 3–4cm (1¼–1½in)

Family ZYGAENIDAE	Species *Zygaena filipendulae*	Author Linnaeus

SIX-SPOT BURNET

As its common name suggests, this species is distinguished by having six large, red spots on each greenish black forewing.
• **EARLY STAGES** The yellowish green caterpillar has yellow and black spots. It feeds on bird's-foot trefoil *(Lotus corniculatus)* and related plants of the pea family (Leguminosae).
• **DISTRIBUTION** Widespread and common throughout Europe.

PALAEARCTIC

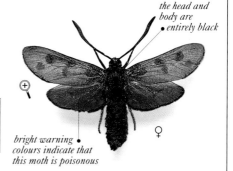

*the head and
body are
entirely black*

♀

*bright warning
colours indicate that
this moth is poisonous*

Time of Flight ☼	Habitat 〜〜	Wingspan 2.5–4cm (1–1½in)

Family ZYGAENIDAE	Species *Adscita statices*	Author Linnaeus

THE FORESTER

This is one of a group of species with metallic-green wings. Several other species are similar, but are distinguishable by small differences in the structure of the wings and antennae.
• **EARLY STAGES** The caterpillar is pale yellow or greenish white, suffused with pinkish brown on the sides, and has brown, hairy warts. It feeds on sorrel *(Rumex).*
• **DISTRIBUTION** Europe, extending into temperate Asia.

PALAEARCTIC

*strongly feathered
antennae of male*

♂

*blackish hindwings are
characteristic of all foresters*

Time of Flight ☼	Habitat 〜〜	Wingspan 2.5–3cm (1–1¼in)

Family ZYGAENIDAE	Species *Harrisina americana*	Author Guérin

EASTERN GRAPELEAF SKELETONIZER

This unusual little moth is characterized by its slender, black wings and long, black body. This species has a distinctive red or orange collar behind the head.

• **EARLY STAGES** The caterpillar is yellowish white with black spots that are covered with stinging hairs. The caterpillar feeds on grapevine *(Vinifera)* and Virginia creeper *(Parthenocissus)*.

• **DISTRIBUTION** Widespread in the eastern USA.

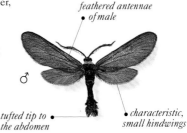

feathered antennae of male

♂

tufted tip to the abdomen

characteristic, small hindwings

NEARCTIC

Time of Flight ☀	Habitat 🌿 🌾 🌾	Wingspan 2–3cm (¾–1¼in)

Family ZYGAENIDAE	Species *Campylotes desgodinsi*	Author Oberthür

FIERY CAMPYLOTES

This handsome and distinctive moth belongs to a genus of about fifteen species, all brightly coloured with black and red as a warning that they are distasteful and probably poisonous.

• **EARLY STAGES** Nothing is known about the caterpillar or its foodplants.

• **DISTRIBUTION** This species can be found from northern India and Tibet to South China and throughout Borneo.

long, almost rectangular forewings

slender, slightly feathered antennae

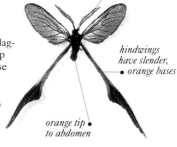

♂

INDO-AUSTRALIAN

Time of Flight ☀	Habitat 🌴	Wingspan 5.5–7cm (2¼–2¾in)

Family ZYGAENIDAE	Species *Himantopterus dohertyi*	Author Elwes

DOHERTY'S LONGTAIL

This unusual little moth belongs to a small genus of south-east Asian species that are characterized by their long, streamer-like hindwings. This species has black forewings; its hindwings have strange, black, triangular, flag-like extremities. If disturbed when at rest, the moths drop to the ground and feign death as a defence strategy. These moths have a slow flight.

• **EARLY STAGES** The caterpillars live in the nests of termites.

• **DISTRIBUTION** Can be found throughout India and Malaysia.

strongly feathered antennae

hindwings have slender, orange bases

♂

orange tip to abdomen

INDO-AUSTRALIAN

Time of Flight ☀	Habitat 🌴	Wingspan 2–2.5cm (¾–1in)

COSSIDAE

THIS IS A WORLDWIDE FAMILY of some 500 species of medium-sized to very large moth. They are usually rather dull in colour, ranging from grey and brown to white, and are patterned with contrasting streaks or spots. The caterpillars feed mainly on wood, boring holes in the branches and trunks of trees, and are therefore commonly known as carpenterworms.

•

Because of the low nutritional value of their food, some species take several years to complete their development.

Family COSSIDAE	Species *Xyleutes strix*	Author Linnaeus

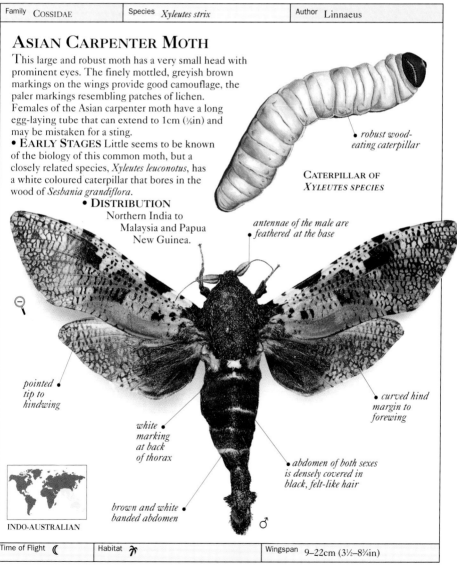

ASIAN CARPENTER MOTH

This large and robust moth has a very small head with prominent eyes. The finely mottled, greyish brown markings on the wings provide good camouflage, the paler markings resembling patches of lichen. Females of the Asian carpenter moth have a long egg-laying tube that can extend to 1cm (⅜in) and may be mistaken for a sting.

• **EARLY STAGES** Little seems to be known of the biology of this common moth, but a closely related species, *Xyleutes leuconotus*, has a white coloured caterpillar that bores in the wood of *Sesbania grandiflora*.

• **DISTRIBUTION** Northern India to Malaysia and Papua New Guinea.

• *robust wood-eating caterpillar*

CATERPILLAR OF
XYLEUTES SPECIES

antennae of the male are • *feathered at the base*

pointed • *tip to hindwing*

• *curved hind margin to forewing*

white • *marking at back of thorax*

abdomen of both sexes is densely covered in black, felt-like hair

brown and white banded abdomen •

♂

INDO-AUSTRALIAN

Time of Flight ☾	Habitat 🐾	Wingspan 9–22cm (3½–8¾in)

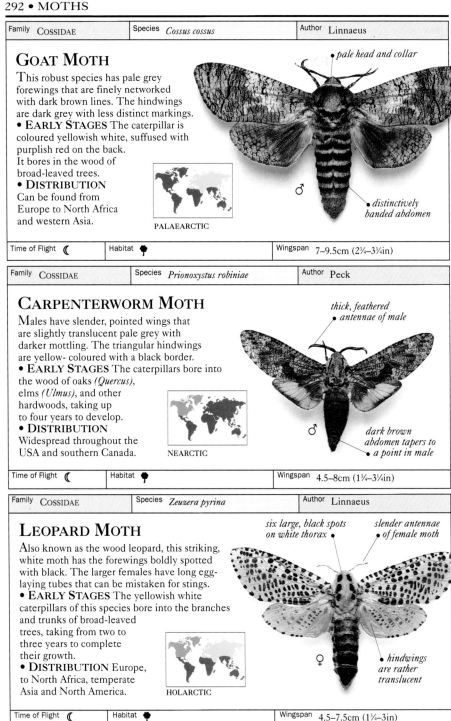

| Family COSSIDAE | Species *Cossus cossus* | Author Linnaeus |

GOAT MOTH

This robust species has pale grey forewings that are finely networked with dark brown lines. The hindwings are dark grey with less distinct markings.
• **EARLY STAGES** The caterpillar is coloured yellowish white, suffused with purplish red on the back. It bores in the wood of broad-leaved trees.
• **DISTRIBUTION** Can be found from Europe to North Africa and western Asia.

PALAEARCTIC

pale head and collar •

♂

• *distinctively banded abdomen*

| Time of Flight ☾ | Habitat ⚲ | Wingspan 7–9.5cm (2¾–3¾in) |

| Family COSSIDAE | Species *Prionoxystus robiniae* | Author Peck |

CARPENTERWORM MOTH

Males have slender, pointed wings that are slightly translucent pale grey with darker mottling. The triangular hindwings are yellow- coloured with a black border.
• **EARLY STAGES** The caterpillars bore into the wood of oaks *(Quercus),* elms *(Ulmus),* and other hardwoods, taking up to four years to develop.
• **DISTRIBUTION** Widespread throughout the USA and southern Canada.

NEARCTIC

thick, feathered antennae of male •

♂

dark brown abdomen tapers to a point in male •

| Time of Flight ☾ | Habitat ⚲ | Wingspan 4.5–8cm (1¾–3¼in) |

| Family COSSIDAE | Species *Zeuzera pyrina* | Author Linnaeus |

LEOPARD MOTH

Also known as the wood leopard, this striking, white moth has the forewings boldly spotted with black. The larger females have long egg-laying tubes that can be mistaken for stings.
• **EARLY STAGES** The yellowish white caterpillars of this species bore into the branches and trunks of broad-leaved trees, taking from two to three years to complete their growth.
• **DISTRIBUTION** Europe, to North Africa, temperate Asia and North America.

HOLARCTIC

six large, black spots on white thorax •

slender antennae • of female moth

♀

• *hindwings are rather translucent*

| Time of Flight ☾ | Habitat ⚲ | Wingspan 4.5–7.5cm (1¾–3in) |

| Family COSSIDAE | Species *Xyleutes eucalypti* | Author Herrich-Schäffer |

ACACIA CARPENTER MOTH

This is one of the most attractive and distinctive
Australian carpenter moths. The forewings are grey
with a fine network pattern of black and dark brown,
while the hindwings are reddish brown with fine,
dark brown markings. The body is banded with white.
• **EARLY STAGES** The robust, white caterpillar
has a large, brown,
shield-like plate
on its back
behind the
head. It attacks
acacia species.
• **DISTRIBUTION**
Occurs in NSW and
Queensland.

*distinctively
patterned, black
and grey thorax*

*delicate
forewing
patterning*

♂

INDO-AUSTRALIAN

*striking, black
abdomen has
narrow, white rings*

*white fringe to
inner margin of
hindwing*

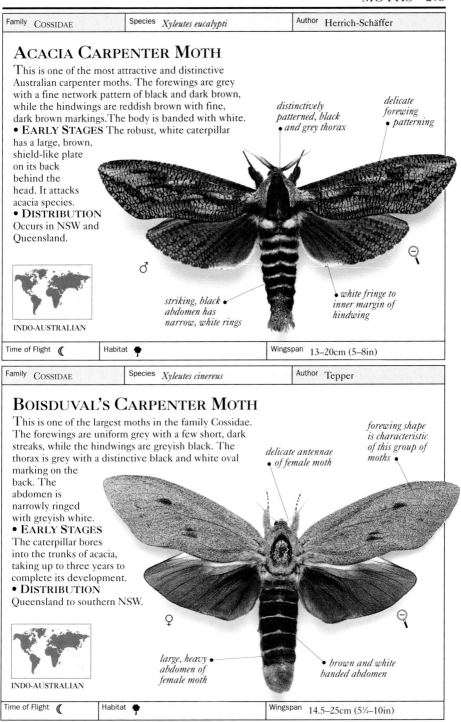

| Time of Flight ☾ | Habitat ❦ | Wingspan 13–20cm (5–8in) |

| Family COSSIDAE | Species *Xyleutes cinereus* | Author Tepper |

BOISDUVAL'S CARPENTER MOTH

This is one of the largest moths in the family Cossidae.
The forewings are uniform grey with a few short, dark
streaks, while the hindwings are greyish black. The
thorax is grey with a distinctive black and white oval
marking on the
back. The
abdomen is
narrowly ringed
with greyish white.
• **EARLY STAGES**
The caterpillar bores
into the trunks of acacia,
taking up to three years to
complete its development.
• **DISTRIBUTION**
Queensland to southern NSW.

*forewing shape
is characteristic
of this group of
moths*

*delicate antennae
of female moth*

♀

INDO-AUSTRALIAN

*large, heavy
abdomen of
female moth*

*brown and white
banded abdomen*

| Time of Flight ☾ | Habitat ❦ | Wingspan 14.5–25cm (5¾–10in) |

HEPIALIDAE

T HIS FAMILY OF SOME 300 species of moth displays a number of primitive features that distinguish them from all other large moths. The wings lack the usual bristle-and-catch linking system and instead have a lobe on the forewing that overlaps the hindwing, thus holding them together when in flight. Another more obvious and primitive feature is that the

hindwing and forewing are usually very similar in shape and have a similar arrangement of wing veins.

Hepialid moths vary in size from small to very large. They are worldwide in distribution, and are very strongly represented in Australia where some of the largest species occur. They are generally most active at dusk.

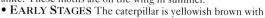

Family HEPIALIDAE	Species *Zelotypia stacyi*	Author Scott

BENT-WING GHOST MOTH

The forewings of this large and beautiful moth are intricately patterned with brown and white and have a distinct eyespot at their centres. The hindwings are orange with brown markings at the extreme tip but are otherwise quite plain. The sexes are alike. These moths are on the wing in summer.
• **EARLY STAGES** The caterpillar is yellowish brown with stout, reddish brown plates on the back immediately behind the head. Along the back is a series of yellowish white, oval markings. Caterpillars bore in the stems and branches of Sydney blue gum (*Eucalyptus saligna*) and related trees. They are sometimes pests of young trees used for paper pulp.
• **DISTRIBUTION** Occurs in eastern Australia from Queensland to NSW.

INDO-AUSTRALIAN

shape of forewing tips gives rise to the common name •

distinctive forelegs have the appearance • of pipe-cleaners

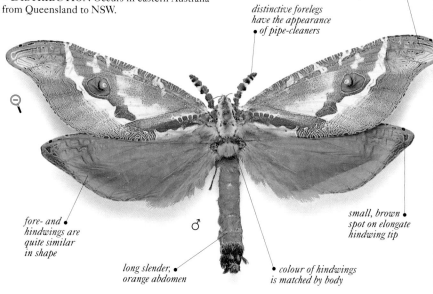

fore- and • hindwings are quite similar in shape

♂

long slender, orange abdomen

small, brown • spot on elongate hindwing tip

• colour of hindwings is matched by body

Time of Flight ☾	Habitat ⚲	Wingspan 19–25cm (7½–10in)

Family HEPIALIDAE	Species *Aenetus eximius*	Author Scott

COMMON AENETUS

There are fifteen Australian species in this genus, often called splendid ghost moths. They are remarkable not only for their large size, but for the difference between the sexes. The males of the common Aenetus have pale bluish green forewings and white hindwings tinged with green on the hind margin. The much larger females have rich, mottled, moss-green forewings with a diagonal line of brown-ringed, white markings. The hindwings are a pinkish red which continues onto the abdomen. The abdomen tip is coloured a vivid green.

INDO-AUSTRALIAN

male forewings are shorter and more sharply pointed at the tips than those of female •

• **EARLY STAGES** The caterpillar feeds on *Waterhousea*, eucalyptus, *Doryphora*, *Glochidion*, *Nothofagus*, and *Dodonaea* species. They bore into the stem or trunk of the plant, and tunnel down into the main root. Some of the *Aenetus* caterpillars take up to five years to complete their development.

• **DISTRIBUTION** Range extends from Queensland to Victoria and Tasmania in Australia.

♂

brightly coloured forelegs •

brown spotting on forewing edge •

• *male abdomen is white with a pale green tip*

♀

hindwings are dusky orange-red •

• *yellow margins to hindwings*

• *orange colour of body matches hindwings*

abdomen has a green tip •

Time of Flight ☾	Habitat 🜨 🌺	Wingspan 8–12.5cm (3¹/₄–4¹/₄in)

Family HEPIALIDAE	Species *Leto venus*	Author Stoll

VENUS MOTH

As its common name suggests, this is probably the most beautiful of all Hepialid moths, with its rich orange-brown forewings brilliantly patterned with silver spots. The hindwings are a uniform salmon-pink with slightly darker veins. Males have long, orange hairs on the underside of the wings.
• **EARLY STAGES** Little is known of the early stages of this moth and the caterpillar appears to be undescribed. It bores into the trunks of Keurboom trees and it probably feeds between the wood and the bark.
• **DISTRIBUTION** Confined to Cape Province, South Africa.

AFROTROPICAL

distinctive, triangular, silver spots along forewing margin

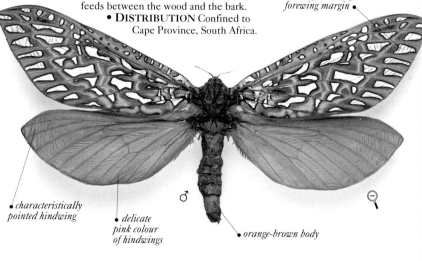

characteristically pointed hindwing

delicate pink colour of hindwings

orange-brown body

♂

Time of Flight ☾	Habitat ⚘	Wingspan 10–16cm (4–6¼in)

Family HEPIALIDAE	Species *Hepialus fusconebulosa*	Author De Geer

MAP-WINGED SWIFT

The intricate pattern of brown and white on the forewings of this moth gives rise to its common name. It is extremely variable and one form is uniform brown with little visible pattern. The hindwings are dark brownish grey with pale fringes. The sexes are similar, but females are larger and paler with the markings less distinct.
• **EARLY STAGES** The caterpillar is yellowish white with pale yellowish brown spots. It feeds on the roots of bracken (*Pteris*) and other plants, living two years.
• **DISTRIBUTION** Occurs from Europe, including the British Isles, to temperate Asia.

short antennae

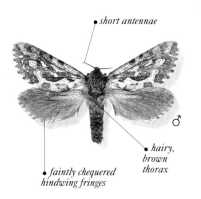

♂

hairy, brown thorax

PALAEARCTIC

faintly chequered hindwing fringes

Time of Flight ☾	Habitat ⠇⠇	Wingspan 3–5cm (1¼–2in)

Family HEPIALIDAE	Species *Hepialus humuli*	Author Linnaeus

GHOST MOTH

The silvery white males are appropriately named as they look quite ghostly when hovering over vegetation at dusk. A northern form exists in which the male wings are patterned with brown. Females are generally larger and have pale yellow forewings patterned with pink or pinkish brown.

• **EARLY STAGES** The yellowish white caterpillar has small, dark brown spots. It feeds on the roots of grasses and other plants and is sometimes an agricultural pest. Presumably because of its burrowing habits, this species is also known as the otter.

• **DISTRIBUTION** Widespread from Europe, including the British Isles to Asia.

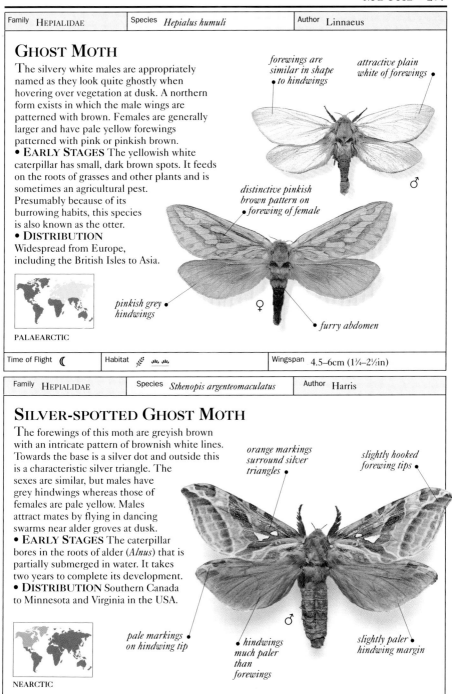

forewings are similar in shape to hindwings

attractive plain white of forewings

♂

distinctive pinkish brown pattern on forewing of female

pinkish grey hindwings

♀

furry abdomen

PALAEARCTIC

Time of Flight ☾	Habitat	Wingspan 4.5–6cm (1¼–2½in)

Family HEPIALIDAE	Species *Sthenopis argenteomaculatus*	Author Harris

SILVER-SPOTTED GHOST MOTH

The forewings of this moth are greyish brown with an intricate pattern of brownish white lines. Towards the base is a silver dot and outside this is a characteristic silver triangle. The sexes are similar, but males have grey hindwings whereas those of females are pale yellow. Males attract mates by flying in dancing swarms near alder groves at dusk.

• **EARLY STAGES** The caterpillar bores in the roots of alder (*Alnus*) that is partially submerged in water. It takes two years to complete its development.

• **DISTRIBUTION** Southern Canada to Minnesota and Virginia in the USA.

orange markings surround silver triangles

slightly hooked forewing tips

♂

pale markings on hindwing tip

hindwings much paler than forewings

slightly paler hindwing margin

NEARCTIC

Time of Flight ◑	Habitat	Wingspan 6–10cm (2½–4in)

GLOSSARY

Technical expressions have been avoided wherever possible, but a limited use of them is unavoidable in a book of this nature. The terms listed below, many of them peculiar to butterflies and moths, are defined in a concise manner. Some definitions have been simplified and generalised in order to avoid obscure language, and they are to be regarded as definitive for this book only. Words in bold type are explained elsewhere in the glossary.

- **Abdomen**
Rear part of the body behind **thorax**
- **Cardenolide Poison**
A heart poison
- **Claspers**
False, sucker-like legs on the **abdomen**
- **Cocoon**
Protective enclosure for the pupa, usually made of silk

- **Eyespot**
Circular colour markings found on the wings
- **Lunule**
Small, moon-like shape
- **Melanic**
Black or dark form of species, due to increased melanin
- **Mimetic group**
Species which mimic one another to gain protection

- **Palps**
Sensory mouthparts used for investigating food
- **Scent scales**
Scales that release an aphrodisiac scent
- **Sclerophyll Forest**
A forest of hard-leaved trees
- **Thorax**
Middle of the body immediately behind the head

USEFUL ADDRESSES

Butterfly Conservation
PO Box 222
Dedham
Colchester CO7 6EY
Tel: 01206 322342/323402

National Museums and Galleries on Merseyside
William Brown Street
Liverpool L3 8EN
Tel: 0151 207 0001

Worldwide Butterflies
Compton House
Sherborne, Dorset DT9 4QN
Tel: 01935 474608
www.wwb.co.uk/home.html

Edinburgh Butterfly and Insect World
Dobbies Garden Centre
Lasswade nr. Edinburgh
Midlothian EH18 1AZ
Tel: 0131 663 4932

Conwy Butterfly Jungle
Bodlondeb Park
Conwy LL32 8DU
Tel: 01492 593149
www.marketsite.co.uk/conwy/bfly/index.htm

London Butterfly House
Syon Park
Brentford, Middlesex
Tel: 020 8560 7272
www.butterflies.org.uk

Booth Museum of Natural History
194 Dyke Road
Brighton, East Sussex BN1 5AA
Tel: 01273 292777

The Natural History Museum
Cromwell Road
London SW7 5BD
Tel: 020 7942 5000
www.nhm.ac.uk/

Stratford-Upon Avon Butterfly Farm
Tramway Walk
Swan's Nest Lane
Stratford-Upon-Avon
Warwickshire CV37 7LS
Tel: 01789 299288

INDEX